Managing Classrooms and Student Behavior

Managing Classrooms and Student Behavior provides the essential information necessary for understanding and applying classroom and behavior management techniques with a Response to Intervention (RTI) approach. The presentation and application of information more closely resembles the actual decision-making approaches used by individuals and teams of teachers, schools, and districts. This introductory, reader-friendly textbook can be used in undergraduate or graduate level courses with special education or both special and general education candidates. A companion website provides key ancillary materials, such as PowerPoint presentations, a test bank, and an instructor's manual.

Catherine Lawless Frank is Clinical Faculty in the School of Education and Health Sciences, University of Dayton, USA.

Jennifer T. Christman is Clinical Faculty in the School of Education and Health Sciences, University of Dayton, USA.

Joni L. Baldwin is Associate Professor in the School of Education and Health Sciences, University of Dayton, USA.

Stephen B. Richards is Associate Professor of Teacher Education in the College of Education and Human Performance at West Liberty University, USA.

Managing Classrooms and Student Behavior

A Response to Intervention Approach for Educators

Catherine Lawless Frank,
Jennifer T. Christman, Joni L. Baldwin,
and Stephen B. Richards

NEW YORK AND LONDON

First published 2019
by Routledge
711 Third Avenue, New York, NY 10017

and by Routledge
2 Park Square, Milton Park, Abingdon, Oxon, OX14 4RN

Routledge is an imprint of the Taylor & Francis Group, an informa business

© 2019 Taylor & Francis

The right of Catherine Lawless Frank, Jennifer T. Christman, Joni L. Baldwin, and Stephen B. Richards to be identified as the authors of the editorial material, and of the authors for their individual chapters, has been asserted in accordance with sections 77 and 78 of the Copyright, Designs and Patents Act 1988.

All rights reserved. No part of this book may be reprinted or reproduced or utilised in any form or by any electronic, mechanical, or other means, now known or hereafter invented, including photocopying and recording, or in any information storage or retrieval system, without permission in writing from the publishers.

Trademark notice: Product or corporate names may be trademarks or registered trademarks, and are used only for identification and explanation without intent to infringe.

Library of Congress Cataloging-in-Publication Data
Names: Frank, Catherine Lawless, editor. | Baldwin, Joni L., editor. | Christman, Jennifer T., editor. | Richards, Steve, 1954– editor.
Title: Managing classrooms and student behavior : a response to intervention approach for educators / edited by Catherine Lawless Frank, Joni L. Baldwin, Jennifer T. Christman, and Stephen Richards.
Description: New York, NY : Routledge, 2019. | Includes bibliographical references and index.
Identifiers: LCCN 2018023060 (print) | LCCN 2018032790 (ebook) | ISBN 9781315193205 (e-book) | ISBN 9781138723122 | ISBN 9781138723122 (hardback) | ISBN 9781138723115 (paperback) | ISBN 9781315193205 (ebk)
Subjects: LCSH: Classroom management. | Behavior modification.
Classification: LCC LB3013 (ebook) | LCC LB3013 .M32598 2019 (print) | DDC 371.102/4—dc23
LC record available at https://lccn.loc.gov/2018023060

ISBN: 978-1-138-72312-2 (hbk)
ISBN: 978-1-138-72311-5 (pbk)
ISBN: 978-1-315-19320-5 (ebk)

Typeset in Minion
by Apex CoVantage, LLC

Visit the companion website: www.routledge.com/cw/lawlessfrank

Printed in the United Kingdom
by Henry Ling Limited

CONTENTS

Part I	**FOUNDATIONS OF CLASSROOM AND BEHAVIOR MANAGEMENT**	1
Chapter 1	Response to Intervention and the Law: An Overview CATHERINE LAWLESS FRANK	3
Chapter 2	Principles of Managing Behaviors STEPHEN B. RICHARDS	26
Chapter 3	Data Collection STEPHEN B. RICHARDS AND SARAH SCHIMMEL	50
Part II	**APPLICATION OF CLASSROOM AND BEHAVIOR MANAGEMENT STRATEGIES: TIER 1**	65
Chapter 4	Schoolwide Positive Behavior Support JENNIFER T. CHRISTMAN	67
Chapter 5	The Teacher's Role CATHERINE LAWLESS FRANK	87
Chapter 6	Building a Culturally Inclusive Classroom CATHERINE LAWLESS FRANK	111
Chapter 7	Motivation CATHERINE LAWLESS FRANK	140
Chapter 8	Group Strategies for Improving and Maintaining Appropriate Behavior JENNIFER T. CHRISTMAN	167

Chapter 9	Strategies for Decreasing Behavior Challenges in the Classroom JENNIFER T. CHRISTMAN	182

Part III	**APPLICATION OF CLASSROOM AND BEHAVIOR MANAGEMENT STRATEGIES: TIER 2**	**197**
Chapter 10	Tier 2 CATHERINE LAWLESS FRANK	199
Chapter 11	Strategies for Externalizing Behaviors JENNIFER T. CHRISTMAN	221
Chapter 12	Internalizing Behaviors JONI L. BALDWIN	239

Part IV	**APPLICATION OF CLASSROOM AND BEHAVIOR MANAGEMENT STRATEGIES: TIER 3**	**261**
Chapter 13	Tier 3 and Special Education JONI L. BALDWIN	263
Chapter 14	Functional Behavioral Assessment JONI L. BALDWIN	285
Chapter 15	Behavioral Intervention Plans JONI L. BALDWIN	302

Index		325

Part I
Foundations of Classroom and Behavior Management

Part 1

1

RESPONSE TO INTERVENTION AND THE LAW

An Overview

Catherine Lawless Frank

CHAPTER OBJECTIVES

After reading this chapter, students should be able to:

1. Summarize the laws that guide special education and protect the rights of people with disabilities.
2. Explain the ongoing cycle of assessment, analysis, decision-making, and instruction used in the Response to Intervention process.
3. Understand the components of each tier in the Response to Intervention process and how the ongoing cycle is used.

THE LAWS

In order to understand special education and to promote an inclusive classroom, which is essential to behavior and classroom management, it is important to be familiar with the legal framework. In the United States, there are three main laws that provide the framework, protect the rights of people with disabilities, and promote an inclusive society: the Americans with Disabilities Act (ADA), Section 504 of the Rehabilitation Act (Section 504), and the Individuals with Disabilities Education Act (IDEA). These laws ensure that people with disabilities receive reasonable accommodations and an appropriate education.

Americans With Disabilities Act

The Americans with Disabilities Act (ADA) is a civil rights law that is designed to protect people with disabilities, including those that affect a person's behavior, from discrimination by promoting accessibility in places of employment and entities that provide services, regardless of whether they receive federal funding. Under the ADA, a disability is a physical or mental impairment that affects one or more major life activities, such as walking, talking, working, or learning. This law guarantees a person "reasonable accommodations" based on the needs of their disability. What constitutes a reasonable accommodation varies depending on the environment and situation. Providing reasonable accommodations may mean allowing fidgets or movement breaks to accommodate a child when completing an activity in an extracurricular club, but it does not necessarily constitute changing the club's meeting schedule for all children to accommodate one child. This law has limited influence on schools because most schools receive federal funding (Smith, 2001).

Section 504 of the Rehabilitation Act

Section 504 of the Rehabilitation Act is similar to the ADA but is designed for businesses and other entities that receive federal funding. It is also a civil rights law similar to the ADA, with the same definition of a disability (a physical or mental impairment that affects one or more major life activities) and the same requirements of reasonable accommodations. Section 504 differs from the ADA in that it is applicable to any place, program, and/or organization that receives federal financial assistance.

Because the majority of schools in the United States receive federal assistance, they must abide by Section 504. This law prevents discrimination to students with disabilities (including disabilities that impede behavior) by providing access to and reasonable accommodations within the school environment. It is not designed to provide special education services but the accommodations necessary to mitigate a person's disability (Wright & Wright, 2015). A student who qualifies under Section 504 as having a disability could receive reasonable academic and/or behavioral accommodations but would not necessarily be entitled to the provisions of special education under IDEA. Section 504 has a broader definition of a disability than IDEA and allows students who qualify with a disability (that affects learning and/or participation in school) accommodations that they might not otherwise receive.

Determining what constitutes reasonable accommodations should be a multidisciplinary team decision. The team, consisting of general education teachers, special education teachers, parents (throughout this book, the term *parents* will be used to represent a student's legal guardian or primary caregiver), school administrators, and possibly the student, may decide that reasonable accommodations for a student with attention deficit disorder are extended time on tests, preferential seating, and assistive technology to aid in writing. These accommodations are then typically written into a 504 Plan or Individualized Accommodation Plan, which is used to document the services and accommodations to be provided by the school. The components of a 504 Plan are not federally mandated as in the case of an Individualized Education Program (IEP), but this plan should outline the students' needs and the reasonable accommodations and services provided to meet those needs (DREDF, n.d.; Skalski & Stanek, 2010; Stanberry, 2014).

An illustration of these two laws is Bobby, an eight-year-old boy who has recently been identified by a medical professional as having attention deficit hyperactivity disorder (ADHD). Through a multi-tiered system of support and a pre-referral process (discussed later in the chapter), it is determined that Bobby does not meet the eligibility requirements under IDEA. A multidisciplinary team consisting of Bobby's general

Table 1.1 Sample 504 Plan

Sample 504 Plan
Jaidyn Christopher Elementary School

Date of plan: **Date of next review:**
Student's name: Bobby Washington   **Date of birth:**   **Grade:**
Parents/guardians: Nicole and Alfred Washington
Student's areas of strength:
Bobby is a very social child who is friendly and outgoing. He has good relationships with his classmates and is often the first to volunteer to help a teacher or peer.

Description of eligibility determination and need:
Bobby was recently diagnosed with ADHD, which causes him to have difficulties with his time management, organization, and impulse control.

Area of Need	Accommodations	Responsible Party
Time management	Preferential seating near the teacher	General education teacher is responsible for all accommodations
Organization	Teacher supervision in writing down assignments	
Impulse control		
	Seat breaks (run errands, get drink of water, etc.)	
	Extended time on tests	

education teacher, a special education teacher, Bobby's mother, and the school principal determines that Bobby's disability does affect one or more major life functions, and in Bobby's case it affects his time management, organization, and impulse control. The team determines that Bobby qualifies for services under Section 504 because the school receives federal funding. Bobby's 504 Plan lists his accommodations as preferential seating near the teacher, teacher supervision in writing down assignments, seat breaks (run errands, get a drink of water, pass out papers), and extended time on tests. When Bobby goes to camp that summer, his mother shares with the counselors his 504 Plan. The camp is under the requirements of the ADA because it does not receive federal funds and provides Bobby with reasonable accommodations, including extended time on certain activities and seat breaks during meeting and craft times. In regard to the school and the camp, reasonable accommodations were provided to Bobby that allowed him to participate. See Table 1.1 for a sample 504 Plan.

Individuals With Disabilities Education Act
In 1975, President Gerald Ford signed Public Law 94–142, the Education for All Handicapped Children Act. This law was later reauthorized as the Individuals with Disabilities Education Act (IDEA). It governs and guarantees an appropriate education for children with disabilities from birth to age 21. IDEA differs from the ADA and Section 504 in that it provides greater legal provisions than reasonable accommodations but has a narrower definition of what constitutes a disability.

Table 1.2 Thirteen Disability Categories Under the Individuals with Disabilities Education Act

Disability	Description
Specific learning disability (SLD)	Affects the way a person learns, processes, understands, and/or uses language (listen, think, speak, read, write, spell, or do mathematical calculations)
Intellectual disability (ID)	Deficit in intellectual ability (reasoning, planning, problem-solving, abstract thinking, comprehension, speed of learning, and learning from experience) and adaptive behaviors, which consist of learned skills used in everyday life, such as conceptual (time, money, language, literacy), social (interpersonal skills, gullibility, social responsibility, problem-solving, self-esteem), and practical (daily living, health care, transportation, financial awareness) skills
Emotional disturbance (ED)	Student's mental health or behavior interferes with their ability to learn and/or participate in school
Speech and language impairment (SLI)	Affects a student's ability to communicate
Autism	A neurological disorder that impedes behavior, communication, and socialization
Deaf-blindness	A significant degree of both hearing and vision loss
Deafness	The inability to hear most, if any, sounds
Hearing impairment	Limited ability to hear
Multiple disabilities	A combination of two or more severe disabilities
Orthopedic impairment	A physical impairment, such as neuromotor impairments (spina bifida, cerebral palsy), degenerative diseases (muscular dystrophy), and musculoskeletal disorders (rheumatoid arthritis, limb deficiency)
Other health impairment	An umbrella category for other disabilities that adversely affect a student's ability to learn and/or participate in school
Traumatic brain injury	An acquired injury to the brain that affects a person's ability to learn and/or participate in school
Visual impairment, including blindness	An impairment to a student's sight that even with correction affects their ability to learn and/or participate in school

IDEA has six major provisions and identifies 13 different disabilities, each with a qualifying definition, that influences a student's ability to learn and/or participate in school. See Table 1.2 for a list of disabilities and a summary of the qualifying definitions under IDEA. In order for a student to qualify for special education, the disability as identified under IDEA must negatively affect their ability to learn and participate in school. The student is then guaranteed the right to zero rejection, nondiscriminatory testing, a free and appropriate public education, a least restrictive environment, due process, and parental participation. An explanation of these provisions can be found in Table 1.3.

Imagine that Olivia is a fourth-grade, 10-year-old girl diagnosed with ADHD and a learning disability. Because Olivia has a learning disability (unlike Bobby in the previous example), she is guaranteed the provisions under IDEA. For Olivia, this means that she has a right to a free and appropriate public education regardless of the severity of her disability (academic and/or behavioral severity). In determining

Table 1.3 Six Provisions of the Individuals with Disabilities Education Act

Provision	Description
Zero rejection	Students have the right to a publicly funded education regardless of the severity of their disabilities.
Nondiscriminatory testing	Eligibility must be determined through a multi-factored evaluation using unbiased assessments.
Free and appropriate public education	An appropriate individualized education is provided at no additional cost to the student or parents. This includes curriculum, instruction, and any related services, transportation, or supports needed for an appropriate education.
Least restrictive environment	Education must occur in the environment alongside students' general education peers to the greatest degree appropriate.
Due process	The process and procedures for determining eligibility, developing an Individualized Education Program, and providing services must be followed in a nondiscriminatory and timely manner.
Parental participation	Ensures parents' or guardians' rights and participation in the eligibility, design, and implementation of their child's education program.

Olivia's eligibility for special education, a multi-factored evaluation was conducted using nondiscriminatory testing. As part of this testing procedure, several people used multiple means of assessments in a nonbiased manner to ensure that Olivia met the requirements for special education. Once it was documented that Olivia was eligible, a multidisciplinary team, consisting of general education teachers, special education teachers, her parents, and a school administrator, determined the appropriate education, including any related services, for her. This appropriate education was documented on her IEP, which stated her academic and/or behavioral goals and objectives for the following year. The IEP also documented her least restrictive environment and appropriate accommodations. The procedures of this process were followed in a timely and collaborative manner under due process. Olivia's parents were considered equal members of the multidisciplinary team, gave consent to the process, and were involved in the design of their child's IEP.

If Olivia were to go to summer camp with Bobby, she will also be eligible for reasonable accommodations under the ADA. The ADA and Section 504 have broader definitions of a disability than IDEA; therefore, everyone covered under IDEA is also eligible for reasonable accommodations under the ADA and Section 504. Thus, when Olivia is at a non-federally funded summer camp, her rights are ensured under the ADA. She is also still covered under Section 504 at school, but she receives greater rights under IDEA.

It is important to remember that these three laws protect people with disabilities and include the behaviors manifested or caused by the disability. These laws do not protect a person against the consequences of their actions or behaviors but ensure that they are not discriminated against because of these behaviors. The behavioral components of special education will be covered in greater detail in Chapter 12.

> *Comprehension Check*
> 1. What are three laws that protect people with disabilities in the United States?
> 2. How do IDEA and Section 504 differ?
> 3. How are IDEA and Section 504 alike?

RESPONSE TO INTERVENTION

Although the Education for All Handicapped Children Act and IDEA made great strides in providing support for students with disabilities, the education of all students who struggle academically and/or behaviorally continues to be a concern. During the 1970s and early 1980s, reform efforts began to focus on improving instruction for all struggling students, not just those with disabilities, and preventing the inappropriate identification and referral of students into special education. Response to Intervention is designed to do just that. Response to Intervention, or RTI, is a multi-tiered system of support designed to meet the academic and behavioral needs of all students by providing increasing levels of support based on individual student needs. RTI is not strictly a special education or general education initiative but a team-based, problem-solving process with the goal of better meeting the needs of all students by collecting student data, identifying potential problems, brainstorming interventions, implementing the interventions, employing progress monitoring, and revising the process as needed (Nellis, 2012; NJCLD, 2005).

Although not federally mandated, most states implement some form of a multi-tiered system of support. These support systems share common features and emphasize data-driven, evidence-based instruction, progress monitoring, and increasing levels of instructional support, with the most common type of these being a three-tiered RTI (Berkeley, Bender, Peaster, & Saunders, 2009). The concepts and framework of RTI are similar to other systems of support and intervention processes. This text will use RTI as the framework, but the information is applicable to any multi-tiered system of support or pre-referral process. The pre-referral process provides supports to students who struggle to meet the academic and/or behavioral demands of general education, with the goal of remediating the concern before a referral to special education becomes necessary.

An Overview of Response to Intervention

RTI is a multi-tiered system of support designed around an ongoing cycle of assessment, analysis, decision-making, and instruction (see Figure 1.1). Students are initially assessed, or universally screened, to determine their baselines (levels of performance before instruction or intervention), areas of strengths, and areas of need. The results of these assessments are analyzed and used to make decisions on effective evidence-based instruction that best meets the students' needs. After a period of instruction, the students are reassessed, or progress monitored, and the results are analyzed to determine if the instruction was successful and if students are learning. This ongoing

Figure 1.1 Ongoing Cycle of Response to Intervention

Table 1.4 Components of Response to Intervention

	Components
Tier 1	• **Assessment**—universal screening and progress monitoring • **Analysis** of assessment results • **Decision-making** for instruction based on the analysis • Effective evidence-based **instruction and intervention** • Continued ongoing assessment, analysis, decision-making, and instruction
Tier 2	• **Assessment**—progress monitoring • **Analysis** of assessment results • **Decision-making** for instruction based on the analysis • Effective evidence-based **instruction and intervention** • Continued ongoing assessment, analysis, decision-making, and instruction • Referral to pre-referral intervention team • Pre-referral assessments • Pre-referral interventions • Fidelity assessment
Tier 3	• **Assessment**—progress monitoring • **Analysis** of assessment results • **Decision-making** for instruction based on the analysis • Effective evidence-based **instruction and intervention** • Continued ongoing assessment, analysis, decision-making, and instruction • Referral for special education services • Multi-factored evaluation for special education services • Determination of eligibility for special education services • Individualized Education Program • Fidelity assessment

cycle is used to establish the needed instruction and supports for each student. Tier 1 is designed for implementation in the general education classroom. Tier 2 is often considered part of the pre-referral process and provides an increasing level of support for students who struggled in Tier 1. Tier 3 provides more and/or specialized support and typically a referral to special education for students who did not make adequate progress in Tiers 1 or 2 (see Table 1.4 for an overview of the components in each tier).

This section will examine the components of the ongoing cycle of assessment, analysis, decision-making, and instruction as they relate to each tier. It is important to note that the term *intervention* may also be used to represent the instructional phase of this cycle. An intervention delivers additional instruction and support to students who struggle academically or behaviorally.

THE ONGOING CYCLE OF RESPONSE TO INTERVENTION

Assessment: Universal Screening

In order to provide effective instruction, it is essential to understand what students know and are able to do. Without knowing where students are academically or behaviorally, it is almost impossible to determine their strengths, areas of need, and appropriate instruction in a timely manner. The cycle begins with initial assessments or universal screenings. Universal screenings are provided to all students at the beginning of the year in order to determine their baselines, strengths, and areas of need in core academic areas, such as comprehension, reading fluency, writing, and/or math. These initial assessments are not designed to determine who receives Tier 2 support or a referral for special education but are a means to closely monitor student growth in order to provide early intervention. The universal screening assessments are typically repeated one or more times in an academic year (two to three times total) as a continuing measure of students' overall progress (Center on Response to Intervention, n.d.).

Universal screenings are typically academic in nature and are usually not conducted to determine students' behavioral strengths or needs. Formal behavioral screenings are impractical to conduct class wide, especially at the beginning of a school year. Behavioral screenings normally ask a teacher to rate each individual student on several behavioral indicators. These indicators are dependent on the teacher knowing the student to a greater degree. Teachers can use previous school records or speak with past teachers to gain some insight into or indication of a class or student's behavioral strengths, but typically there is no formal behavioral universal screening.

Although there is typically no formal universal screening or behavioral assessments in Tier 1, the students are screened and assessed informally through teacher observations. As teachers observe their students, they begin to determine students' patterns of behaviors. A teacher may observe that Tamika is quiet and begins work independently. Raphael is talkative and often needs teacher prompts to begin working. Jamal

Figure 1.2 Ongoing Cycle of Response to Intervention

appears more engaged in a lesson when he is seated next to Tamika and less engaged when seated next to Raphael. Although this information tends to be more informal and subjective, it is used as assessment data in the ongoing cycle to make behavioral decisions in regard to the class and individual students.

Because the cycle is ongoing, assessments, both formal and informal, are used on a continuing basis after instruction has occurred. These later assessments are used to determine if students are making adequate progress and are referred to as progress monitoring. Progress monitoring results are then analyzed and used to make decisions on providing effective instruction, and the cycle continues.

Analysis

Once the formal universal assessments (and later progress monitoring) are completed, the results are analyzed to determine students' baselines, strengths, and areas of need. This analysis should examine the whole class, individual students, and possibly subgroups of the class (males compared to females, different races, students with disabilities, English as a second language). These academic results should then be graphed (line graph or bar graph) to provide a visual that will aid in comparing scores and interpreting the results (School Improvement in Maryland, 2016).

As part of the analysis, it is important to establish criteria or a benchmark as to what determines an at-risk score. Sometimes schools determine a specific number as a benchmark (The IRIS Center, 2016). For example, the average reading fluency rate for early second grade is 70 words per minute (wpm). This average can be used to set a benchmark. If the benchmark were set at 60 wpm, it would mean that any student who scored less than 60 wpm would be identified as being at risk in terms of reading fluency. If the benchmark were set at 65 wpm, then the standard would be higher and more students (those who read at less than 65 wpm) would most likely be identified. Schools can also set behavioral benchmarks, such as three office referrals (student sent to the office for behavioral concerns) per semester as a way of determining who is at risk for having a behavioral challenge. Those students sent to the office more than three times per semester would be considered as having a behavior challenge and in need of some form of intervention (social skills class, meeting with parent, etc.).

Another way to establish a benchmark is to rank order students. Instead of establishing a specific score or number, a percentage of students receiving intervention is used (The IRIS Center, 2016). For example, students could be ranked order in terms of second-grade reading fluency rather than establishing a benchmark number. The

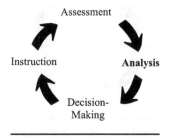

Figure 1.3 Ongoing Cycle of Response to Intervention

school or teacher would then identify a specific number or percentage of students to provide intervention—for example, the lowest 10%. This would mean that if a second grader scored in the lowest 10% of their class, no matter what the wpm, they would be identified as at risk in terms of reading fluency and receive interventions. The same is true for behavioral benchmarks. Instead of three office referrals, a school could establish a benchmark of the seven students within the school with the most office referrals to consider at risk and in need of intervention.

It is important to thoroughly analyze the data and a teacher or school's resources when setting an appropriate benchmark. If the benchmark is set too low (meaning fewer students qualify), then some students may not receive needed supports. If the benchmark is set too high (more students qualify), then students who do not need interventions may be receiving them, which may strain a teacher or school's resources and ability to provide appropriate interventions to those students who truly need them. Academic benchmark decisions must align the needs of the students and the resources available to the school.

In informal behavioral assessments, such as observations, the benchmark is typically based on the expectations of the teacher and the behavioral norms of the classroom. The teacher determines the strengths and needs of a class in regard to behaviors based on their own criteria, making this analysis more subjective in nature. The expectations of one teacher or class may differ to some degree from that of another teacher or class. Tamika's quiet nature may meet the teacher's expectations in language arts class but may be seen as a challenge in another teacher's drama class. Raphael's talkative nature may be acceptable in social studies but not in science due to the characteristics of the classroom and the expectations of the teacher. In either case, the information is analyzed and evaluated in terms of the behavioral benchmarks established by the teacher. It is important for teachers to be aware of their benchmarks and behavioral expectations in order to enforce them in a consistent and equitable manner.

Decision-Making

Once the data are properly analyzed and a benchmark is established, the next step is to decide how to use the information to improve student learning and behavioral outcomes. Decisions must be made on what factors the teacher or school believes are promoting or inhibiting students' learning and what can be done to enhance or mitigate these factors and improve student outcomes (NAESP, n.d.). These decisions are

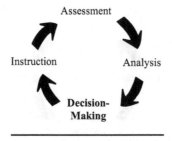

Figure 1.4 Ongoing Cycle of Response to Intervention

often made based on a variety of information and not a single assessment score (work samples, observations).

Teachers may decide to use the results of the universal screening to guide the overall instruction for the class, to group their students based on their strengths and areas of need, or to determine which students need closer monitoring. For example, if an analysis of the assessment results indicates that a teacher's third-grade students have all mastered addition, then they could decide to switch from teaching addition to teaching subtraction. If the analysis of the assessment results indicates that some of the students have mastered their addition but a small group of students have not, then the teacher could decide to develop interventions and/or additional monitoring of student progress for the small group while teaching subtraction to the class as a whole.

Teachers use the results of their behavioral analysis to help facilitate classroom management. This information is used to help teachers make a variety of decisions, such as seating arrangements, groupings for class projects, class contracts or rewards (if the class receives three complements about their behavior at lunch this week, then the class can have extra recess on Friday), and adjusting the classroom routines and rules to better meet students' needs. This analysis is also used to determine interventions for specific students and the entire class. It plays a critical role in adjusting behavioral strategies to provide the appropriate structure to a classroom.

It is important to understand and determine the potential factors that are positively and negatively affecting the assessment results (NAESP, n.d.). What instructional or curricular aspects from the previous year positively and/or negatively influenced the universal screening results? Did last year's teacher use multisensory approaches that substantially increase student learning? Was the curriculum used too easy or too difficult? Are a student's low scores due to a lack of basic skills or knowledge? Are the behavioral expectations too low or too high? Is there a mismatch between the teaching style and the students' learning styles? Are peers positively or negatively influencing one another's behavior? Asking questions such as these is necessary for determining the appropriate instruction.

Progress monitoring decisions are made as to whether the current instruction is effective and should continue or not effective and should be changed or adjusted. If the analysis shows student growth, then the decision could be that the instruction continues as it is. If the analysis shows that a student or students are not making adequate growth, then the decision could be that the instruction needs to be adjusted. Sometimes the decision is to leave the instruction as it is, even if a student is not making adequate progress, until the next round of progress monitoring. This would allow the student more time to adjust or react to the instruction. Other times the decision will be to change the instruction in some way, such as more time per day or week on the instruction, more individualized support, or a different type of instruction. Either way, students continue to be progress monitored, the data analyzed, and the decisions adjusted to guide instruction.

Instruction

The basis of RTI is effective evidence-based instruction designed to meet students' academic and behavioral needs by providing increasing levels of support in each of the three tiers. Student assessment data, analysis of that data, and decision-making

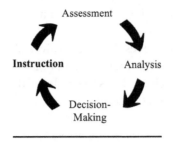

Figure 1.5 Ongoing Cycle of Response to Intervention

based on that analysis are used to guide effective evidence-based instruction. Effective evidence-based instruction is instruction that has been shown to increase student learning. This instruction encompasses more than just the curriculum and teaching. Part of effective instruction includes ensuring that the academic curriculum is research validated. Most, if not all, curriculums from major publishing companies adopted by schools have been shown to be research validated in that they are designed and tested to teach what a student is expected to learn. Evidence-based teaching practices are based on the theories and theorists typically covered in university methodology courses. Theorists and theories, such as Piaget's cognitive theory, Vygotsky's sociocultural theory, and Gardner's multiple intelligence theory, provide a framework for effective teaching practices. A research-validated curriculum and the use of established teaching practices are fundamental to effective teaching and provide a basis for the delivery of both academic and behavioral instruction. But any veteran teacher knows effective instruction requires much more than a research-validated curriculum and established teaching practices. Effective instruction also requires an understanding of the role of the teacher (Chapter 5), developing and maintaining an inclusive classroom environment (Chapter 6), motivating students and keeping them engaged (Chapter 7), managing appropriate classroom behavior (Chapter 8), and knowing how to address behavioral issues (Chapter 9). All these components, along with the ongoing cycle, are incorporated to provide effective instruction.

Progress Monitoring

Remember that the cycle is ongoing. Once the students have been formally or informally assessed, the data analyzed, curricular decisions made based on the analysis, and instruction provided, the students are reassessed, which is referred to as progress monitoring. Progress monitoring assesses a specific skill over a period of time to measure growth and determine if a student is receiving effective instruction (Center on Response to Intervention, 2016). Weekly or biweekly progress monitoring is conducted on the specific skills that assessment results indicated a student is struggling to master in order to provide academic and behavioral supports in a timely manner. Universal screening assessments are repeated two to three additional times per year to monitor the whole class while progress monitoring is completed weekly or biweekly on specific skills for individual students who are at risk in that particular area.

Progress monitoring is different from typical tests, chapter tests, or end-of-year assessments. Progress monitoring assesses the same skill, either academic or behavioral,

Figure 1.6 Ongoing Cycle of Response to Intervention

over time while curriculum tests typically assess different material or skills. The test for the first chapter in a reading book will contain different material and/or skills from the test for the second chapter. Progress monitoring for reading fluency will assess the same skill, reading fluency, multiple times to determine if a student's fluency or rate of reading is improving. Progress monitoring for a behavior, such as following the classroom procedure for answering a question (raise hand, wait quietly to be called on, if called on answer the question, if not call on lower hand), assesses the same behavior multiple times until the predetermined goal is reached.

Although the ongoing cycle may seem more structured and formal for academics, the same cycle of assessment, analysis, decision-making, and instruction is used for both academic and behavioral interventions and support. Teachers routinely use informal screening and observations of students' behavior to base their analysis, decision-making, and instruction. Teachers may screen their grade book to see which students have missing assignments. They observe patterns in students' behaviors to determine who is out of their seat and who is having difficulty staying on task, completing assignments, raising a hand to ask a question, or even staying awake in class. These informal screenings and observed patterns are then analyzed and decisions are made as to the interventions needed, which are then implemented, and the results are progress monitored. This ongoing cycle will be further discussed throughout this text.

Comprehension Check
1. What are the components of the ongoing cycle of RTI?
2. What is the purpose of a universal screening?
3. Why is it important to determine why a student is struggling?
4. What is progress monitoring, and how is it used to guide instruction?

THE TIERS OF RESPONSE TO INTERVENTION

Tier 1

Tier 1 of RTI incorporates the ongoing cycle into the general education classroom for whole-class instruction. It is in this tier that students are formally and informally screened academically (universal screening) and behaviorally (observations) and the process of analysis, decision-making, instruction, and progress monitoring begins. The screenings are designed to identify struggling students early, before they have a history of failure, in order to provide the needed instruction and interventions. It serves as the baseline from which student growth is measured.

The general education teacher analyzes the data, makes instructional decisions, and provides additional supports, interventions, and instruction to address these areas of concern. The supports can be offered to the entire class, such as providing more remediation or instruction in a basic skill (daily basic math fact drills), incorporating more cooperative learning projects, or reinforcing or establishing additional classroom rules and procedures. The interventions could also be provided to small groups or individual students, such as differentiated reading groups, additional instruction during independent work times, or greater proximity in order to provide immediate behavioral feedback and support. The students who struggle to meet the classroom academic and behavioral expectations are progress monitored, and the data are used as part of the ongoing cycle to measure student growth and guide instruction.

ILLUSTRATIVE CASE STUDY 1.1

Raul is a fourth-grade teacher who began his school year by universally screening his students academically in the areas of reading fluency, comprehension, and basic math skills. Based on these assessment results, Raul planned lessons using evidence-based instruction and effective classroom practices designed to meet his students' needs. In math class, Raul analyzed the assessment results and decided to provide interventions to his students based on their ability to fluently answer basic addition, subtraction, and multiplication problems. He defined his criterion for fluency as the ability to correctly answer 60 basic individual operation fact questions. Raul used this information to guide his review practices and to progress monitor students, especially those who had not met the criteria for addition fact fluency. The students were progress monitored on a weekly basis, and Raul used the continuous cycle of assessment, analysis, and decision-making to guide his classroom instruction.

After four weeks of school, Raul screened his students in terms of late and missing assignments. He analyzed the course grade book and established a criterion of two missing assignments and/or three late assignments as his benchmark for considering a student struggling in terms of work completion. Raul's analysis showed that three of his students, Jamaal, Allie, and Leslie, fell below this benchmark. Raul knew that in order to provide the appropriate interventions, he needed to determine why these three students were not completing their assignments.

Jamaal had recently missed three days of school due to an illness, and all his late and missing assignments fell on the dates he was absent. Raul determined that Jamaal's missing assignments were due to his illness. He decided to speak with Jamaal to determine a plan for completing the rest of his missing assignments. Raul continued to progress monitor Jamaal until all the missing assignments were completed.

Allie and Leslie's missing and late assignments were all in math. Raul looked at their universal screening and progress monitoring data and realized that Allie and Leslie were two of the lowest-performing students in his math class. Raul decided to observe them both later that day. Based on that observation, Raul theorized that Leslie and Allie were struggling to complete assignments because of a lack of fluency in math facts. They both seemed to know the process but struggled to complete independent assignments due to a lack of fluency in basic math facts. It took them longer than their peers to solve each individual problem because it took them longer to figure out basic math facts. For example, when multiplying 7×3, Leslie added three plus three seven times (3+3+3+3+3+3+3) and ultimately came up with the wrong answer. The majority of her peers had memorized 7×3 = 21 and more quickly answered the problem. All but four students, including Allie and Leslie, did not complete that day's assignment during independent work time. Although the two other students turned in their assignment the following morning, Leslie and Allie did not.

Raul decided that his intervention needed to focus on providing additional instruction and supports for basic math facts (identify strategies to compensate for difficulties with memorization, multiplication tables). Raul incorporated daily computation and fluency instruction for Leslie, Allie, and the two additional students. He also established a system to check Allie and Leslie's homework journals at the end of the day to ensure that the assignment was properly recorded. He continued to progress monitor Allie and Leslie's basic math fluency and work completion rates on an ongoing basis to ensure that both were making progress toward meeting the goals.

If a student does not make adequate academic and/or behavioral progress in Tier 1, they may be referred to Tier 2 for more intensive and individualized support. There are no strict guidelines as to the criteria for a referral to Tier 2. When that referral is made is a school and/or teacher decision and is based on the needs of the students and the policies and resources of each particular school.

APPLICATION CASE STUDY 1.2

After nine weeks of school, Raul has the following progress monitoring data on five students who have not reach the goal of answering 60 single-digit addition questions correctly.

These data show the number of questions each student correctly answered in five minutes.

Addition Fluency Goal: Sixty Questions Correct

	Week 1	Week 2	Week 3	Week 4	Week 5	Week 6	Week 7	Week 8	Week 9
Samuel A.	53	54	53	57	58	58	58	59	62
Allie D.	32	34	35	33	37	38	40	42	45
Liam J.	28	32	33	36	38	41	41	44	47
Leslie N.	23	25	24	25	24	25	26	27	24
Olivia P.	45	44	46	45	48	48	49	50	51

Case Study Comprehension Check

For this case study, independently or in a small group:

1. Analyze the data to determine which students have failed to meet Raul's goal (it may be beneficial to graph the scores using a line graph).
2. Discuss what other types of information would be beneficial to know in order to fully analyze the information.
3. Determine the different types of decisions that could be made based on these assessment results.

Tier 2

A referral to Tier 2 is typically initiated by a general education teacher after assessment data and observations document a student's failure to make adequate academic or behavioral progress in Tier 1. The components of Tier 2 typically incorporate what has traditionally been referred to as the pre-referral process and is designed to provide more individualized supports and interventions beyond what is provided during whole-class instruction. The interventions and instruction provided in this tier are more intensive and focused on the specific needs of an individual student in an attempt to remediate academic and behavioral concerns before a referral to special education becomes necessary. These interventions are based on the same ongoing cycle of assessment, analysis, decision-making, and instruction but also incorporate a fidelity check to verify that interventions and instruction are implemented appropriately (NJCLD, 2005).

Because of Tier 2's more intensive nature, it is typically a team-based process consisting of general education, special education, and administrative support, parents, and possibly the student. The team is responsible for engaging in and collaborating within the ongoing cycle to determine the interventions needed to increase academic and behavioral progress. The team supports the implementation of those interventions and the collection of student progress data to analyze its effectiveness and to determine any necessary future action (Nellis, 2012).

In Tier 2, assessment information is gathered through multiple means, including screenings, progress monitoring, observations, evaluation of student work, developmental checklists, interviews, and behavioral rating scales (Polloway, Patton, & Serna,

2008). This process tends to be more informal than gathering data for a referral to special education.

The assessment data are analyzed to determine a clear picture of the student's specific strengths and areas of need. The cause for the behavior or academic area of concern is established in order to help specifically define the problem. The cause could be a failure to comprehend the information, deficits in skills (reading fluency, social skills, anger management), lack of background knowledge, a desire to avoid work or embarrassment, or an attempt to get attention. For academic issues, the cause is often determined with an error analysis that looks for patterns in mistakes made to determine why the error occurs. For example, if the area of concern is mathematics, then an error analysis may point to a lack of knowledge of basic math facts (multiplication of numbers greater than six). If the area of concern is behavior, then the cause may be determined by analyzing the factors that may contribute to motivating or reinforcing the behavior. For example, it may be established through observations that a student disrupts language arts class in order to avoid having to read in class. It may be necessary to conduct a functional behavioral analysis to identify the antecedents and consequences of the behavior in order to determine its cause and reinforcers (see Chapter 13 for more information on a functional behavior analysis).

For determining interventions, the team examines the area of concern and its cause before determining the appropriate interventions and instructional changes needed. These interventions are typically implemented by either the general education or the special education teacher and progress monitored to determine their effectiveness. This process is specific and focused on an individual or small group of students rather than on the whole class. A fidelity check is typically administered by someone familiar with the curriculum to ensure that the interventions are provided in the manner in which they are designed. Proper identification and implementation of interventions is crucial for the success of Tier 2 in terms of remediating the area of concern and preventing inappropriate referrals to special education (Daly, Martens, Barnett, Witt, & Olson, 2007). These interventions may include providing more instruction (longer reading classes or social skills classes), different types of instruction (more hands-on or collaborative activities), more individualized attention (small group or one-on-one), or a different curriculum or added supports that address the student's area of need. The student's progress continues to be monitored, and the results are graphed and compared to the baseline to determine if the interventions are successful and if the student is making adequate progress.

If a student does not respond to instruction in Tier 2, they may be referred to Tier 3 for even more intensive instruction and possible referral to special education. Again, there is no set criteria for when a student should be referred to Tier 3, and the decision is typically made by the team.

Tier 3

Tier 3 of RTI is based on the same ongoing cycle of assessment, analysis, decision-making, and instruction as the other two tiers, but it typically incorporates referral, eligibility determination, and special education. It is designed for the few students who failed to respond to interventions in both Tiers 1 and 2. In this tier, students are referred to special education and assessed through a multi-factored evaluation to determine eligibility for services under the requirements of IDEA. If the student is deemed eligible and identified with a disability, then the student is provided with an IEP and the provisions guaranteed under IDEA, as discussed earlier in this chapter.

It is important to note, however, that not all students with special needs go through the referral and eligibility process. IDEA provides protection for students with disability from birth through age 21, and children who receive special education services at birth or before beginning traditional school are typically automatically referred for school-age special education services. The students will still be assessed using a multi-factored evaluation to determine eligibility, which is then repeated every three years, but they may forgo the pre-referral or Tier 2 process.

Parents play a key role in the referral and eligibility team-based process. Besides being equal members of the eligibility and IEP teams, parents must also give written consent prior to any eligibility assessments conducted. If a student is found to have a disability under IDEA, parents must again give consent before the student is officially identified. Parental consent is needed a third time for approval of their child's IEP.

After the initial parental consent is given for eligibility testing, a multi-factored evaluation (MFE) is conducted. An MFE is a team-based assessment process that gathers information that is analyzed to determine if a student is eligible for special education. This means that the evaluation is conducted by multiple people and includes information from multiple sources. Eligibility for special education cannot be based solely on one person administering one assessment (IQ test). An MFE is designed to be a clear and unbiased determination of a student's strengths and areas of need based on a variety of assessments that accurately determine if a student qualifies for special education. This is to prevent the inappropriate identification of students. Imagine, for example, that a teacher suspects a child has a disability and refers that student for an MFE. A school psychologist then assesses that student using an IQ test and determines that the child has intellectual disability (IQ score of 70–75 and below) based on the IQ score alone. Under IDEA, a student cannot be diagnosed with a disability or be eligible for special education based on one test alone. Although the student's score may show that they met one of the requirements of an intellectual disability, it does not provide an overall unbiased picture of the student's strengths and areas of need. There could be a multitude of reasons for that student's assessment results that are only partially due to the student's actual IQ. The student could have a previously undiagnosed mild hearing loss and therefore could not clearly hear or correctly distinguish the assessor's words. The student's primary language may not have been English, causing language to be a barrier in comprehending and completing the assessment. The assessor may not have established rapport, making the student feel uncomfortable and inhibiting their performance. There are multiple reasons why a student's single assessment result may be skewed. Multiple assessments conducted by multiple assessors in various settings is essential in developing an objective, unbiased, and complete evaluation of a student in order to determine eligibility for special education.

This comprehensive evaluation of the student's abilities includes a variety of formal and informal assessments depending on the suspected disability. The pre-referral

Table 1.5 Types of Formal Assessments Used to Determine Eligibility

Formal Assessment	Definition
Developmental assessments	A rating scale for children birth to five years used to identify strengths and needs in such areas as communication and language, fine and gross motor, social, cognitive, and self-help skills
Screening	A short assessment designed to identify potential problems, the most common of which are hearing and vision screenings
Individual intelligence tests	Measures a student's cognitive ability or intelligence quotient (IQ)
Individual academic achievement test	Assesses specific content knowledge, such as reading comprehension, phonetic awareness, and mathematics
Adaptive behavior scales	Assesses strengths and needs in general areas, such as daily living skills and community participation, and more specific areas, such as social skills, motor skills, communication, and generalizing basic academic skills
Behavior rating scale	Assesses the intensity or frequency of the behavior(s)

intervention team typically provides the MFE team with data and with a suspected disability. The suspected disability designation provides guidance to the MFE team as to what assessments are most appropriate. The types of formal assessments used in an MFE may include developmental assessments, screenings, individualized intelligence tests, individualized academic achievement tests, adaptive behavior scales, behavior rating scales, and specific related services assessments (speech and language assessment, occupational therapy evaluation). For more information on the types of formal assessments that may be used in an MFE, see Table 1.5. Informal assessments often include background information, observations, curriculum-based assessments, and a review of the student's academic history and current levels of academic performance. The assessments used in an MFE vary based on the student's strengths, areas of need, and suspected disability. Which assessments are used is a team decision and not all students will receive the same assessments.

Once all the assessments are completed, the information is compiled into an evaluation team report that summarizes the formal and informal assessment results. The evaluation team report is analyzed by the team to determine if the student meets the eligibility requirements for special education in one of the 13 disability categories (see Table 1.2 for a summary of the disability categories). Before a student is officially identified as having a disability, the parents or guardians must agree to have their child identified with the disability and provide their consent in writing.

If the analysis determines that a student is eligible for special education and written parental consent is obtained, then the team decides on the appropriate IEP. If the team decides that a student is not eligible for special education under IDEA, then the team must decide if the student qualifies for a 504 Plan under Section 504 of the Rehabilitation Act (see Table 1.1 for a sample 504 Plan). As you may recall,

Table 1.6 Components of an Individualized Education Program

Component	Explanation
Present Levels of Performance (PLOP) or Present Levels of Academic Achievement and Functional Performance (PLAAAFP)	A summary statement that objectively details the student's current levels of performance (summative and formative assessment results or frequency, duration and/or intensity of a behavior) in an area of need. It serves as a baseline on which to measure a student's growth and justifies the student's need for a particular goal.
Annual goals	Observable, measureable statements aligned with a PLOP and details a learning target (what they will know and be able to do) the student will work toward during the course of a year.
Short-term objective or benchmarks	Observable and measurable learning targets that mark a student's progress toward their annual goal.
Special education and related services	The specific special education and related services that a student needs in order to participate in school and to reach their annual goals and short-term objectives.

Section 504 has a broader definition of a disability than IDEA and enables a student reasonable accommodations in school. If the student does not qualify under IDEA or Section 504 or parents do not give consent, then the student may still receive interventions through Tier 2 of RTI or a pre-referral process.

The IEP is an annual legal written contract that details the team's decisions in regard to an individual student's instruction in terms of their free appropriate public education and least restrictive environment. It documents the interventions, services, and supports that a school will provide for a student to help meet their academic, behavioral, and/or functional needs. IEPs may look different across the United States, but all must contain the student's present levels of performance, annual goals and short-term objectives, and the needed special education and related services. For an explanation of the key components of an IEP, see Table 1.6. For a sample IEP goal page, see Table 1.7.

Once the appropriate education is agreed upon and the IEP is written, then the instructional decisions are implemented. The IEP documents include where this instruction will take place (general education classroom, resource room, self-contained classroom or a more restrictive environment) and who is responsible for providing the instruction (general education teacher, special education teacher, related services personnel). No matter where the instruction takes place or who provides the instruction, the student must be assessed and monitored to determine their progress toward meeting the goal. This progress monitoring must be documented so that the results can be analyzed and decisions made on what, if any, instructional changes are necessary. For more information on identifying students for Tier 3 and IEPs, see Chapter 12.

Throughout this book, the ongoing cycle of assessment, analysis, decision-making, and instruction will be referenced as a way to provide effective instruction to meet students' behavioral needs.

Table 1.7 Sample Individualized Education Program

Background Information

Max is a fifth-grade student with a learning disability.

Present Levels of Performance: Academics

Based on the results of curriculum-based measurements, Max is able to solve single-digit addition and subtraction problems with 95% accuracy and double-digit problems with 85% accuracy. Max struggles with word problems, especially determining needed information, key words, and the appropriate strategies to correctly solve the problem. Max averages 20% on curriculum-based measurements involving addition and subtraction word problems while the class average is 85%. Being able to determine needed key words and information from a word problem and solve it correctly is a skill that is necessary for Max to be successful in the general education mathematic curriculum.

Goal

When given grade-level word problems, Max will be able to identify the relevant information and operations needed to correctly solve the problem with a minimum accuracy rate of 80% or eight out of ten correct with zero teacher prompts in five consecutive trials.

Objectives

1. When given a grade-level word problem involving addition or subtraction, Max will identify (highlight, underline, or circle) needed information to solve the problems in four out of five trials.
2. When given a grade-level word problem involving addition or subtraction, Max will identify the key words necessary in determining the correct operations and steps involved in solving the problems with 100% accuracy and no more than one teacher prompt.
3. When asked by the teacher, Max will state the strategies needed to solve the problem with no more than one teacher prompt in four out of five trials.

Present Levels of Performance: Behavior

Max is a very social student who easily makes friends but has difficulties completing in-class assignments in a timely manner. While his peers on average have zero to one late or missing assignments and can typically complete in-class assignments with zero to one teacher prompt, Max averages three late and one missing assignment per week and often requires four to five prompts to continue working before completing an assignment. These late and missing assignments are negatively affecting his grade and are causing him to fall farther behind in the general education curriculum.

Goal

Given in-class assignments, Max will complete the assignment within the teacher's allotted time with at least 75% accuracy and no more than two teacher prompts.

Objectives

1. When asked by the teacher, Max will restate the directions for an assignment in his own words.
2. When given an in-class assignment, Max will independently begin the assignment with no more than one teacher prompt.
3. Before beginning an assignment, Max will get out all the necessary materials and clear everything off his desk with 100% accuracy in four out of five consecutive trials.
4. Given a check sheet, Max will self-monitor his ability to work on a given task for 10 consecutive minutes before taking a brief (fewer than two minutes) break with 100% accuracy in four out of five trials.

Comprehension Check

1. How does of the ongoing cycle of RTI fit into each tier?
2. How does instruction change in each tier?
3. What components of instruction remain the same in each tier?
4. How does the decision-making process affect each tier?

CHAPTER SUMMARY

There are three laws that protect the rights of people with disabilities and promote an inclusive society.

- The Americans with Disabilities Act requires reasonable accommodations for people with disabilities (physical or mental impairment that affects one or more major life activities) in places of employment or entities that provide services whether or not they receive federal funding.
- Section 504 of the Rehabilitation Act requires reasonable accommodations for people with disabilities (physical or mental impairment that impedes one or more major life activities) in any place, program, and/or organization that receives federal funding.
- The Individuals with Disabilities Education Act guarantees free and appropriate public education to students exhibiting specific disabilities that affect their ability to learn and/or participate in school.
  - It also guarantees students the right to zero rejection, nondiscriminatory testing, a least restrictive environment, due process, and parental participation.

Response to Intervention is a multi-tiered system of support designed to meet the academic and behavioral needs of all students by providing appropriate education and increasing levels of support.

- This system is based on an ongoing cycle of assessment (universal screening and progress monitoring), analysis, decision-making, and instruction.
- Tier 1 incorporates the ongoing cycle into the general education classroom for whole-class instruction.
  - Students are universally screened, results are analyzed, instructional decisions are made based on that analysis, and instruction is provided.
  - Students who are at risk are progress monitored and may be referred to Tier 2.
- Tier 2 is also part of the pre-referral process and offers support and interventions beyond what is provided to the typical general education student using the ongoing cycle of assessment, analysis, decision-making, and instruction.
- Tier 3 typically incorporates the ongoing cycle (assessment, analysis, decision-making, and instruction) and is designed for the few students who failed to respond to interventions in both Tiers 1 and 2.
  - Students are assessed using a multi-factored evaluation, which is then analyzed to determine if a student is eligible for special education.
  - Decisions are then made as to what the appropriate education is for that student and incorporated into an Individualized Education Program.

REFERENCES

Berkeley, S., Bender, W., Peaster, L. G., & Saunders, L. (2009). Implementation of response to intervention: A snapshot of progress. *Journal of Learning Disabilities, 42*(1), 85–95.

Center on Response to Intervention. (2016). *Progress monitoring*. Retrieved from www.rti4success.org/essential-components-rti/progress-monitoring

Center on Response to Intervention. (n.d.). *RTI implementer series* [PowerPoint slides]. Retrieved from www.rti4success.org/resource/rti-implementer-series-module-1-screening

Daly, E. J., III, Martens, B. K., Barnett, D., Witt, J. C., & Olson, S. C. (2007). Varying intervention delivery in response-to-intervention: Confronting and resolving challenges with measurement, instruction, and intensity. *School Psychology Review, 36,* 562–581.

Disability Rights Education & Defense Fund (DREDF). (n.d.). *A comparison of ADA, IDEA, and Section 504.* Retrieved from http://dredf.org/advocacy/comparison.html

The IRIS Center. (2016). *Universal screening.* Retrieved from http://iris.peabody.vanderbilt.edu/module/rti-math/cresource/q1/p03/#content

National Association of Elementary School Principals. (n.d.). *Student assessment: Using student achievement data to support instructional decision making.* Retrieved from www.naesp.org/sites/default/files/Student%20Achievement_blue.pdf

National Joint Committee on Learning Disabilities (NJCLD). (2005). *Responsiveness to intervention and learning disabilities.* Retrieved from www.ldonline.org/article/11498

Nellis, L. (2012). Maximizing the effectiveness of building teams in response to intervention implementation. *Psychology in the Schools, 49*(3), 245–256. doi:10.1002/pits.2159

Polloway, E. A., Patton, J. R., & Serna, L. (2008). *Strategies for teaching learners with special needs* (9th ed.). Columbus, OH: Pearson.

School Improvement in Maryland. (2016). *Analyzing and using the data.* Retrieved from http://mdk12.msde.maryland.gov/instruction/progress/using.html

Skalski, A. K., & Stanek, J. (2010). *Section 504: A guide for parents and educators.* National Association of School Psychologists. Retrieved from http://www.bpsd.org/Downloads/Section%20504.pdf

Smith, T. (2001). *Section 504, the ADA, and public schools.* Retrieved from www.ldonline.org/article/6108?theme=print

Stanberry, K. (2014). *Understanding 504 plans.* Retrieved from www.understood.org/en/school-learning/special-services/504-plan/understanding-504-plans

Wright, P., & Wright, P. (2015). *My child with a 504 plain is failing, school won't help: Your eligibility game plan.* Retrieved from www.wrightslaw.com/info/sec504.idea.eligibility.htm

2

PRINCIPLES OF MANAGING BEHAVIORS

Stephen B. Richards

CHAPTER OBJECTIVES

After reading this chapter, students should be able to:

1. Identify and describe methods for increasing behavior and define key terms and concepts related to positive and negative reinforcement, including the Premack principle, shaping procedures, token economies, and behavioral contracts.
2. Differentiate between types of reinforcers, describe how the quality and quantity of reinforcers affect student behavior, identify how reinforcement schedules are used, and describe how to encourage generalization.
3. Identify and describe methods of decreasing behavior, including differential reinforcement, extinction, and positive and negative punishment.

METHODS FOR INCREASING BEHAVIOR

As noted in Chapter 1, a major key to managing student behavior is to focus on Positive Behavioral Interventions and Supports (PBIS—also known as Schoolwide Positive Behavior Support, Sugai & Horner, 2006), particularly in Response to Intervention (RTI) or any similar multi-tiered system of supports. PBIS as integral to RTI are discussed in Chapter 3. Within each tier of RTI, educators address what students need to do to be successful in all school environments. Although consequences for inappropriate behavior are a necessary component of PBIS, these are not the primary tools in PBIS within RTI. Instead, educators use various teaching and positive reinforcement strategies to encourage appropriate behavior rather than using punishment to suppress inappropriate behavior. This approach to managing behavior is universally acceptable to families of students, students themselves, educators, school boards, advocates, and other vested parties in the education and treatment of children and adolescents.

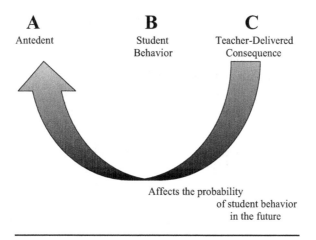

Figure 2.1 ABC Chart

To understand the principles of increasing (and decreasing) behavior, it is necessary to understand the basic principles of behavioral interventions. The paradigm for behavioral interventions includes an antecedent (A) that occurs before student behavior (B), which in turn is followed by a consequence (C) that affects the future occurrence of B under the same or similar A conditions (see Figure 2.1). The emphasis on the *future* occurrence of behavior cannot be overstated. Only by collecting data on how a student behaves (B) under the same conditions (A) can educators truly determine if consequences (C) are having the desired influence on student behavior. Remember, only a student (or anyone) can actually change their behavior. As an educator, you cannot change a student's behavior, but you can arrange A and C to *encourage* students to behave (B) in a manner that is in the student's best interests and in concert with the behavioral expectations within the school environment (Kazdin, 2013). As background, readers may review online various videos that explain the principles outlined by researchers John Watson and B. F. Skinner in establishing the power of A and C in affecting the future occurrence of B. Since that early research, educators have expanded and refined those principles outlined by Watson and Skinner.

Positive and Negative Reinforcement

When referring to interventions that may be used to increase or maintain behavior, we are referring to *positive* and *negative reinforcement*. Reinforcement occurs when the probability that a behavior will happen in the future under the same or similar antecedent conditions is increased (or maintained) by the delivery of a consequence following the behavior (Alberto & Troutman, 2017), as shown in Figure 2.2.

There are important aspects of reinforcement, including:

- Positive and negative reinforcement are not "good and bad" or refer to reinforcing "good or bad behavior."
- Positive and negative refer to the consequences delivered following a behavior.

	A	B	C
+ reinforcement	Antecedent (e.g., bell rings)	Student behaves appropriately	Consequence delivered by teacher that is desired by the student
- reinforcement	Antecedent is aversive	Student behaves appropriately	Consequence delivered by teacher is removal of the aversive
		Future occurrence of behavior is increased in either + or - reinforcement	

Figure 2.2 Positive and Negative Reinforcement

- Positive means you *add* something to the student's life as a result of performing a behavior.
- Negative means you *take away* something from the student as a result of performing a behavior.
- In negative reinforcement, what is taken away as a consequence is an aversive antecedent; negative reinforcement relies on students wishing to escape or avoid the negative aversive.
- Behaviors may need to be defined. For example, "Respect others" is not clear enough for students to fully understand the rule. Teachers must inform and demonstrate for students what exemplifies respecting others as well as non-examples of the rule.
- In both positive and negative reinforcement, the consequences are intended to help the student learn how to behave (what actions to take) under the same or similar antecedent conditions in the future.
- Finally, teachers can accidentally reinforce inappropriate behavior as well as systematically reinforce appropriate behavior.
- RTI is a multi-tiered system for reinforcing appropriate behavior.
- Progress monitoring is necessary (through collection of data) to validate that the student is or is not responding to the interventions at any of the tiers of RTI.

Here is an example of systematic intervention using positive reinforcement in Tier 1. Students receive praise and "tickets" they can later exchange for desired rewards for being on time to class, having all their materials needed, completing their work on time, and respecting others. The students have been systematically taught that respecting others means keeping hands and feet to yourself, asking others if you can borrow their possessions, saying nice things to your peers, and following teachers' directions. Over time, teachers may need to do additional teaching to further define respecting others (e.g., later in the school year, students are taught through discussion and demonstration that making fun of other students' clothing or appearance is *not* respecting others). It is important to provide non-examples of behavioral expectations as well as examples for students to have a better understanding of what are appropriate and inappropriate behaviors. Also, it is important to note that using tickets and praise to reinforce appropriate behavior is a scientific, evidence-based behavioral intervention. Positive reinforcement can also be applicable in Tiers 2 and 3 of RTI.

An example of accidental negative reinforcement follows. A student who is disruptive in her classroom is systematically removed from the direct instruction (sits facing away from the class but still can hear and participate in instruction) in Tier 2, as she has not responded appropriately to the evidence-based behavioral interventions in Tier 1. The RTI team originally hypothesized that the student was receiving accidental positive reinforcement from peers for disrupting class through laughter and other forms of attention, such as smiles and gestures. Through collecting data (progress monitoring), the RTI team recognizes that the student's behavior is increasing as a result of being removed from having visual contact with peers. The team now hypothesizes that while peer attention may indeed have had some effect, the student may be disruptive in order to escape or avoid work. Despite her presence still in class, it appears the teacher's expectations for work completion and participation dissipate when the student is removed. The team now believes that the student is being negatively reinforced (student finds work aversive, student disrupts, consequence is student is able to escape or avoid the aversive work). The team needs to rethink the intervention once again. An important aspect of negative reinforcement in schools is that it may occur more often accidentally than it does systematically. That is, the student may discern how to engage in inappropriate behavior to escape or avoid undesirable school expectations when removal from the teaching situation is the consequence. An example of using negative reinforcement systematically would be offering students a pass from doing homework or taking a final course exam by performing very well on in-class activities and assignments (assuming homework and final exams are aversive to the student). This example of systematic use would likely be a Tier 1 intervention.

Because teachers want to avoid accidentally reinforcing inappropriate behavior, it is important that reinforcement, positive or negative, be delivered immediately after the behavior is performed and only when the desired behavior is performed (contingently and immediately delivered upon meeting behavioral expectations). The student learns the behavioral expectations by the consistent pairing of antecedent to behavior and behavior to consequence. These pairings result in the student learning that when certain conditions are in effect (A), then a particular behavior (B) results in a desired consequence (C). For example, when a teacher raises her hand, her students know to stop talking, look, and listen to the teacher. The teacher praises her students for their behavior. The teacher has taught this to students systematically through praise and perhaps other reinforcement strategies over a period of time. These pairings can be so effective that the teacher's students may learn to monitor their own noise levels and behavior and encourage one another to be quieter and to listen, even without the teacher raising her hand or in the absence of her direct praise.

Premack Principle

One of the more available positively reinforcing interventions that is evidence based is the Premack principle (Premack, 1959). The Premack principle relies on a student engaging in a lower preference activity (such as the student who needs to do their schoolwork) to obtain a higher preference activity (time to engage in computer-based activities at the end of the day). The RTI team in the negative reinforcement example preceding this discussion decided on the use of the Premack principle as a different intervention in Tier 2. The Premack principle is sometimes referred to as grandma's rule because the basics of this principle have been well established for many generations. Children are told to do their chores before going outside to play or to complete homework before engaging in video game play. The child engages in a less preferred activity to gain access to the more preferred activity. Teachers use the Premack principle through offering higher preference activities (engaging in free reading time, sitting next to a friend, engaging in a computer-based academic game, being the line leader, being the teacher's helper) to students for meeting less preferred behavioral expectations, particularly for completing academic work but also for avoiding inappropriate behavior, such as disrupting class. One key factor in applying the Premack principle is that the high-preference activity must be under teacher control. That is, if the student may obtain the activity freely, it may not have a reinforcing quality. For example, if the student in the negative reinforcement example can obtain access to computer games freely at home, then they may not value the activity at school sufficiently to actually perform their schoolwork. Teachers typically use activities that are available only at school or are not available at home. The Premack principle is equally applicable in Tiers 1, 2, or 3 of RTI. Progress monitoring is necessary to validate the effective use of the Premack principle.

Shaping Procedures

Shaping is another commonly used application of positive reinforcement in all tiers of RTI. Shaping relies on systematically reinforcing a student's behavior as it more closely approximates the end behavioral expectation. Shaping involves offering reinforcement (often in the form of praise or some form of tokens or points to be exchanged for desired rewards) for behavior that is showing improvement toward meeting the behavioral expectation. Shaping is a process that takes time and is used when teachers expect a student is not likely to alter their behavior all at once. For example, a student regularly blurts out answers to questions in class without following the rule "Raise your hand and wait to be recognized by the teacher before speaking during class discussions." The teacher may recognize that the student has impulsive behavior as a consequence of their attention deficit hyperactivity disorder. The student has engaged in this behavior for an extended period of time. The teacher decides that shaping is her best approach in RTI Tier 1. She works by explaining the rule and demonstrating how it is done properly as well as non-examples of following the rule. Initially, the teacher praises the student for raising their hand, even though they still blurt out answers. She continues to explain the rule and having the student and other students demonstrate examples and non-examples. She praises the student for raising their hand, waiting for some period of time, but then blurting out the answer before another student can answer. Eventually, the student is able to follow the rule regularly. The teacher has shaped the student's behavior by reinforcing closer approximations to the actual expected behavior until the student has mastered that behavior. Other examples of using shaping include teaching students how to line up, walk through the halls, turn in homework, sit properly in their seats, obtain and pay for lunch in the cafeteria, and almost any behavior that students need to learn but may not accomplish all at once. Shaping requires patience and some judgment on the teacher's part in determining when and if the student is making a closer approximation to the target behavior. Academic behaviors, such as handwriting, social behaviors, such as engaging in conversations, and athletic behaviors, such as shooting a basketball, are other examples of behaviors that lend themselves to shaping procedures. Shaping is useful in any tier of RTI but particularly has applications when students have experienced behavioral "failures" for a period of time and truly do not understand how to meet those expectations. Shaping offers a means for providing evidence-based, additional instruction in Tiers 2 and 3 for students to experience behavioral success. Again, progress monitoring is needed to validate the effectiveness of shaping.

Token Economies

Token economies are a comprehensive system for applying reinforcement for establishing and maintaining behavioral expectations, particularly at the outset of the school year in Tier 1 (and sometimes punishment through response cost, which is discussed later in this chapter). Token economies may also function as point systems, sticker systems, and any approach that uses a generalized reinforcer (discussed later in this chapter) that can be exchanged for individualized, desired rewards. The payment of money is the ultimate example of such an economy in the adult world. Money, intrinsically, has no value. It is paper and pieces of metal. However, money is prized because it can be used by each individual to obtain goods and services that are valued by that person.

Establishing a token economy requires several components.

- First, teachers must establish and teach the behavioral expectations for earning tokens. Both examples and non-examples of expectations are taught. Teachers often engage the students themselves in establishing individual classroom expectations in particular.
- Teachers select a token (poker chips, points, stickers) to be used such that students can bank their tokens. Tokens should not be easily counterfeited by students (e.g., pennies could be brought in by students "illegally" to increase their bank) and should be easily delivered to students with minimal disruption to the class activities. Teachers often use teacher dollars with students' names, teachers' names, or the school name. This adds the benefit of teaching mathematical money skills as well.

- Teachers set up a banking system to keep track of tokens earned. Students are often engaged in keeping track of their own token bank.
- Teachers establish a reinforce menu (how to accomplish this is discussed later in this chapter) with a wide variety of positive reinforcers that appeal to all students. Reinforcers often include tangible items (candy, homework passes, discount coupons for local businesses), social rewards (sitting with a friend, having lunch with the teacher), and activities using the Premack principle (self-selected reading, choice of a free-time activity, choice of a game to play at recess).
- Teachers establish the amount of reinforcement delivered for meeting behavioral expectations (two tokens, points, or stickers for arriving on time, three tokens for turning in completed homework, one token for paying a peer a compliment). The amount of reinforcement should be in line with the student effort required to meet the expectations.
- Teachers establish the cost of the reinforcers (5 tokens for sitting with a friend, 10 tokens for choosing a game at recess, 15 tokens for access to engaging in a computer-based academic game). Costs of reinforcers should also be in line with the effort required to earn the reinforcer.
- Teachers establish a system for cashing in tokens. With very young students, this may need to be daily or every two days. With older students, or after the token economy is firmly established, this may occur once a week.
- Teachers implement the economy and make adjustments as needed. For example, teachers may find that they create inflation by distributing so many tokens that they have to raise the price of reinforcers. Similarly, teachers may create deflation by distributing so few reinforcers that students must wait much too long to obtain their desired reinforcer. Teachers may need to adjust the system to ensure that all students can obtain reinforcers within a reasonable amount of time. Teachers may also need to require students to occasionally cash in tokens, as some students may hoard tokens simply because the tokens become reinforcing in and of themselves.
- Teachers should be mindful that the personal expense of the economy is very limited. Offering students pizza parties, free fast-food lunch, or expensive tangible items, such as compact discs, may lead to a breakdown of the economy. Teachers must be mindful that praise, always included with the delivery of a token, should eventually replace the tokens.
- Finally, as students master the behavioral expectations, the token economy should be faded, as just noted. Teachers use the token economy to establish behavioral expectations and then lessen the number of tokens delivered, raise the costs of reinforcers, and/or remove or substantially limit the use of the token economy. Students should learn to meet behavioral expectations because it leads to personal success, social recognition through occasional praise, and that a predictable, consistent school environment leads to better learning and better relationships among students and school personnel.

Behavioral contracts often work well with token economies for Tier 2 and 3 interventions. Students who are not entirely successful at Tier 1 need additional PBIS. In behavioral contracts, teachers establish a signed, "If you, the student, do _____, then the teacher will provide you with _____." Contracts are negotiated with the student, agreed to, and signed by the teacher and student. Contracts are used for meeting behavioral expectations, such as reducing disruptive behavior through shaping procedures. For example, a student who continues to engage in disruptive behavior (defined as talking out of turn, making inappropriate noises and comments, moving about the room when the student should be in-seat) may be entered into a contract to reduce disruptions from an average of 10 per day to no more than seven per day for five consecutive school days. The contract could include provisions for additional reductions or be renegotiated to set an upper limit of disruptions to no more than five per day, to three per day, and finally to no more than one disruption per day. The teacher agrees that if the student meets the contract, they will provide the student with X number of tokens or a particular desired reinforcer valued by the student. Behavioral contracts work well when students need to focus on a particular behavioral expectation. Teachers should also spell out in the contract any additional consequences for the student not meeting the expectations, although withholding of the reinforcer may be sufficient as a consequence. As with all the methods discussed in this chapter, progress monitoring is essential to determine if a student is responding to PBIS in the RTI system.

Comprehension Check
1. How are positive and negative reinforcement alike? How are they different?
2. What is the Premack principle? Provide an example.
3. How is shaping used in teaching behavioral expectations?
4. What are the major steps in establishing a token economy?
5. How can behavior contracts be used to promote student learning?

USE OF REINFORCERS

We have already discussed reinforcers and their application within RTI and as PBIS for students in all three tiers of RTI. There are particular factors influencing the use of reinforcers with which teachers should be aware so that they may choose and apply them most appropriately. Among those factors are the types of reinforcers used, the quality and quantity of reinforcers, schedules of reinforcement, and how teachers may encourage generalization through reinforcement.

Types of Reinforcers

We have described various types of reinforcers, such as tangible items, social reinforcers, activity reinforcers, and tokens. There are general descriptors for these various reinforcers that are helpful in designing interventions because students respond to and value reinforcers differently. Each of us has an individual history of reinforcement that influences how we respond to positive reinforcers. For example, for some students, praise is very effective because, over time, those students have learned that attention and recognition from adults and others is desirable. Other students, particularly those who are very young or experience more severe disabilities, may require tangible reinforcers, such as food or beverage items, at least until they have learned to associate those reinforcers with being praised. Still other students may value access to preferred activities as a result of earning those activities or privileges through token or point systems. These various types of reinforcers are generally referred to as primary, secondary, and generalized reinforcers. The use of these terms is helpful to teachers because their use allows team members to share a common vocabulary and understanding of what types of PBIS they wish to implement.

Primary Reinforcers

Primary reinforcers are sometimes thought of as life-sustainers (food, beverages, heat or clothing in cold weather, housing, affection, safety). There is not absolute agreement as to exactly what are *all* the primary reinforcers, but a good definition is that these reinforcers do not require experience for them to be valued. In a very real sense, we could say that the value of primary reinforcers is hardwired into human beings. When we are deprived of these reinforcers or we have a serious lack of them, we may be less able to attend to other tasks, such as schoolwork. Maslow's hierarchy can be viewed within this framework. A student who is hungry, frightened, freezing with inadequate clothing, and/or deprived of affection from family members may indeed have a very difficult time being successful in school behaviorally or academically. These primary reinforcer needs must be met for students to devote their attention and energy to other matters. Otherwise, they may spend much or all of their energy in pursuing these very basic human needs.

However, primary reinforcers are generally not desirable in their abundant use as PBIS if these basic needs *are* being met. Certainly, any PBIS and RTI system must recognize when these needs are not met and address them. Examples of implementing these types of supports could include having a free clothing bank at school, free breakfasts and lunches, social services to address housing needs, food banks, counseling and family supports for those experiencing particularly difficult circumstances, such as homelessness, loss of a loved one, or loss of parental employment, students experiencing bullying or abuse, and many other possibilities. Once it is clear that these needs are being met, teachers may consider other forms of evidence-based interventions to support struggling students.

Two important variables affect the use of all types of reinforcers but are particularly applicable to primary reinforcers. The first is *deprivation*. Deprivation could refer to the types of dire circumstances just outlined. However, in terms of designing more typical school-based effective PBIS, deprivation is used as a term to describe that a student does not have unlimited access to a reinforcer and in fact desires obtaining the reinforcer. Deprivation, in this use, can refer to primary, secondary, or generalized reinforcers. A student experiences deprivation when they desire a reinforcer and should meet behavioral expectations in order to obtain that reinforcer. We cited an earlier example when a student did not consider access to a computer at school as a reinforcer because there was considerable access at home. In short, this student was not deprived of access to computers sufficiently for that access to be positively reinforcing at school. This is why we suggest that when choosing reinforcers, teachers try to select those that they can have control over their access. *Satiation* is a term used to describe when a student has received a reinforcer in such abundance that whatever reinforcing quality it had is greatly diminished or lost altogether (Alberto & Troutman, 2017). Many, if not most, students are not in a state of deprivation with primary reinforcers. These are best used when no other type of reinforcer can be easily identified. For example, with a very young child or a child with severe disabilities, an edible reinforcer, such as a raisin or a piece of cereal, can be delivered immediately and contingently. These primary reinforcers should always be presented with praise, with the intention that praise will eventually replace the primary reinforcers. Primary reinforcers are particularly susceptible to satiation. Because people often tire of eating (or drinking) the same food (or beverage), such primary reinforcers may quickly lose their reinforcing quality, at least for a period of time. Therefore, varying edible reinforcers is encouraged, but again, replacing them with secondary or generalized reinforcers is strongly recommended. Of course, primary reinforcers may be included on reinforcer menus sparingly, as students may occasionally choose such items as candy or a favored snack in exchange for tokens, as nearly everyone occasionally appreciates this type of reinforcer.

Secondary Reinforcers

Secondary reinforcers are "learned" by humans by being paired with primary reinforcers. Praise and positive attention paired with primary reinforcers begins early in life and typically replaces any need for regular use of primary reinforcers. Parents smile, coo, talk to, laugh, and socially interact with their children regularly so that their children recognize that these types of social reinforcers are desirable without the presence of a primary reinforcer. After children enter school, they begin to appreciate other secondary reinforcers. Grades, for example, are not meaningful in and of themselves, but when consistently paired with praise and attention for completing work well, the grades themselves become reinforcing, with only occasional praise paired to the grades. Other secondary reinforcers include privileges (such as being the line leader, eating lunch with a special friend), a smiley face on a paper, various activities, and any item or event that acquires its reinforcing quality (as opposed to primary reinforcers that require no history of reinforcement to be valued). Secondary reinforcers, such as praise and attention, can be used to establish other secondary reinforcers. In other words, teachers often use their attention and praise paired with another consequence (such as obtaining that computer-based academic game) to establish new secondary reinforcers. In fact, it is recommended that teachers use praise liberally for appropriate behavior when also applying other consequences to assist the student in learning that these new consequences, which may have little intrinsic value, become reinforcing. This process helps to establish a sense of intrinsic reinforcement in students. That is, the student accepts the smiley face or the good grade as a reinforcer, and over time, the student develops the ability to self-reinforce (e.g., "I really studied hard and did well on that test."). Toward this effort to establish self-reinforcement, teachers often fade reinforcement by providing fewer secondary reinforcers less frequently and less predictably. This process is discussed at greater length in the later section addressing reinforcement schedules.

A special type of secondary reinforcer is the generalized reinforcer. These were discussed earlier in regard to token economies. Generalized reinforcers are established by being paired with already established secondary reinforcers (especially praise and attention) but also are backed up by other primary and secondary reinforcers that the students choose themselves.

Generalized Reinforcers

Generalized reinforcers, as suggested earlier, are actual tangible items (tokens, points, stickers) that are delivered immediately and contingently for meeting behavioral expectations. Generalized reinforcers are typically used in a token economy system, but they are also used in a PBIS system, often in a less structured manner than in a token economy. Generalized reinforcers derive their value from being used to "purchase" or exchange for a variety of back-up reinforcers (Alberto & Troutman, 2017). These back-up reinforcers are typically selected by the teacher, with considerable input from the students. The back-up reinforcers comprise a reinforcer menu. Prices for items on the menu are established, and students may bank their generalized reinforcers in order to save up for desired items. However, there should always be back-up reinforcers at various prices, allowing nearly any student to make some type of selection when tokens or other similar generalized reinforcers are exchanged. Items of some cost or effort on the teacher's part should require commensurate effort on the student's part to earn the sufficient tokens to obtain such items.

It is important, no matter what type of reinforcers are delivered, that they are valued and sought by the students (deprivation). The *quality* of the reinforcers should be in line with the effort required on the part of students to meet the behavioral expectations. High-quality reinforcers should take greater effort and vice versa. This is one reason why token economies can be quite effective in establishing behavioral expectations in any tier of RTI but particularly in Tier 1. The *quantity* of reinforcers must be managed such that students don't tire of the reinforcers and no longer value their delivery (satiation). Generalized reinforcers are useful in avoiding satiation because they are backed up by a wide variety of reinforcers that are tangible, social privileges or activities. Even when primary and secondary reinforcers are used, they should be occasionally varied. Praise, for example, can be offered in many different forms (e.g., "Good work." "I like how you _____." "You were an example today."). Teachers, through progress monitoring of student behavior, particularly in Tiers 2 and 3 of RTI, should evaluate if consequences are

- functioning as reinforcers, leading to increases or maintenance of appropriate behaviors;
- of sufficient quality to merit the student effort required to meet behavioral expectations; and
- sufficient in number to avoid encouraging students to change behavior yet not so frequently delivered that satiation occurs.

By using reinforcer schedules, teachers are better able to manage the balancing act of delivering enough but not too many reinforcers.

Reinforcer Menus

Reinforcer menus are often used with token economies but can be created to avoid satiation in any classroom. One may find online any number of reinforcer menu questionnaires appropriate for various grade levels. See Figure 2.3 for an example we created for an elementary-level classroom.

Reinforcer menus typically include tangible reinforcers (school items, such as pencils, notebooks, erasers; edibles, such as candy, thumb drives, books, coupons) and secondary reinforcers (privileges, such as free time, opportunities to serve in a special role in class, opportunities to engage in activities with a friend, homework pass). The reinforcer menu informs teachers as to what primary and secondary reinforcers students desire and wish to earn (Hall & Hall, 1980). Remember, the reinforcer menu includes the back-up reinforcers for which students exchange their generalized reinforcers (tokens, points, stickers). Teachers may also take notes about activities that students enjoy when given opportunities to make choices at school (opportunities to read a book, use a computer for an academic game, work on a special project with a friend, engage in art, music, or physical activities). Such observations can provide additional insight into what students enjoy, particularly when working with young

---

Before beginning:
1. Ensured approval from administrator to implement program.
2. Informed parents of program and sought input regarding reinforcers and any restrictions on reinforcers (e.g., food reinforcers).
3. Discussed with students, explained program, sought input on behavioral expectations.
4. Administered reinforcer menu questionnaire.
5. Directly taught examples and non-examples of the behavioral expectations.

Behavioral Expectations:
1. Follow directions of the teacher at all times.
2. Be ready to work and complete your work.
3. Participate in learning activities.
4. Treat other students like you want to be treated.
5. Take care of your belongings.

Selected Tokens (Generalized Reinforcer):
1. Used paper money illustrated by students including teacher's name.
2. Used denominations of $1, 5, & 10.
3. Copied bills from students' drawings.
4. Created a log sheet to keep track of students' accounts.
5. Created a bank where students store their dollars.

Selected Back-Up Reinforcers (Primary and Secondary Reinforcers):
1. From student questionnaires obtained tangible reinforcers such as erasers, pencils, candy, stickers, donated books, coupons, etc.

Figure 2.3 Example of a Reinforcer Menu Questionnaire for Fourth Graders

2. Determined from questionnaires activity reinforcers in concert with those available such as free reading time, work on academic games, engage in artwork or media production exercises, eating lunch with the teacher, being the teacher's aide, etc.
3. Every 2 weeks, will evaluate students' selections and add to or remove reinforcers based on popularity/scarcity. Observe students for other clues as to reinforcers to add.

Set Rewards for Meeting Behavioral Expectations:
1. Follow directions of the teacher at all times. 1-10 dollars for immediate compliance.
2. Be ready to work and complete your work. 1 dollar for daily work, 1 dollar for homework, 5-10 dollars for multi-day work
3. Participate in learning activities. 1 dollar for each participation including listening attentively, making appropriate comments, answering questions, asking questions, taking notes, other participation activities.
4. Treat other students like you want to be treated. 1-10 dollars for helping another student, 1 dollar for making a reinforcing comment to another student, 1 dollar for appropriate interactions with other students, 1-10 dollars for collaborating with other students, other examples 1-10 dollars.
5. Take care of your belongings. 1 dollar for having school materials in place, desk neat and tidy, coat/hat hung up, cleaning up behind self at lunch.

Set Prices for Reinforcers:
1. Varied based on value of reinforcer

    5 dollars for erasers, pencils, other basic school supplies

    5 dollars for each piece of candy or other edible

    5 dollars for each sticker

    20-40 dollars for donated books and coupons

    20 dollars for every 5 minutes of free reading time

    20 dollars for every 5 minutes of academic games

    30 dollars for 10 minutes of artwork or media production

    30 dollars for being teacher aide

    40 dollars for lunch with the teacher (may include a friend for an additional 10 dollars)
2. Will reevaluate every 2 weeks to determine if students' rewards are commensurate with prices of reinforcers. Be prepared to increase/decrease rewards and/or increase/decrease prices. Fade awarding of dollars over time and increase/maintain prices based on progress monitoring (charting of behavioral violations/incidents).
3. Set banking hours for Friday afternoon for last half-hour of day for students to count dollars in their accounts and purchase desired reinforcers.
4. Use last half-hour of Tuesdays/Thursdays of the following week for activity reinforcers selected on Friday.

Follow-Up
1. Every 2 weeks review data regarding frequency and severity of behavioral violations/incidents.
2. Note any student who is having more violations/incidents than others and consider using a behavioral contract or individualized modification of program.
3. Communicate to students how they are performing individually and collectively. Communicate to parents how their students are performing.
4. Communicate to administrator success or lack thereof. If not successful, seek advice or additional support.
5. When feasible, consider replacing token economy with a lottery. Dollars are still awarded in $1 increments, placed in a common bank, and 3 "winners" of the lottery drawn each Friday who can then choose reinforcers.

Figure 2.3 (Continued)

children who may not fully understand that the teacher is using questions to establish a reinforcer menu. They key to reinforcer menus is to ensure that there are a sufficient number of various reinforcers that appeal to each and every student (Hall & Hall, 1980) so that satiation is unlikely when students can choose their own rewards. Teachers can also add or delete reinforcers over time. For example, students may desire items associated with a popular new movie that could be added. Similarly, students may lose interest in earning the same items after a period of time or with the release of a new movie. Finally, rather than absorbing expenses for the items on reinforcer menus, teachers should include items that are free to them and/or seek donations from local businesses, the PTO, or other entities invested in student success.

Reinforcement Schedules

There are numerous scholarly sources to assist teachers in the systematic and precise use of the various reinforcement schedules. Possibilities include continuous, fixed ratio, variable ratio, fixed duration, and variable duration schedules as well as variations of these basic schedules. In general, these schedules can be thought of as continuous and intermittent schedules (Ferster & Skinner, 1957). Additionally, natural schedules of reinforcement are important.

Our experience is that classroom teachers do not typically engage in all the steps necessary to systematically employ ratio and duration schedules, with the exception of fixed ratio schedules. In token economies, when teachers establish, raise, or lower the number of generalized reinforcers to earn particular rewards, they are actually using a fixed ratio schedule. Teachers may also use duration schedules to teach students to engage in activities for more or less time (spend more time working on assignments before asking for teacher help, taking less time to move between classes during passing periods).

Because the precise use of these schedules is less common among classroom teachers, we will discuss the *principles* involved in using these schedules. In our experience, unless engaged in action research, applying the principles are sufficient for accomplishing the overall goal of encouraging lasting change in student behavior. However, we also want to stress that at Tiers 2 and 3 it may become necessary to use a systematic schedule with a particular student. In this case, we recommend consulting a source that fully describes and explains these schedules. Most teachers can apply the principles of using continuous, intermittent, and natural schedules of reinforcement and successfully implement interventions at all three tiers of RTI.

Continuous Schedules of Reinforcement

A continuous schedule of reinforcement involves reinforcing each and every correct behavioral response a student makes. That behavioral response is a targeted response. For example, a teacher may reinforce a student each and every time they arrive to class on time, have all their materials, or complete any in-class assignments. Continuous schedules are used to establish new behaviors or strengthen existing ones that are not occurring with sufficient frequency. Continuous schedules should not be maintained for extended periods or the student may become dependent on receiving reinforcement and may, in fact, not respond if the student perceives reinforcement is not going to be delivered following the response. For example, a teacher might reinforce a student each and every time they complete their classroom work. However, if the teacher uses this schedule for too long, when the teacher fails to deliver the reinforcer following work completion, the student may not complete their work on the next assignment because the student perceives they are not going to be rewarded. For this reason, teachers must thin the schedule of reinforcement from a continuous to an intermittent schedule. Once a new behavior is established or the student achieves an initial criterion, such as completing 10 consecutive assignments, the teacher should thin the schedule. As mentioned, this could be done systematically (the teacher now reinforces every second complete assignment, then every third, every fifth, and so on—this would be a fixed ratio schedule). Eventually, the teacher could reinforce the student on an average of every five completed assignments (this would be a variable ratio schedule). However, the teacher can thin the reinforcement by simply weaning the student from receiving reinforcement for every assignment completed so long as the student continues to respond correctly. The systematic approach does provide additional data that may aid in intervening with particularly difficult situations. For example, a student with more severe disabilities may respond to the level of reinforcement delivered such that systematic thinning is necessary to maintain improved or steady responding of the student. However, it is also quite appropriate for the teacher to thin the schedule non-systematically so long as the teacher does sufficient progress monitoring to ensure that the reinforcement is encouraging a student to strengthen or maintain their behavior. This is particularly applicable to students with whom the teacher can communicate. For example, a teacher might tell the student that they are doing so well at completing their work that they no longer need to be praised and given tokens for *each* assignment. The teacher would then continue to reinforce the student with frequency but not for each completed assignment. Over time, the teacher can continue to praise the student (and award tokens) more and more occasionally so long as data confirm that the student is continuing their success. If success does erode, the teacher would increase the frequency of reinforcement once again until the student is responding appropriately, and the teacher would then pay attention to lessening the frequency of reinforcement but at a slower pace. The same principles would be applied if the student's targeted behavior was time-based, such as taking more time to eat, less time to get to class, or more time engaged in cooperative play or cooperative learning.

Intermittent Schedules

Intermittent schedules have already been described in the previous section. When teachers thin the schedule, they are using an intermittent schedule. Teachers need progress monitoring data to analyze that the student behavior is continuing to improve or be maintained as they progressively (systematically or not) lessen the frequency of reinforcement. Intermittent schedules have the distinct advantage over continuous schedules in that intermittent ones tend to strengthen student behavior such that the student requires less and less reinforcement and may in fact develop intrinsic reinforcement. For example, the student who is reinforced each time they come to class on time may have their schedule thinned but they continue to come to class on time.

Eventually, the student comes to class on time with only very occasional praise or perhaps in the absence of praise altogether. The student begins intrinsically reinforcing themselves for getting to class on time. In short, this and all students may develop a sense of a job well done for the sake of doing the job well. This clearly is an expectation in the adult world, and teachers should work toward development of these intrinsic beliefs and values. Although reinforcement is available in the adult world (bosses praise workers, workers earn raises, entrepreneurs grow successful businesses, parents take pride in their children's accomplishments), generally, adults are expected to recognize the worth of their own efforts without an abundance of extrinsic recognition. Also, economies do provide generalized reinforcers (money for working) that do help to maintain behavior through the exchange of goods and services desired by adults. Teachers may continue to use a token economy or point system, but the level of reinforcement delivered should be significantly thinned so that students appreciate their own work and are less dependent on the exchange for reinforcer menu items for maintaining appropriate behavior.

Natural Schedules of Reinforcement

If teachers thin schedules of reinforcement effectively, students will eventually be on a natural schedule of reinforcement. This can work in at least two ways. One is that students become much less dependent on reinforcers delivered by teachers such that the students develop their own sense of intrinsic or self-reinforcement. Ideally, students come to rely on little more reinforcement from the teacher than occasional praise and the other built-in reinforcers of school, such as good grades and academic, performing arts, and athletic success. In short, they learn to recognize natural reinforcers available in the environment, including the praise of peers, better relations with peers and adults, opportunities opened by success, and a general sense of well-being, among many others. Ultimately, we want students and adults alike to recognize and derive reinforcement in these naturally occurring ways.

Second, students respond to natural schedules of reinforcement as well. Both natural reinforcers and schedules can be taught by using praise paired with primary and other secondary as well as generalized reinforcers, such as tokens, and by thinning schedules of reinforcement. The praise helps students understand that good grades are a reinforcer, as are social, academic, and other types of success achieved through their own (and supported) efforts. The thinning of reinforcement schedules teaches students to continue to work hard for success and to value natural reinforcers and the occasional praise and recognition provided by others.

Generalization of Behavior

The use of natural reinforcers and schedules through the thinning process includes students using learned behaviors in new situations and settings and even developing related behavior not directly taught through RTI and PBIS. For example, a student learns to interact with peers by offering compliments, using appropriate language, and engaging in conversation more competently. This same student is taught these behaviors directly through RTI and PBIS, and over time the "more pleasant" student is now finding that peers and adults interact more with them, provide them with attention, and praise them for accomplishments. This natural reinforcement encourages the student to maintain their behavior. The student also begins using their learned behaviors in environments outside of school and learns to engage in more sophisticated and fulfilling conversations as they become more and more skilled in interactions with others. The student begins to express sympathy and empathy for other students who struggle with social acceptance. The student has learned new but related behaviors that they were not taught directly and uses them in situations and settings where they were not directly taught to do so. The student has generalized their social interactions and conversational skills. Generalization is a desired outcome of teaching in all types of skills, including academics, career skills, everyday living skills, and particularly social skills. The end result is that the student develops appropriate behaviors that elicit reinforcement naturally from others.

Despite the efforts of educators and students themselves, it is necessary at times to teach students to stop engaging in inappropriate behavior. There are several evidence-based strategies designed for this purpose, and we will present them in the following section.

> *Comprehension Check*
> 1. How are primary, secondary, and generalized reinforcers different from one another?
> 2. At what stage of learning should continuous schedules of reinforcement be used? What are the advantages of intermittent schedules in maintaining learning of behavioral expectations?
> 3. How do natural schedules and natural reinforcers affect generalization of student behavior?

METHODS FOR DECREASING BEHAVIOR

Educators have strategies to contend with persistent inappropriate behavior that is not naturally replaced through positive reinforcement of appropriate behavior alone. These strategies can be quite intrusive, but we focus on strategies that are less so. The strategies we discuss are generally more acceptable to all stakeholders concerned with safe, effective learning environments than are strategies that focus primarily on punishment or similar procedures.

Differential Reinforcement

Differential reinforcement involves particular techniques to *replace* inappropriate behavior with more adaptive responses. Differential reinforcement, as the term suggests, involves changing the positive reinforcement being received that maintains the inappropriate behavior to a focus on a behavior that achieves the same level of reinforcement but is more adaptive behavior that benefits the student's own functioning and education (Dietz & Repp, 1983). In general, differential reinforcement involves interrupting or ignoring inappropriate behavior when it does occur, encouraging the more adaptive, targeted behavior, and "catching the student being good" to further strengthen the replacement behavior. Differential reinforcement comes in various forms depending on the targeted replacement behavior. In the first strategy, which is a bit different from the other differential reinforcement strategies, the aim is to reduce the level of an appropriate behavior that is occurring at an inappropriate level.

Differential Reinforcement of Lower Rates of Behavior

Occasionally, a student is engaging in an appropriate behavior that is occurring at an inappropriate level (too frequently, too long in duration). Examples include asking or actually leaving the classroom to get a drink of water or go to the restroom. Clearly, the examples are appropriate behavior but could be occurring at a higher rate or for a longer duration than is acceptable. Differential reinforcement of lower rates of behavior (DRL) relies on teaching a student to gradually lessen the frequency, duration, and so forth. Teachers may consider that when students engage in behavior at an inappropriately higher rate, it may be that the student is being negatively reinforced accidentally. That is, the student is escaping or avoiding work or some situation that is aversive to the student.

DRL relies on establishing an achievable, acceptable rate of occurrence and gradually working toward that outcome. For example, if a student asks to go to the restroom at a higher than typical rate and there is no physical reason for the student to do so, the teacher would reinforce gradual reductions in the behavior. The teacher would likely rely on initial baseline student performance in comparison to peers' performance to establish the DRL intervention. Again, the student may be asking to go the restroom on average eight times per day while peers ask only about once per week to go to the restroom outside of established break times for getting water and using the restroom.

The teacher discusses the issue with the student and other stakeholders (parents, other educators). The team decides to establish an expectation that the student will ask to go to the restroom no more than four times per day. If the student meets the expectation, a positive reinforcer chosen from a reinforcer menu is delivered. If the student exceeds the expectation, no reinforcer is delivered and the situation is typically discussed again, stressing to the student the expected performance level. Once the student achieves the expectation of no more than four requests per day, the expectation is lowered and so forth, until the student's requesting behavior is at a level much closer or equal to that of their typical peers. DRL should be only with behaviors that can take some time to reduce.

Differential Reinforcement of Alternative Behavior

Differential reinforcement of alternative behavior (DRA) relies on interrupting a targeted maladaptive behavior and reinforcing a replacement behavior. The student may need to be taught the alternative behavior or it may already be behavior the student possesses. For example, a student may need to be taught to interact with peers in more appropriate ways to replace inappropriate interaction behavior (student uses disrespectful language and comments and must learn how to ask questions, respond to questions, and seek assistance from adults). DRA usually involves interrupting the inappropriate behavior when it occurs and redirecting the student to engage in the targeted appropriate responses and then to be reinforced to do so. An example where the student already possesses the behavior would be a student who arrives to class late and is being reinforced for arriving on time. Teachers will need to consider the reinforcement schedule and the reinforcer for meeting the behavioral expectation. Generalized reinforcers paired with praise are often considered desirable because of the ease of delivery immediately following the desired behavior. Over time, the reinforcement is reduced toward natural schedules. The key to DRA is identifying a replacement behavior that, over time, will likely result in the same or similar level of natural reinforcement that was derived from the inappropriate behavior. In other words, the appropriate replacement behavior ideally should result in the same levels of attention and types of reinforcement (tangibles, social reinforcers, control over a situation) as did the inappropriate response.

Differential Reinforcement of Other Behavior

In some instances, students engage in a behavior or cluster of similar behaviors that are more difficult to identify replacement behaviors. For example, a student may engage in some self-defeating behavior, such as chewing their fingernails, making too many and too strong erasures on papers, or touching others inappropriately. In such cases, differential reinforcement of other behavior (DRO) may be a good choice. DRO interventions rely on using a timer to deliver reinforcement after a period of time in which the student does not engage in the inappropriate behavior. It is important to understand that the timer is used for establishing a duration of time in which the student engages in any behavior other than the targeted inappropriate behavior. For example, a student who is chewing on their fingernails may be delivered praise and a generalized reinforcer, such as a token, for every five minutes they do not engage in chewing their nails. If success is achieved, the timer is set for progressively longer periods of time until the targeted behavior is eliminated altogether or at least reduced to an acceptable level. When the student does engage in the inappropriate behavior, the teacher interrupts the student and resets the timer, typically explaining to the student what they did. One potential issue with DRO is that teachers should reinforce the student for not engaging in the inappropriate behavior, but the student may engage in some other inappropriate behavior not targeted. The teacher should still reinforce the student but may want to add this new behavior to the program. For example, a student may disrupt class by speaking out and making irrelevant and inappropriate remarks. The student is included in a DRO intervention. The student begins making inappropriate noises instead of the remarks. Technically, the student should be reinforced for not making remarks, but the teacher will need to include noise-making as an additional behavior in the DRO intervention. When such circumstances arise, students may display similar behavior intended to achieve the same purpose (gaining attention from the teacher or peers, avoiding or escaping work or class) and the teacher and educational team will need to adjust the program, informing the student of the addition of the new behavior to the DRO intervention. When differential reinforcement is not suitable for interventions intended to decrease behavior, then there are other more intrusive interventions available, although these may be less acceptable by parents, other educators, and students themselves.

Extinction

Extinction is probably best used when inappropriate behavior is reinforced through the acquisition of some tangible item or the inappropriate behavior is relatively recently acquired and more likely to change without heroic effort. Extinction involves withholding access to the reinforcer(s) that are maintaining a behavior (Alberto & Troutman, 2017). Therefore, it is necessary to know that the reinforcer is maintaining the targeted behavior. For example, a younger child may exhibit tantrum behavior in order to obtain some tangible item (a toy) or perhaps attention (teacher or aide intervenes to comfort the child) or perhaps to avoid some aversive situation (the child wishes to avoid some school task). The teacher would make the toy unavailable, or ignore the child's tantrum-seeking attention, or ensure that the child does not escape the school task. Unfortunately, the longer the inappropriate behavior has been used, the more resistant to extinction is the behavior. That is, the student's efforts to obtain the desired reinforcer may actually *increase* initially when an extinction intervention is implemented (Kazdin, 2013). In our example, the child's tantrums may get louder and longer at first as the child doubles up on their efforts to achieve the reinforcer. For this reason alone, extinction interventions can be difficult to maintain, particularly when the student seeks attention and becomes increasingly disruptive in the class in attempts to achieve that attention. In such situations, DRA is likely a better choice for intervention, as this strategy provides a more acceptable means of obtaining teacher attention. If reinforcement is being derived from some tangible item that can be removed or have very controlled access, then extinction may be the preferred choice for intervention so long as any of the child's reactions to the loss of the reinforcer are not too disruptive, interfere with the learning or safety of themselves or others, and the behavior declines in frequency, duration, and intensity rather quickly. Because a teacher can accidentally reinforce a student on a very intermittent schedule if they cave in and the student obtains the desired reinforcer, it is likely best to use extinction only when there is a significant degree of confidence that intervention will work and rather quickly. If the student is accidentally reinforced on this intermittent schedule (the tantrums become so severe they cannot be ignored), the teacher may actually worsen the behavior over time because the student is learning that if they engage in the inappropriate behavior long enough with intensity, they may very well achieve the aim of obtaining reinforcement and thus strengthen or maintain the maladaptive response.

Positive Punishment

As with reinforcement, positive punishment refers to a consequence immediately following a behavior that is added to the individual's life. In positive punishment, the aim is for the consequence to result in a future decrease in the targeted behavior under the same or similar antecedent conditions. Positive punishment is used in schools, primarily through mild verbal reprimands. For example, a child who is behaving in some manner outside of the behavioral expectations, interrupting the student verbally and instructing the student to stop and engage in some other behavior may serve the desired purpose of the teacher. Such positive punishment is likely most effective in Tier 1 of RTI when students can be mildly reprimanded for violating expectations but also are still receiving positive reinforcement for meeting those expectations. Administration of corporal punishment, contingent exercise, or other possible positive punishments are not likely to be acceptable or even an option for educators. Mild verbal reprimands can be effective when teachers are making many more positively reinforcing comments (praise) than reprimands and the student's behavior is relatively mild in rate, duration, and intensity. One type of positive punishment teachers should absolutely avoid is assigning academic work as punishment for misbehavior. Such interventions send a clear message that academic work is undesirable and to be avoided, even if the outcome of suppressing the undesirable response is achieved. Requiring a student to write 100 times "I will not _____" teaches the student that writing is punishing, and that is not a message teachers want to send.

Negative Punishment

Negative punishment, similar to negative reinforcement, involves removing something from the person's life that results in a future decrease in behavior under the same or similar antecedent conditions. Negative punishment is most appropriately used within a token economy or similar system. Tokens (generalized reinforcers) are delivered for meeting behavioral expectations, while tokens may be taken away for infractions. This is referred to as *response cost* in the literature. In essence, the student is fined for misbehavior. Because the delivery of generalized reinforcers is above and beyond what students would typically receive in school, many educators believe it is then acceptable to take back such reinforcers for not meeting behavioral expectations. Be aware, however, that some adults may feel it is not right to give something to a child only to take it away later. Another manner in which negative reinforcement is sometimes used is in the removal of privileges. For example, a student who throws food in the cafeteria may lose the privilege of eating there and is then required to eat alone for a day or some period of time. However, in removing privileges, teachers should be aware if the privilege is expected as a routine part of schooling. One common example is the removal of recess for not meeting expectations. However, the frequent use of such loss of privilege is contrary to what educators believe is developmentally appropriate. Recess is in the school day for younger children because it is beneficial, and its regular removal from a child is likely to prove counterproductive if not unacceptable to parents or other educators.

Punishment, positive or negative, can have undesirable side effects. It may suppress the undesirable response only in the presence of adults or in the classroom. A student may continue to bully when unobserved or outside of the school environment. Punishment can lead to students wishing to avoid the teacher by whom or class in which they are punished. Punishment can send the message that this is a good strategy for controlling the behavior of others. Students may respond to punishment (and extinction) in unpredictable and possibly volatile ways, such as verbal or physical aggression. For these and other reasons, punishment, except in its very mildest forms and when used only very occasionally and when the side effects of its use can be reasonably predicted, is likely best avoided altogether. If an educational team decides that punishment may be a potentially useful intervention in Tier 2 or 3, that team is also likely to find the requirements in terms of obtaining approval are time consuming, tedious, and difficult. Even when punishment might be approved, it is typically a provision of its use that a parent or even a student can demand immediately to have the procedure stopped. It is always preferable to use reinforcement strategies to teach new or replacement behaviors that result in natural reinforcement from others.

Remember, progress monitoring is always necessary to determine if the intended outcome of an intervention is being achieved. Teachers can think they are punishing a student when data reveal that the behavior is worsening, suggesting that positive reinforcement is occurring. The student kept from the cafeteria may actually prefer eating alone with the teacher than being in the classroom, even though the teacher may believe their actions are resulting in punishment. In all these intervention strategies, teachers should keep in mind that it is the effect on student behavior that signals what is actually occurring and not necessarily what the teacher intends to occur. Many teachers have accidentally reinforced or punished behavior when they intended to do the exact opposite. In the next chapter, we discuss PBIS systems and how they are effective in preventing misbehavior and in teaching behavioral expectations using positive reinforcement.

Comprehension Check

1. How are DRL, DRA, and DRO used to decrease inappropriate student behavior?
2. When are extinction interventions more appropriate? What are the hazards of using extinction procedures?
3. What mild forms of positive and negative punishment might teachers use in the classroom?
4. What are the potential side effects of using extinction and punishment interventions?

CHAPTER SUMMARY

Identify and describe methods for increasing behavior and define key terms and concepts related to positive and negative reinforcement, including the Premack principle, shaping procedures, token economies, and behavioral contracts.

- Positive reinforcement refers to the presentation of a reward immediately following a behavior that results in an increase in the future rate of that behavior under the same or similar antecedent conditions.
- Negative reinforcement refers to the withdrawal of an aversive antecedent immediately following a behavior that results in an increase in the future rate of that behavior under the same or similar antecedent conditions.
- The Premack principle refers to the practice of allowing students access to high-preference activities as a reward for engaging in low-preference activities.
- Shaping is the process of positively reinforcing successively closer approximations of a behavior so that the behavior is learned.

- Token economies involve several steps on the part of the teacher and are useful in establishing and maintaining behavioral expectations.
- Behavioral contracts are written agreements between a student and teacher that specify if the student meets specific behavioral expectations, the teacher will provide the student with reinforcement.

Differentiate between types of reinforcers, describe how the quality and quantity of reinforcers influence student behavior, identify how reinforcement schedules are used, and describe how to encourage generalization.

- Reinforcers may be primary, secondary, or generalized reinforcers. Primary reinforcers require no learning to have value to humans. Secondary reinforcers acquire value through being paired with primary or already established secondary reinforcers. Generalized reinforcers acquire their value through being exchanged for a variety of reinforcers. Natural reinforcers may be any of these but occur without systematic application by the teacher.
- The quality and quantity of reinforcers delivered affects student behavior and both should be commensurate in value to the behavioral effort required to obtain them.
- Reinforcement schedules can be continuous, intermittent, or natural. Continuous schedules are used when students are first learning behavioral expectations. Intermittent schedules are used to strengthen and maintain learned behaviors. Natural schedules are those that occur in the environment without systematic application by the teacher.
- Generalization of behavior is encouraged when behavioral expectations have been learned and are maintained through natural reinforcers and schedules.

Identify and describe methods of decreasing behavior, including differential reinforcement, extinction, and positive and negative punishment.

- Differential reinforcement of lower rates, alternative, and other behaviors are available interventions for decreasing behavior that rely on positive reinforcement to shape or teach appropriate behavioral expectations.
- Extinction relies on withholding the identifiable reinforcer for an inappropriate behavior. Extinction interventions can be difficult to maintain and should be used sparingly.
- Positive punishment most often comes in the form of mild and occasional verbal reprimands. Such positive punishment should occur in the presence of more abundant positively reinforcing comments (praise).
- Negative punishment, also known as response cost, is most often used in conjunction with token economies or similar systems. Removing privileges from students on a regular basis is inadvisable.
- Punishment and extinction interventions come with the threat of many potential undesirable side effects.
- Progress monitoring must be used to validate how interventions are affecting student behavior.

REFERENCES

Alberto, P. A., & Troutman, A. C. (2017). *Applied behavior analysis for teachers* (9th ed.). Boston, MA: Pearson.

Dietz, D. E. D., & Repp, A. C. (1983). Reducing behavior through reinforcement. *Exceptional Education Quarterly, 3*, 34–46.

Ferster, C. B., & Skinner, B. F. (1957). *Schedules of reinforcement.* Englewood Cliffs, NJ: Prentice-Hall.

Hall, R. V., & Hall, M. C. (1980). *How to select reinforcers.* Lawrence, KS: H & H Enterprises.

Kazdin, A. E. (2013). *Behavior modification in applied settings.* Long Grove, IL: The Waveland Press.

Premack, D. (1959). Toward empirical behavior laws: I. Positive reinforcement. *Psychological Bulletin, 66*, 219–233.

Sugai, G., & Horner, R. R. (2006). A promising approach for expanding and sustaining school-wide positive behavior support. *School Psychology Review: Bethesda, 35*(2), 245–259.

3

DATA COLLECTION

Stephen B. Richards and Sarah Schimmel

CHAPTER OBJECTIVES

After reading this chapter, students should be able to:

1. Identify schoolwide data collection methods that yield individual behavioral data.
2. Identify individual behavioral data collection methods for use within the Response to Intervention process.

INTRODUCTION

Positive Behavioral Interventions and Supports (PBIS) as a topic has been introduced and discussed briefly in the previous two chapters. PBIS is a natural fit with Response to Intervention (RTI). Although these two processes were not conceived of and implemented simultaneously, they both rely on similar principles and procedures. RTI, we have learned, is a multi-tiered system of supports that is applicable to academic learning as well as to behavioral interventions. PBIS includes preventing and addressing behavioral expectations in a multi-tiered system as well. Without successful academic engagement, school personnel should expect more behavioral challenges among students. Without a successful preventive and proactive approach to school, classroom, and behavior management, there is less likelihood of successful academic learning.

PBIS relies on these fundamental principles (Sugai & Horner, 2006; Taylor, Smiley, & Richards, 2019):

- Collect data to determine current performance of the student body (and individuals as needed) in relation to behavioral infractions in particular.
- Develop behavioral expectations that are useful in all school environments and with all students. The expectations should cover a wide range of student behavior and expectations.

- Identify a team of school personnel to coordinate training of both faculty and staff as well as the student body.
- At the beginning of the school year, use direct instruction to teach students how the expectations are operationalized and what examples and non-examples of the expectations look like (model, provide guided feedback as students practice following the behavioral expectations, and promote maintenance, transfer, and generalization of the behavioral skills learned).
- Continue with guided practice and feedback in all classrooms and in all school environments.
- Provide rewards and recognition to students for meeting the behavioral expectations (and generalizing them). Provide consequences for behavioral infractions.
- Continue to collect data, particularly on behavioral infractions but also on academic success.
- Evaluate data regularly to determine if the PBIS are resulting in improved behavioral and academic outcomes.
- Revise training, expectations, rewards and recognition, or data collection as needed.
- Identify students (anywhere in the steps already mentioned) who are not meeting expectations, even with training, guided practice, and feedback.
- Provide additional small-group or individualized instruction for these identified students to ensure that they understand the expectations, what examples and non-examples look like, and how students can demonstrate those expectations.
- Identify students who are still not meeting behavioral expectations, even with additional intervention supports within small groups or provided individually.
- Conduct a functional behavioral assessment and develop a behavioral intervention plan for these students as necessary if students are on Individualized Education Programs. Functional behavioral assessments and behavioral intervention plans are discussed in detail in Chapter 14 and Chapter 15, respectively.
- If students are not on Individualized Education Programs, the team should consider if students need referral for a multidisciplinary evaluation for special education and related services.
- If students are not referred, continue to provide individualized interventions, such as those discussed in Chapter 2.

PBIS is a multi-tiered system of supports intended to proactively address any potential behavioral issues, teach students what to do to be successful, recognize and reward their achievements, and address any student issues that continue.

As noted earlier, data collection is paramount to successful implementation of RTI. In Chapter 2, you read about a variety of behavior management strategies that rely on direct observation of individual student behavior to collect data. In Chapter 4, you will read about implementation of RTI schoolwide and some of the data concerns from that perspective. In this chapter, we will discuss data collection that uses schoolwide methods for individuals (attendance records, academic results) as well as specific individual methods of observational data (frequency, percentages, duration).

> *Comprehension Check*
> 1. List three fundamental principles of PBIS.
> 2. Why is data collection important?
> 3. When is a functional behavioral assessment needed?

SCHOOLWIDE METHODS THAT YIELD INDIVIDUAL DATA

Schools regularly collect a variety of data that can be useful in identifying students who are at risk for or in need of Tier 2 or 3 RTI supports. These data may also reveal at least some possible causes for not meeting behavioral expectations. These methods may also be helpful in identifying interventions and/or other assessments needed.

Vision and Hearing Data

Vision and hearing screening is often conducted in schools at various grade levels, particularly with young children. Whenever a student displays inappropriate behavior, particularly if it can be associated with possible vision or hearing loss (not following written or oral directions) because of repeated actions and patterns, it is advisable to consider if there is some sensory issue that may be the cause or contributing significantly to the behavioral issue. Additionally, if a student has a sudden change in behavior patterns for no discernible reason at school, it may also be helpful to ask the student's caregivers about changes at home or any conditions they may be aware of that could cause the behavior change.

Attendance and Tardy Data

Research throughout the years has demonstrated the effect of attendance on success in school. This is common sense. A student is not likely to be learning if they regularly miss school. Schools collect attendance on every student, every day. Reasons why students may not be attending can be investigated when it is apparent a student has missed an excessive number of school days. For example, a child may have missed several school days due to illness, injury, or a family issue, such as homelessness. The RTI team would want to know if the situation leading to school absences was temporary and, if so, how long the situation is likely to persist. Some students may miss school regularly due to issues of neglect (parents do not help a child get ready for school or get to the bus stop). Others may miss school simply because the child does not want to go to school and parents do not enforce the need to go to school. For older students, particularly in high school, parents may be unaware that the student is skipping school or classes, although schools typically have a system to report absences to parents to avoid this circumstance. The reasons as to why students miss school are abundant and may reveal life situations or circumstances (abuse or neglect, homelessness) that must be addressed. Attendance records provide fundamental data that may be critical in understanding why a student is struggling academically or behaviorally.

Students with truancy issues are at risk of not being successful during their schooling. The reasons for tardies can be similar to those for poor attendance (not getting ready in time to catch the school bus) and a desire not to be in school or class (low motivation to attend class in high school). Importantly, tardies and absences resulting from skipping may reveal that a student is struggling academically and is attempting to avoid or escape engaging in tasks that are too challenging given their knowledge and skills. Tardies may reveal social or behavioral circumstances to be monitored (a boyfriend and girlfriend are both tardy regularly) or addressed directly. One possible issue in collecting data on tardies is the degree to which teachers in the same school address and report them. Ideally, the RTI team will ensure that teachers are consistent in both addressing and reporting tardies.

Office and Behavioral Referrals

As a component of RTI, schools include when students should be sent to the office and for what behavioral infractions. Schools keep records of such referrals for administrator and/or counselor intervention. Clearly, such referrals may be the result of an isolated incident (a student vandalizes school property) or reveal a regular pattern of not meeting behavioral expectations. Schools typically record the reasons for referrals, including behavioral or social or emotional issues. Referrals need not always represent behavioral problems (a student is upset because of a family or personal issue), but they may still indicate a need for intervention (counseling). Referrals resulting from not meeting behavioral expectations should be regularly analyzed by the RTI team for patterns among students and for identifying students receiving too frequent referrals. It is also important for the RTI team or administration to analyze which teachers are making referrals and why. These data might yield information that suggests teachers are using office referrals for different reasons and for different levels of behavioral infractions. In short, these data might suggest that a particular teacher needs additional in-service on when and why to send a student to the office.

Academic Data

Universal screening typically occurs two to three times per year across all grade levels, particularly in elementary schools. Universal screening involves assessing each and every student in a variety of academic areas and may involve behavioral screening as well. Typically, assessments are conducted at the outset of a school year and toward the end of the school year. Some schools may also conduct an additional screening at the midpoint of the school year. Universal screening involves assessing students' basic academic skills (sight vocabulary, correct words read per minute, percentage correct on a timed math assessment) toward identifying students who are exceeding expectations, meeting expectations, or not meeting expectations based on grade or age level in development of academic and/or social or emotional skill development. Usually, each student's results are categorized with a particular focus on students whose performance indicates that they may be at risk or in need of intervention based on the difference between their scores and the typical achievement levels at that grade level and at that particular time of the school year. RTI teams (other names include intervention assistance teams, student assistance teams, and child study teams, among other possibilities) identify students who may require Tier 2 assistance either academically and/or behaviorally. Although behavioral assessments may not be involved in any particular school's universal screening protocol, identifying students who are lagging behind peers in academic achievement may be useful in understanding students who are having behavioral difficulties as reported by teachers (in running records that are discussed in a subsequent section).

Similar to universal screening, school achievement tests may also be helpful in identifying students who are struggling academically. These tests are, however, given only in certain grades and are a relatively "gross" measure of student learning.

All schools require grade books to be kept and regular progress reports to be sent home to parents or caregivers. The data from actual classroom performance are included and are likely the best academic data one could gather. It allows the team to identify patterns across and within content areas (math is average but English language arts is poor) but also likely yields additional information about turning in homework and completing other assignments. These data may provide insight into inappropriate behavior in school, particularly in the classroom.

Behavior Scales Data

To determine areas of significant concern, rating scales are common practice. Rating scales are used to identify social, emotional, and behavioral concerns. The items on the scale typically are listed with a Likert scale (from very frequently to never occurs). Characteristics of attention, behavior, social, and emotional concerns are rated by multiple individuals and the data are compared. Ideally, a guardian, an educator, and the student, when applicable, fill out the rating scale. This provides data from home and school to identify if the same areas of concern are seen in multiple settings. These scales may or may not be used in any particular school.

The information collated from these various sources may be useful in identifying students at risk for behavior problems (habitually absent or tardy, struggling academically) or those who have exhibited behavior problems (acting out in the classroom or other school environments). Usually, RTI teams use these data, along with behavioral observations of students in their classrooms, to specify behavioral issues and to develop intervention plans to alleviate the issues. These issues may stem from students not understanding expectations to deliberately breaking the rules. In either case, the RTI team addresses how to teach students to meet the behavioral expectations of the school. Also, the RTI team may include academic interventions when it is apparent that the behavioral and academic issues go hand in hand.

Cultural Context

A vital area for review of any student is the cultural context in which the behavior is occurring. One behavior can be considered culturally appropriate in one area of the United States and considered inappropriate in another geographic area. Cultural and linguistic background can have a profound effect on a student's understanding of what is appropriate and inappropriate behavior. Some areas for consideration include the following:

- Ethnic and linguistic background of the student and family
- Cultural norms of the student and family

- Geographic area of the school and community (rural, suburban, urban, crime rate in the area in which the student and family live, specific neighborhood in which the student and family live)
- Educational background of the student and other family members (experience in US schools)
- Socioeconomic status of the family
- Drug and alcohol use or abuse of the student, family, and community

These are just a few of the cultural context areas for RTI teams to consider among many possibilities. The key is that when identifying students for Tier 2 and 3 interventions, the possibility that there is a mismatch between typical K–12 school behavioral expectations and those of the student should be reviewed. It is possible that a student doesn't understand those expectations or there is some conflict with the behavioral norms expected at home and/or in the student's community.

Comprehension Check
1. Why are vision and hearing screenings important?
2. What might attendance, tardy, and office referral data provide?
3. How is cultural context important in identifying students at risk for behavioral challenges?

INDIVIDUAL STUDENT DATA COLLECTION METHODS

There are many possible methods for collecting data on the behavioral performance of individual students (Alberto & Troutman, 2013). However, we will address those methods that would be used more commonly in classrooms. These include anecdotal records (or ABC recording), frequency counts, duration, and latency timing. Other methods for recording academic behavior can also be useful but need not be addressed in this text. Typically, pre- and in-service teachers are familiar with these methods, such as the number of items correct, the percentage correct, the rate of words read correctly in one minute, achieving a particular number of points on a grading rubric, and so on. Here we address behaviors that are nonacademic. Alberto and Troutman (2013) and Richards (2019) are two sources among many from which educators can obtain additional information on the many nuances and variations of recording student behavior, academic or otherwise.

Anecdotal Records

In the previous section, we discussed how teachers might use running records for behavioral and academic performance assessment. Running records may be informal and not intended to be shared with others or they can be used for formal progress monitoring (e.g., in monitoring progress in reading). However, here we are concerned

Date:				
Time:	A	B	C	Comments

Figure 3.1 ABC Recording Sheet

with a more formal use of anecdotal records. Sometimes before an RTI team can begin monitoring progress for student performance with any particular behavior, a teacher would need to specify the behavior of concern. This may mean operationally defining the behavior so that it is observable and measurable (Alberto & Troutman, 2013). Operationally defining a behavior may involve the use of anecdotal records.

Sometimes this type of data collection is referred to as ABC recording because of the information collected. *A* stands for antecedents to the occurrence of a behavior. *B* stands for the behavior of concern (or target behavior). *C* stands for any consequences delivered intentionally or unintentionally as a result of the student performing or emitting the behavior. A typical format for ABC recording is included in Figure 3.1. ABC recording has been used for many years by teachers, school psychologists, other professionals, and teams charged with managing the RTI process, particularly when inappropriate behavior of a student is the issue.

Anecdotal recording is useful for figuring out what is happening in a situation. For example, a teacher might report that a student who began the year with mildly disruptive behavior from time to time is increasing in frequency and intensity of disruptions. An observer (a co-teacher, a school psychologist, an administrator) may sit in on the class to record the student's behavior. Suppose at 10:01 a.m. the teacher directs the class to get out their literacy program books as they will be working on their literacy block skills (speaking, listening, writing, and reading) for the next 60 minutes. The observer records the teacher's remark as an antecedent on the recoding form. The student being observed delays responding to the teacher's directions by talking to a peer (the behavior). The teacher asks the student individually to please follow directions and to stop talking (the consequence). Note that the consequence could also serve as an antecedent for another behavior occurring very shortly thereafter. Now, at 10:02 a.m., the observer notes speaking directly to the student to follow directions and stop talking (the antecedent). The student responds, "I don't want to! I hate reading!" loudly enough for the whole class to hear (the behavior). Some peers giggle (one consequence), and the teacher remarks to the student, "We need to work on this. Won't you do this for me?" (another consequence). The recording continues, and the anecdotal record is later analyzed and presented to the teacher and child study team (a group of educators who assist in the RTI process and implement individual interventions within PBIS). The group reaches consensus that it appears that teacher and peer attention may very well be positively reinforcing the student's disruptive behavior. This hypothesis gives the classroom teacher and the team some ideas as to how to address the behavior. It also helps the classroom teacher and the team to specifically define the behavior as "one or more remarks that are not relevant to the present class task or activity and are audible to others." This also helps the teacher and team to identify how to monitor progress through data collection (they decide on counting the frequency of the remarks at varying times during the week). They are also able to devise a plan for interventions, how and when data will be collected to monitor progress, set a criterion for success on how much the student must change their behavior for the interventions to be deemed acceptable, and set a timeline for testing their hypothesis that the disruptive remarks are being reinforced through peer and teacher attention.

Anecdotal recording can be used as a means for progress monitoring. ABC data may be used for a student behavior that occurs infrequently (once a day or every two days) but still interferes significantly with the student's learning and/or the learning of others. For example, a younger child exhibits tantrums only occasionally, but the tantrums are still lengthy and intense. In this example, anecdotal recording may be the best possible option because frequency (how often the behavior occurred) would underestimate the effect of the behavior. Duration recording (how long the behavior occurs) might indicate the length but not necessarily all aspects of the situation that tend to trigger tantrums or their end. However, more often, frequency recording is used versus anecdotal recording when teams using PBIS in an RTI framework are concerned with problem student behavior that is not academic.

FREQUENCY RECORDING

Frequency recording may be the most easily understood data collection method. Virtually everyone, educators and others alike, understand that counting how often a behavior occurs is a useful method for assessing progress in whether a behavior is improving or not. Frequency recording can be useful in both reducing inappropriate behavior and increasing appropriate behavior. Educators use this method often.

Frequency recording has a few basic principles to consider.

- The behavior must be defined so that it is observable and measurable.
- The behavior must occur often enough that counting it will yield useful data as to whether the behavior is increasing or decreasing.
- The behavior must *not* occur so frequently (several occurrences each minute) that counting it would be impractical. In this case, counting *episodes* of a

behavior might be more useful (Alberto & Troutman, 2013; Richards, 2019). This is explained later.
- A method for recording frequency may be devised that requires an observer in the classroom. In this case, the actual recording of behavior would not likely be all day, every day. Rather, a sample of behavior would be recorded. Again, this is explained later.
- A method for recording frequency may be devised that does not require an observer and does not substantively interfere with teaching and learning. For example, a teacher recording a student's behavior could move pennies from one pocket into another while teaching to keep track of how often a behavior is occurring. There also are actual clickers for this purpose (push a button and the behavior is recorded, and the number of occurrences increases by one with each click—the frequency is displayed on the clicker). A simple tally chart often serves the purpose. A team might also choose to videotape teaching sessions to allow recording of behavior.
- A student could be taught to record the frequency of their behavior using a clicker or simple tally chart. Self-recording can be an effective method in and of itself to have a desirable effect on increasing or decreasing behavior.
- Finally, regardless of the specific means for recording frequency, there should be occasional interrater reliability checks (also known as interobserver agreement checks) (Alberto & Troutman, 2013; Richards, 2019). Again, this is explained later.

See Figure 3.2 for a sample of a simple tally chart for recording frequency of a behavior. Typically, counting the number of occurrences of a behavior is possible and sufficient for progress monitoring.

We mentioned that, occasionally, the frequency of the behavior may be such that recording episodes of the behavior may be more practical, and this is still a form of frequency recording. That is, an educator would not count every discreet occurrence of a behavior but episodes of the occurrence. In our example of the student who makes irrelevant remarks that are reinforced through peer and teacher attention, consider that the student may make several remarks following a teacher direction. In fact,

Date/Time:	Total Frequency:
Date/Time:	Total Frequency:

Figure 3.2 Frequency Recording Sheet

knowing the actual number of remarks made could be important, or it could suffice for progress monitoring purposes to record this as one episode. In other words, knowing how often the student makes remarks is quite adequate to determine if the goal of reducing this behavior is being achieved. The actual number of specific remarks may not be so important.

If the actual number of specific remarks made is important, then recording frequency may require an observer in the classroom, as the teacher could not perform their job while simultaneously recording every remark. Also, a student's behavior could be occurring with such frequency that counting all day, every day, is not practical. In these cases, it is likely that the team would decide to record frequency by taking samples of the frequency of behavior. For example, the team might have an observer in the classroom at random 30 minutes per day for two or three, or all days, per school week (other team members observe the student for 30 minutes during their planning periods; they go into the student's classroom and record frequency so that the student's teacher is able to do their job without having to also try to count behavior). The team would, of course, have to decide if this sampling method was working for capturing a true picture of how often the behavior occurs and whether it is decreasing, increasing, or remaining at the same level of frequency. This is not usually a difficult determination, as the classroom teacher would be aware if the true frequency of the behavior was quite different from what was being captured in the various samples.

The team may recognize that episodes of the behavior (four to five occurrences daily) is such that the teacher can record all day, every day, by simply making a tally, using a clicker, or moving a penny from one pocket to another. This method does not interfere with teaching and learning and the data will be good for progress monitoring because the team knows all episodes of the behavior are being captured by this method.

The team could also select rate recording that is a combination of frequency and duration recording (discussed in the next section). Rate involves counting the number of occurrences of a behavior and dividing it by the length of the observation. Rate is useful for recording behavior when it is necessary to break up the recording across the day or week. A common use of rate recording is in academics and is used frequently in RTI. Correct words read per minute (often used as progress monitoring in earlier grades) is an example of using rate. Similarly, one could record behavior for one hour one day, two hours the next day, and 30 minutes the third day. The frequency of the behavior is 10, 18, and 7, respectively. Rate would yield (using one hour as the time element) data of 10 responses per hour, 9 responses per hour, and 14 responses per hour. Although not precise in capturing all episodes of when a student might display an inappropriate behavior, it can be useful for progress monitoring if the observations are sufficiently frequent and long enough to give a good picture of what is actually occurring all day and all week.

Ideally, the team would conduct interrater reliability checks. Occasionally, the team may wish to have two observers record behavior (the teacher and a colleague on the team) for a period of time and determine if the two observers/raters are obtaining the same or very similar results. Ideally, 90% or better reliability is desirable, with 80% being considered acceptable. In reality, the team should have little difficulty in determining if both observers are counting frequency exactly the same or closely enough that behavioral occurrences are being accurately recorded. The basic formula for determining the percentage of reliability between two observers is provided in Figure 3.3. Also, see Richards (2019) for an extensive discussion of reliability checks, examples, and various formulas for determining reliability.

Duration and Latency Recording

Duration recording and latency recording differ from many academic achievement measures and frequency recording in that each involves measuring time. To understand duration recording (and latency as well), we must revisit our discussion of ABC or anecdotal recording, where *A* stands for antecedent, *B* for behavior, and *C* for consequence. Duration recording involves measuring the time from when a behavior begins to when it ends. Duration can be recorded as total duration or by each occurrence, depending on the behavior and the overall goal. See Figure 3.4 for a typical duration recording sheet.

Total duration would be used when the behavior of concern occurs repeatedly, and it is the overall time spent displaying the behavior that is important to the team. Overall, time spent engaged in cooperative play with a young child across the day is an example for a behavior to increase. Time spent engaged in off-task behavior might be an example of a behavior to decrease.

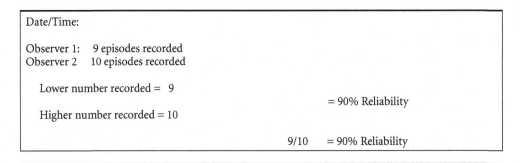

Figure 3.3 Basic Formula for Determining Reliability

Date:		
Time Behavior Began:	Time Behavior Ended:	Duration:
Time Behavior Began:	Time Behavior Ended:	Duration:
Time Behavior Began:	Time Behavior Ended:	Duration:
Time Behavior Began:	Time Behavior Ended:	Duration:
Time Behavior Began:	Time Behavior Ended:	Duration:
Time Behavior Began:	Time Behavior Ended:	Duration:

Figure 3.4 Duration Recording Sheet

Date:		
Time Antecedent is Given	Time Behavior Begins	Latency

Figure 3.5 Latency Recording Sheet

Duration per occurrence is useful because it also includes the frequency of the behavior. For example, time spent reading could be an example of a behavior expected to occur several times per day and at a minimum level (e.g., 15 minutes). Duration per occurrence could also be used for a young child who engages in temper tantrums several times per day. This behavior would need to be decreased.

Duration is typically recorded using a stopwatch or similar device. Total duration recording is simpler, as all one must do is repeatedly start and stop the watch as the behavior occurs and then record the total time at the end of the observation period (e.g., the entire school day). Again, this variation of duration recording does not provide frequency, just total time spent engaged in the behavior. Duration per occurrence involves recording the time spent engaged in the behavior each and every time it occurs. One can also calculate total duration by simply adding up the duration for each occurrence across the observation period (the school day).

Latency recording, practically speaking, works exactly the same as duration in terms of using the timer and recording data. However, with latency recording you are measuring the time elapsed from when an antecedent occurs (teacher directions) and when a behavior begins. Latency recording is used typically when the goal is to reduce the latency. The more common example is recording how long it takes a student to begin work after the bell rings, the teacher gives a command, or some other antecedent cue is given indicating to begin a particular behavior. Remember, with latency recording one is recording how long it takes behavior to begin. Dawdling or getting ready to work are examples. Figure 3.5 depicts a latency recording data collection sheet.

Using Data to Support Referral for Multidisciplinary Evaluation

The Individuals with Disabilities Education Act requires that the team working with students throughout the RTI process collect data that indicates actual classroom performance. These data potentially include each of the areas we have discussed. Of course, given the particular situation, different types of data will be collected. Additionally, if a student is suspected to have a disability (specific learning disability, intellectual disability, emotional or behavioral disorder), the RTI team provides that to the multidisciplinary evaluation team to guide the individual assessments it will conduct to determine if a student is eligible for special education and related services.

In summary, RTI requires data to be collected through a variety of sources and to reflect actual student performance. These data guide the decision-making processes of the RTI team. These data help the team to understand that a behavioral issue is the result of possible medical conditions, environmental conditions, academic problems, or behavioral issues that are demonstrated for repeatedly and/or substantially not meeting the behavioral expectations of students in a school. PBIS is a process for addressing these behavioral expectations whose effectiveness has been demonstrated extensively.

Comprehension Check
1. What are two simple ways to record frequency data?
2. Why is interrater reliability important?
3. What are the differences between duration and latency recording?

CHAPTER SUMMARY

Identify schoolwide data collection methods that yield individual behavioral data and identify individual behavioral data collection methods for use within the Response to Intervention (RTI) process.

- Positive Behavioral Interventions and Supports are useful in addressing behavioral challenges in students.
- Positive Behavioral Interventions and Supports draw on many of the principles of RTI and RTI teams.

Schoolwide Methods That Yield Individual Data

- Vision and hearing screening are important to rule out sensory issues.
- Attendance and tardy data may provide insight into whether a student is in school frequently enough, if there might be issues of abuse or neglect, and a student's motivation to be in school.
- Office or behavioral referrals allow the RTI team to determine the frequency of serious behavioral infractions and the types of infractions; these referrals may also indicate a need for counseling or other supports not directly related to behavioral difficulties.
- Academic data are particularly helpful in determining if behavioral difficulties may be related to poor school performance, frustration, or anxiety about academics.

- Behavior rating scales involve parents, students, and teachers in rating the degree of behavioral strengths and weaknesses of students.
- Cultural context is important in determining if not meeting behavioral expectations may be due to cultural and/or linguistic differences.

Individual Student Data Collection Methods

- Anecdotal records can be useful in identifying antecedents and consequences of a student's behavior, useful in more precisely defining a student's behavior, and for hypothesizing the function of problem behavior.
- Frequency recording is easily understood and involves counting how often a behavior occurs; frequency recording may also involve recording episodes of behavior and may include student's self-recording of behavior.
- Interrater reliability checks are needed to ensure that everyone is recording behavior accurately; 80% reliability is acceptable, with 90% being desirable.
- Duration involves recording the time from when a behavior begins to when it ends; duration recording may include duration across an entire observation period or the duration for each occurrence of the behavior.
- Latency involves recording the time from when an antecedent is given for behavior to begin to when the behavior actually begins; latency recording may include latency across an entire observation period or the latency for each occurrence of the behavior.
- Behavioral data are required for a multidisciplinary evaluation to be conducted, particularly when an emotional or behavioral disorder is the suspected disability.

REFERENCES

Alberto, P. A., & Troutman, A. C. (2013). *Applied behavior analysis for teachers* (9th ed.). Columbus, OH: Pearson.

Richards, S. B. (2019). *Single-subject research and design: Applications in educational and clinical settings* (3rd ed.). Boston, MA: Cengage.

Sugai, G., & Horner, R. R. (2006). A promising approach for expanding and sustaining school-wide positive behavior support. *School Psychology Review: Bethesda, 35*(2), 245–259.

Taylor, R. L., Smiley, L. R., & Richards, S. B. (2019). *Exceptional students: Preparing teachers for the 21st century* (3rd ed.). Columbus, OH: McGraw-Hill.

Part II

Application of Classroom and Behavior Management Strategies: Tier 1

Part II

4

SCHOOLWIDE POSITIVE BEHAVIOR SUPPORT

Jennifer T. Christman

CHAPTER OBJECTIVES

After reading this chapter, students should be able to:

1. Summarize a three-tiered support model.
2. Explain the components to a quality Schoolwide Positive Behavior Support system.
3. Discuss hurdles to effective Schoolwide Positive Behavior Support models.

Traditionally in schools, problem behaviors are dealt with in reactive and punitive ways: time-outs, punishments, office referrals, loss of privileges, detentions, and suspensions. Researchers suggest that these forms of punishment are ineffective in the long run (Positive Behavioral Interventions and Supports, 2018). School-based problem behaviors are believed to be increasing and more frequently escalating into violent offenses. Proactive means of addressing these problem behaviors are needed. These proactive strategies may include zero-tolerance policies, implementation of metal detectors in schools, and hiring of school resource officers. Although these strategies do help to prevent the most serious problems, they do not address most of the issues that teachers and administrators face in the classrooms, Hallways, and other school environments. It is through the implementation of Schoolwide Positive Behavior Support (SWPBS) programs that positive behavior changes are seen in schools.

BEHAVIORAL SUPPORTS IN A THREE-TIERED FRAMEWORK

The goal of SWPBS is to create a predictable, positive school climate in which students feel comfortable and can learn. The school environment and classrooms are organized with predictable rules that are taught. Positive reinforcement for appropriate behavior is encouraged with feedback and instruction when inappropriate behavior occurs and

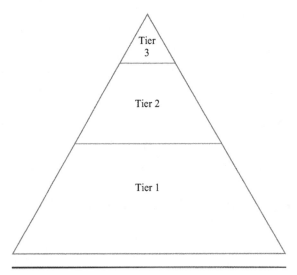

Figure 4.1 Response to Intervention Triangle

clear consequences when rules are obviously and voluntarily broken. By creating a proactive and positive climate, these behavior supports encourage academic success as well. As noted in Chapter 1, academic struggles and behavior problems are often associated with each other. SWPBS strategies are systematic approaches to proactively address challenging behaviors within school systems. As you learned in Chapter 1, in a three-tiered model (see Figure 4.1), behavioral supports are implemented at increasing levels of intensity to maintain all students at a level appropriate to their needs and abilities. At Tier 1, the approach is intended for all students and implemented throughout the school in a universal fashion. It is at this tier of support that typically about 80% of students are successful. At Tier 2, additional supports are implemented to aid those students who have not responded adequately to Tier 1 interventions and may display persistent behavior problems or who are at risk of behavioral problems. These supports will be implemented for 15% of the school population, typically not successful with the SWPBS strategies in Tier 1. Tier 2 includes more specific interventions to address particular behaviors for that 15% of students. At Tier 3, more intensive, specific interventions are implemented for students who continue to need additional supports because they have not responded to Tier 2 interventions. Tier 3 interventions are more intrusive and may include changing the setting of learning or may require additional personnel resources. Under most circumstances, approximately 5% of the student population requires this intensive level of supports, as typically 95% of students are following school rules with interventions used in Tiers 1 and 2. At Tier 3, if a student is not responding to interventions, an evaluation may take place to determine whether a student has an emotional or behavioral disorder that is igniting the behavioral problems (Center on Response to Intervention, n.d.). If the evaluation results in the identification of an emotional or behavioral disorder, the multidisciplinary team discussed in Chapter 1 will develop an Individualized Education Program for the student and recommend services as required under the

Individuals with Disabilities Education Act (IDEA), so long as parental consent has been obtained throughout the referral and identification processes, also discussed in Chapter 1. Keep in mind, as we have discussed in earlier chapters, that students may also be identified as having disabilities other than emotional or behavioral and still exhibit behavioral issues. Again, academic struggles may result in behavioral difficulties. When students are not engaged in learning, they may shut down or act out because of that lack of engagement.

Throughout this three-tiered model, it is imperative that teachers and school personnel are collecting data to analyze the effectiveness of the interventions used in each tier. This data analysis is essential to determine if and when students move through the various tiers. As noted in previous chapters, the four-part cycle of assessment—assessment, analysis, decision-making, and instruction—continues to be applicable throughout the SWPBS model. Assessing student responses at the Tier 1 level, analyzing for whom schoolwide supports are appropriate and for whom more intensive interventions are needed, and determining instructional aids based on this data analysis are critical to scaffolding support in the most appropriate way and to identifying those students in need of more assistance.

> *Comprehension Check*
> 1. What is the goal of SWPBS?
> 2. Describe a three-tiered model of SWPBS.

COMPONENTS OF A QUALITY SCHOOLWIDE POSITIVE BEHAVIOR SUPPORT SYSTEM

SWPBS is the foundation of this integrated support model. It is imperative that the strategies are evidence based and implemented with fidelity. SWPBS looks different in schools across the country; however, educators in each model intend to teach students behavioral expectations in a direct format, create consistency across environments within the school, and motivate students to achieve high behavioral expectations. These SWPBS systems are often the impetus for other positive changes within a school, such as increased academic success. Another consistent factor across variations of SWPBS is that there is usually a core team. Often this core team is trained in a specific behavioral support program or philosophy and expected to then train the other staff members in the school. This employs an efficient model for involving all school personnel in SWPBS. It is critical that the adults in the building support the SWPBS model adopted (Carr et al., 2002). This common understanding and skills lead to consistency. Staff members must be consistent, using the same terms with students regarding behavior, and the behavioral expectations must remain steady regardless of where the students are on the school campus. This consistency is needed in the classroom, cafeteria, gymnasium, and even on the school bus for optimal success to be derived. Consistency of expectations leads to more desirable behavioral outcomes.

South Kings Elementary School
SWPBS Core Team Mission

At South Kings Elementary School, we are dedicated to creating safe and positive learning environments for all students. To uphold this mission, our SWPBS Core Team will:

- Encourage all members of the school community to embrace the Schoolwide Positive Behavior Support program
- Continue to grow in our knowledge of SWPBS
- Communicate our understanding of SWPBS to our colleagues to build capacity within our school
- Analyze data collected from classroom teachers
- Make team-based, data driven-decisions regarding South Kings Elementary implementation of SWPBS
- Communicate our school's dedication to a safe and positive learning environment to parents, district administrators and local representatives

---

Figure 4.2 Schoolwide Positive Behavior Support Core Team Mission Statement

The core team is made up of administrators, teachers, and other school employees. See Figure 4.2 for a SWPBS core team mission statement. This team analyzes data to identify student needs, discusses the successes and failures within the program, and works to modify the plan to yield the most positive results. Because each school environment, as well as educators and students, is unique, adaptability is a hallmark of SWPBS. Models are fine-tuned and changes are implemented to best meet the needs of individual school communities.

There is no universally accepted set of fundamental elements of SWPBS. However, most guidelines include (1) a few (three to five) specific, positively written behavioral expectations developed within the school, (2) a description of what the desired behaviors look like (what students need to know and do to follow each rule), (3) lesson plans for teaching the expected behavioral skills, (4) consequences when the rules are not followed, (5) recognition and positive reinforcement when the expectations are met, and (6) a system to monitor progress through data collection and analysis (Coffey & Horner, 2012; Ogulmus & Vuran, 2016; Horner et al., 2004). Because a SWPBS system is only as strong as the knowledge of the adults who implement it and the students who follow it, ownership is critical. This ownership can be established by allowing students to be engaged in the creation of aspects of the system. For example, students often help to write the schoolwide rules, and higher grade-level students demonstrate for new students what the appropriate behaviors look like when the rules are being followed.

Positively Written Behavioral Expectations

Students thrive when they know what is expected of them in the school environment. Therefore, it is important to establish behavioral expectations through school and classroom rules and routines. Rules and routines are not the same. Rules provide for safety and a positive school climate while routines facilitate efficiency in the school and classroom. An example of a rule is: "All students must raise their hands to participate in class." (Keep in mind how to follow this rule is defined, demonstrated, and taught to and by students.) An example of a routine is how to purchase lunch in the cafeteria or how to turn in homework before the bell rings. These routines, when completed as expected, allow for efficiency and increased productivity in the school building or in the classroom. Student commitment to the rules and routines—behavioral expectations—leads to successful outcomes. Knowing this, it is important that teachers allow students to participate in the creation of the behavioral expectations. Collaboratively, students, general education teachers, special education teachers, school counselors, and administrators create three to five specific and positively written behavioral expectations. It is important that these expectations are written to focus on the desired behaviors, not the behaviors to be avoided. For example, "The students will keep their hands and feet to themselves" rather than "The students will not hit, kick, punch, or otherwise aggressively touch another student." When written positively, the focus remains on what is expected to be achieved. When the focus is on what will be achieved through positively written behavior expectations, the message suggests that the adults believe all students can achieve the expectation set. This empowers students to feel that the behavior expectation is attainable. Keeping this list to three to five expectations (or rules) focuses student attention on the important skills, and the shorter list enables students to remember the expectations. The rules should be posted in the school as visual reminders to students and staff. These brief, positively written behavioral expectations imply a belief that all students can perform the expectations set within the system. This implied belief follows a growth mindset philosophy versus a fixed mindset. In a *fixed mindset*, the belief is that student performance is largely influenced by intelligence, behavior, character traits, and the like that tend to be innate and are not easily changed. This fixed mindset is especially important to avoid with particular groups of students (students receiving special education services, English language learners, learners from different racial or ethnic groups). Conversely, with a *growth mindset*, the belief is that human behavior can be developed and changed over time, given an encouraging, consistent, and positively oriented environment. When students believe that adults have a fixed mindset regarding their potential, they often perform to the levels implied by that fixed mindset. A teacher who believes that students receiving special education services will not be able to achieve success in the general education curriculum may very well communicate that low level of expectation in implicit if not explicit ways. For example, this same teacher may always group the students receiving special education services together for small-group learning activities, implying that they are not able to participate with and succeed at the levels of non-disabled peers. Students often do not exceed low expectations when they are consistently evident. When behavior expectations are written implying a growth mindset, there tends to be a can-do level of expectation for success. Students strive to exceed expectations, particularly when recognition and positive reinforcement are provided.

When establishing routines, it is important that students work collaboratively with adults to determine how students will complete routines. While collaboratively establishing these routines, adults can maintain control of the process by being strategic in the presentation to students. For example, if the teacher would like homework turned in following a specific routine but would like the students to feel in control of the decision-making, the teacher may present the choice to students: "Do you think it is best to complete your lunch count first or to turn in your homework first?" Students should feel that they are decision makers in the process, but the teacher is maintaining control by presenting two options that both lead to the task completion routine they desire.

Description of How the Expected Behaviors Look

As stated previously, students thrive with clear expectations. As these expectations are presented to students, an explanation of how these behaviors look helps to solidify how students should act. An operational definition of a behavior describes the behavior without value or opinion. This operational definition of the desired behavior should make clear to educators and students alike what is expected. By doing so, the definition reduces personal interpretations of the expected behaviors and provides consistency in the school and classroom, likely producing the desired performance of the expected behaviors. Again, with positively written and operationalized definitions of the expected behaviors, there is an implied belief that students can and will be able to meet those expectations.

First, it is important for the teacher to provide the students with a clear definition of what the behavior looks like. Avoiding cultural, gender, ability, and other potential biases helps to create an inclusive classroom. Only verbally describing what the behavior looks like may restrict the student's understanding of the behavioral expectation. By verbally stating the expectation, writing and posting it, demonstrating examples and non-examples of following the expectation, and providing immediate positive reinforcement, as well as constructive and corrective feedback when the expectation is not followed, more students may retrieve how to follow the rule or routine, decreasing the need for re-teaching or reducing the number of students requiring Tier 2 or 3 interventions. Illustrative Case Study 4.1 demonstrates how teachers can authentically model classroom rules.

ILLUSTRATIVE CASE STUDY 4.1: MODELING COLLABORATION

After reading *Freak the Mighty*, fifth-grade students were presented with a comprehension assignment requiring them to work collaboratively in pairs to demonstrate their understanding of the character development throughout the novel. The students were permitted to present their project in any format of their choosing. At this school, one rule was: "Students work collaboratively to achieve learning." This rule was written, verbally explained, and demonstrated to and by students from the outset of school, but some students were still less successful at working collaboratively.

After observing Leah and Sarah struggling to collaborate on their presentation format, Ms. Reynolds, the language arts teachers, decided to model how to work collaboratively. The following school day, Ms. Reynolds and Mr. Henry, the special education teacher, modeled how to collaborate when two learners have different opinions. Each teacher presented their opinion, shared common ideas, and then decided why to allow Mr. Henry's presentation format to be selected while Ms. Reynolds decided who would present the material and what examples would be used from the text. Modeling specific steps relevant to the choosing of a collaborative presentation format helped Sarah and Leah and provided clarification for several other pairs of students on what it means to work collaboratively. Ms. Reynolds made it a point to praise Sarah and Leah and other student pairs as they decided on their presentation formats and again after their presentations.

This example illustrates that rules may be stated positively but may require continued constructive feedback to students, particularly as expectations become more complex. Schools may adopt rules like the one in this example because they reflect the mission statement and school philosophy concerning the focus on how learning takes place as well as what students learn. Although simple rules, such as "Raise your hand to participate in class," are typically easier to operationally define and teach, including one or more (but not all) rules that encourage more complex behavioral skills may also be beneficial. They will require more time and effort to define and teach and will likely require ongoing demonstration of examples and non-examples, but they can be especially appropriate for older students who have acquired the basic behavioral expectations in school.

Lesson Plans to Teach Desired Behavioral Expectations

As students work to achieve behavioral expectations, direct instruction on the desired behaviors is necessary at times. Direct instruction, the explicit teaching of a skill set through structured teaching (Gersten, Woodward, & Darch, 1986), is effective in teaching a variety of skills, including appropriate behaviors. It is desirable to have available for classroom use a bank of lesson plans, developed by the core team and other staff members, that support teaching skills and routines in a SWPBS model. These lesson plans may be used at the teachers' discretion or on a scheduled basis and can increase student awareness of behavioral expectations, improve outcomes regarding expectations, and help students learn lifelong skills. Lesson plan ideas should address the specific rules and routines but may also include those for anger management, social skills training, bullying prevention, and conflict resolution and mediation among friends for use as the need arises and to help students in learning more complex positive behaviors and skills. These skills can be taught at all grade levels but must be presented in a developmentally appropriate format. As students grow older, the expectations generally increase. See Figure 4.3 for a sample lesson plan for elementary school students.

Consequences When Rules or Routines Are Not Being Followed

Another element of the successful implementation of SWPBS is the use of consequences. It is merely reactive to enforce consequences (time-out, loss of privileges,

Social Skills Training Lesson Plan
Topic: Anger Management
Grades: Elementary

Lesson Objectives:
- At the conclusion of this lesson, the first-grade students will be able to distinguish between sad, mad, frustrated, lonely, jealous and bored.
- At the conclusion of this lesson, the first-grade students will be able to match a feeling with a situation that may elicit that feeling.

Lesson Opening:
- Read aloud the children's book: "Mad Isn't Bad: A Child's Book About Anger" by Michaelene Mundy
- Ask the students, "Is it okay to be mad?"

Body of Lesson:
- Show students pictures of faces displaying various negative feelings (mad, sad, lonely, etc.)
- Ask students to guess how the person in the picture is feeling
- Discuss how, though they are all not feeling "good," they are not all feeling the same
  - Ex. Anger is not the same as sadness, etc.
- In collaboration with another adult, act out scenarios and discuss feelings that come from scenarios

Conclusion:
- Provide students with worksheet of feeling words on left side and picture of situations on the right side. Have students draw line to match word to situation.

What comes next?
- Now that negative feeling vocabulary has been discussed, next lesson is on coping strategies... What do you do when you feel sad, mad, frustrated, lonely, jealous or bored?

Simulation scenarios:
1. Several third graders are outside playing baseball at recess. The first three batters have all hit homeruns. Skip gets up to bat and strikes out. Skip walks away with his head hung low, feeling like he never wants to play baseball again.
2. Two team captains are selected in gym class. The team captains will choose teams for Gaga Ball. Emma is chosen last.
3. The students are assigned a timed math test. The teacher says "When I say, 'Go,' flip over your paper and answer as many problems as you can in 60 seconds." The teacher says, "go" and as soon as Henry starts to write his first answer, his pencil lead breaks.
4. The teacher says, "Everyone find a partner to practice flashcards for 10 minutes". There are 25 students in the classroom so everyone finds a partner except for Becky.
5. After Winter Break, the students return to school. Amy, Diane, Sam, and Jen all have on new shoes they received during the holidays and call themselves the "New Shoe Club." Because Katie did not get any new shoes she is excluded from the club.
6. Tyler finished technology time and his parents told him he needed to find a toy to play with. He walked around his house, could not find a toy to play with and decided to sit in a chair and wait until dinnertime.

Figure 4.3 Sample Lesson Plan

office referral) for rule or routine infractions. Students, particularly those receiving special education services, may exhibit inappropriate behavior because some cause rooted in their prior experience is influencing that behavior. Rather than punishment only for infractions, SWPBS stresses teaching rules and routines and reinforcing appropriate behavior.

Analyzing a student's behavior through a functional behavioral assessment (FBA) will help to determine the function or purpose behind the student's challenging behavior. The precise cause of the behavior may not be identifiable (e.g., who first modeled and/or reinforced the inappropriate behavior) but *why* the student continues to engage in the behavior, despite Tier 1 and possibly Tier 2 interventions, must be considered. FBA teams attempt to determine what is maintaining the behavior (what is reinforcing that behavior) and what function or purpose the behavior serves. All behaviors serve some function(s). At a basic level, all behaviors either seek to gain something (attention, a tangible, serving a sensory need) or to avoid something (a task, attention, pain). Discovering the function of the behavior is essential in the FBA process. FBA will be discussed in depth in Chapter 14, but it is important to understand that in the SWPBS model, educators assume students are engaging in inappropriate behavior because they learned through equally inappropriate reinforcement and/or modeling. The identification of the function of the behavior allows for school staff to design a plan that replaces the undesirable behavior with a desirable one that serves the same function, eventually eliminating the undesirable behavior. If, for example, a student's out-of-seat behavior is in violation of one of the behavioral expectations set and agreed upon by members of the school, a teacher, special educator, or school psychologist may examine the student's behavior and determine that the student is getting out of his seat and walking around the classroom to serve a sensory need (e.g., the student has attention deficit hyperactivity disorder) and that the student has received considerable attention over time (e.g., the teacher saying, "How many times do I have to tell you to get back in your seat?" "You should not be walking around right now." "Why are you out of your seat?"). Other students laugh when the teacher addresses the student repeatedly, reinforcing the undesirable behavior. Therefore, the replacement behavior of sitting on an exercise ball during seatwork time attends to the sensory needs of the child but doesn't address the attention-getting reinforcement available to the student when they do get up. Therefore, the teacher must intervene with a minimum amount of attention when the student is out of their seat (physically redirecting the student back to their seat without comment) and provide reinforcement regularly for sitting on the exercise ball ("I really like how you are sitting on the ball." "You are working hard today." "It is so nice to see you in your seat."). The teacher may also enlist the support of other students to praise the child for sitting and to ignore the child when they are out of their seat. These interventions could occur in Tiers 1, 2, or 3 of Response to Intervention (RTI) in a SWPBS model, depending on the severity of the inappropriate behavior and how it affects the student's learning and that of their peers. The FBA and the interventions would be developed and progress monitored by a team, and especially in Tiers 2 and 3, would likely involve the parents and possibly the student. It is also important to note that when behavioral issues do occur in a SWPBS model, sometimes others in the environment may need to change their behaviors to assist with a particular student's behavior. Inappropriate behavior can have internal drivers (such as this student's attention deficit hyperactivity disorder) but often do include or are almost entirely driven by external factors (such as the attention provided by the teacher and other students that reinforce being out of seat). The FBA team also developed interventions that were positive rather than punitive, stressing appropriate behavior and reinforcement.

Despite systematically designed behavioral expectations, it is inevitable that there will be times that a student needs redirection outside of the SWPBS itself. When the behavioral expectations are not followed and a student's behavior requires intervention, there must be a consistent plan for handling challenging behaviors. The example of the FBA in the previous passage illustrates how such a formal plan might be implemented for a student being served under IDEA. However, educators must have planned, positive responses to behavioral issues that lead to behavior change in students who are not served under IDEA. Again, SWPBS stresses a proactive rather than a reactive (and often punitive) approach. Office discipline referrals (ODR) are a frequent response to undesirable behaviors in the classroom or other school setting. An ODR is a written report addressing a student's infraction of the rules and a tool for communicating this infraction among teachers, administrators, parents, and the student. Often the student would be required to write down what they did that was an infraction, what should have been done, and what their own plan is for avoiding similar infractions in the future. However, with the use of ODRs, learning time is lost. Students are removed from the learning environment, spend time in the hallway and administrative office, and lose instructional opportunities. This time away from learning can be reinforcing to students as it may be viewed as free time and an escape from the demands of the classroom. When discipline problems are reduced through a proactive approach, such as a SWPBS system, more learning opportunities are accessible for all students and teacher time is used in instruction. Office referrals are sometimes necessary in any school, when learning has been seriously disrupted or the student's behavior is egregious (e.g., having brought a weapon to the classroom). However, in a SWPBS system, most infractions can be managed within the classroom by the teacher and/or with additional support from other educators. Again, in SWPBS, educators devote their time to teaching and reinforcing appropriate behavior rather than devoting time to punishing students.

REINFORCEMENT, RECOGNITION, AND REWARD

People are often reinforced or motivated by recognition and rewards (Cooper, Heron, & Heward, 2007). For example, when a baby stacks up cups and Mom claps for the baby, the baby smiles and repeats the stacking behavior. When a child begins reciting her ABCs and Dad sings along and dances with the her, the child feels motivated to continue singing the ABCs. When a middle school student studies for several hours for a social studies test, performs well on the test, and earns an A for the semester, they are more likely to study as hard for the next test. This principle of recognition and reward (positive reinforcement) continues into adulthood when professionals work hard to achieve employment status (title, pay raise, benefits), and upon achieving the desired status, continue to work hard to seek the next higher level because of the recognition obtained. What these situations all have in common is the need to be caught performing the desired behavior. Over time, being caught doing what is appropriate (and in our own best interests) serves to develop an internal sense of accomplishment and self-reinforcement that lessens the need for external recognition from others. The SWPBS model used must outline what will happen when a student is observed performing to or exceeding the behavioral expectation. This recognition or reward may come in the form of individual specific praise. For example, the teacher quietly says to a student, "Nora, I really like the way you are taking a deep breath and calmly speaking with Yaseen right now. I know you are upset, but you are keeping your body calm and working through your frustration. You are demonstrating the rule 'Respect the rights and feelings of all.'" Recognition may also be public. For example, the school principal announces "Happy-Grams" on the schoolwide morning announcements at the end of each month. Students are called by name during the morning announcements for exemplifying high behavioral expectations, asked to report to the office to receive a certificate, and their names are entered into a lottery for a tangible prize. This is a combination of public and individual recognition, either or both of which may be important to any student. These individual, behavior-specific praise acknowledgments are effective in reinforcing the student to continue to achieve a high level of performance. This may also be motivating for other students, if they find the acknowledgment desirable, to act in the same way that their peer acted, in the hopes of being acknowledged similarly. Whole-class praise can also be effective. Perhaps the principal walks down the hallway, sees an entire class quietly walking down the hallway, and states, "Wow, Ms. Jenkins, your class sure is following our school rule of being quiet and orderly in the hallway!" This class recognition may motivate students in that class to continue to transition in a quiet and orderly fashion, and it may also encourage other students in other classes, who may have heard the praise from the principal, to try to earn the same recognition for following the transition routine.

Another way that adults can acknowledge that they have caught a student meeting or exceeding behavioral expectations is through the distribution of tangible reinforcing items. There is a debate in education as to whether teachers should reinforce student behavior with the use of tangible items (Akin-Little, Eckert, Lovett, & Little, 2004). Intrinsic motivation comes from the desire to know, learn, and grow while extrinsic motivation often comes from a desire to attain something that serves as a reinforcer (Vallerand et al., 1992). Reinforcers are a form of reward and, by definition, are motivational. Reinforcers can be used with a range of student ages and developmental levels. These reinforcers can be a piece of candy, a sticker, a certificate, praise, good grades, access to preferred activities, or a collectible, to name a few. Items are reinforcing to the student when obtaining the item is meaningful to that student. Principles of reinforcement were discussed earlier in this text, and the reader should refer to Chapter 2 to refresh understanding. The key principle to remember is that different students respond to different reinforcers, although a teacher may make some assumptions about likely reinforcers given various student traits, including age, developmental level, background, and so on. For example, most younger children and adolescents like candy as a reward for following rules and routines. Younger students may

Figure 4.4 Interest Inventory

Source: The Picture Communication Symbols © 1981-2015 by Mayer-Johnson LLC a Tobii Dynavox company. All Rights Reserved Worldwide. Used with permission. Boardmaker © is a trademark of Mayer Johnson LLC.

prefer rewards like pencils or erasers, while older students may prefer a reward like a homework pass. Interest inventories can be helpful in identifying common reinforcers for a class as well as individual reinforcers (see Figure 4.4 for a sample picture based interest inventory). This is another example of how the implementation of the four-part ongoing assessment cycle improves instruction. Analyzing reinforcers that are most effective for students and using that information to determine the motivators to be used in a classroom to maintain or improve student behaviors provides evidence of the effectiveness of the data analysis process. As to the debate about whether students should receive extrinsic reinforcers or be motivated solely by intrinsic reinforcers, it is safe to assert that nearly all students need some extrinsic reinforcement (praise, good grades) at least occasionally, but the use of extrinsic reinforcers, such as tangibles, special privileges or activities, or other intrusive items or events, should be eventually faded from use. Extrinsic reinforcers are typically used to establish new learning, such as when students are first learning and demonstrating the expectations in a SWPBS model and then less frequently once the appropriate behaviors are established. By using such fading procedures, the teacher encourages students to build intrinsic motivation and self-reinforcement for a job well done.

It is critical that the adults in the building support the SWPBS system (Carr et al., 2002). Universal knowledge is important, but it is universal implementation that leads to consistency. Staff members must use the same terms with students regarding behavior, and the expectation must remain constant regardless of where the students are on the school campus. This consistency must be maintained in the classroom, cafeteria, gymnasium, and even on the school bus for optimal success to be derived. Consistency of expectations leads to more desirable behavioral outcomes.

Monitoring Progress Through Data Collection and Analysis

As for any change process, including the implementation of SWPBS, it is essential to monitor progress. This can be done through data collection and analysis. The information yielded from this collection and analysis process provides a means by which to assess the effectiveness of the SWPBS system as it is implemented (throughout implementation). The progress can be monitored in the form of comparing the number of ODRs prior to the implementation of the SWPBS system to the number of ODRs after the implementation of the system. Another way to monitor the success of the program is to compare data on individual student behaviors (out of seat, aggressive behaviors) in a baseline fashion (prior to Tier 1 interventions) to those after the interventions have been implemented. To show true cause and effect between the interventions at any tier and subsequent changes in behavioral outcomes, a research design is required that some schools may use, but it can be complex and present many challenges to the school's resources. The advantage to this more sophisticated type of data analysis is that it does clarify that the interventions used at any tier in RTI are evidence-based. However, most schools do not implement such a specific research design. Instead, the SWPBS core team members and other interested adults (staff members, parents) review data from a variety of sources (number of office referrals, number and degree of acknowledgements given to students, academic achievement, direct classroom and school environment observations) to determine if progress has been achieved. If that progress is achieved by a significant majority of students and is maintained over time with new and existing students, the team continues the plan as it exists, considering it successful. Certainly, most schools must adjust their SWPBS system over time, but the essential elements should be demonstrably beneficial through improved behavioral and academic outcomes as well. The core team may also gather data through such sources as interviewing teachers, parents, and students as to how effective they believe the SWPBS model to be. Evaluators from outside the school, who are considered to be more objective compared to the core team, are sometimes employed to assist in developing evidence that the SWPBS interventions are effective. The key to providing an evidence base is derived from consistent results whenever and with whomever the SWPBS system is employed within the RTI framework. Interventions at Tiers 1, 2, and 3 should yield data that demonstrate consistent results within the overall school, the classrooms, and with individual students at Tiers 2 and 3. However and whatever data are collected, it is critical to monitor progress and to use the data to determine the continuation of the system, the need for a modified version of the system, or implementation of a different system to ensure the greatest success for students. See Figure 4.5 to increase your knowledge of this ongoing cycle.

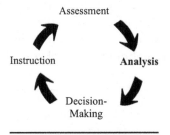

Figure 4.5 Ongoing Cycle of Response to Intervention

> *Comprehension Check*
> 1. What are the six critical elements to the successful implementation of a SWPBS system?
> 2. Why is it important to collect data?
> 3. Explain the four-part ongoing assessment cycle and how it applies SWPBS.

HURDLES TO A SUCCESSFUL SCHOOLWIDE POSITIVE BEHAVIOR SUPPORT SYSTEM

SWPBS systems are most effective when the six elements, as previously stated, are followed with fidelity. As discussed earlier in this text, fidelity requires observations to be made to verify that RTIs are being implemented consistently by all educators and staff involved and that data are being collected honestly and consistently. Additionally, there are a few other factors that can hinder the success of a SWPBS program. First, a lack of staff acceptance and implementation is detrimental to the success of the program (Carr et al., 2002). Because in Tier 1 the commitment to this program must be at a schoolwide level, all staff must embrace the program. Staff across the school building must use common language, agree on reinforcements and consequences, and acknowledge and implement schoolwide behavioral expectations. Consistency is essential for student success. New programs are often met with resistance, although typically this resistance fades with training and time. Administrative support of a program is evidenced by providing staff with in-services to learn and practice implementation of the SWPBS system. Second, the more transient the school population (staff and student body), the more inconsistent the results *may* be because a SWPBS system requires both understanding of the program by all staff and consistency in its implementation. The greater the student and staff turnover, the more time and repeated effort are required to learn the program, the school rules and routines, and the implementation of the consequences and rewards. Third, a SWPBS system that is designed without recognizing the diversity of the school population in terms of staff and students is less likely to yield the desired learning outcomes. It is essential that the schoolwide program is designed to embrace the student body inclusively, without undue emphasis on the expectations of the majority culture. Eliminating biases based on gender, class, racial, and/or ethnic differences and ability creates an inclusive program, recognizing that the student body is diverse and that supports must reflect that diversity. Last, it is critical to implement a SWPBS model at the start of the school year. The execution of proactive strategies creates an environment for success, starting at day one of and continuing throughout the school year (Taylor-Greene et al., 1997).

> *Comprehension Check*
> 1. Name three hurdles to effective SWPBS systems.
> 2. What are ways to mitigate these hurdles?

BULLYING PREVENTION WITHIN SCHOOLWIDE POSITIVE BEHAVIOR SUPPORT SYSTEMS

"Bullying is described as aggressive behavior normally characterized by repetition and imbalance of power" (Smith & Brain, 2000). Bullying is a growing concern among students, parents, and educators today. Social and emotional learning play a significant role in academic achievement, and when teaching social skills and addressing problem behaviors, such skills as conflict management, respecting others, and building relationships are critical (Zins, Bloodworth, Weissberg, & Walberg, 2004). These are critical skills to decrease bullying. Bystanders, victims of bullying, and students who bully all have lessons to learn regarding prevention and response to this ongoing problem. Bullying has grown from the bothersome behavior of one student teasing another to a schoolwide safety concern when violence could be involved. Bullying often continues because the bully is reinforced for the bullying behavior by an assumed increase in social status among peers, although that perceived peer status may be derived from fear of the bully. It is critical that supports are implemented to diminish bullying in schools. Creating a learning environment that provides social reinforcement in positive ways teaches students to stand up to and speak out against bullying and structures school to be positive, safe, and predictable, which can decrease bullying in schools. Hence, SWPBS is well designed to incorporate anti-bullying efforts, and rules can be written to emphasize teaching positive behaviors in a proactive manner (e.g., "Respect the rights, property, and feelings of all.").

ADDITIONAL BENEFITS OF SCHOOLWIDE POSITIVE BEHAVIOR SUPPORT

The benefits of SWPBS are many and varied, but some of the more commonly recognized benefits include improved morale in the school, increased achievement of behavioral expectations, and enhanced positive school culture. Furthermore, there is a decrease in office referrals, referral for and identification of students for special education, and bullying in schools, along with an increase in academic achievement when evidence-based SWPBS strategies are practiced (Bohanon et al., 2006; Meraviglia, Becker, Rosenbluth, Sanchez, & Robertson, 2003; Lassen, Steele, & Sailor, 2006). Supplementary advantages include greater faculty effectiveness in teaching, retention of teachers leading to consistent staffing over time, and lower absenteeism rates for both students and faculty (Horner & Sugai, 2007). When school is a positive environment, students and adults want to be there because both are engaged in learning; the environment is safe, consistent, positively reinforcing; and the ongoing cycle yields evidence that all are benefitting from the SWPBS program. This leads to recognition from students, staff, parents, and community members that good things are happening in school.

Comprehension Check

1. How can SWBPS programs decrease bullying, and what skills are interrelated?
2. What are the benefits to an effective SWBPS program?

APPLICATION CASE STUDY 4.2

South Kings Elementary School (SKES) is a suburban elementary school in the Midwest. There are approximately 600 students at this school, from kindergarten through fourth grade. The school has moderate socioeconomic diversity, minimal cultural and racial diversity, and an average percentage (9–13%) of students with disabilities. The staff and students are committed to creating a safe and positive learning environment for all students through the implementation of SWPBS, along with classroom and individual supports, when necessary.

SKES has a core SWPBS team. This volunteer team, made up of the principal, school counselor, four classroom teachers, two special education teachers, two paraprofessionals, and the music teacher, attended a three-day state training on SWPBS. The core team then trained the rest of the staff at SKES. The core team has a mission statement, holds monthly meetings, and troubleshoots with the staff when needed. The core team also analyzes data provided by the classroom teachers to determine the effectiveness of the program and to make data-driven decisions.

Students, staff, and administration have collaboratively written and are committed to the following four rules:

1. Keep hands and feet to yourself.
2. Take care of yourself, your friends, your teachers, and the school building.
3. Complete your work to the best of your ability at all times.
4. Be honest.

These school rules were written during the first week of school in August and posted in the school's multipurpose room. Also during the first week of school, building and classroom routines were established. Staff members modeled for students how to transition from the bus into the classrooms, how to walk in the hallway to various rooms in the building, how to purchase lunch in the lunch line, and other processes that occur throughout the school day. The third and fourth-grade students demonstrated for the younger students the behavioral expectations when completing these procedures.

Teachers and other staff members routinely model expected behavior, use behavior-specific praise to draw attention when students are performing desired behaviors, provide examples and non-examples of behavior expectations, use consistent language across the building with students, and have agreed-upon protocol when rules are not followed.

Administrators, teachers, and staff are also committed to using rewards and recognition and to acknowledging the value of reinforcement. Students are rewarded with coins to be turned in for more valuable prizes at the end of each quarter, state the school promise at the beginning of each week, and have the opportunity to earn social praise in various school situations.

Each month, the school counselor spends time teaching social skills in group lessons based on character traits. The students learn how these character traits help to build a positive school climate, practice the traits in both simulated situations and authentic situations, and learn songs about them in music class.

The staff at SKES use FBAs to determine the purpose that problem behaviors fulfill and to design a plan for replacing undesirable behaviors with acceptable behaviors that serve the same function. This proactive approach to behavior change reduces the loss of instructional time that occurs when time-outs, office referrals, and suspensions are implemented.

The SWBPS strategies are in place at all times for all students throughout the school building. For those students who require more structure or are at risk for behavior problems despite the schoolwide program, classroom supports are in place as well as small-group and individual supports. Between the schoolwide program and the more specific classroom and small-group interventions, about 95% of the students are behaviorally successful in school. For the remaining students, intensive interventions are provided in a structured setting to optimize their access to the curriculum and to bridge the gap created by their undesirable behaviors.

The staff retention rate at SKES is very high; many of the teachers in the building have been teaching at SKES for the entirety of their careers. The average teaching experience is 14 years. There is a low absenteeism rate, and substitute teachers report that it is one of the least stressful buildings to work in because the students are well behaved, know the school expectations, and are respectful to one another on a consistent basis.

SKES values their SWPBS program, and the staff and students respond positively to the structures in place. This model has proven effective as evidenced by high scores on state report cards, high staff retention, successful advancement in curriculum, and student and adult positive outlook on their school.

Case Study Comprehension Check

Apply what you have learned in Chapter 4 to this case study.

1. What elements of SWPBS are implemented at SKES?
2. What collaborative efforts are evidenced through this model?
3. Describe the importance of the use of reinforcement through the eyes of the students, teachers, and administrators. Why is this important?

APPLICATION ACTIVITIES

1. In a field experience, discuss with your mentor teacher or building principal the SWPBS strategies that are implemented in the school. Look for rules posted, procedures followed, and common language used throughout the building. Discuss your experiences with your classmates.

2. Consider standard behavioral expectations (e.g., "No hitting." "No late homework will be accepted." "Don't call out answers.").
   - How can these expectations be positively written?
   - How would you, as the teacher, explicitly teach these skills?
   - How could you use direct instruction, reinforcement, and the like?

CHAPTER SUMMARY

Behavioral Supports in a Three-Tiered Framework

- At Tier 1, the approach is intended for all students and implemented throughout the school in a universal fashion.
- At Tier 2, additional support is given to those students who were not successful with Schoolwide Positive Behavioral Support (SWPBS) in Tier 1.
- At Tier 3, specific interventions are executed for students who need additional support beyond Tier 2. Approximately 5% of the student population requires these intense interventions.
- It is crucial during this three-tiered model for data to be collected and analyzed appropriately for the effectiveness of the interventions in each tier.

Components of a Quality Schoolwide Positive Behavior Support System

- Consistency of expectations among all is key to more desirable behavioral outcomes.
- SWPBS models should be fine-tuned and implemented as needed in each school.
- It is important to establish behavioral expectations through school and classroom rules and routines.
- When adults have a growth mindset, students are seen to have the ability to develop and change behavior over time given an encouraging, consistent, and positively oriented environment.
- When teachers and students work collaboratively in the process of creating rules and routines, students feel they are a part of the process.
- When determining rules and routines, written and verbal communication as well as demonstration is significant for student comprehension.
- Functional behavioral assessment is a way to analyze a student's behavior to help determine the function or purpose behind the behavior.
- An office discipline referral is a frequent response to undesirable behaviors in the classroom or school setting.
  - Office discipline referrals can cause negative reinforcement among students. Rather, a more proactive approach, such as SWPBS, can create learning opportunities for the student to reverse the negative behavior.
- Monitoring the progress of the SWPBS model through data collection and analysis is crucial for its effectiveness.
  - Data from a variety of sources are reviewed to determine progress and achievement.
  - Core teams may need to adjust the system or model over time.

Hurdles to a Successful Schoolwide Positive Behavior Support System

- The lack of staff support and implementation is detrimental to the success of the program.
- Staff throughout the school building must use common language, agreed-upon reinforcements, and consequences of behavioral expectations.
- Consistency is crucial for student success.
- The more transient the school population, the more inconsistent the results may be.
- A SWPBS system should be designed to recognize diversity across the school population. If it does not recognize diversity, the system is less likely to yield the desired learning outcomes.
- The implementation of this system has its best results if it is put into effect at the start of the school year.

Bullying Prevention Within Schoolwide Positive Behavior Support Systems

- "Bullying is described as aggressive behavior normally characterized by repetition and imbalance of power" (Smith & Brain, 2000).
- SWPBS systems incorporate anti-bullying efforts by designing prevention programs that create a learning environment for students to stand up to and speak out against bullying in a positive manner.

Additional Benefits of Schoolwide Positive Behavior Support

- Increased morale, achievement of behavioral expectations, enhanced positive school culture, and academic achievement.
- Decrease in office referrals, referral and identification for special education, and bullying.
- Greater faculty effectiveness in teaching, retention of teachers, and lower absenteeism for students and faculty.

REFERENCES

Akin-Little, K., Eckert, T., Lovett, B., & Little, S. (2004). Extrinsic reinforcement in the classroom: Bribery or best practice. *School Psychology Review, 33,* 344–362.

Bohanon, H., Fenning, P., Carney K. L., Minnis-Kim, Anderson-Harriss, S. Morozn, K. B., . . . Pigott, T. D. (2006). Schoolwide application of positive behavior support in an urban high school: A case study. *Journal of Positive Behavior Interventions, 8,* 131–145.

Carr, E., Dunlap, G., Horner, R., Koegel, R., Turnball, A., Sailor, W., & Anderson, J. (2002). Positive behavior support: Evolution of an applied science. *Journal of Positive Behavior Interventions, 4,* 4–20.

Center on Response to Intervention. (n.d.). *The essential components of RTI.* Retrieved from www.rti4success.org

Coffey, J., & Horner, R. (2012). The sustainability of schoolwide positive behavior interventions and supports. *Exceptional Children, 78,* 407–422.

Cooper, J., Heron, T., & Heward, W. (2007). *Applied behavior analysis* (2nd ed.). London, England: Pearson.

Gersten, R., Woodward, J., & Darch, C. (1986). Direct instruction: A research-based approach to curriculum design and teaching. *Exceptional Children, 53,* 17–31.

Horner, R., & Sugai, G., (2007). *Schoolwide positive behavior support* [PowerPoint presentation]. Retrieved from www.pbis.org

Horner, R., Todd, A., Lewis-Palmer, T., Irvin, L., Sugai, G., & Boland, J. (2004). The school-wide evaluation tool (SET): A research instrument for assessing school-wide positive behavior support. *Journal of Positive Behavior Interventions, 6,* 3–12.

Lassen, S., Steele, M., & Sailor, W. (2006). The relationship of school-wide positive behavior support to academic achievement in an urban middle school. *Psychology in the Schools, 43,* 701–712.

Meraviglia, M., Becker, H., Rosenbluth, B., Sanchez, E., & Robertson, T. (2003). The expect respect project: Creating a positive elementary school climate. *Journal of Interpersonal Violence, 18,* 1347–1360.

Ogulmus, K., & Vuran, S. (2016). Schoolwide positive behavioral interventions and support practices: Review of students in the Journal of Positive Behavior Interventions. *Educational Sciences: Theory and Practice, 16,* 1693–1710.

Positive Behavioral Interventions and Supports. (2018). *Home page.* Retrieved from http://www.pbis.org/default.aspx

Smith, P., & Brain, P. (2000). Bullying in schools: Lessons from two decades of research. *Aggressive Behavior, 26,* 1–9.

Taylor-Greene, S., Brown, D., Nelson, L., Longton, J., Gassman, T., Cohen, J., . . . Hall, S. (1997). Schoolwide behavioral support: Starting the year off right. *Journal of Behavioral Education, 7,* 99–112.

Vallerand, R., Pelletier, L., Blais, M., Briere, N., Senecal, C., & Vallieres, E. (1992). The academic motivation scale: A measure of intrinsic, extrinsic, and amotivation in education. *Education and Psychological Measurement, 52,* 1003–1017.

Zins, J., Bloodworth, M., Weissberg, R., & Walberg, H. (2004). The scientific base linking social and emotional learning to school success. In J. E. Zins, R. P. Weissberg, M. C. Wang, & H. J. Walberg (Eds.), *Building academic success on social on emotional learning: What does the research say?* (pp. 3–22). New York, NY: Teachers College Press.

5

THE TEACHER'S ROLE

Catherine Lawless Frank

CHAPTER OBJECTIVES

After reading this chapter, students should be able to:

1. Discuss the importance of fostering the teacher-student, student-student, and teacher-parent relationships.
2. Develop an awareness of cultural differences and nonverbal communication and the effect these have on relationships.
3. Understand the leadership qualities necessary for an effective teacher.

The previous chapters in this text have examined the components of Response to Intervention (RTI), the principles of behavior management, methods for collecting data, and Schoolwide Positive Behavior Support strategies. These first four chapters provide the background information, concepts, and tools necessary for developing a behavior management system. The concepts discussed in Chapters 1 through 4 will be reinforced and built on in the following chapters. The ensuing four chapters will begin examining the foundation of classroom behavior management. Just as the academic components of Tier 1 are incorporated into all three tiers (see Table 5.1), so are the behavioral components. These four chapters will examine the basis of effective academic and behavioral instruction by examining the role of the teacher as the guiding force in the classroom (Chapter 5), structuring an inclusive classroom (Chapter 6), motivating and engaging students (Chapter 7), and implementing strategies for improving and maintaining overall classroom behavior (Chapter 8). These four chapters are applicable to and the foundation for classroom and behavior management in all three tiers of RTI in both general and special education classrooms. These chapters will not only focus on the ongoing cycle of assessment, analysis, decision-making, and instruction (see Figure 5.1) but also are the foundations necessary to make the cycle effective.

Table 5.1 Components of Response to Intervention

	Components
Tier 1	• **Assessment**—universal screening and progress monitoring • **Analysis** of assessment results • **Decision-making** for instruction based on the analysis • Effective evidence-based **instruction and intervention** • Continued ongoing assessment, analysis, decision-making, and instruction
Tier 2	• **Assessment**—progress monitoring • **Analysis** of assessment results • **Decision-making** for instruction based on the analysis • Effective evidence-based **instruction and intervention** • Continued ongoing assessment, analysis, decision-making, and instruction • Referral to pre-referral intervention team • Pre-referral assessments • Pre-referral interventions • Fidelity assessment
Tier 3	• **Assessment**—progress monitoring • **Analysis** of assessment results • **Decision-making** for instruction based on the analysis • Effective evidence-based **instruction and intervention** • Continued ongoing assessment, analysis, decision-making, and instruction • Referral for special education services • Multidisciplinary evaluation for special education services • Determination of eligibility for special education services • Individualized Education Program • Fidelity assessment

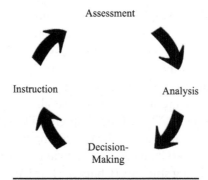

Figure 5.1 Ongoing Cycle of Response to Intervention

According to the *Cambridge English Dictionary* (2018), inclusion is "the act of including something as a part of something else." Although in education it is often interpreted to mean the act of including special education students as part of the general education population, in reality it is a conscious attempt to ensure that all students, parents, and faculty (teachers, co-teachers, paraprofessionals) feel like a welcomed and valued part of the classroom community. All students (special education, general education, gifted, culturally diverse, ethnically diverse, English language learners, at risk for school failure), parents, staff, and faculty who play a role in the classroom should feel welcomed and an integral part of the classroom community. This inclusive environment allows learners to work together to become pro-social members of the classroom and school community. This approach benefits all students by providing greater access to an effective curriculum, allowing them to develop to their fullest potential behaviorally and academically, and better prepares them to more effectively thrive in the workplace as well as in a diverse society (The IRIS Center, 2012).

This chapter will discuss components of classroom management by examining the teacher's role in an effective and inclusive classroom environment. Effective classrooms have a structured behavior management system that in turn increases academic achievement. The teacher is responsible for providing that structure and is the main determinant of academic and behavioral success within the classroom. Haim G. Ginott (1975), a child psychologist, author, and teacher, described the importance of the teacher as follows:

> I've come to a frightening conclusion that I am the decisive element in the classroom. It's my personal approach that creates the climate. It's my daily mood that makes the weather. As a teacher, I possess a tremendous power to make a child's life miserable or joyous. I can be a tool of torture or an instrument of inspiration. I can humiliate or heal. In all situations, it is my response that decides whether a crisis will be escalated or de-escalated and a child humanized or dehumanized.
> (www.goodreads.com/quotes/81938-i-ve-come-to-a-frightening-conclusion-that-i-am-the)

Ginott defines the teacher as the "decisive element" with "tremendous power" in the lives of students in the classroom. Teachers determine the culture and climate of the classroom, no matter the diversity of the population or the learning needs of the students. Teachers have the power to make a classroom "joyous," "inspirational," "heal(ing)," and "humaniz(ing)." They are the guiding force in a classroom with the ability to make the students feel like a valuable part of an inclusive classroom.

The role of the teacher is greater than simply developing lesson and behavior management plans in regard to guiding students' behavior and academic achievement. This chapter will examine the role of the teacher in becoming that "deciding factor" in the classroom as it relates to building relationships and dispositions.

BUILDING AND PROMOTING RELATIONSHIPS
Teacher-Student Relationship

To promote academic achievement and behavior management, teachers must develop a community in the classroom where every student feels accepted, cared for, and supported. This community is essential to making students feel safe and valued. The most essential ingredient in this is the relationship teachers establish with their individual students. This teacher-student relationship is often seen as the key ingredient in positive and successful classroom management (Wang, Haertel, & Walberg, 1993). Teachers with strong, high-quality, and caring relationships with their students have fewer discipline and behavioral issues than teachers without such a relationship (Marzano & Maranzo, 2003).

Relationships do not happen by chance, and the teacher-student relationship must be consciously developed and fostered by the teacher, who must willingly reach out and actively form a quality relationship with every student. Each student must feel that the teacher cares about them as a person. The teacher's verbal and nonverbal behaviors must support this message, and extra effort should be given to developing relationships with students who are struggling either academically and/or behaviorally. Research has shown that students will make decisions about how to behave in a classroom, both academically and behaviorally, based on their perception of whether a teacher cares about them (Weinstein, Tomlinson-Clarke, & Curran, 2004). The key is that it is the student's perception of whether a teacher cares. A teacher may truly care about a student, but it is the student's perception that matters. When students feel that their teacher cares about them, they tend to put greater effort into academics and are more likely to behave in an appropriate manner in that classroom. When a student feels a teacher does not care, they tend to put less effort into the class academically and behaviorally. A student may feel that if the teacher does not care, then why should they care?

The teacher-student relationship is too important to be left to chance. Fundamental to this is the teacher's belief that they are responsible for developing and maintaining this teacher-student relationship. Each and every student must be viewed as an important member of the classroom and deserving of a supportive classroom community that encompasses and enriches all students. In such a community, the teacher is committed to the behavioral and academic success of each student and views all students as equally important parts of the learning community.

Although developing relationships may seem obvious and simple, that is not always the case. Having the belief that it is the teachers' responsibility to develop quality relationships requires teachers to be aware of their own biases and actions. It requires ongoing critical reflection by teachers on their own thoughts and actions and a willingness to admit mistakes and change behaviors.

Developing a quality relationship is often easier with students with strong social and relationship skills. These students have typically learned how to interact and to foster quality relationships with peers or other adults. Their behavior is considered respectful and appropriate for the classroom, making it easier for teachers to develop and maintain a relationship. Some students may not know or employ these same relationship and social skills, making it more challenging for the teacher to develop a relationship with them. Students may have different cultural norms (different standards of personal hygiene, ways of engaging in conversation, showing respect), behavioral characteristics (disrupting the teacher, off task, sleeping during class), or difficulty developing relationships with adults or peers (poor social skills, disrespect toward the teacher, fighting). These student differences may challenge teachers and require them to make a conscious and determined effort to build a quality relationship. These challenging students are often those most in need of a caring, quality teacher-student relationship. Students often make decisions about their classroom behavior based on their beliefs about their relationship with their teacher. Developing strong relationships is essential for the structure and well-being of the classroom community (Weinstein et al., 2004).

CASE STUDY 5.1

Patricia is a student in Ms. Lisset's class. As Ms. Lisset begins teaching a lesson, Patricia raises her hand and asks to go to the restroom. Ms. Lisset reminds Patricia of the classroom procedures for when students are allowed to use the restroom (during independent works times and not while Ms. Lisset is teaching) and asks Patricia to wait until the appropriate time. Patricia complains that she "really, really, really has to go." Ms. Lisset goes on with her lesson but soon stops to redirect Patricia, who is talking to her neighbor. The neighbor quickly sits quietly and looks at Ms. Lisset, while Patricia sighs loudly and begins doodling and looking at her desk rather than at Ms. Lisset. When asked to put her pencil down and look at the board, Patricia follows the teacher's directions and sits quietly for few minutes. She then gets up to get a tissue, blows her nose (loudly), and walks to the front of the room to throw away the tissue. Ms. Lisset continues on with the lesson but notices that many of the students are watching Patricia blow her nose rather than focusing on her lesson.

When she finishes her lesson, Ms. Lisset assigns independent work to the students. Most students quickly transition to the assignment, but Patricia does not and begins again talking to her neighbor. Ms. Lisset intervenes and tells Patricia to start working. When Ms. Lisset walks over to Patricia's desk a few minutes later, she notices that Patricia still has not started the assignment. Patricia states that she has not started the assignment because she does not have a pencil (she broke the one she had earlier). Exasperated, Ms. Lisset hands Patricia a sharpened pencil and tells her to begin working. After working quietly for a few minutes, Patricia wanders over to Ms. Lisset to ask a question. Ms. Lisset redirects her back to her desk and tells her to raise her hand. Patricia goes back to her desk, raises her hand, and asks a question about the first problem. After receiving the answer, Patricia writes down the answer and then quickly completes the rest of the assignment, calling out, "I'm done." Patricia is the first one finished with the assignment but answered only 45% of the problems correctly.

At the end of the class period, Ms. Lisset is tired and frustrated. As she reflects on her day, she thinks primarily about Patricia. Patricia's behaviors in the classroom are a distraction both to Ms. Lisset and to the rest of the class, and Patricia is struggling academically. As she tries to determine what she could do differently to help Patricia, she thinks back over their interactions throughout the class. She soon realizes that she could not recall a single positive interaction between Patricia and herself all class period. Although she gave Patricia plenty of attention, none of it was positive. Ms. Lisset tried to examine class from Patricia's perspective

> and realized that if she were Patricia, she would not enjoy being in that class. She doubted that Patricia felt they shared an authentic caring relationship. Because Ms. Lisset knew the value of that relationship, she vowed to work harder to develop a positive one with Patricia. Ms. Lisset set a goal for herself of at least three positive interactions with Patricia every class period (greeting her when she arrived, praising her, catching her being good, complimenting her, showing interest).

For example, Jackie is a student in Mr. Allen's class. The bell has rung, and Mr. Allen is beginning his lecture on the day's topic. Five minutes later, Jackie arrives late to class (again), walks in, shuffles to Mr. Allen's desk, tosses her tardy slip on his desk, and shuffles to her seat, acting as though this class is the last place on earth she would like to be. Mr. Allen stops his lecture, welcomes Jackie to class, and patiently waits (taking class time away from the rest of the students) for Jackie to take her seat. When he asks Jackie to "please get out her homework," she replies, "I didn't do it." Jackie then proceeds to put her head on the desk, using her sweatshirt as a pillow. When Mr. Allen finishes his lesson, he instructs the students to begin working on that day's assignment. While most students begin working within a minute or so, Jackie does not. Mr. Allen approaches her desk and asks her to begin working. Jackie replies, "I don't know what to do."

In this example, Mr. Allen may feel frustrated with Jackie. She showed up late (again) and disrupted class in the process. Her homework was not completed and because her head was on her desk, she appeared to make no obvious attempts to listen or pay attention in class. She did not ask questions or seek help when she was confused. Students such as Jackie, who demand more time and energy for nonacademic reasons, can cause a teacher to feel aggravated or annoyed. Teachers may feel that the student does not care so why should the teacher care? This makes it difficult for teachers to provide the extra effort and energy needed to support students and to work to form a quality relationship. Mr. Allen has the right to feel frustrated but not the right to give up on Jackie. It is Mr. Allen's responsibility to educate Jackie, and to do so he must work to provide supports and to build a quality relationship with her. Students make decisions on how to behave and how much effort to put into a class based in part on the relationship they have with the teacher (Weinstein et al., 2004). Whatever the reason for Jackie's behavior (life circumstances, disconnect in teaching and learning styles, learned helplessness, academic challenges), it is Mr. Allen's responsibility to address the issue and work to resolve it.

It is also possible that Mr. Allen has already developed this relationship with Jackie. He may be tolerant of her behavior because he is aware of the circumstances that may contribute to Jackie being late to class, unprepared, and tired (working in the evenings, helping to take care of younger siblings, sleep disorder). This knowledge then allows him to meet Jackie's needs in a caring, supportive manner.

Two challenges to building authentic relationships are social skills deficits and cultural differences. It is important to remember that some students, especially those with disabilities and other learning needs, may also have social skills deficits that may make it more difficult for them to build relationships. Social skills are culturally based patterns of behavior that guide the norms of how humans interact with one another. These skills are typically not explicitly taught but are learned through modeling. For instance, a child watches a parent to see how they should act or respond in a given situation. They may see the parent greet another person, such as a neighbor, coworker, or stranger, by smiling and saying hi. As the child grows, this behavior is modeled time and time again, and typically the child learns that when greeting someone, a person should smile and say hi. How to greet someone typically is not explicitly taught because the majority of people learn how to do so (and most other social skills) through modeling and observation. Some students struggle to learn through modeling alone though, causing them to have deficits in social skills because of this lack of knowledge.

Social skills are also culturally based. Each culture has its own accepted patterns of behavior, and what is considered appropriate in one culture may not be considered appropriate in another. A child who learns to smile and say hi when greeting someone may be at a disadvantage if they immigrated to another culture with different norms for greeting (a handshake or kiss instead of a smile, a hierarchical structure that deems it disrespectful for a child to speak without first be spoken too or that dictates the type of greeting based on age or status). The child would most likely not be given a book or pamphlet on how to greet someone (or for any other social skill), and this lack of knowledge of the cultural norm may cause others to view and treat them differently.

It is important for teachers to be cognizant of deficits and cultural differences in social skills. When someone's (teachers and students) behavior fails to adhere to the cultural norms, they are often viewed or treated differently. This may then affect a teacher's ability and willingness to put forth the effort to build an authentic relationship. For example, Steve is a student in the school where Mrs. Russell teaches. When she noticed him in the hall or cafeteria, Mrs. Russell thought Steve's behaviors were a little odd but assumed he was young and a little immature. In the hall one day, Mrs. Russell asks him about his weekend and Steve responds with a long story about his cousins that seemed off topic and confusing. When she asked a follow-up question, Steve made eye contact, turned and walked away down the hall without answering the question or finishing the conversation. He simply left in the middle of the conversation without answering her question for no apparent reason and walked away.

This interaction may cause Mrs. Russell to no longer view Steve as a little odd or immature and to view him now as self-absorbed and rude. Mrs. Russell took the time to engage him in conversation and to build a relationship. In return, he turned and walked away without answering the question, saying, "Goodbye. I gotta get to class," or even asking a follow-up question about her weekend. This interaction left an impression on Mrs. Russell and, most likely, a negative one. It is often difficult to extend common courtesies much less actively build a caring relationship with someone who is perceived as self-absorbed and rude.

It is also possible (and hopeful) that Mrs. Russell is cognizant of social skills differences and deficits. She may be sensitive to the possibility that Steve has a social skills deficit or a culturally different way of engaging in or ending a conversation. Rather than assuming that Steve's behavior was purposefully rude or self-absorbed, she could talk to him about her impression of his behavior and use the interaction to teach Steve a mini social skills lesson. She could teach him the social skills for ending a conversation ("Steve, when you want to end a conversation, it is considered rude to turn and walk away. What you should do is say something like 'Goodbye. I gotta get to class now.' So what should you say to end a conversation?") or engaging in conversational turn taking ("Steve, when I was confused and asked you a question, you did not respond. When you are asked a question in a conversation, it is expected that you respond to the question. So when you are asked a question, what should you do?"). Next week, Mrs. Russell could then remind Steve of what they discussed the previous week and again ask him about his weekend to verify that it was a social skills issue and to allow Steve an opportunity to practice his new skills.

ILLUSTRATIVE CASE STUDY 5.2

Edward is a Native American student in Mr. Murray's class who recently got in trouble for an incident in the cafeteria. The principal asked Mr. Murray to join her and Edward in her office to discuss his behavior and the consequences for his actions. Although typically teachers are not asked to participate in conferences between the principal and students about behaviors in the cafeteria, Mr. Murray's presence was requested because the principal was becoming frustrated with Edward belligerence.

Edward refused to answer any of the questions the principal asked him and would not look at her when she addressed him. The principal quickly became aggravated because when she asked Edward a direct question, he stared down at the floor and refused to answer. He would not defend himself or offer any explanation for his behavior. When she asked him to look at her, he briefly raised his head and then quickly lowered it again. He just sat there staring at the floor. The principal asked Mr. Murray to attend the conference hoping that he could help her reach this student and find out what happened in the cafeteria.

If Mr. Murray is aware that there is a cultural difference in terms of showing respect to a person in authority between the principal and Edward, he will be able to navigate the situation and advocate for Edward in terms of this cultural difference. Mr. Murray could explain to the principal that remaining quiet and avoiding eye contact in Edward's culture is a sign of respect for the principal. Edward is not answering the questions as a sign of respect, and he is not refusing to answer because he is disrespectful or belligerent. Because Mr. Murray knows this cultural difference between the principal and Edward, it not only helps Edward and the principal in this situation but also reaffirms to Edward that his teacher cares for him enough to understand his culture and to advocate for him.

If Mr. Murray was not aware of the cultural difference between the principal and Edward, then he would not able to advocate on Edward's behalf. Edward may have been labeled belligerent and given a harsher consequence when in fact he was trying to be respectful. The relationship between Edward and Mr. Murray may have also suffered because of this misunderstood cultural difference. Mr. Murray may have viewed Edward more negatively, and Edward may have felt as if Mr. Murray did not understand, care about, or support him. Neither Mr. Murray nor Edward may understand or be aware of this cultural difference, and this lack of knowledge may have negatively affected their relationship.

Table 5.2 Ways to Increase Cultural Knowledge and Awareness

- Be aware of your own cultural biases.
- Research cultural differences.
- Ask other teachers in your building.
- Talk to, survey or interview parents, students and/or other community members.
- Visit museums and other cultural centers.
- Engage with students' community and culture by shopping where they shop, visiting neighborhoods, attend festival, fairs, and/or religious events.
- Attend cultural awareness classes or other trainings offered by your school and the community.

When building a relationship with students, it is important to be respectful of and sensitive to the cultural and communication style differences that may exist between the teacher and the student. Different cultures hold different beliefs on the dynamics of appropriate relationships between teachers and students and many have differing communication styles that influence those relationships. When teachers' cultural backgrounds are different from their students' backgrounds, misunderstanding can affect a teacher-student relationship, especially if the teacher is not cognizant of those differences. See Table 5.2 for ways to increase cultural knowledge and awareness.

Another example, is a student named Samuel that often yells out comments when the teacher is instructing the class. Samuel's comments are typically on topic but inappropriate because he is interrupting class by calling out answers instead of raising his hand and waiting to be called on. When he is asked to be quiet, he is for a brief period of time but then quickly seems to yell out whatever comment is in his head. The teacher has tried asking him (repeatedly) to be quiet and to wait his turn, has written his name on the board, and has taken away recess and free time, but he still continues the same behavior. This disruptive and noncompliant behavior is making it difficult for the teacher to build a quality relationship with Samuel. What the teacher may not realize is that in Samuel's culture it is expected for him to be actively engaged in conversations. Samuel may not understand why a teacher would ask him to sit quietly when he has learned at home that sitting quietly is inappropriate and means that a person is not paying attention. Samuel may think that he is showing interest in the lesson by actively commenting and that quiet students are either shy or not engaged. This cultural difference and lack of understanding that both Samuel and his teacher have about this difference can be interpreted as a behavior problem and can interfere with building a relationship. The teacher may feel that Samuel is disrespectful or noncompliant while Samuel may be confused about the teacher's expectations and why he is getting into trouble. It may become easy for Samuel to perceive that his teacher does not understand or care about him, which may then negatively influence his behavior and academics.

Developing a high-quality relationship with every student is essential. All students need a classroom community that fosters an inclusive environment where students feel a sense of belonging, support, and care. The teacher's role in developing that community and building relationships is essential. Classrooms that foster community and belonging have been linked to positive student outcomes, such as an increased desire to learn. Not having that sense of community and belonging has been linked to negative student outcomes, such as truancy and dropping out of school (Mansor, Eng, Rasul, Hamzah, & Hamid, 2012).

Almost anything teachers do that show they care about, and are interested in, a student has a positive effect in the classroom (Marzano & Maranzo, 2003). When teachers take an interest in every student and engage students in social interactions and not just academic ones, students respond positively both academically and behaviorally. These interactions often correspond to better-behaved students, with fewer disrupting behaviors, more tolerance, openness to divergent views, creativity, and a safer school environment (Wang et al., 1993). For ways for teachers to build authentic relationships with students, see Table 5.3.

Table 5.3 Ways to Begin Building Caring Relationships With Students

- Welcome students into the classroom and greet them by name ("Hi, Sam. Welcome to school today.").
- Welcome students of different nationalities in their primary or native language (*buenos dias* for a student from Honduras or *bonjour* for a student from France).
- Comment on a haircut, new jacket, new shoes, or anything that you notice ("I like that shirt. That is a beautiful color." "Did you get a haircut? It looks good on you.").
- Ask about their weekend ("What did you do that was fun this weekend?" "On Friday you said you were going to go _____. Did you go? How was it?").
- Congratulate them on all accomplishments, not just academic ones ("I heard you won your basketball game. Congratulations." "The principal said you were very polite and helpful this morning when you opened the door for her and helped her carry in some boxes.").
- Ask about television shows or movies ("Who watched the Super Bowl over the weekend? What was your favorite commercial from the Super Bowl?").
- Take an interest in what the students have an interest in ("I took your advice and watched _____, and I did/did not like it." "What music are you listening to?" "What is your favorite band?").
- Remember important events in students' lives (wish them a happy birthday, ask about a sporting, cheerleading, club, scouting, or band event).
- Ask about a student's family or pet ("How is your mother/father/sister/brother doing?" "Did you take your dog for a walk last night?").
- Share stories about what is happening in your life ("Last weekend I went to _____. Has anyone been there?" "At dinner last night my dogs _____.").
- Share stories about your own childhood ("When I was a third grader _____." "My younger brother used to _____.").
- Use specific praise with students for academic and nonacademic behaviors both inside and outside your classroom ("I really like how your used your resources to find that answer, Carl. Nice job." "Thank you for helping Simaya pick up the pens she dropped. That was very nice of you." "I heard from Mrs. Peterson that you got an A on your social studies test. Nice job.").
- Attribute ideas and suggestions back to the student ("Layla suggested that we _____. What do the rest of you think?" "I like Vince's idea to _____.").
- Offer the students choices ("Would you rather do your math independently or as a group?" "You can use a pen or a pencil for this assignment.").
- Reach out to parents, guardians, and other family members (introduce yourself to a parent or guardian at student pick-up or drop-off time, introduce yourself to a student's sibling at school).

Remember that everything teachers do to show they are interested in a student counts and matters in terms of building an authentic relationships (Marzano, Marzano, & Pickering, 2003).

Building Relationships Among Students

Teachers also must encourage and promote positive interactions and relationships among students. Peer-to-peer relationships are essential in fostering a sense of classroom community. People, in general, tend to feel more accepted when surrounded by people with whom they have a positive relationship. This does not mean that all students must or will be friends with one another, although friendships within the classroom do matter. It does mean that students treat one another in a respectful and positive manner. Students are typically more willing to follow the goals and structure of the classroom when they feel accepted and have a sense of belonging.

The teacher-student relationship begins the process of building positive relationships among all students by modeling and demonstrating acceptance. When teachers develop quality relationships with every student, it demonstrates that all students, especially those with more challenging behaviors, are worthy. Teachers then also model for other students how to develop these relationships.

Teachers should go further than just modeling, however. They must consciously foster an environment where students are accepting and respectful to one another. This accepting peer-to-peer relationship is something that teachers must cultivate and should not be left to chance. See Table 5.4 for ideas on how to foster quality relationships among students.

Table 5.4 Fostering Quality Relationships Among Students

- Focus on the positive (rather than the negative) actions of students.
  - Praise students for what they do well both academically and behaviorally.
  - Aim for 10 positive comments for every negative or punitive comment.
  - Pay particular attention to students with behavioral difficulties to identify and praise positive behaviors.
- Create opportunities for students to be interactive.
  - Use collaborative and problem-solving activities rather than competition.
  - Play games.
  - Do community-building activities
- Use flexible grouping.
  - Use heterogeneous grouping whenever possible.
  - Consciously assign students to specific groups to help build and foster relationships.
  - Change student groups regularly rather than keeping students in the same groups all quarter, semester, or year.
  - Keep groups small (three students if possible) to encourage more interactions.
- Be aware of cultural differences.
  - Support and educate students about similarities and differences.
  - Celebrate cultural differences.
  - Be prepared and willing to intervene if necessary.

(Continued)

Table 5.4 (Continued)

- Be firm in your expectations as to appropriate interactions among students.
  - Praise positive interactions ("Thank you, JaVon, for helping Ellie pick up her papers.").
  - Have a zero-tolerance policy (and enforce it consistently) for bullying and teasing, and intervene early and firmly.
  - Educate students on the appropriate ways to express feelings and different points of view.
- Focus on social skills.
  - Teach students the appropriate ways to disagree and resolve conflict.
  - Identify social skills deficits in students, address those deficits, and teach the appropriate skills.

Table 5.5 Ways to Promote Parental Involvement

- Send a weekly or monthly newsletter, and offer the newsletter in a variety of forms (email, paper copy, podcast).
- Send positive notes and make positive phone calls home about a student's behaviors.
- Encourage involvement within the classroom.
- Promptly respond to emails, phone calls, and notes from parents.
- Greet parents when they enter the classroom and make them feel welcome.
- Be flexible with meeting times and ways of communication.
- Greet parents when they drop off or pick up their child.
- Always begin and end meetings with a positive comment about the student.
- Ask parents for guidance in working with their child.
- Learn about family backgrounds and cultures.
- Encourage and promote family involvement.

Teacher-Guardian Relationships

Parental involvement in the school has been shown to positively influence a student's performance, making it essential for teachers to strategically develop relationships with parents, guardians, and caregivers (Grolnick & Slowiaczek, 1994). Teachers must be cognizant of the benefits of parental involvement and foster a strong school-home connection. It is the teacher's, not the parents', responsibility to develop and foster this relationship (Metropolitan Center for Urban Education, 2008). For ways to promote parental or guardian involvement, see Table 5.5.

When meeting with parents, it is important to include positive information about their child. Teachers must be aware of how they present information and how a parent may interpret that information.

For example, Mr. Joseph, a teacher, is meeting with a parent, Jamie Barrett, to address concerns about her daughter, Connie. Connie often disrupts class, and Mr. Joseph is hoping for support from Ms. Barrett in addressing these concerns. The following are two examples of how Mr. Joseph could conduct the conversation.

Example 1

Hi, Ms. Barrett. Thank you for meeting with me. I requested this meeting to discuss some behavioral concerns I am having with Connie. Before we begin, however, I want to tell you that I enjoy having Connie in my class. She is inquisitive and has made friends with everyone in the room. The problem is that this causes Connie to become distracted in class. Connie engages her classmates in conversations, which means that both Connie and the classmate miss key information in lessons or directions. This causes both students to be off task and to fall behind. I have tried moving her seat away from her friends, reminding her of the class rules, and meeting with her about this, but none of this has been very successful. I was hoping you could provide some insights into or ideas on how to help your daughter be more successful in class. I do not want to discourage her ability to develop relationships, but I want to teach her the appropriate time and place to do so.

Example 2

Hi, Ms. Barrett. Thank you for meeting with me. I requested this meeting because Connie has become a disruption in class. Connie engages her classmates in conversations, which means that both Connie and the classmate miss key information in lessons or directions. This causes both students to be off task and to fall behind. I have tried moving her seat away from her friends, reminding her of the class rules, and meeting with her about this. I was hoping you could provide some insights into or ideas on how to help your daughter be more successful in class.

In both instances, Mr. Joseph's concern was Connie talking and disrupting class, and five of the six sentences in example 2 were exactly the same as those in example 1 (the sixth sentence in example 2 was reworded slightly). Example 1 tends to be viewed as more collaborative and positive, especially from a parent's perspective. In this example, Mr. Joseph began and ended the conversation on a positive note about Connie's behavior. This is important when working with parents. Example 2 may lead Ms. Barrett to have a much more negative view of Mr. Joseph, which can affect her desire to form a working relationship with him. When teachers take the time and effort to acknowledge the strengths in students and to begin and end conversations on a positive note, it helps facilitate quality relationships between school and home.

It is also important to be aware of cultural norms and differences, which may become more apparent in parental interactions. Interactions with students primarily involve group interactions, and students tend to conform to peer pressure and group expectations and norms. Interactions with parents tend to be more one on one with fewer group norms guiding the interaction, allowing the culture and cultural differences to be more pronounced. It is important to remember that cultural differences may not always be physically apparent. It may seem obvious that a mother is Muslim because she is wearing a hijab (headscarf) or a father is an Orthodox Jew because he is wearing a kippah (skullcap), but most cultural differences are not physically apparent. Physical demonstrations of a religion or culture may make a culture more obvious and may make it easier for a teacher to be cognizant of differences, but most differences tend to involve differing attitudes, beliefs, and practices rather than physical traits or appearances.

Misunderstandings about cultural differences may inadvertently cause tensions between teachers and parents. For example, a teacher and a parent may differ in the value of time or, more specifically, being on time. A teacher may see being on time as a life skill and something to be strictly maintained. If a parent-teacher conference is scheduled for 3:00 p.m., then the teacher may interpret that to mean that both the teacher and the parent are in the same location at 3:00 p.m. or 3:05 at the latest. The teacher may also assume that if one of the parties is more than five to 10 minutes late without notifying the other party, it is a violation of the cultural norm and is considered rude. A parent, on the other hand, may be from a culture that is more relaxed or flexible in terms of time and may even view arriving at the exact appointed time as a violation of cultural norms and even rude. The parent may assume that when the teacher sets an appointment for 3:00 p.m., the teacher really means sometime between 3:15 and 4:00. The parent may see arriving at 3:00 p.m. as rude because 3:00 may be when the teacher begins preparing for the meeting, and arriving at the appointed time may interfere with the teacher's time to prepare. In an interaction such as this, what the teacher sees as rude, the parent sees as respectful. If the parent were to invite the teacher over for coffee or dinner, and the teacher arrived at the exact appointed time, then the parent may view that as a violation of their culture norms and consider it rude. Misunderstanding may occur if neither party is aware of the cultural differences. For a list of potential cultural differences in communicating, see Table 5.6.

Table 5.6 Cultural Differences in Communication Styles

Communication Style	Meaning	Difference
Conversing	How did the conversation start, and what was the topic addressed?	Is it direct and straight to the point or less direct, easing into the topic with an emphasis on how the message is received?
Emotional style	How much emotion is appropriate to display during a conversation in terms of tone of voice, gestures, facial expressions, and volume?	Should emotions be expressed or subdued?
Movement	How much movement (hand and/or body movement) is used while communicating?	Do people remain still or move part or all of their body while communicating?
Turn taking	When is it a person's time to talk, turn take, or respond?	Does the communication partner wait until the speaker has completely finished talking before responding, or is it appropriate to interrupt or talk over one another?
Consideration	Is an individual's rights or the group's rights more important?	Is it appropriate to refrain from behaviors that may disturb others at the expense of individual rights, or should others be tolerant of an individual's rights at the expense of their rights?

Communication Style	Meaning	Difference
Personal space	What is the amount of personal space that is appropriate when engaged in a conversation?	Should communicating partners maintain a specific distance between them, and, if so, how much distance? In what instances is that personal space allowed to be violated?
Ownership	How are resources shared or owned?	Are resources shared among those in need, or are they the individual property of the person who bought or owns them?
Authority figure	What constitutes an authority figure?	Is a person's authority earned, or is it by right of their position?
Respect	What are the nonverbal ways in which respect or deference is shown?	What specific body language or customs are used to signify respect (eye contact, body posture)?
Behavior management	How much structure is necessary or appropriate?	Should there be leniency employed in managing behaviors to allow students more freedom and individuality, or should there be more structure?

(The IRIS Center, 2012)

The Importance of Nonverbal Communication

It is not just what a person says but how they say it that makes nonverbal communication important. Nonverbal communication is how a person converses without spoken language and includes facial expression, body language, tone and pitch of voice, gestures, and proximity between the speaker and listener. Nonverbal communication is the primary way people communicate attitudes, emotions, sarcasm, and moods. It can convince the speaker that the listener is interested and engaged or disinterested and bored. When a person's nonverbal communication matches their verbal message, then the message sent is more likely to be believed as authentic. When the verbal and nonverbal messages do not match, then the message is more likely to be viewed as sarcastic, untrustworthy, or dishonest. The interpretation of nonverbal communication is subjective and rarely verified. The message sent may be intentional (a smile and a wave to greet a person) or unintentional (yawning in the middle of a meeting with a parent) (Fortenot, 2014). The norms for nonverbal communication are also culturally based. The same nonverbal communication can be interpreted in multiple ways based on subjective impressions and cultural differences. People often use another's nonverbal communication to form an impression or attitude about that person (Richards, Lawless Frank, Sableski, & Arnold, 2016).

It is important for teachers to be aware of the nonverbal message they are sending. Because impressions are formed and judgments are made based on nonverbal communication, teachers must become consciously aware of their nonverbal actions and the messages they are sending.

Imagine a teacher is working at his desk, and a student comes in at recess to talk to him. If the teacher stops working, physically turns his body toward the student, makes eye contact, and places his arms at his side, the teacher typically conveys that he is invested in the conversation and listening to the student. If instead the teacher continued working or does not turn toward the student, or even crosses his arms when turning toward the student, then the message the teacher conveys may be completely different, even if the teacher did not intend it to be different. The teacher may think he is multitasking and can listen to the student and work at the same time. The student may interpret this as the teacher is not invested in the conversation or just does not care. If the teacher does turn to face the student and makes eye contact but crosses his arms in from his chest, it may convey a position of authority, and the student may interpret it as if they are in trouble.

Sometimes the message sent by nonverbal communication is intentional, while other times the message is not intentional and the sender may not even realize they are sending that message. The teacher with the crossed arms may just like to rest his arms in that position and have no communicational intent in crossing his arms. The teacher may never know or realize how a student interpreted that simple nonverbal gesture.

Teachers must also be aware of how they are interpreting students' nonverbal communication and what impressions (either positive or negative) are formed. These impressions can affect their relationship with or attitude toward a student. A teacher's attitude toward a student may be affected if the student rolls their eyes when given a direction as opposed to smiles at a teacher when they walk into the classroom. Or if the student puts their head down on the desk as opposed to sitting up straight and looking at the board. Each of these behaviors can influence a teacher's attitude, and it is the teacher's responsibility to be cognizant of this and the effect it may have on building a quality relationship.

Comprehension Check
1. Why is the teacher-student relationship important in an inclusive classroom environment?
2. How can cultural differences influence teacher-student, teacher-parent, or peer relationships?
3. What are some ways a teacher can foster a relationship with parents?
4. What is nonverbal communication, and how can it affect a teacher's impression of a student and a student's impression of a teacher?

TEACHER DISPOSITIONS

Although relationships are extremely important in establishing an effective and inclusive classroom, they alone are not enough. Teachers must also possess certain characteristics or dispositions that facilitate their ability to successfully fulfill their role in a classroom. Although there is not consistency in or agreement of the specific number and types of dispositions a teacher should possess, certain ones are required to successfully facilitate classroom management. These necessary dispositions help teachers provide leadership and foster the determination needed to meet the challenges of the classroom. Leadership includes not only the ability to manage behaviors but also the capacity for consistency, flexibility, fairness, and persistence. These dispositions are not fixed within a person and can evolve and become stronger with resolve and practice. Just as the behaviors of students can evolve and grow, so can those of a teacher.

Leadership

An authentic relationship means there must be separation between the teacher and the students, with the teacher assuming a leadership role. Although the classroom should be collaborative in nature, it is up to the teacher to be the authority figure who provides structure and guidance both academically and behaviorally. Teachers must communicate a sense of authority or an "appropriate level of dominance" to be in charge and in control of the classroom. As a leader, they should be collaborative and flexible (rather than bossy and inflexible) but realize that they are responsible for the final decision, which should reflect their high behavioral and academic expectations for the students (Marzano & Marzano, 2003).

Research has shown that students actually prefer a teacher with a sense of authority and high expectations over a more permissive teacher (Chiu & Tulley, 1997). Students prefer a teacher who is capable of providing guidance and maintaining classroom structure over a teacher who is more lenient, unclear, and/or inconsistent with behavioral and academic expectations.

One of the keys to leadership is consistency. Rules, procedures, and expectations must be implemented in a consistent manner in order for them to be effective. This consistency provides the structure that allows students to know the clear boundaries and expectations. More importantly, however, consistency allows students to know that the teacher means what they say.

For example, Mrs. Raymond established a procedure for getting her attention during independent work time, which consists of the student raising their hand and waiting quietly at their desk until she acknowledges them by walking over to their desk to provide assistance. At the beginning of the year, Mrs. Raymond and her class practiced this procedure with both examples (how to do it correctly by remaining quiet and at their desk with their hand up) and non-examples (getting out of their seat or calling out to ask a question). Mrs. Raymond practiced and reinforced this procedure until she was sure that her students understood and were able to implement it. At this point, Mrs. Raymond must be sure that she consistently enforces this procedure every time and with every student who needs assistance during independent work time. When a student calls out, gets out of their seat, and fails to raise their hand, Mrs. Raymond must ensure that the student follows the procedure correctly before responding to the student's inquiry. If she does enforce the procedure consistently, then the students will learn to follow the procedures and, more importantly, learn that Mrs. Raymond means what she says. When Mrs. Raymond says the students are to follow a procedure, then the students know that they are to follow the procedure. This consistency helps solidify Mrs. Raymond's role as an authority figure. She means what she says. If Mrs. Raymond answers students' inquiries when they are not following the procedure (calling out her name, getting out of their seat, and approaching her), the students learn the opposite. Mrs. Raymond says a student needs to raise their hand and wait quietly at their desk, but she does not really mean this. Even though she says students must follow a procedure, sometimes it is acceptable to walk over to her and ask her a question. Other times it may be acceptable to call out her name and ask for help ("Will you help me, Mrs. Raymond?"). When Mrs. Raymond allows students to break the procedure and still have their inquiries met, then the students begin to learn that Mrs. Raymond does not really mean what she says. She says one thing, but students can actually ignore her and do something else. The students may begin testing other procedures and standards set by Mrs. Raymond to find other inconsistencies between what she says and what she does.

Leadership and Nonverbal Communication

Providing this sense of guidance includes not only verbal but also nonverbal components of communication. Teachers must convey a sense of assurance in their role as an authority figure, which is done not only through words but also the manner in which those words are spoken (Marzano, Marzano, & Pickering, 2003). It is not only what is said but also how it is said. Teachers must be mindful not only of their words but also of their tone of voice, posture, and proximity in order to communicate confidence in their role as an authority figure.

The tone and pitch, or strength and quality, of voice is often what students use to decide how serious a teacher is. Teachers need what is sometimes referred to as a teacher's voice or a tone of voice that lets a student know that the teacher is serious and means business. Teachers must be able to use a tone that is clear, intentional, and slightly louder in order to convey a sense of authority (Marzano, Marzano, & Pickering, 2003). Students often determine when a teacher means business or is unsure and wavering strictly by the teacher's tone of voice.

Posture is another nonverbal component that teachers use to convey leadership (Marzano, Marzano, & Pickering, 2003). A straight spine with shoulders back and chin up expresses a teacher's confidence in their role as a leader. A curved spine, rounded shoulders, and/or chin down signifies a lack of confidence and undermines the role of an authority figure. Students read nonverbal cues to make judgments about their teachers; therefore, teachers must be aware of their nonverbal communication and the message it is sending. Hunched shoulders and chin down sends a completely different message than that of shoulders back and chin up.

The use of proximity, as discussed in Chapter 2, is also a nonverbal cue that can be used to signify authority. Students tend to respond in a more appropriate manner to a teacher who is nearby as opposed to across the room. Just as drivers are more likely to drive the speed limit when a police officer is nearby and within sight, the same is true with students. Students are more like to obey rules and expectations when the teacher is visible as opposed to less visible or across the room. Although a teacher should expect and enforce standards of behavior throughout the school and school day, their sense of authority is greater when they are near the students. It is especially important to remember to use proximity when correcting or praising a student's behavior. The message is stronger when the teacher is nearby.

Flexibility and Fairness

Two components of leadership that are especially relevant to building authentic relationships and an inclusive environment are flexibility and fairness. Students need structure and consistency, but they also need to feel as though their thoughts and opinions matter. Teachers affirm that students matter by their willingness to, at times, be flexible and, at times, give students choices. The classroom should be a collaborative environment, with the teacher being the decisive element. An effective teacher is not a strict dictator or a permissive friend. Being a strict dictator makes it difficult for a student to feel that a teacher cares about them or that their thoughts and opinions matter. Teachers also cannot provide the structure and guidance students need if they are overly permissive or inconsistent in their expectations. In between the dictator and the permissive friend is a teacher with the right amount of flexibility in lessons and structure who still provides support and guidance while giving students ownership and choice in the classroom. This flexibility is essential to building quality relationships and a supportive classroom community that promotes academic and behavioral success (Marzano, Marzano, & Pickering, 2003).

APPLICATION CASE STUDY 5.3

Mr. Habad knows that he has to build authentic relationships with his students while maintaining control of his classroom. He prides himself on his ability to be an authority figure and has established rules and procedures that he strictly and consistently enforces. He tells his students often that he has high academic and behavioral expectations for them and that it is his job to ensure that they meet those expectations.

In order to help build relationships, Mr. Habad greets each student by name as they enter the classroom, asks about their weekend or evening, and tries to show an interest in their lives. Although he feels he has been successful in building quality relationships with most students, there are other students he has had difficulties reaching.

One of the students that Mr. Habad does not feel he has an authentic relationship with is Roland. Mr. Habad has consciously tried to engage Roland in social conversations and build that relationship, but so far he has not been successful. Roland has even complained that Mr. Habad doesn't like him and just doesn't care. Mr. Habad does not understand why Roland would feel that way when in fact he truly does care. Roland gave the following example to justify his belief:

> During independent work time in class, you said we have to raise our hand and sit at our desks and wait quietly for you to come to us to answer our questions. I sit in the back of the room. When I raise my hand, it takes you forever to get to me and help me. You stop and help other students, even those who raised their hands after me, and I am always the last one to get help. I tried to go up to you and ask a question so I could get my work done, but you would

not let me because that wasn't the procedure. When I complain about the wait time, you just give me a look. You know I have a question and you still make me wait. I did not ask to sit in the back of the room, and you know I can't do my work until I find out the answer to my question, but you still make me wait. I end up with extra homework because I could not get my work done in class because it took you so long to answer my questions. It is not fair. I usually just give up, do the work wrong, and use the extra time to draw or talk to my friends. You do not care to help me, so why should I care if I do the work right or behave in your classroom?

Case Study Comprehension Check
1. What is the problem between Mr. Habad and Roland?
2. Is Roland correct in his belief that Mr. Habad does not care?
3. Should Mr. Habad address Roland's concerns, even though consistency is important in classroom management? Why or why not?
4. How has Mr. Habad's strict enforcement of his rules and procedures hindered his relationship with Roland?

Fairness

Fairness does not mean everyone is treated in the same way. Fairness means that each individual student is given the structure, support, and instruction to maximize their success. This means that students are treated differently based on their needs and individuality. Treating a student fairly does not mean lowering expectations. It means differentiating and providing students with what they need individually to be successful.

Teachers are often more cognizant of the need for differentiation and fairness in terms of academics and use different strategies with different learners to support academic growth. They may use different reading strategies in different reading groups and spend more time providing instruction to struggling readers. Different supplies and books may be purchased based on individual needs. Teachers use flexible seating or offer a variety of accommodations and supports with the knowledge that one size does not fit all. In these instances, each student in a class may not be given the exact same thing, but each is treated fairly and provided what they need.

Teachers may be less cognizant of the need to treat students differently in terms of behavior and classroom management. To be effective, teachers must also apply different behavioral strategies, accommodations and supports in order to be fair. Again, fairness does not mean treating every student the same, nor does it mean lowering expectations for certain students. Teachers must uphold high expectations but realize the need for and allow individual differences in working toward and meeting those standards. The rewards, consequences, and motivational strategies that work for one student may not work for another. While one student may be highly motivated by praise, for another student it may cause embarrassment and make them less likely to repeat the praised behavior. It requires more effort and time to build relationships with some students than it does other students. Some students may be on behavior management plans that allow them to earn extra computer time, prizes, gym time, or lunch with the teacher that are not available to students not on behavior plans. In order to be fair to students, teachers must be willing to provide different levels of support both academically and behaviorally.

Persistence

Another crucial attribute held by effective teachers is persistence and perseverance. Becoming an effective teacher is a lifelong process in which skills are constantly evolving and growing in order to better meet the needs of students. It requires teachers to set high expectations for themselves and to find that inner grit and determination to meet and exceed those standards. The adage "If at first you don't succeed, try, try again" is extremely relevant to the life of a teacher. Many times first, second, and even third attempts to help or reach a student may not be successful, but teachers must have the persistence and perseverance to keep trying.

Comprehension Check
1. Why are leadership skills important in teaching?
2. How does nonverbal communication influence leadership?
3. What does flexibility and fairness have to do with teaching?
4. Why are persistence and perseverance essential attributes of an effective teacher?

APPLICATION ACTIVITIES

1. Have candidates reflect on past teachers who have had a positive effect on them and list the characteristics those teachers possessed. Discuss how those teachers made a difference in the candidates' lives.
2. Have candidates interview a teacher to determine the characteristics they think are important to being an effective teacher. Have the teachers describe how they building authentic relationships and learning about their students' cultures.
3. Have candidates research ways to build relationships with students and parents and how to foster peer relationships and collaboration in the classroom.
4. Have candidates reflect on the dispositions needed to be an effective classroom manager and self-evaluate in terms of their own strengths and weaknesses.

CHAPTER SUMMARY

The teacher is the main determinant of academic and behavioral success of the classroom.

- Teachers are the guiding force and have the ability to make students feel they are an important part of the classroom.

- Inclusion is the act of including all students regardless of their culture, ethnicity, or learning needs as part of the general education population and curriculum to the greatest extent possible.

Teacher-Student Relationship

- To promote academic achievement and behavior management, the teacher must develop a community in the classroom.
- A key component to developing a community is the relationship between the teacher and their students.
- The teacher must reach out to every student and form a quality relationship, and extra effort should be given to developing relationships with students who may be struggling behaviorally or academically.
- When a student feels that their teacher cares for them, the student puts forth greater effort in the classroom.
- Teachers may find it difficult to develop relationships with students who are challenging.
- When developing teacher-student relationships, it is vital for the teacher to understand each student individually.
- Two challenges in developing these relationships are social skills deficits and cultural differences.

Building Relationships Among Students

- Peer-to-peer relationships are important in developing a sense of community in the classroom.
- Students should treat one another in a respectful and positive manner.
- It is vital for teachers to be a model in their relationship with each student as a demonstration of how their students should interact with one another.

Teacher-Guardian Relationships

- Parental involvement in the school has a positive influence on a student's performance.
  - Therefore, teachers must take the responsibility of developing a positive relationship with all parents.
- Teacher should always include positive information about the student to the parent.
  - They should focus on how they present information to the parent and how the parent may interpret that information.
- Teachers must also recognize cultural differences with the parents.

Nonverbal Communication

- Nonverbal communication is how a person converses without spoken language and includes facial expression, body language, tone and pitch of voice, gestures, and proximity between the speaker and listener.

- When a person's nonverbal communication matches the message they are conveying, the person is more likely to be seen as authentic.
- Nonverbal communication can be interpreted in multiple ways based on cultural differences.
- It is important for teachers to be aware of their own use of nonverbal communication.
  - Nonverbal communication may be intentional or unintentional.
- Teachers also must be aware of how they are interpreting the nonverbal communication of their students.

Teacher Dispositions

- Teachers must possess certain characteristics to be successful in the classroom.
- Although it is important for the classroom to be a collaborative environment, the teacher is still responsible for taking on the leadership position.
- Students prefer teachers who provide guidance and structure.
  - Students respond better when they are given direction and know the teacher's expectations.
- A key component of leadership is consistency.
- Teachers must be mindful of their nonverbal communication as the authority figure.
- These nonverbal behaviors include tone of voice, posture, and proximity.
- Being flexible and fair allows students to feel as though their thoughts, abilities, and opinions matter.
- Fairness means differentiating and providing students with what they need individually to be successful.
- Persistence and perseverance are crucial dispositions for teachers to possess.
- It requires teachers to set high expectations for themselves and to find their inner grit and determination.

REFERENCES

Cambridge English Dictionary. (2018). *Inclusion*. Retrieved from http://dictionary.cambridge.org/us/dictionary/english/inclusion

Chiu, L. H., & Tulley, M. (1997). Student preferences of teacher discipline styles. *Journal of Instructional Psychology, 24*(3), 168–175.

Fortenot, K. A. (2014). *Nonverbal communication and social cognition*. Hackensack, NJ: Salem Press Encyclopedia of Health.

Ginott, H. G. (1975). *Teacher and child: A book for parents and teachers*. New York, NY: Macmillan.

Grolnick, W. S., & Slowiaczek, M. L. (1994). Parents' involvement in children's schooling: A multidimensional conceptualization and motivation model. *Child Development, 65*, 237–252.

The IRIS Center. (2012). *Classroom management (part 2): Developing your own comprehensive behavior management plan*. Retrieved from https://iris.peabody.vanderbilt.edu/module/beh2/

Mansor, A. N., Eng, W. K., Rasul, M. S., Hamzah, M. I., & Hamid, A. H. (2012). Effective classroom management. *International Education Studies, 5*(5), 35–42.

Marzano, R. J., & Marzano, J. S. (2003). The key to classroom management. *Educational Leadership, 61*(1), 6–13.

Marzano, R. J., Marzano, J. S., & Pickering, D. J. (2003). *Classroom management that works*. Alexandria, VA: ASCD.

Metropolitan Center for Urban Education. (2008). *Culturally responsive classroom management strategies*. New York, NY: New York University Press.

Richards, S. B., Lawless Frank, C., Sableski, M. K., & Arnold, J. M. (2016). *Collaboration among professionals, students, families and communities*. New York, NY: Routledge.

Wang, M. C., Haertel, G. D., & Walberg, H. J. (1993). Toward a knowledge base for school learning. *Review of Educational Research, 63*(3), 249–294.

Weinstein, C., Tomlinson-Clarke, S., & Curran, M. (2004). Toward a conception of culturally responsive classroom management. *Journal of Teacher Education, 55*(1), 25–38.

6

BUILDING A CULTURALLY INCLUSIVE CLASSROOM

Catherine Lawless Frank

CHAPTER OBJECTIVES

After reading this chapter, students should be able to:

1. Understand the effect of culture on behavior and its implications for behavior management.
2. Identify the necessary components of a classroom management plan.
3. Recognize the steps necessary for implementing a classroom management plan.
4. Define the components of the ongoing cycle of assessment as it relates to the classroom management plan.

Inclusion is a process of making the classroom a community of learners, and it does not happen by chance. It requires a proactive approach by the teacher to develop and implement a classroom structure that provides the supports necessary for all students to achieve. This structure enables students to perform academically and behaviorally in a manner that fosters community, enhances growth, and provides a context for all students to develop skills necessary for the future. This structure benefits teachers and students alike. Students tend to be more cooperative if they feel part of a safe, secure, and supported classroom community (Soodak, 2003).

The way a classroom is structured influences the way it makes students feel. Developing that structure requires teachers to be proactive in understanding their students' diverse cultures and developing the appropriate classroom design and management plan. Chapter 5 discussed the teacher's role in developing an inclusive classroom, and Chapter 6 examines the structures necessary to support its success.

CULTURE

When developing a management plan, it is important to keep in mind diversity and the cultures present in the classroom. Although some classrooms may appear more culturally diverse than others, in reality all classrooms are diverse. Teachers must realize that diversity extends beyond skin color, religion, and nationality and affects many aspects of a person's life beyond the food the student eats, the church they attend, or the holidays they celebrate. Culture is a way of life. It can influence language, behavior, clothing, religion, priorities, communication styles, and so much more. Although every country, region, area, clan, or family may have cultural tendencies, keep in mind that these are generalizations of culture. These generalizations provide clues as to what is typical about a culture, but each region, family, and individual is different. For example, there is a cultural tendency in Guatemala to have a different value of time than the cultural tendency of the United States. In Guatemala, time tends to be more flexible and fluid. For instance, an invitation for dinner at 5:00 p.m. in the United States means 5:00 p.m., and it would be considered rude to arrive late (or early) without first contacting and informing the hosts. In Guatemala, a 5:00 p.m. dinner invitation generally means sometime between 6:00 and 7:30 p.m., and it would be considered rude to arrive at 5:00 p.m. This is a generalization of the culture of each country, but the reality for a specific family and/or individual may be different. In some homes in the United States, it would be considered rude to arrive at 5:00 p.m., and in some homes in Guatemala, it would be rude to arrive late. Regional, religious, or ethnic culture is a generalization of the individuals rather than an absolute about everyone.

It is also important to keep in mind that there is no right or wrong in regard to culture. Cultures are different, and none is better (or more right) than another. People may disagree with a specific cultural tendency, but that does not make that cultural tendency wrong. Five p.m. meaning exactly 5:00 p.m. is not more correct but a different interpretation of time than 5:00 meaning sometime around 6:30 p.m.

A person's behavior is influenced by their culture, and students of different cultures often have different values and standards of behavior, which they bring into the classroom. Conflicts may arise when a student's culture differs from that which is typically expected in the classroom or by the teacher or peers. Teachers must be able to recognize and respect the cultural difference in the classroom (Weinstein, Curran, & Tomlinson-Clarke, 2003).

For example, Isfahan is a student from a culture that tends to be louder and more boisterous than that of his classmates. Isfahan speaks loudly and passionately, using large hand and arm motions, and at times even stands up and leans over his desk when speaking in class, particularly when he is excited (either positively or negatively) about a topic, answer, or idea. This emotional response is not typical of most of the other students in Isfahan's class. Although some of the other students may imitate Isfahan's behavior, for the most part they are significantly more reserved in their interactions in the classroom. The other students tend to raise their hands, wait to be called on, and respond calmly, with little to no hand or body movement while answering questions or participating in class discussions. Because of his outbursts, Isfahan's behaviors may be seen as threatening or inappropriate for the classroom. These outbursts may be viewed as behavioral issues rather than as cultural differences. In reality, cultural communication styles differ in terms of the amount of emotion and movement that is appropriate (The IRIS Center, 2012b). Isfahan's behavioral issue is in reality a cultural difference in communication style rather than a conscious attempt to threaten or intimidate. Although Isfahan's teacher may (or may not) deem his response inappropriate for the classroom, it is not wrong while his classmates culture is right. The communication styles are different, and teachers must acknowledge and recognize those differences. Isfahan's teacher may need to teach him about classroom expectations in terms of tone of voice and movement but, the teacher must also realize that this is a cultural difference rather than a behavior issue or problem. Neither culture is right, but Isfahan's cultural tendencies may not be in line with his teacher's behavioral expectations. These cultural differences at times lead to behavioral conflicts in the classroom, but it is the teacher's responsibility to educate and instruct rather than simply to punish.

These differences can cause discord or conflicts not only between the teacher and student but also among students themselves. For example, cultures vary on the amount of personal space that is appropriate. When two acquaintances from differing cultures are in a conversation, the difference in personal space may make one or both of them uncomfortable. The person from the culture that dictates more personal space may be confused and uncomfortable that their personal space is being violated. The person from the culture that dictates less personal space may be confused or hurt that the other person is trying to get away. Consider, for instance, this encounter between two sixth graders, Sahai and Jenny. At recess one day, a conflict arose when Sahai, a recent immigrant to the United States, attempted to hold hands with her new female friend Jenny. In Jenny's culture, it is considered inappropriate for two sixth-grade girls to hold hands at recess (or anywhere). In Sahai's culture, physical contact (holding hands, arms across shoulders, hugging) is a typical and appropriate sign of friendship. If these cultural differences are not acknowledged and understood by the teacher and students, there is a potential for misunderstandings, hurt feelings, and, possibly, conflict. Neither student nor culture was right or wrong, but what is considered appropriate in one culture may be inappropriate in another culture (Weinstein et al., 2003).

Culturally Responsive Teachers

All classrooms are diverse. It is the teacher's responsibility to be culturally aware and responsive to their students and their students' families in order to appropriately manage behaviors and provide effective instruction. The behavioral effect of cultural tendencies can be easily apparent or very subtle, but it influences how a person is viewed and treated by others. When teachers are culturally aware, they are able to appropriately respond to the students' behavior. In order to do this, teachers must develop relationships with their students, create an inclusive and culturally responsive classroom environment, be able to recognize and acknowledge their own biases, and use a behavior management system that is culturally appropriate (Weinstein et al., 2003).

As discussed in Chapter 5, it is essential for teachers to develop authentic caring relationships with their students. In developing this relationship, teachers should also deepen their background knowledge of their students' culture. They should get to know their students' interests, families, and hobbies as well as the cultural aspects of their lives. Developing authentic relationships also includes observing and learning

Table 6.1 Cultural Differences in Communication Styles

- *Conversing.* How did the conversation start, and what was the topic addressed? Is it direct and straight to the point or less direct, easing into the topic with an emphasis on how the message is received?
- *Emotion.* How much emotion is appropriate to display during a conversation in terms of tone of voice, gestures, facial expressions, and volume? To what degree should emotions be expressed or subdued?
- *Movement.* How much movement (hand motions and body movement) is used while communicating? Do people stand or sit still or move some or all of their body while communicating?
- *Turn taking.* When is it a person's time to talk? Does the communication partner wait until the speaker has completely finished talking before responding, or is it appropriate to interrupt or talk over one another?
- *Consideration.* Is an individual's rights or the group's rights more important? Is it appropriate to refrain from behaviors that may disturb others at the expense of individual rights, or should others be tolerant of an individual's rights at the expense of their rights?
- *Personal space.* What is the amount of personal space that is appropriate when engaged in a conversation? Should communicating partners maintain a specific distance between them, and, if so, how far apart should they be? In what instances is that personal space allowed to be violated?
- *Ownership.* How are resources shared or owned? Are resources shared among those in need, or are they the individual property of the person who bought or owns them?
- *Authority figure.* What constitutes an authority figure? Is a person's authority earned, or is it by right of their position?
- *Respect.* What are the nonverbal ways is which respect or deference is shown? What specific body language is used to signify respect (eye contact, body posture)?
- *Behavior management.* How much structure is necessary? Should there be leniency employed in managing behaviors to allow students more freedom and individuality, or should there be more structure and conformity?

(The IRIS Center, 2012b)

differences in behavioral and communication styles (see Chapter 5 and Table 6.1 for more information on cultural differences in communication styles) as well as learning about students' backgrounds and previous educational experience. Teachers must demonstrate an openness and willingness to learn about their students' cultures and use that knowledge to develop relevant instructional and behavioral practices (Weinstein et al., 2003).

To be culturally responsive, teachers must also develop and facilitate an inclusive classroom environment. As discussed earlier, inclusion involves meeting the academic and behavioral needs of all students in a manner that facilitates a caring and supportive classroom community. An inclusive and culturally responsive classroom environment goes beyond merely hanging diverse posters or using literature representing different cultures. Although those are both important, it is more important for teachers to incorporate provisions and structures into their classroom that benefit and support all learners. Teachers should engage students in discussions about the behavioral expectations and cultural norms of the classroom and use clear, supported, and precise communication regarding behavioral expectations. Teachers must be cognizant of how their expectations may differ from that of their students and allow for differences while maintaining expectations. When differences occur, it is important for teachers to discuss these differences with their students. Until a teacher is willing to acknowledge and discuss cultural differences, there is a potential for misunderstandings and confusion. Teachers must clearly communicate and teach their behavioral expectations to students in the same manner as an academic subject. Clearly communicating and teaching expectations helps develop the cultural norms and allows everyone to be familiar with and educated on the behavioral standards of the classroom (Weinstein et al., 2003).

CASE STUDY 6.1: A CULTURALLY DIVERSE CLASSROOM

Ms. Dobson is a white middle-class teacher who is currently teaching in an urban school, the Hope School of Excellence. The students in the Hope School are primarily African American and Latino and of lower socioeconomic status. The school has an 86% free and reduced lunch rate. Ms. Dobson knows that there are cultural differences between herself and her students. She tries to be very aware of her cultural biases, and although it is difficult at times, she tries to be open to the cultural differences in her classroom.

When Ms. Dobson first began teaching at the Hope School, she googled the culture of her students by asking questions such as "What is the culture of Latino students?" and "What is the culture of African American students?" Although what she learned was interesting and somewhat useful, Ms. Dobson eventually realized that her students' culture was not easily determined through a google search. The information she learned about culture did provide her with some overview, but through trial and error, Ms. Dobson realized that what she learned was a generalization. Her research on cultural tendencies was an overview but not necessarily specifically tied to her individual students. There were direct links to some of what she read to some of her students some of the time but not most of her students most of the time.

Ms. Dobson began conducting her own research. She spoke with other teachers in the building who she admired and asked for their advice on and suggestions for how to connect with and engage her students in the lessons (Ms. Dobson realized that keeping students engaged in learning is one of the best forms of behavior management). She also asked about how to handle and manage specific behavior issues and concerns. Ms. Dobson contacted parents using a variety of means (emails, phone calls, newsletters, face-to-face meetings, greeting and speaking with them before and after school and when they were in the building) to build relationships and to learn more about her students' interests and cultures. She also realized that the school secretary, counselors, and janitorial staff provided a wealth of insight into the culture of the school and in some cases her students in particular. Finally, Ms. Dobson also spoke with her students and began building relationships with them. She asked them about their weekend, sporting events, clubs, and even specific questions about differences in behavior and culture.

> Over the course of the year, Ms. Dobson became a more culturally responsive teacher, and her classroom became a more inclusive environment. She realized that although she had made many mistakes along the way, she had learned a lot about her students, which in turn improved her teaching and behavior management. Her lessons became more relevant to the students, and she adapted her classroom management system and style (multiple times) to better reflect the culture of her students. Ms. Dobson maintained high expectations throughout the year but adjusted her mindset to better meet the needs of her students. Although the process was not quick or easy, the outcome for both the students and Ms. Dobson was worth it. The students were more actively engaged in their lessons, and the behavioral concerns decreased. It became apparent to Ms. Dobson that learning about culture was not a one-time thing but an ongoing daily, weekly, and yearly process, but what she learned was enriching to her students, to their families, and to herself.

It is also important for teachers to be aware of their own cultural biases and prejudices. Teachers must develop a self-awareness of their cultural biases and be willing to mitigate the effects of it. Being aware of biases helps a teacher appropriately respond to cultural differences, especially in terms of differences in classroom behavior and allows teachers to respond to situations in a more just and equitable manner (Weinstein et al., 2003). There are many stereotypical prejudices and biases against (and for) different religions, nationalities, skin color, ethnicity, socioeconomic status, and so forth that teachers must be aware of, but they also must be cognizant of their own personal bias. Often biases are not conscious thoughts and are not easily recognized in oneself. These hidden biases often influence behaviors in subtle ways and may be consciously justified in other ways. For example, Ms. Higgins loves her job as a teacher at a racially diverse school and works hard to build an inclusive classroom community and authentic caring relationships with all her students. Ms. Higgins is also consciously aware of the fact that she is tougher on students who have the same ethnic background as she does and is nicer to students of different ethnic backgrounds. When talking after school one day with another teacher, Ms. Brubaker, Ms. Higgins said, "The students cannot say I am prejudice. I am tougher on the kids from my ethnic background than on those who are not. I do not think I am biased against kids from other ethnicity but biased for them." After a moment, Ms. Brubaker responded, "Maybe it is not a question of being biased against people of different races but a question of expectations. Maybe you have higher expectations for the students with your own ethnic background than students from different ethnicities. That is why you are tougher on them because you expect more from them." Ms. Higgins thought that her caring, quality relationship with her students and being nicer to students of different ethnicities indicated a lack of bias. Although she was consciously aware that she had a soft spot for certain students, she was not cognizant of how that soft spot was actually a hidden bias. She cared about and supported all her students, but she actually had higher expectations for certain

Table 6.2 Developing a Culturally Responsive Classroom

Develop authentic relationships with students that involve the following:
- Learning about the cultural aspects of students' lives
- Observing and learning about cultural differences in behavior and communication styles
- Learning about students' backgrounds and histories
- Learning about students' previous experiences with education
- Incorporating aspects of student culture into academics
- Being cognizant of cultural differences when interpreting and responding to behavior

Create an inclusive classroom that includes the following:
- Physical representations of different cultures in the classroom (posters, bulletin boards, displays)
- Culturally relevant academic materials and lessons
- Acknowledgment of cultural differences and the facilitation of discussions about behavioral expectations and cultural norms
- Teaching and supporting behavioral expectations

Be aware of personal biases and mitigating their influence.

---

students based on their ethnicity. It took a comment from her coworker, Ms. Brubaker, for her to realize this bias. This bias did not mean that Ms. Higgins was a bad or unjust teacher. It meant that she, like all people, had biases that she was not consciously aware of. An equally important part of this story is what Ms. Higgins decides to do with this new self-awareness and how it will influence her instruction and expectations for all her students in the future. Teachers must make the effort to become self-aware of their biases and to be willing to mitigate the effects of it.

Understanding cultural influence on behavior is important. The more teachers know, the better they are at facilitating effective classroom management (see Table 6.2 for ideas on developing a culturally responsive classroom). Some behaviors that may appear to be misbehaviors are actually the result of cultural differences rather than a conscious attempt by a student to misbehave. Although culture does affect behavior, it is not the only influence on behavior. Culture is something teachers should be aware of when designing and implementing a behavior management system, but it is not the only reason students behave (positively or negatively) the way they do (Weinstein et al., 2003).

> *Comprehension Check*
> 1. Why is it important to be cognizant of cultural differences in the classroom?
> 2. How can cultural differences influence classroom management?
> 3. What can teachers do to develop and facilitate a culturally inclusive classroom?

MANAGEMENT PLAN

For a classroom to be effective both academically and behaviorally, it must have structure. This structure is partially derived from a management plan that is proactively constructed by the teacher and ideally before the first day of class. By developing such a plan, teachers have a basis on which to build and enforce structure in the classroom. Having a plan allows teachers to solidify their expectations in a manner that is understood by all who enter the classroom and ensures that teachers and students are consciously aware of the plan (The IRIS Center, 2012a).

A classroom management plan, when properly employed, helps ensure that students behave in a pro-social manner and meet the expectations of the classroom community. It helps eliminate behavioral problems by defining the expectations, rules, and procedures. Once the plan is developed, it must be taught and reinforced in a systematic way. It cannot be assumed that students will know how to follow the rules and expectations without them first being taught and continuously reviewed (Rademacher, Callahan, & Pederson-Seelye, 1998).

The goal of this plan is to enhance learning, increase appropriate classroom behavior, and promote personal responsibility. The purpose of a classroom management plan is that students learn to behave out of a sense of personal responsibility rather than out of a fear of punishment or hope of a reward (Weinstein et al., 2003).

In order to help develop a sense of community and ownership, teachers may have students help develop the plan. It is important, however, for teachers to start the year with structure, and therefore they must have a concrete idea of their expectations before the first day of class. Students may help develop the plan, but the teacher should guide that development to reflect their ideals.

The classroom environment is essential to establishing a community that fosters learning and classroom order. This environment is partly established through the classroom design and a management plan that encompasses the overarching philosophy or guiding principles for the classroom as well as establishes the rules and procedures. It is also essential to consider the manner in which the plan will be taught and reinforced.

Classroom Design

A classroom must be a welcoming and inclusive environment but also one that is organized and promotes classroom management. Part of this organization and management is the design and layout of the classroom. Classrooms must be intentionally designed to be inviting and also meet the organizational needs of the students and the teacher. The design of the classroom provides an opportunity to facilitate the culture of the classroom. How a room is designed may affect the degree to which a student feels part of the community, and the inclusivity is reflected in both the physical layout and the decorations. Table 6.3 identifies some questions to consider when designing a classroom layout.

Guiding Principles

The guiding principles are the philosophy of the classroom. They are developed from the core values or overarching behaviors that teachers expect from their students. This is the starting point of the management plan that defines the main values and guides the climate of the classroom and the development of the rest of the plan. This statement is based on attributes that are more civil minded and long term in development, but they are essential components of a classroom and ultimately of a larger

Table 6.3 Questions to Consider When Designing a Classroom Layout

Student Seating Arrangements
- What type of lessons will be the focus? Will the students be doing more individual work or group work? Is the seating arrangement appropriate for both individual and group work?
- Can all students see the board and teaching areas?
- Do specific seating accommodations need to be made for any students?
- Will the students be using tables or desks?
- What type of seating will students be using? Will all students sit in the same types of chairs? Use adapted seating (balance balls or activity chairs)?
- Will all seating be the same size, or will some be larger and need more space than others?

Teacher Seating Arrangements
- Where will the teacher's desk be positioned?
- If necessary, is there a desk or space for co-teachers or paraprofessionals?
- Can the teacher see all students at all times?

Traffic Flow
- How will the students maneuver through the classroom?
- What will the student traffic flow look like?
- Is this traffic flow pattern accessible to all students? Are the aisles wide enough for students who may need additional room?
- Will any desks or students be overly disturbed by students moving throughout the classroom?

Group Work
- How will collaboration and collaborative groups be arranged?
- Is there a space or easy way to transition from individual activities to collaborative ones?

Wall Hangings
- Do the posters, bulletin boards, and decorations depict all the diverse cultures in the classroom?
- Is there a place to exhibit student work?
- Does the room look too cluttered or too bare?

Other Considerations
- Are supply bins and places labeled and easily accessible?
- Is there adequate space for students to store their items?

community and society (Curwin & Mendler, 1988). Unlike the rest of the plan, the guiding principle is not necessarily based on behaviors that are easily observable and measurable. It may include attributes like respecting everyone, being responsible for all you say and do, being a problem solver, developing good work habits, respecting diversity, being responsible for your own actions, being a good neighbor or a good citizen, or respecting yourself and others (Rademacher et al., 1998). These statements are elements of a pro-social society and classroom rather than specific observable and measurable behaviors and are used to guide the classroom and to facilitate an inclusive classroom community.

The guiding principle is short (usually two to three sentences) and should be expressed in writing in a positive manner that directs students (and teachers) as to the behavioral expectations. It states what is expected (be kind and considerate, be respectful, complete your best work) rather than what is not expected (do not be mean, do

Table 6.4 Examples of Classroom Guiding Principles

Elementary School

This classroom is a community of learners that works together to be the best that we can be. We will share, treat one another kindly, take care of our things, and be the best learners possible. We will work together to be the best class ever.

Middle School

This classroom is a respectful community where everyone works to be their best. We treat one another with kindness, respect one another's differences, and are responsible for our own actions.

Resource Room

This classroom is a safe and caring learning environment. We are responsible for our own actions, support one another, and strive to do our best.

High School

This classroom is a positive learning environment that fosters respect and responsibility. We (students and teachers) treat one another with dignity, are accountable for what we say and do, and support positive growth.

---

not be disrespectful, do not turn in work that is not your best effort) (The IRIS Center, 2012a). See Table 6.4 for examples of classroom guiding principles.

The example statements in Table 6.4 illustrate the overarching expectations for the classroom in two to three sentences. The first sentence in each example states the expectations for the classroom environment (This classroom is a _____.). This is the opportunity to communicate the main goal for the culture or community of the classroom (community of learners, respectful community, safe and caring learning environment, and positive learning environment) and helps define its meaning (works together to be the best that we can be, works to be their best, and fosters respect and responsibility) (The IRIS Center, 2012a).

The second and third (if needed) sentences focus on the specific responsibilities and expectations of all the teachers and students in the classroom (We _____.). It states the specific types of behaviors expected by everyone in that classroom (treat one another kindly, take care of our things, be the best learners possible, respect one another's differences, responsible for our own actions) (The IRIS Center, 2012a).

The guiding principle clearly and specifically articulates the core values of the classroom. It should be posted in a prominent place to allow all who enter (teachers, parents, administrators, students, related service personnel) to quickly discern the classroom expectations. When creating a management plan, this statement should be developed first to ensure that the other components of the plan are aligned with the classroom core values (The IRIS Center, 2012a).

Classroom Rules

A main part of the management plan is the classroom rules. Rules should be aligned with and help give structure to the guiding principles and reiterate some of the behavioral expectations of the classroom. The guiding principle is the core values of the classroom, and the rules should help support it. For example, if the guiding principle includes being responsible, then there should be rules (bring all needed materials to class, be in your seat before the bell rings) to help define and make this concept more concrete. Rules should help clarify the behaviors that are expected under the guiding principle (Rademacher et al., 1998).

Typically, there are three to five specific, observable, and measurable rules in a classroom. It is usually limited to three to five rules in order to have enough rules to define expectations but not too many that they become difficult for students to remember. Rules must be clear, specific, observable, and measurable to accurately state the behaviors a student should exhibit. For example, the rule "Raise your hand quietly and wait to be called on before answering a question" is clear, specific, observable, and measurable. This rule is clear and specific in that it tells the student exactly what to do (raise your hand quietly and wait to be called on before answering a question). It is clear enough to avoid confusion (such as simply "raise your hand") about when a student should raise their hand (to answer a question) or how a student should go about answering a question (raise their hand quietly). It is observable, and a teacher can easily determine whether a student has followed the rule or not (raised their hand, was quiet and waited to be called on, or did not raise their hand or do so quietly or wait to be called on). The rule is measurable. The teacher can measure or count (if necessary) the number of times that a student does or does not follow the rule. Being clear, specific, observable, and measurable allows the students to be certain of what is expected of them and allows the teacher to positively identify compliance or noncompliance. See Table 6.5 for examples and non-examples of specific, observable, and measurable classroom rules.

Rules should be positively stated and let students know what they should be doing rather than what they should not be doing. Rules such as "Do not yell out answers" appear to have a similar intent as "Raise your hand quietly and wait to be

Table 6.5 Examples and Non-Examples of Specific, Observable, and Measurable Classroom Rules

Non-Example	Example	Explanation
No cell phones or other electronic devices.	Cell phones and other electronic devices must be kept turned off and in your backpack.	The non-example is **not stated positively** and does not tell students how they should behave or what they should do with their cell phones.
Bring everything you need to class.	Come to class prepared with all needed materials, including: • Textbook • Pen or pencil • Notebook • Homework	Although this non-example is positive, observable, and measurable, **it is not specific**. The example details exactly what the needed materials are and makes it easier for the students to interpret and follow.
Follow directions.	Follow the teacher's directions quickly (within 30 seconds) the first time the teacher asks.	This non-example is **not specific** and can be somewhat open to interpretation. It is also **difficult to observe and measure**.
Respect other people's property.	Ask and obtain permission before borrowing someone else's supplies.	This non-example is stated positively but is **not specific, observable, or measurable**. It allows for different interpretation by the teacher, students, and parents.

called on" but do not tell students what behavior they should perform and therefore leave it open for the students to interpret. When a rule is left open to interpretation, there is a possibility that a student's interpretation (shout, rather than yell, out an answer, whistle or jump up and down to answer a question) will be different from what the teacher anticipated (raise your hand quietly and wait to be called on before answering a question) (The IRIS Center, 2012a). See Table 6.6 for examples of classroom rules.

Table 6.6 Sample Classroom Rules

Elementary School
  1. Get permission to use someone else's supplies before using them—ask first.
  2. Stay in your seat unless the teacher tells you differently.
  3. Follow the teacher's directions quickly (within 30 seconds) the first time the teacher asks.
  4. Raise your hand and wait quietly to ask a question.

Middle School
  1. Turn in all work on time. This includes:
     - Homework—due at the beginning of class
     - Classwork—due at the end of class (unless otherwise stated)
     - Projects—due at the beginning of class (unless otherwise stated)
  2. Come to class prepared with all needed materials (book, notebook, homework, and pen).
  3. Arrive to class on time (be in the classroom before the bell rings).
  4. Clean up after yourself before you leave the classroom.
     - All materials returned to their designated places
     - All trash in the trash can
     - Take all your personal materials with you
  5. Remain in your seat at the end of class until you are dismissed.

Resource Room
  1. Enter the classroom quietly and on time.
  2. Bring all your needed materials:
     - Math book
     - Pencil
     - Any papers given to you by your classroom teacher (assignments, tests, quizzes)
  3. Get permission from the teacher before leaving your seat.

High School
  1. Bring all needed materials to class. This includes:
     - Book
     - Notebook
     - Laptop
     - Paper
     - Pen or pencil
     - Homework
  2. Be in your assigned seat before the bell rings.
  3. Cell phones and all electronic devices are turned off and in a closed bag (e.g., backpacks, purses) or in a locker.
  4. Complete and turn in all assignments within the allotted time frame.
  5. Follow teacher directions the first time they are given within a reasonable amount of time (30 seconds).

Procedures

Procedures are specific directions as to how certain routines are to be performed in the classroom. They clearly define the necessary steps required to complete a typical classroom routine. By delineating the steps, teachers clearly communicate what is to be done during specific times throughout the day. Table 6.7 identifies a list of some daily

Table 6.7 Classroom Procedures

Elementary School Classroom Procedures
- Entering the classroom in the morning
- When and how to sharpen a pencil or get supplies (including the appropriate time to do so)
- Walking in the hall
- Getting the teacher's attention or asking a question
- Transitioning between subjects
- Turning in assignments
- Turning in homework
- Getting a drink of water
- Going to the restroom as a class
- Going to the restroom independently (including the appropriate time to do so)
- Leaving school at the end of the day

Middle School Classroom Procedures
- Entering the classroom in the morning
- When and how to sharpen a pencil or get supplies (including the appropriate time to do so)
- Getting the teacher's attention or asking a question
- Changing classes
- Leaving at the end of class
- Transitioning between subjects
- Turning in assignments
- Turning in homework
- Getting a drink of water
- Going to the restroom (including the appropriate time to do so)
- Leaving school at the end of the day

Resource Room Procedures
- Entering the classroom
- When and how to sharpen a pencil or get supplies (including the appropriate time to do so)
- Getting the teacher's attention or asking a question
- Turning in assignments
- Getting a drink of water
- Going to the restroom (including the appropriate time to do so)
- Leaving at the end of class

High School Classroom Procedures
- Entering the classroom
- When and how to sharpen a pencil or get supplies (including the appropriate time to do so)
- Getting the teacher's attention or asking a question
- Turning in assignments
- Turning in homework
- Getting a drink of water
- Going to the restroom (including the appropriate time to do so)
- Leaving at the end of class

Table 6.8 Example Procedures for Entering the Classroom

Elementary School Procedures for the Entering the Classroom
    Enter the classroom quietly.
    Hang your coat on your hook.
    Take your backpack to your desk.
    Put the contents of your backpack where they belong.
        Place your school books in your desk.
        Place completed homework in the tray.
        Place notes to the teacher and any other papers on the teacher's desk.
    Hang your backpack next to your coat.
    Begin working on the problem of the day.

Resource Room Procedures for Entering the Classroom
    Enter the classroom quietly.
    Greet your teacher (say, "Hello, Mrs. Walker.").
    Sit in your designated seat.
    Begin working on your warm-up assignment before the start of class.

Middle or High School Procedures for Entering the Classroom
    Enter the classroom quietly.
    Sit in your designated seat.
    Place completed homework on the upper right-hand corner of your desk.
    Place a pen or pencil on your desk.
    Place the remainder of your books and supplies under your desk.
    Begin working on the problem of the day before the bell rings.

routines for which teachers should develop clear procedures. Procedures may also be developed for less routine events, such as attending an assembly or leaving class early.

Procedures are designed to allow transitions to run smoothly and class time to be used effectively. When expectations are clearly presented and non-instructional time or downtime is decreased, students are more likely to be actively engaged in learning and less likely to misbehave. See Table 6.8 for example procedures for entering the classroom.

A classroom management plan should include a guiding principle as well as classroom rules and procedures. Teachers may want to consider including other components in the plan, such as a medical emergency or crisis situation plan. It is advised that teachers check with their school personnel or administrators to determine what, if any, additional information should be included.

This plan should be implemented beginning on the first day of school. Although teachers may decide to collaborate with their students to develop the guiding principle and/or classroom rules, teachers must begin on day one with a structure of that plan in mind. Students begin to learn a classroom's values and structure the moment they enter the room. Teachers must be prepared to teach and implement those values and structures on the first day of school. Preparations for the first two weeks of school will be discussed in more detail in Chapter 8.

APPLICATION CASE STUDY 6.2: MANAGEMENT PLAN

Mr. Patterson wants to write a guiding principle for his class that focuses on the following concepts:

- Being a community of learners
- Developing good work habits
- Being problem solvers
- Respecting one another

Using the following format, help Mr. Patterson write a guiding principle for his class.

This classroom is _____
_____.

We _____
_____.

Review the following classroom rules and answer the questions.

1. Listen carefully.
2. Come to class prepared with your homework and needed supplies.
3. No talking without permission.
4. Be responsible for all you say and do.
5. Remain in your seat unless given permission to get up.

Which rules are clear and specific?
Which rules are observable?
Which rules are measurable?
Which rule is not stated positively? Rewrite that rule and make it positive.

Imagine your future (or current) classroom. Write a procedure for the students to use when going to the restroom. Questions to consider include:

- When during class are they allowed to go to the restroom? Anytime? At the beginning or the end? When the teacher is not lecturing or teaching?
- Will students need to ask permission? If so, how should they get the teacher's attention?
- Will they need to carry a hall pass or sign out?
- How many students are allowed to go to the restroom at one time?
- Although this may not be part of your procedures, keep in mind how you will handle emergency situations (a student says they need to use the restroom outside of the procedure time).

> *Comprehension Check*
> 1. What are the main components of a classroom management plan?
> 2. How does the guiding principle help structure the classroom climate?
> 3. Why is it important to have specific, observable, and measurable classroom rules?
> 4. List three routines for which a teacher should develop specific classroom procedures.

IMPLEMENTING THE MANAGEMENT PLAN
Teaching

The first step in implementing the plan is teaching it to the students. Just like students must be taught academics, they also must be taught behavioral expectations. It is unfair for a teacher to assume that a student knows how to do a math lesson prior to being taught. It is equally unfair for a teacher to assume that a student knows the teacher's behavioral expectations prior to being taught those behaviors. Math concepts are routinely reviewed and reiterated, just as behavioral expectations should be routinely reviewed and reiterated. Teachers should not assume that students at any age or grade know the behavioral expectations of their classroom. Even when students help develop the classroom guiding principle or rules, they still must be taught what exactly those behaviors look like. Failure to teach, reinforce, and review the management plan in a systematic manner often creates needless behavior problems.

Behavior expectations must be taught in a manner similar to teaching an academic content area. Academic subject areas are taught using clear, precise language with the necessary assistance, models, and guided practice. When students struggle, they are not punished for not knowing but retaught and supported in a manner that allows them to work toward learning and meeting expectations. Behaviors should be taught applying the same instructional concepts as academics. In an inclusive, culturally responsive classroom, behavioral expectations must be clearly stated, taught, modeled, and reinforced in the same manner (Weinstein et al., 2003).

The management plan should be taught using a direct instruction model in which teachers clearly communicate their expectations, model examples and non-examples, and provide guided and independent practice. The first step in the process involves getting the students' attention and providing a motive or rationale for learning (why this information is important to students). This step could involve a discussion (What is the purpose of the classroom? Why have classroom rules?). It could be a comparison between procedures at home (What do you do when you walk in the door after school?) versus procedures in the classroom (What should you do when you walk into the classroom?). It could involve the use of children's literature (*Do Unto Otters: A Book About Manners* by Laurie Keller, *What If Everybody Did That?* by Ellen Javernick and Colleen M. Madden, *My Mouth Is a Volcano* by Julia Cook and Carrie Hartman). Whatever the means, teachers should begin the lesson in a manner that engages the students. Teachers also should use this step to make the lesson relevant to students, and should discuss with students how it will benefit them (individually and as a class) to know the classroom rules and procedures (less likely to get in trouble so more time at recess, more learning, less homework due to more efficient classes). In this step, teachers must ensure that students are interested and paying attention and that students realize the information is relevant and important.

After engaging the students, teachers should then precisely teach the behaviors as they expect them to be performed. This includes stating the guiding principle, rules, and procedures clearly, both orally and in writing and possibly in picture form. Each aspect of the plan should be modeled with examples and non-examples of appropriate behavior. Teachers can have students write rule books, draw pictures, or make classroom posters. They can have students write a letter to their parents explaining the guiding principle and rules. Students can participate in role-plays, puppet shows, or skits on what to do and what not to do in the classroom. Students with a history of behavior concerns should be responsible for modeling or acting out the examples of appropriate behaviors rather than the non-examples or inappropriate behaviors. Having a student with a history of behavioral concerns model inappropriate behaviors may reinforce the inappropriate behavior. These skits or puppet shows could be videotaped and viewed throughout the year as one way to review the rules. It is important that all aspects of the plan are clearly articulated to the students, even if the students helped develop the plan. It may be more practical and beneficial to teach the procedures throughout the first few days or even weeks as the situations arise rather than all at once on the first day. Breaking the information into small pieces may make it more manageable for students.

After teaching the rules and procedures, students should be given a chance to practice what they have learned with guidance from the teacher. They can practice the proper way to enter the class while the teacher supports each step (orally, written, and/or picture form) and provides guidance (positive praise and corrective feedback). Students can practice raising their hands and waiting to be called on, turning off their cell phones and putting them away in their backpacks or lockers, or having the necessary supplies out for the start of a class period. All these behaviors should be practiced with guidance and feedback from the teacher to assure that students are aware of the expectations and know how to perform them correctly. It is critical to use this step to provide clear guidance and feedback to all students, but special attention should be provided to students with diverse learning needs (English language learners, special education, diverse cultures, history of behavior concerns).

After the rules are practiced with guidance, they should be practiced independently multiple times. Teachers can use this time to assess whether students can independently demonstrate each behavioral expectation. Behaviors that are not correctly portrayed should be practiced. Teachers can use the concept of positive practice. In positive practice, the behavior is repeated correctly multiple times to ensure that students know and understand the expectations. For example, the expectation when walking to lunch is that the students walk quietly. If a student(s) talked during the walk to lunch, then the student(s) would turn around, walk back to the classroom, sit back in their chair, and repeat the procedure of walking to lunch quietly. This process is repeated three or more times correctly, in a row, before the student is allowed to go to lunch. This is not a punishment but a way for the student to practice a behavior similar to how they would practice an academic concept. Once the students know and can demonstrate the behavior, it does not mean that the process is over. The students' ability to follow the management plan should be assessed using the ongoing cycle of assessment first addressed in Chapter 1.

As the students get older and advance in grades, it may not be necessary to implement all the lesson components discussed. Teachers should never assume, however, that any student knows the behavioral expectations of the classroom. The lesson may be more condensed in later grades, but the information must still be conveyed and reinforced on a regular and consistent basis.

It is important to inform parents of the behavioral expectations, including the guiding principle and rules, for the classroom. As discussed in Chapter 5, it is essential to foster a collaborative relationship with families and to keep them informed as to what is happening in their child's classroom. Parents can be a wonderful and important resource for teachers, and it is the teacher's responsibility to build a strong school and family connection.

Assessing the Classroom Management Plan Using an Ongoing Cycle

Teaching behavioral expectations is a process and not a one-time action. Developing and managing the structure of the classroom requires the teacher to proactively and continuously assess all aspects of the management plan. Teachers should use the ongoing assessment cycle (assessment, analysis, decision-making, and instruction) to evaluate what works and what does not work in regard to their behavioral expectations (see Figure 6.1).

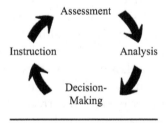

Figure 6.1 Ongoing Cycle of Response to Intervention

ILLUSTRATIVE CASE STUDY 6.3

Mrs. Fulner knows the importance of starting the beginning of the school year on the right foot. She dedicated the first few days of the school year to ensuring that her students knew the classroom rules and procedures. She worked with her students to develop a guiding principle and classroom rules. She used guided practices to ensure that each student knew the rules and procedures and how to perform them. For the first couple of weeks, Mrs. Fulner closely observed her students' compliance with the rules and procedures. She reviewed and reinforced the rules as necessary, and the students all seemed able to perform each rule and procedure as she had envisioned.

Although Mrs. Fulner always had a strong focus on her behavioral expectation in the beginning of the year, she has learned the hard way that that is not enough. Teaching behavioral expectations is an ongoing process requiring assessment, analysis, decision-making, and instruction throughout the entire year. Mrs. Fulner learned the value of this and now includes a monthly behavior assessment cycle week in her calendar. During those weeks, Mrs. Fulner makes a special point to closely observe her students to ensure that they are following the rules and procedures correctly. Although she is with her students and observes them often, it is difficult to closely observe whether students are following the management plan on a daily basis. Sometimes it is easy to observe who is misbehaving in the classroom (Johnny yelling out in math class, Trisha talking in the hallway, Sam texting on his cell phone), but other behaviors go unnoticed or overlooked. Mrs. Fulner has learned that if she lets a pattern of noncompliance begin and continue, then the amount of noncompliance (behavior problems) increases. If one student gets away with a misbehavior, then other students begin to assume that misbehavior is okay.

Mrs. Fulner learned her lesson a couple of years ago. At the beginning of the year, she taught her students the management plan by motivating her students and then providing guided practice followed by independent practice. She then made a mental note to assess and review the plan monthly throughout the year, but that did not happen. The students seemed to be following the plan, and there were no real behavior concerns in September, so Mrs. Fulner decided to wait on her assessment until October. When October came, she forgot about the assessment but was starting to notice some minor violations (Steve never seemed to be prepared with his needed materials at the beginning of class, Johnny seemed to be talking out more in math, Trisha had her phone out at least three times in a week). She thought the increase in behavior problems was mainly due to summer being over and the full moon.

Things had not improved by November, but she decided to wait until after Thanksgiving to assess and review the rules and procedures. She figured that the students would not remember after the Thanksgiving break anyway, and she could use the time before the winter break to assess and review. Mrs. Fulner figured she could use the free time, movie, or party that she planned before the start of winter break as the incentive for her lesson review, but she forgot how short and busy the time was between Thanksgiving break and winter break. The students' compliance to the rules however was decreasing (one day five students were not prepared with the needed materials at the beginning of class, Johnny and three other students were yelling out answers and not just during math, and four students had their phones out).

Mrs. Fulner started the new year determined to be stricter, but by then the students had developed a pattern of behavior that was difficult for her to break.

The students had different behavior expectations for the classroom from what had been taught at the beginning of the year. This made it difficult for Mrs. Fulner to enforce rules and procedures that had not been consistently reviewed and enforced throughout the year. But Mrs. Fulner was determined. But, right after Christmas break there was a long weekend, and she really needed the time she had planned for reviewing behaviors to prepare for testing. There also seemed to be a reason or an excuse for the students' behavior (changing weather, springtime, full moon, break coming up, just got back from break, the year is almost over) and content to be covered so that the assessment and review of the rules never happened.

The problem was that as the students became less and less compliant with the rules and procedures, it took more and more of her instructional time to deal with them. The problem behaviors were mostly minor (talking, not being prepared for class, not following procedures for sharpening a pencil or getting a drink) but dealing with them was consuming instructional time. Mrs. Fulner did not do the assessment and reviews in order to spend more time teaching, but the opposite happened. She spent more time dealing with behavior problems she could have avoided, causing her to increase her frustration and lose instructional time.

The following year, Mrs. Fulner was determined to use the ongoing cycle not only in the beginning of the year but also all year long. Each month, she scheduled a week devoted to assessing behaviors using observations and progress monitored her findings. She analyzed the findings and used that information to make instructional decisions. She reviewed and retaught procedures as necessary to the entire class and provided additional instruction, intervention, and supports to individual students who were struggling to meet behavioral expectations. Although she continued to devote one week a month to assessments, Mrs. Fulner found that doing so made her more consciously aware of behaviors all month long. This allowed her to more consistently intervene when the need arose and to keep behavior problems to a minimum. Academically, Mrs. Fulner noticed that this year's students were progressing more quickly through the curriculum and even seemed to be more inclusive and accepting of one another.

Ever since that first year, Mrs. Fulner has continued to use the ongoing cycle throughout the year. She has realized that this cycle is essential to establishing and maintaining an effective and inclusive classroom. In the end, it allows her students to learn more and to be a more cohesive and inclusive class, and it has made teaching a much more enjoyable and productive experience.

Assessment

The assessment component used in evaluating the management plan (see Figure 6.2) is typically an informal observation done by the classroom teacher. Although at times a formal structured observation conducted by an outside observer (principal, another

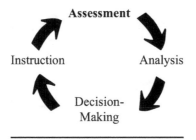

Figure 6.2 Ongoing Cycle of Response to Intervention

teacher, staff member) may be required or appropriate, typically the ongoing assessment is conducted by the classroom teacher based on their observations and reflections. Teachers observe their classrooms on a daily basis, but for this observation to be truly effective, it should be more focused in nature.

Although it may be natural for some teachers to reflect on an ongoing basis on what is happening in their classroom, this reflection should be more purposeful and evaluative in order to determine not only what is working and not working but also to determine who, what, where, and when. The most obvious part of an observation is typically who and what. Who is behaving or not behaving? What are those who are misbehaving or behaving doing? For example, Ezekiel (who) threw a paper wad (what), or Marissa (who) was talking during class (what).

Besides who and what, the assessment should also encompass the setting of the behavior, or the where and when. Where and when are important pieces of information needed to make an informed analysis and decision. For example, Ezekiel (who) threw a paper wad (what) at a trash can (where) at the end of a class period (when) should constitute a different analysis than if he threw it at another student (where) during the middle of class (when). Or Marissa (who) is talking during class (what) in a collaborative group (where) working on a class project (when) is different from talking out during class in the middle of a teacher's lecture. It is helpful to be as specific as possible in the observations in order to analyze the situation accurately and to determine the appropriate response. Although observations typically focus on what is not working, it is equally, if not more, important to determine what is working. Identifying what is working may help focus on the positive aspects of the classroom and provide a foundation for the necessary changes needed to improve behaviors.

Analysis

The analysis of the assessment (see Figure 6.3) attempts to determine the why, or the motivation for the behavior. Instead of focusing only on who is "bad" and who is "good," teacher observations should be expanded to determine why certain behaviors are occurring and not occurring. Behaviors happen for a reason and determining that reason is essential to developing the appropriate classroom management strategies. It

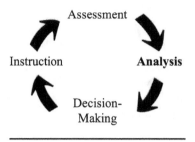

Figure 6.3 Ongoing Cycle of Response to Intervention

is important to remember that often more than one person is involved in a behavior, and the why may involve the student, other students, the teacher, or any and all of the above.

One way to determine the why is to look for patterns of behavior. Identifying patterns helps provide a larger and clearer frame of reference. For example, Matthew has not completed three out of the last eight homework assignments in math. Looking for patterns in which type of assignments (never completes assignments involving word problems but tends to complete assignments without them) or which days he has completed assignments (always completes Monday night's homework but never Wednesday and Thursday) provides a larger and clearer picture of the problem that then helps to determine an appropriate intervention. If a teacher observes that Symia frequently gets in trouble for talking out during class, and the analysis later shows Symia is more likely to talk out if she is seated next to Racheal, then the intervention (which includes not letting her sit next to Racheal) is a clearer process.

Although motivations and causes of behaviors will be discussed in Chapter 7 and throughout this book, a general and simplified rule in determining why students misbehave is because they either want something or want to avoid something. When students misbehave because they want something, it may be that they want an object, a basic need met, or, more typically, attention from a peer or an adult. When students misbehave to avoid something, it typically involves avoiding class work or embarrassment due to a perceived inability or lack of skills. Sometimes the why involves both wanting something and avoiding something, but typically one or the other is dominate. Demetri may act out and seek attention from his peers during reading class but does so because he would rather get attention for misbehaving than have to read in front of his classmates (to avoid reading and being embarrassed about his reading skills).

When determining the why, it is also important for teachers to consider their role in the process. Is the teacher doing something or not doing something that may be contributing to the issue? Is there an academic or cultural issue that may be contributing to the problem? Has the teacher built an authentic caring relationship with each student? Does each student realize that the teacher cares? Is the teacher being consistent in their expectations? The teacher is the guiding force in the classroom and must ensure that they are working with the students to have an effective classroom.

Often teachers contribute to the problem unknowingly and therefore must reflect on and analyze the situation and their own behavior to determine why specific student behaviors may be occurring.

Decision-Making

Once the who, what, where, when, and why are identified, the teacher can determine the appropriate course of action (see Figure 6.4). As stated earlier, the more precise the answers to the who, what, where, when, and why questions, the easier the decision-making process will be. This discussion as to how to intervene should be directly tied to the answers determined in the assessment and analysis. The stronger the link between the assessment, analysis, and decision-making, the more likely the intervention will be successful and mitigate the behavioral concern. In determining the course of action, it is important to remember that the appropriate intervention may involve the student(s), teacher(s), or both.

A teacher may decide to implement some of the strategies discussed in Chapter 2, such as positive and negative (group or individual) reinforcement (remembering to reinforce and praise appropriate behaviors), group reinforcement contingencies (a movie if the class reaches a specific goal), planned ignoring (ignoring the inappropriate behavior), or even the Premack principle (if a student does their work, then they can have five minutes of computer time). It may be more appropriate to implement strategies from Chapter 8, such as teaching social skills (specific steps on how to get a person's attention), self-regulation (self-monitoring chart), or emotional intelligence (teaching empathy). The instruction may involve using some of the strategies for common behavioral issues (speaking out of turn, staying on task, organizational skills) as discussed in Chapter 9. Whatever instruction or intervention the teacher decides to implement, it should be specifically tied to the analysis. The more logical and natural the intervention is, the more likely it is to be effective.

It is also important that teachers consider what role they should play in the intervention. It might be that the teacher needs more cultural awareness to understand the diversity in their classroom. It may be that the teacher is inconsistent or too flexible in their enforcement of the rules and/or procedures. A student(s) may need more academic support than what is currently being provided. Or possibly the teacher has not built an authentic caring relationship with each student or that the students do not

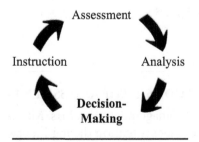

Figure 6.4 Ongoing Cycle of Response to Intervention

see the teacher as an authority figure (see Chapter 5). Whatever the case, it is important for teachers to seriously consider thier role in the decision-making process. Teachers are the guiding force in the classroom, and are essential to building an effective and inclusive classroom.

Successful classroom management does not simply focus on who is behaving and who is not and rewarding those who behave and punishing those who do not. Teachers should reflect on their observations and analyze why a student is doing what they are doing. Consequences, both positive and negative, are more successful in shaping behaviors if they are tied to the behavior and motivation behind the behavior.

Instruction

The final component in the cycle is instruction (see Figure 6.5). The assessment, analysis, and decision-making allow the teacher to implement the appropriate intervention and instruction. Although instruction was discussed previously in this chapter, it is important to note that whatever intervention is determined, it must also include instruction. The students need direct instruction as to what the intervention is and why it is necessary. This does not need to be a 45-minute lesson on the proper way for a student to answer a question in class (although it might). The instruction could be a mini lesson on why students should raise their hands in class, along with some guided and independent practice. It may also include a written list of the procedural steps (quietly raise hand, remain quiet and wait for the teacher to call on you, answer the question if the teacher calls on you, quietly lower your hand if the teacher does not call on you) on a form for the students to self-monitor whether or not they follow each step. The instruction provided must meet the students' needs as determined by the assessment and analysis.

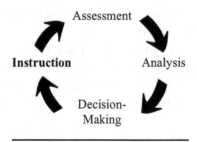

Figure 6.5 Ongoing Cycle of Response to Intervention

CASE STUDY 6.4: THE ASSESSMENT CYCLE

As part of her classroom management plan, Mrs. Maneski implemented a procedure for getting the teacher's attention during independent work time (raise your hand and wait quietly until the teacher responds to you). At the beginning of the year, she taught the procedure using a direct instruction model. As part of her ongoing assessment, Mrs. Maneski noticed that one student in particular, Sally, was having difficulty following this procedure.

Mrs. Maneski decided to observe Sally during independent practice time in math class and determined that Sally called out five times while correctly following the procedure for getting attention only one time in a 45-minute period (assessment of who, what, when, and where).

Upon reflecting on the situation and analyzing what had happened, Mrs. Maneski realized that the one time Sally correctly followed the procedure was when she was near Sally and could quickly answer her question. The five times Sally called out were times when Mrs. Maneski was across the room from her. She also realized that she did not know if, or for how long, Sally's hand had been up on three of those occasions because she was working with other students. Mrs. Maneski realized that both she and Sally were part of the problem. Sally was most likely not following the procedures because of the amount of time she had to wait, and Mrs. Maneski was not monitoring and responding to her students' needs in a timely manner (analysis of why the behavior was occurring).

Based on the analysis, Mrs. Maneski decided that her instruction needed to include both Sally and herself. Mrs. Maneski decided to conduct a mini lesson with Sally with the goal of increasing the amount of times she correctly followed the procedure. Sally's goal for next week was to seek attention following the procedure three times (up from one time) per math period. Mrs. Maneski also set a goal for herself to respond to students needs in a timelier manner. She planned to do this by moving around the classroom in a predictable pattern so that students would know when to expect her near their desk. She also decided that she must acknowledge students who raise their hands within a timely manner (30 seconds). Although she may not be able to provide assistance that quickly, she needed to at least acknowledge the students ("Sally, I see you have your hand up. I will help you after I finish helping Zachary.") (decision-making linked to the assessment and analysis).

Mrs. Maneski then implemented her decision. She conducted a mini lesson with Sally to revisit the procedures for getting the teacher's attention and set a goal with Sally to reduce the amount of times she incorrectly sought attention and to increase the number of times she did so correctly. Sally was given a task analysis of the procedures to check off as they were performed and taught how to use it. Before each math class, Mrs. Maneski reviews the procedure for seeking attention with the entire class and privately reminds Sally of her goal. Mrs. Maneski makes sure to praise Sally and other students when they follow the procedure correctly. Mrs. Maneski followed through on her part by more efficiently and quickly moving around the classroom and acknowledging students in a timely manner when they raised their hands. After each math class, Mrs. Maneski discusses with Sally how well she performed toward her goal. She praises Sally when she makes progress toward her goal and had Sally practice the procedure if she fails to reach her goal (instruction linked to assessment, analysis, and decision-making). Mrs. Maneski continued to assess the situation and to reflect on ways to improve the climate of her classroom.

The instruction and intervention may also relate specifically to the teacher. Teachers may need to learn more about the cultural norms of their students and how they influence behaviors. They may need to focus on building relationships, learning more about their students, and learning different teaching strategies or ways to support their students. Teachers may simply need to learn to recognize and reinforce positive behaviors to provide the attention students are seeking. Whatever the case, teachers must be reflective and willing to learn and to make the necessary changes to help students learn and grow academically and behaviorally.

Comprehension Check
1. Why is it important to teach the classroom management plan?
2. What are the direct instruction components that should be used in teaching a classroom management plan?
3. How is an ongoing cycle of assessment used to evaluate the classroom management plan?

The classroom management plan should be systematically taught to guide students toward managing their own behaviors and creating an inclusive classroom community. Teachers with effective management plans teach their students both how and why to follow the rules and consistently enforce the plan. Violations of the plan (not following the rules) are dealt with quickly but in a manner that educates students rather than punishing them. The student's behavior is monitored in relation to the plan using an ongoing cycle, and instruction and interventions are provided as needed (Rademacher et al., 1998).

Although there is a need for consistent implementation of the plan, there also must be a degree of flexibility. There will be times when the appropriate course of action demands flexibility in the implementation of the plan. For example, during a fire or fire drill, the class procedure for lining up may be suspended in order to get the students out of the classroom as quickly and orderly as possible. Or if a class rule requires students to arrive to class on time but extenuating circumstances interfere (bus broke down, another teacher wanted to talk to a student, or a sprained ankle), then the need for flexibility is paramount to the need for consistency. Although the need for consistency is important, there is also a need for a degree of reasonableness and flexibility. Having this reasonable flexibility also increases the likelihood that students will follow the classroom rules (Rademacher et al., 1998).

APPLICATION ACTIVITIES

1. Interview a teacher or observe a classroom to determine how they address culture in the classroom. What does the teacher do to meet the needs of diverse cultures in their classroom? How does this impact his or her classroom management?

2. Conduct an internet search for classroom rules and procedures. Have candidates independently or in small groups evaluate them in terms of strengths and weaknesses.
3. Have the students develop their own classroom management plan, including a guiding principle, three to five rules, and procedures for one or more of the following:
   - Turning in assignments
   - Sharpening a pencil
   - Entering the classroom at the beginning of the day or class period
   - Leaving the classroom at the end of the day or class period

CHAPTER SUMMARY

Culture

- Culture is a way of life, and there is no right or wrong in regard to culture.
- Behaviors are often influenced by a person's culture.
  - Communication styles as a cultural difference can sometimes lead to behavioral conflicts in the classroom.
  - The teacher must recognize and respect these cultural differences and discuss with students the expectations they have as the teacher in the classroom.

Culturally Responsive Teachers

- When teachers are aware of their students culturally, they are able to manage behaviors and to provide appropriate responses and/or instruction when certain events arise in the classroom.
- To be culturally aware, teachers should observe and learn differences in behavioral and communication styles and develop an inclusive classroom environment.
- Teachers should guide discussion over behavioral expectations and cultural norms with their students in the classroom.
- Teachers should also be aware of their cultural biases and prejudices; this will help them respond appropriately to cultural differences.
- Sometimes behaviors that appear to be misbehaviors are actually a result of cultural differences.

Management Plan

- A management plan is a plan created by the teacher before the first day of class to help ensure that students behave and meet the expectation the teacher has set for the classroom.
- The plan helps eliminate behavioral problems.
- This plan must be taught and reinforced in a systematic way.
- The goal of a management plan is to enhance learning, increase appropriate classroom behavior, and promote personal responsibility.
- The plan provides students the opportunity to develop a sense of personal responsibility.

Classroom Design

- Classrooms must be intentionally designed to be inviting and to meet the organizational needs of the students and teachers.

Guiding Principle

- This principle is based on characteristics that are more civil minded and long term in development but are essential elements of a classroom.
- The guiding principle is not necessarily based on behaviors that are easily observed or measured.
- This is a short statement that is usually two to three sentences that positively directs students as to how they should behave.
- The guiding principle articulates the core values of the classroom.
- It is displayed in a prominent place in the classroom for anyone who walks in to see.

Implementing the Management Plan

- The first step is teaching the plan to the students.
- Failure to teach, reinforce, and review the management plan in a systematic manner often creates needless behavior problems.
- The plan should be taught using a direct instruction model.
- Attain the students' attention and provide a motive for learning.
- Make the lesson relevant to the students.
- Teach the behaviors as the teacher expects them to be performed.
- Breaking the information into small pieces over the course of the first few weeks of school may make it more manageable for students.
- Students are given the chance to practice what they have learned.
- Students should practice independently multiple times.
- Teachers can use the concept of positive practice.
- The students' ability to follow the management plan should be assessed using the ongoing cycle of assessment.
- Consistency, flexibility, and reasonability are needed.

Ongoing Assessment Cycle

- Assessment
  - Informal observation done by the classroom teacher.
  - Determine who, what, when, and where.
- Analysis
  - Determine the why or the motivation for the behavior.
  - Look for patterns of behavior.
  - A general rule in determining why a student misbehaves is because the student either wants something or wants to avoid something.
  - Teachers must determine their role in any behavioral concern that arises.

- Decision-Making
  - Determine the appropriate course of action.
  - The stronger the link between assessment, analysis, and decision-making, the more likely the intervention will be successful.
  - Reflect on the observations and analyze why the student is doing what they are doing.
- Instruction
  - Students need direct instruction as to what the intervention is and why.
  - Consider a mini lesson on why a student should complete a certain behavior with some guided and independent practice.

REFERENCES

Curwin, R.L. & Mendler, A.N. (1988). Packaged Discipline Programs: Let the Buyer Beware. *Educational Leadership, 46*(2), 68-71.

The IRIS Center. (2012a). *Classroom management (part 1): Learning the components of a comprehensive behavior management plan.* Retrieved from https://iris.peabody.vanderbilt.edu/module/beh1/#content

The IRIS Center. (2012b). *Classroom management (part 2): Developing your own comprehensive behavior management plan.* Retrieved from https://iris.peabody.vanderbilt.edu/module/beh2/

Rademacher, J. A., Callahan, K., & Pederson-Seelye, V. A. (1998). How do your classroom rules measure up? Guidelines for developing an effective rule management routine. *Intervention in School and Clinic, 33*(5), 284–289.

Soodak, L. C. (2003). Classroom management in inclusive settings. *Theory Into Practice, 42*(4), 327–333.

Weinstein, C., Curran, M., & Tomlinson-Clarke, S. (2003). Culturally responsive classroom management: Awareness into action. *Theory Into Practice, 42*(4), 269–276.

7

MOTIVATION

Catherine Lawless Frank

CHAPTER OBJECTIVES

After reading this chapter, students should be able to:

1. Define extrinsic and intrinsic motivation and how they are used in the classroom.
2. Explain the components of expectancy theory and how they relate to teaching.
3. Understand how the needs identified in Maslow's hierarchy of needs theory impact learning.

According to the *Cambridge English Dictionary* (2018), to motivate is to cause someone to behave in a particular way or to make someone want to perform well. Motivation helps a person determine which behaviors to perform and how well to perform them. A student can be motivated to complete an assignment and do it well, complete an assignment but not necessarily do it well, or not complete the assignment at all. Almost all human behaviors are motivated. Although it is often assumed that students are either motivated (working hard) or not motivated (not working hard), in reality all students are motivated. One student may be motivated to work hard while another may be motivated to not work hard (and possibly to daydream, doodle, or talk to a friend). What motivates one student is not necessarily what motivates another student. Every student is motivated but not necessarily to do the same thing. Humans are typically motivated to perform the behaviors or tasks that fulfill needs and/or provide the greatest satisfaction or pleasure (Sachau, 2016). When a school meets a student's needs and provides engaging and supportive lessons, then motivation to succeed academically and behaviorally increases.

For example, Christopher may be motivated to complete a task to the best of his ability and therefore will work hard to do well on that task. He may be motivated by the feeling of satisfaction from doing a job well done or even to avoid a sense of guilt for not doing his best work. Jaidyn may be just as motivated to complete the task but is motivated to do so quickly so that she can go out to recess and talk to a peer. Jaidyn has a stronger motivation and derives more pleasure or satisfaction from going out to recess and talking to a peer than doing her best work. Geoff may be motivated to text his friends on his phone rather than to complete the assignment at all. For a variety of possible reasons, Geoff does not derive satisfaction or is not inspired to complete the assignment (too difficult, not relevant or interesting) but is inspired to text on his phone (entertainment, sense of belonging). All three students are motivated and used their motivation to influence their choice of behaviors. All students are motivated but may not be motivated in the way a teacher prefers them to be.

Teachers must design classrooms that facilitate utilizing student motivation to enhance academics and behaviors. The more students are motivated to be engaged in learning, the less they are motivated by inappropriate behaviors. Knowing what influences a person's motivation can help a teacher design a classroom where students are motivated to succeed both academically and behaviorally.

It is important to keep in mind that behavior is a choice and motivation affects, but does not fully determine, that choice. A person may be motivated to stay in bed on a cold, rainy Monday morning but still choose to get out of bed and go to work or school. From our earlier examples, Jaidyn may be motivated to interact with her peers but still go back and proofread the assignment before submitting it. Geoff may choose to do the assignment, even though he would prefer to be texting on his phone. Motivation influences behavior but does not necessarily determine which behavior is chosen.

TYPES OF MOTIVATION

People are both intrinsically and extrinsically motivated. Intrinsic motivation is based on internal rewards. The inspiration to complete a task or behavior comes from within the person (pride, guilt, interest). A person completes the task because the task itself fulfills a need or provides joy or satisfaction within the person. Zoe is internally motivated to learn in science class because she is interested in and finds satisfaction from learning the material. Extrinsic motivation is based on external rewards. The inspiration to complete the task or behavior comes from outside the person (grades, praise, reward). The task itself is not motivating but a means to an end or leads to something that is motivating. Isaac is not intrinsically motivated in science class but is externally motivated to perform well in order to get good grades. The motivation is getting good grades rather than the assignment itself (Sachau, 2016).

Intrinsic Motivation

Christopher and Geoff from the previous examples may have been intrinsically motivated. Christopher may have been motivated by a sense of satisfaction in performing a task well and Geoff a sense of enjoyment or belonging from communicating or texting with friends. Both Christopher and Geoff were motivated to perform their behaviors by a sense of satisfaction or inspiration from within themselves. Geoff and Christopher were both intrinsically motivated in class, but only one (Christopher) may have been motivated in the manner in which the teacher preferred.

Table 7.1 Ways to Support Intrinsic Motivation

Develop an inclusive environment that emphasizes the following:
- Authentic teacher-to-student and peer-to-peer relationships
- High standards of classroom behavior
- A zero tolerance for inappropriate student behavior that negatively affects another student's feeling of safety or belonging (bullying, teasing, physical aggression)
- Representation in posters, books, curriculum and items of all the different cultures present among the teachers and students

Engaging lessons that do the following:
- Incorporate students' interests
- Are relevant to students' lives
- Include collaborative and hands-on activities
- Include materials and points of view from different cultures

Provide needed support by doing the following:
- Embracing such approaches as Universal Design for Learning
- Using data-driven instruction and error analysis to differentiate levels of support
- Teaching and using learning and organizational strategies (mnemonics, text structures, graphic organizers)
- Making accommodations as needed

Teachers can use intrinsic motivation in a proactive way to enhance behavioral and academic achievement. The classroom environment and lessons a teacher designs as well as the supports they provide help foster intrinsic motivation within students. A classroom in which students feel included and a sense of belonging helps inspire an intrinsic motivation to achieve. Engaging and relevant lessons foster this internal desire to learn while providing the needed supports allows students to be successful and feel a sense of achievement. Although lessons should be engaging to maintain students' interest, it is equally, if not more, important to provide a safe and inclusive classroom environment and the needed supports and accommodations. Without ensuring a student can successfully engage in a lesson in a safe (physically and emotionally) environment, it is difficult, if not impossible, for a teacher to interest or intrinsically motivate the student. The ability to feel physically and emotionally safe, successful, and properly challenged is a large factor in a student's intrinsic motivation within the classroom. See Table 7.1 for ways to support intrinsic motivation.

Extrinsic Motivation

In the earlier example, Jaidyn was extrinsically motivated. She did not find the school assignment itself intrinsically motivating but was extrinsically motivated by recess. Her inspiration came from the chance to play after the task was completed rather than from the task itself. Jaidyn's teacher may have used the Premack principle (discussed in Chapter 2) to externally motivate her to complete the task. The Premack principle

Table 7.2 Types of Extrinsic Motivators Teachers Can Use in the Classroom

Extrinsic Motivators for School
- Class party or movie for meeting a goal
- Praise (smiling and saying, "Nice job")
- Extra recess, free time, computer or art time
- Prize (earn a pencil, pick from a class treasure chest)
- Help out in another classroom, or in the office
- First in line or line up next to a buddy
- Positive note, email, or phone call home
- Read to or tutor a younger student
- Keep a stuffed animal, special toy, or phone at their desk
- Bring an item or story to show and to share with the class
- Attention or time with the teacher or other faculty or staff member (earn lunch with the teacher, talk to the gym teacher)
- No homework or a homework pass
- Listen to music
- Snack or treat

is based on the notion that a desired behavior can be used as an extrinsic motivator for a less desirable behavior or, in other words, if a student first does what the teacher wants, then the student can do what they want. In the case of Jaidyn, the teacher used the desired behavior, recess, to extrinsically motivate her to do the less desirable behavior, schoolwork.

Teachers often use extrinsic motivators, such as positive and negative reinforcers or rewards and punishments, as a means to motivate students to complete an assignment or to behave in a particular manner. Extrinsic motivators are important tools for teachers to use to inspire students to make behavioral and academic choices that are conducive to an effective classroom environment. See Table 7.2 for a list of possible extrinsic motivators to use within the classroom.

Extrinsic reinforcement should not be the only tool a teacher uses to motivate students. This type of motivator typically does not have a lasting effect on a student's behavior. In the example of Jaidyn, once the reward of recess was over, so was Jaidyn's motivation to complete the assignment. Using extrinsic motivation, such as rewards and punishments, is not equally effective for all students. Some students are motivated by rewards, prizes, and the fear of punishment, but others are not. A teacher could attempt to extrinsically motivate Geoff with the threat of punishment to put his phone away. This threat may or may not be effective. Geoff may choose to put his phone away or he may not. He may also choose to put the phone away but get it back out again when the teacher is not looking because external motivators typically do not produce lasting results. Once the teacher is no longer looking, then Geoff may consider the threat of punishment gone.

> *Comprehension Check*
> 1. How does motivation affect a person's behavior?
> 2. What is intrinsic motivation?
> 3. What is extrinsic motivation?
> 4. List examples of intrinsic and extrinsic motivators that could be used in a classroom.

THEORIES OF MOTIVATION

This chapter examines two different theories of motivation, the expectancy theory and Maslow's hierarchy of needs theory. Expectancy theory states that behavior is a choice and motivation is tied to a person's beliefs about a their ability to be successful, that the success and efforts will be recognized and the expected results are worth the effort. Maslow's theory examines motivation as a desire to fulfill specific human needs. Although these theories differ in their views of motivation, both are applicable in the classroom. Teachers should consider both theories when structuring their classrooms and lessons to motivate students both academically and behaviorally.

Expectancy Theory

Expectancy theory is based on the work of Victor Vroom (1964) and his studies on motivation in the workplace. Vroom's theory views behavior as a choice based in part on a person's perception of their ability, the belief that their efforts will be recognized and the desirability of the outcome (Sachau, 2016). According to the expectancy theory, people are more likely to perform behaviors in which they feel they have the needed ability and resources, in which their efforts will be recognized and that the reward or consequences for doing the task are worth the effort. There are three variables associated with this theory: expectancy, instrumentality, and valence. Expectancy is a person's belief that their hard work and efforts can lead to success. Whether the effort and results of the task or behavior will be recognized is instrumentality. Valence is the degree to which the results are seen as worth the effort. A person's analysis of these three variables influences their degree of motivation to perform the task (Sachau, 2016). See Table 7.3 for an overview of these components.

Table 7.3 Components of Expectancy Theory

	Motivation is based on the degree to which a person believes the following:
Expectancy	They have the necessary skills and resources to contribute to or complete a task and that working hard will increase the chances of success.
Instrumentality	Completing the task or behavior will produce the anticipated results.
Valence	The value or desirability of the results or anticipated outcome is worth the effort.

Expectancy

The first of the three components of expectancy theory is expectancy. This is a person's expectations about their likelihood of success on a given task and if increased effort (working harder) will increase the chances of success. It incorporates a person's belief in their skills or ability level as well as the availability of the needed resources and supports. If a person's expectancy is positive (they believe that they have the necessary skills and needed supports and resources), then they are more likely to believe that their efforts will result in, or contribute to, the successful completion of a task. They believe that they possess the knowledge, skills, and resources to get the job done. If the person believes that they do not possess the knowledge or skills but have the needed resources and support, then their expectation of success may still be positive. This person may believe that, with effort and assistance, they can get the job done. But if a person believes that they do not have the needed skills or resources, then their expectations of success are lower. This person may feel that there is no point in putting effort into the task because they lack the skills and resources to complete it successfully.

A student's belief in their ability to be successful and that the needed resources and supports are available to assist them is crucial. The expectation of success tends to be positive when students believe that they have the skills and/or needed resources to perform a task. If, for example, Lillian believes that she has the necessary skills and resources to complete a math assignment, then her expectation of success tends to be positive. Skyar knows that she struggles in math but also knows that she has the resources (addition chart, manipulatives, calculator) and teacher support to be successful. When students believe that they lack some necessary skills but have the needed resources and teacher support, then their expectancy of success can still be positive. Camila believes she lacks the needed skills in math, does not have access to the necessary supports or resources, and her teacher will not have time in class to help her. This may lead Camila to believe that extra effort on her part will not lead to success because she lacks the needed skills and resources. Camila's expectation of success is low, and therefore she is less likely to be motivated to complete the assignment and be engaged in class. It is important to remember that expectancy theory is based on a student's (not the teacher's) belief about their skill level, the available resources, and the teacher's willingness or ability to provide support.

Students with a history of school failure often have low expectancy of success. For instance, Jeremy is a student with a learning disability who, along with his classmates, has spent years learning to read. Although most of his classmates have learned to be good or fluid readers, Jeremy still struggles to read fluently. Even though Jeremy has in the past put a similar amount of effort (if not more) into learning to read, the effort did not provide in the same positive results as his classmates. He still struggles to read. This history of failure may lead Jeremy to have lower expectations of success and affect his degree of motivation in the classroom. It is up to Jeremy's teacher to change his expectations. The teacher must build a classroom environment and an authentic relationship that inspires Jeremy's trust while providing the supports (graphic organizers, data-driven instruction) and resources (audiobooks, text-to-speech software) for him to be successful. Students must believe that their efforts will result in some academic or behavioral gain and that if they struggle, then the teacher will provide the needed

Table 7.4 Ways to Increase Expectancy

- Use an ongoing cycle to provide data-driven instruction to meet individual student's needs.
  - Use short-cycle assessments.
  - Analyze the results of those assessments to determine patterns of students' strengths and areas of need.
  - Decide on the appropriate instruction.
  - Provide instruction.
- Use teaching strategies, such as Universal Design for Learning.
  - *Multiple Means of Representation.* Present lessons and materials in multiple ways (orally and in writing, videos, audiobooks) while providing the necessary supports.
  - *Multiple Means of Action and Expression.* Allow students to demonstrate their knowledge in an array of ways, allowing them to work toward their strengths and to compensate for their areas of need.
  - *Multiple Means of Engagement.* Provide a variety of ways to keep students actively involved in the learning process.
- Provide the resources and supports that students need to be successful.
- Incorporate classroom rules and procedures to provide the needed classroom structure.
- Develop authentic relationships with all students.

supports and resources. When students have low expectancy, they are less likely to be engaged academically and are more likely to behave inappropriately. For ideas on how to increase expectancy in the classroom, see Table 7.4.

Instrumentality

While expectancy is based on ability and resources, the second component, instrumentality addresses whether the completion of the task will recognized or produce results. If a student works hard in school, will that hard work be recognized or rewarded? If a student does not work hard in school, will there be negative consequences? Students, in part, base their behavioral decisions on their beliefs in the results or consequences. For example, in Mr. Monroe's class, homework is collected at the beginning of class and graded. Homework grades consist of 30% of a student's overall course grade. Students in Mr. Monroe's class are likely to believe that completing homework will be recognized and produce the results of a grade. There is an anticipated consequence (a high or low grade) for doing and not doing the assignment. This anticipated outcome or instrumentality is a component in a student's decision on whether or not to do Mr. Monroe's homework. However, Mrs. Watson rarely grades students' homework. She assigns it, expects students to complete it, reviews it in class, but does not collect or grade it. Students in her class anticipate that homework will not be graded and that the homework itself will not influence grades. This anticipated outcome or instrumentality is a component in whether students' complete homework. Students are more likely to be motivated to complete Mr. Monroe's homework than Mrs. Watson's based on instrumentality. Instrumentality is not affected by a person's skill level, the availability of resources, or the desirability of the outcome. It is based on a person's belief about the chances that a behavior will be recognized or produce the anticipated results.

Table 7.5 Ways to Increase Instrumentality

- Be consistent in enforcing rules and procedures.
- Set classroom goals and practice goal setting with students.
- Praise persistence rather than simply results ("I like how hard you are working, Abdul. You had some problems with question one, but you just kept working on it until you figured it out. I like your dedication and persistence.").
- Provided specific feedback to students in regard to their strengths and areas of need ("Miguel, I like how you did _____ but remember to _____.").
- Acknowledge students' positive behaviors ("Ezekiel, I heard you worked really hard in Mr. Richardson's class today. He said he really tried to challenge your class and you did a nice job meeting his challenge.").
- Promote a safe and inclusive classroom environment where students feel protected and are willing to take academic risks without fear of consequences.

Roberto knows the rules and routines of Ms. Jablanski's class and has positive expectancy about his ability to follow them. His behavior (whether to follow the rules or not) is in part motivated by his belief in the results or consequences. If Ms. Jablanski acknowledges his appropriate behaviors ("Roberto, I like how you are sitting quietly at your desk.") and corrects his inappropriate behaviors ("Sit down, Roberto."), then Roberto may have a higher degree of instrumentality. He knows the anticipated outcome for both positive and negative behavior. He believes that not only will Ms. Jablanski acknowledge when he does something wrong but also will also notice when he does something right. Roberto's instrumentality is that he will receive positive attention for following the rules, which in turn may increase his motivation to do so. If Ms. Jablanski only addresses inappropriate behaviors and never acknowledges appropriate behaviors, then it affects Roberto's instrumentality. He may anticipate that there will be no reward (besides that lack of redirection or punishment) for appropriate behavior. Inappropriate behaviors receive attention but appropriate behaviors do not. If Roberto desires attention, then he is more likely to misbehave in order to receive it. Acknowledging students' positive behaviors may affect their instrumentality and motivation to follow the classroom rules. For ideas on how to increase instrumentality in the classroom, see Table 7.5.

Valence

Expectancy is the belief in ability and available resources, instrumentality is the anticipated outcomes, and valence is the value a person attributes to that outcome. A person determines whether a behavior or task is worthwhile based in part on how much they value the outcome. Valance is the significance (either positive or negative) or desirability a person attributes to the expected or anticipated outcome. The expected outcome may be positive (a reward) or negative (a punishment), and valence is the degree to which a person wants, or wants to avoid, that outcome.

Valence can be intrinsic or extrinsic, positive or negative. The valence for some behaviors may be intrinsic, such as a feeling of satisfaction for a job well done or learning more about a topic of interest. For other behaviors, the valence may be

Table 7.6 Ways to Increase Valence

- Use a reward menu allowing students to choose from a variety of reinforcements.
- Offer choices in terms of assignments, assessments, and/or ways in which students can demonstrate their knowledge.
- Incorporate student interests into lessons and assignments.
- Develop a variety of intrinsic and extrinsic motivators based on the needs and interests of students.

extrinsic, such as a positive reward (teacher attention, a high grade) or negative consequence (losing recess, detention). Teachers must remember that valence is based on the value the student places on the expected outcome. Free time to socialize in class for completing an assignment is a positive extrinsic motivator for some students but not for all students. A shy or introverted student may not have the same value for time to socialize as an extroverted student. Some students will be motivated for extra recess while others would prefer lunch inside with the teacher. After-school detention may be a deterrent for some but not for others. The value of a reward or consequence is determined by each individual person, and teachers should consider this when designing rewards and consequences. For ways to increase valence in the classroom, see Table 7.6.

According to expectancy theory, a person decides which behavior to perform based in part on their belief in their ability to perform the task (expectancy), the predicted outcome or recognition in doing the task (instrumentality), and the value, either positive or negative, of that anticipated outcome (valence). A person consciously decides whether to perform a behavior using an analysis of these three factors to determine if the behavior is worth the effort (Sachau, 2016).

Choices and behaviors do not occur in isolation, however, and at any given time people have a variety of behavioral options. A person has the option to read this textbook, go for a walk, check their email, or text a friend. All behaviors have potential competing behaviors, and rarely do people have only one choice as to what to do (Sachau, 2016). For example, imagine that it is Friday and a college student has a five-page research paper to complete for class on Monday. Although that student may need to do some research on the subject, they believe that, with effort and time, they have the ability and resources to complete the task well. The student has the expectancy that they can complete the task and write the five-page paper. The student also believes that there will be a certain outcome or recognition for completing the task. They are confident in the instrumentality that the professor will recognize, read and grade the paper. Lastly, the college student realizes that completing the five-page paper will most likely result in a positive outcome (or at least more positive than not completing the paper), such as a passing grade. This student is confident in their ability and that the outcome is worth the effort.

But imagine it is Friday and there are other potential competing behaviors that are also under consideration. Imagine that one of those competing behaviors is an invitation from a friend to go to a restaurant or club. The college student expects that they can perform the task of going out with a friend (and have the money) and is pretty confident that the outcome of doing so will be positive (having a good time). In regard to both the research paper and going out with a friend, the college student believes they could perform the task (expectancy), anticipate a certain outcome (instrumentality), and believe the outcome will be positive (valence).

The college student may then begin weighing how much time is really needed to complete the paper, how high of a grade they really need to earn, how busy the rest of the weekend is, if they can to afford to go out, and all other potential factors that influence their choice. Humans are typically motivated to perform the behaviors that fulfill a need and/or provides the greatest satisfaction or pleasure, but motivation alone does not determine which behavior is chosen (Sachau, 2016). Students also have choices of competing behaviors within a classroom. Even if a student has the expectation of success, they still have choices of other competing or conflicting behaviors. Just like the college student, these competing behaviors are not necessarily academic in nature.

CASE STUDY 7.1

Sophie is a struggling reader in Mrs. Thompson's class and has received extensive small-group instruction with a reading specialist since first grade. Despite this additional support, Sophie still reads at a level that is significantly below most of her peers. In the past when Sophie was asked to perform tasks in the classroom that involve reading (reading directions on assignments, reading out loud in class, reading and answering questions in a textbook), she often distracted her peers, was off task, and failed to complete the assignments. One of her teachers from last year told Mrs. Thompson that Sophie was a behavior problem and often off task, causing disruption and bothering her classmates. Her previous teacher felt that Sophie "was just not motivated to try", "would never ask for help when she needed it", and "caused many disruptions in class."

Mrs. Thompson knew that Sophie's behaviors were not due to a lack of motivation but a motivation to avoid reading. Sophie's prior experiences taught her to expect that her efforts in reading would not result in her being able to read well and that the outcome (failed grades, being teased by peers) would be negative. Therefore, other behaviors, such as talking to peers and disrupting class, were more motivating than reading.

Mrs. Thompson knew it would require hard work on her part but vowed to design her classroom in a way that facilitated academic motivation in all her students, including Sophie. She did this by structuring her classroom with rules and procedures that helped students feel safe and secure both physically and emotionally. Mrs. Thompson created a classroom environment that fostered an inclusive climate and worked hard to develop authentic relationships with all her students while holding them accountable to high behavioral expectations. The lessons Mrs. Thompson developed incorporated the supports necessary (directions given orally as well as in writing, the availability of audio and print textbooks for all students, the use of videos and websites to supplement the content, the use of guided notes and graphic organizers) to compensate for Sophie's reading struggles and to support other students' learning needs.

The classroom structure, high expectations, and authentic relationships helped Sophie and the other students trust Mrs. Thompson to provide a safe and nurturing environment. Incorporating supports into the lessons allowed all students, including Sophie, to experience positive academic outcomes and made the hard work needed to succeed worth the effort. This environment provided the structure and supports to engage students in learning which in turn positively impacted classroom behaviors.

Comprehension Check

1. What is expectancy theory?
2. How do the three components of expectancy theory affect motivation in the classroom?
3. What can teachers do to increase a student's expectation of academic and behavioral success in the classroom?

MASLOW'S NEEDS

There are many different resources, blogs, and books on how to motivate students, and often these resources are often based on the work of Abraham Maslow. Maslow, a psychologist, is best known for his motivational theory, Maslow's hierarchy of needs (1943). Unlike expectancy theory, which links motivation to the anticipated outcome, Maslow theorized that human motivation is based on a desire to fulfill certain needs. Maslow ranked his needs in a hierarchy, with originally five (Maslow, 1943) and later seven (Maslow, 1970a) and finally eight (Maslow, 1970b) tiers of needs. Fulfillment of these needs leads a person to become self-actualized and transcendent, which then allows a person to reach their full potential and in turn help others in reaching theirs. Maslow organized and identified the tiers based on these needs: physiological and biological, safety, love and belongingness, esteem, cognitive, aesthetic, self-actualization, and transcendence. See Table 7.7 for a description of the needs and their relationship to education.

Maslow believed that motivation is dependent on the whole person and not based on an individual task. This means that a student's motivation to complete a task in school or to behave in a particular way is dependent on the fulfillment, or desire to fulfill, certain needs rather than simply on the task or behavior itself. When Maslow proposed his theory, he believed that the needs were hierarchical, and that the lowest needs—physiological and biological—had to be fulfilled (all basic survival needs met) before the second-tier needs—safety—could be met. Physiological and biological and safety needs had to be fulfilled before love and belonging needs could be addressed. Those three tiers of needs (physiological and biological, safety, and love

Table 7.7 Maslow's Needs

Need	Implication for Teachers
Physiological and biological	Meeting basic survival needs, such as food and water, elimination of waste, air, and rest
Safety	Developing a physically and emotionally safe classroom environment
Love and belonging	Developing authentic relationships and creating an inclusive classroom where students feel accepted and cared for
Esteem	Nurturing a sense of worth, confidence, and self-regard in students
Cognitive	Inspiring and supporting students' quest to understand and make sense of the world around them
Aesthetic	Fostering an appreciation for beauty and nature in the world
Self-actualization	Helping students reach their full potential
Transcendence	Promoting a desire to share gifts and talents and to focus on the needs of others

and belonging) must then be fulfilled before esteem needs could and so on, with cognitive, aesthetic, self-actualization, and finally transcendence. Fulfilling each need was dependent on the fulfillment of all prior needs.

Research has since supported the existence of the needs identified by Maslow across the human race, regardless of geographical or cultural differences. There is disagreement, however, as to whether the needs are hierarchical. It is now typically believed that all humans have these needs, but the fulfillment of needs is not necessarily hierarchical and higher needs may not be dependent on the fulfillment of needs in lower tiers (Tay & Diener, 2011). A person who is hungry (physiological and biological need) can still feel loved (love and belonging needs), even though hunger is one of the lowest or most basic of human needs (lowest tier). A student who is hungry for lunch can still make plans for recess with their friends but the desire for food may still impacts the student in terms of fulfilling other needs. A person can also have more than one need from more than one tier at any given time. A person can be both hungry (physiological and biological need) and have a low sense of self-worth (esteem need) but still have a desire to learn (cognitive need). Although the hierarchy may be disputed, the needs exist across humanity and influence motivation in the classroom. A teacher must address the needs of the whole student in order to motivate and help them reach their full potential. This text will refer to the needs identified by Maslow as Maslow's needs rather than Maslow's hierarchy of needs to reiterate that although everyone possesses these needs, they are not necessarily hierarchical in nature.

Physiological and Biological Needs

The first and most basic type of needs identified by Maslow are physiological and biological. These are basic survival needs (food, water, sleep) and if deprived of one of these needs, then the desire to fulfill it becomes stronger (McLeod, 2016). If a student is deficient in any of these basic needs, then the motivation to fulfill that need may overpower the desire to complete an assignments or behave in an appropriate manner. When a student is hungry, their desire for food may take precedence

Table 7.8 Ways Teachers Can Meet Students' Physiological and Biological Needs

- Food: Provide snacks (fruit, granola bar, crackers) and/or snack time.
- Water: Incorporate times and procedures for water breaks and/or allow students to bring water bottles.
- Clothing (warmth): Allow students to wear a coat or sweatshirt in the classroom.
- Rest: Incorporate brain breaks, stretching exercises, or short periods of downtime.
- Elimination of waste: Integrate scheduled bathroom breaks into the daily routine and allow for and have a procedure for additional restroom breaks.
- Air: Provide recess, brain breaks or allow students to run class errands (note to the office, physical education class).

over learning to read, behaving in social studies, or completing a math assignment. Although some physiological and biological needs are typically fulfilled outside the classroom (clothing, shelter, cleanliness, air, rest), some can and must be fulfilled within the classroom. Teachers meet students' basic needs in terms of hunger (allowing snacks, free lunch programs), thirst (getting a drink of water), elimination of waste (going to the bathroom), and air and rest (recess, brain breaks). These basic needs have a large influence on a student's academic and behavioral tendencies, motivation, and performance in the classroom. See Table 7.8 for ways to meet students physiological and biological needs in the classroom.

Safety Needs

Safety is the second category of needs and is also considered a basic human need. These needs include both physical (protection from the elements and a secure, predictable, and orderly environment) and emotional (safety from oppression and abuse) safety (McLeod, 2016). Students must feel safe both physically and emotionally at school and in the classroom. Some ways teachers offer physical safety are by being an authority figure and providing structure, such as rules and procedures (including for emergency situations), in the classroom (see Chapter 6 for information on developing classroom structure). Teachers help provide emotional safety by establishing predictable routines and an inclusive classroom community. In order to achieve, students must feel emotionally and physically safe to take academic risks (a struggling student reading out loud, volunteering to answer a math question, participating in a class discussion) without the fear of being teased, bullied, or made fun of. Teachers establish a safe environment by developing authentic relationships with and among all students. Students should have strong relationships with their teachers and feel comfortable and safe in approaching them with serious issues and concerns. Behavioral standards must be established that nurture respect and promote appropriate interactions. Teachers must also intervene early and decisively in any student misbehavior that negatively affects another student's feeling of physical (fighting, stealing, hitting) or emotional (teasing, bullying, tormenting) safety. See Table 7.9 for ideas on how to meet students' physical and emotional safety needs within the classroom. (For more ideas on building a safe classroom environment see Chapter 6.)

Table 7.9 Ways for Teachers to Meet Students' Physical and Emotional Safety Needs

- Establish predictable routines.
- Post daily schedules.
- Clearly state classroom rules and expectations.
- Incorporate a zero-tolerance policy for malicious behavior (teasing, bullying).
- Foster classroom community and culture that allows students to try without fear.
- Set high standards of behavior that are consistently enforced.
- Treat students fairly rather than equally.
- Develop a caring relationship and show respect for all students.

Table 7.10 Ways Teachers Can Meet Students' Love and Belonging Needs

- Foster a sense of classroom community that is accepting of all students.
  - Respect diversity and represent the differing cultures within the classroom.
  - Establish high behavioral standards and a zero-tolerance policy for negative peer interactions.
- Develop authentic caring relationships between the teacher and students.
  - Show an interest in individual students and their lives both inside and outside the classroom.
  - Provide acknowledgment and attention for positive student behaviors.
- Foster student relationships.
  - Use collaborative activities and teach the skills necessary to work together in a respectful manner.

Love and Belonging Needs

Physiological and safety needs are basic human survival needs, while the remaining six (love and belonging, esteem, cognitive, aesthetic, self-actualization, and transcendence) are psychological needs. The fulfillment of these needs are not necessary for human survival but for psychological growth and development (McLeod, 2016).

The first of these psychological needs is love and belonging. Love and belonging are a person's need to feel accepted and cared for by another. For teachers, this means that students need a classroom where all students feel a sense of affiliation, acceptance, and support. As discussed in Chapter 5, the teacher is the essential element in establishing this environment. Fundamental to this are the relationships between the teacher and individual students and among students themselves. Teachers must work diligently to develop quality, caring relationships with all students and especially those students who are the most challenging. Friendship, collaboration, and peer acceptance should also be emphasized within the classroom. This may involve teachers demonstrating, modeling, and teaching friendship and social skills as well as the skills needed to work together in a cohesive and respectful manner. All students must feel valued and cared for and be treated with respect and dignity by peers and teachers alike. See Table 7.10 for strategies on meeting students' needs for love and belonging in the classroom. (See Chapter 5 for ways to foster quality student relationships, and see Chapter 6 for ideas on building an inclusive classroom culture.)

Esteem Needs

Esteem is the need for a person to feel a positive sense of self-worth, confidence, and self-regard. Students need to believe that they are capable and worthy in order to persist and succeed in the classroom (McLeod, 2016). Teachers foster this through their interactions and caring relationships, acknowledging strengths and accomplishments, and providing the supports necessary for a student to succeed. Teachers must make a point of providing students with positive (rather than negative) attention in order to address esteem needs. For some students, it is easier to provide this positive attention than it is for other students. Some students will be strong academically ("Nice job on your social studies test, Peter. Mr. Benson said you had the highest score in the class.") and/or athletically ("Rachel, congratulations on winning your volleyball game last weekend."). Others will have positive classroom behavior ("Thank you for raising your hand and waiting to be called on, Maxine. What is the answer to question one?"), strong social skills ("Dyshaun, I like how you waited patiently for your turn. Thank you for doing so."), and/or social awareness ("Charlie, thank you for helping Monica pick up the pencils she dropped. That was very kind of you."). For other students, though it may be more challenging to foster esteem. Teachers must be diligent in providing positive attention to all students and especially those who struggle academically or behaviorally. Students make decisions about how they behave in a classroom based in part on the relationship they have with their teacher (Weinstein, Tomlinson-Clarke, & Curran, 2004), and teachers should be cognizant of working make that relationship positive.

Esteem needs can also be supported by providing specific feedback on students' strengths and needs. Specific feedback is more than a simple acknowledgment of a good job or great work but specifically details what the student did well and where they continue to struggle ("Bryson, I like how you started the sentence with a capital, but remember that you need to also include ending punctuation." "Peter, thank you for hanging up your jacket. Now please go put your book bag away." "Rochanda, you have the process for division correct, but you need to check your multiplication facts."). Specific feedback acknowledges what the student does well and how they can improve.

One especially important attribute for teachers to specifically praise and acknowledge is persistence. Persistence is a person's ability to persevere and keep trying, even when things get difficult. Everyone struggles at times, and persistence is what helps a person continue trying rather than giving up. It is an essential skill in building esteem that should be positively acknowledged and fostered in all students. Teachers should acknowledge persistence in academics. For example, "Wyatt, I know math is challenging for you, but I appreciate how you keep at it, even when you struggle. Every day you come into class prepared and willing to take on the challenge. Nice job." Behavioral persistence should also be acknowledged. "Mackenzie, I know that we have talked about you calling out in class rather than raising your hand and waiting to be called on. I know that this is a struggle for you, but I also noticed that you have been working on it. Three times in math class today you raised your hand before you yelled out the answer. Raising your hand before calling out is a big improvement. Nice job. But now we need to remember to wait to be called on before answering." Persistence can also be praised in other aspects of students' social and emotional lives. "Julian, I heard that you had a rough morning on the bus, but I am glad to see that you made it to school. I especially like that you completed the morning procedure and have a pen and paper on your desk and are ready to go." In each of these instances, the praise was centered on the students' ability to persevere. Praising perseverance is more important than praising the actual accomplishment. This determination fosters esteem and allows people to keep trying in the face of hardships. It is an invaluable skill for students (and teachers) to develop.

It is important to note that praise and feedback must be genuine, and students (not teachers) must believe it is authentic. Telling a struggling student they did a great job for a grade or assignment that is of lower quality than that of their peers may not be seen by the student as genuine. Feedback or praise that is not seen as genuine can impact a student's trust and belief in the teacher and cause the student to question the teachers authenticity. Making the praise specific is more valid and clearly states what student behavior is being recognized ("Great job finishing your work on time. I like how you stuck with it and stayed focus until you got the job done.") which helps eliminate miscommunications and increase the teacher's legitimacy.

Esteem can also be developed by providing students with a choices and ownership. Allowing students to have choices and to make decisions in the classroom shows that their opinions matters and fosters a sense of ownership ("Okay, class, would you rather do your language arts assignments in small groups or individually?" "Today we are going to do a project on poetry, but the fun part is that you can either write a poem or write a song. It will be your choice."). Choices and ownership also helps foster responsibility for the classroom, which in turn can lead to greater behavioral and academic effort and achievement and strengthen the teacher-student relationship.

Remember that inappropriate student behaviors can often be tied to esteem needs. Students tend to misbehave in the classroom because they want something or want to avoid something. Often when students misbehave because they want something, what they want is attention from peers and/or teachers. Wanting attention is a desire to be noticed and recognized. Students can fulfill this desire in either positive (volunteering to answer questions, offering to tutor a peer) or negative (talking out in class, tapping a pencil, passing notes to friends) ways. The desire is for attention and, for some, negative attention fulfills this need just as well as positive attention. When students behave negatively, teachers typically respond more consistently and quickly in providing attention ("Sit down, Peter." "Stop tapping your pencil Elizabeth." "Be quiet, Tamika.") than when students behave positively. This makes the expectancy for getting noticed for negative behaviors typically greater than for positive behaviors. When teachers work diligently to provide students with positive attention, they increase student expectations for getting attention for positive behaviors. The need is to be noticed and recognized, and how teachers fulfill this need influences their relationship with the student and the behaviors in the classroom.

Students' desire to avoid something may also be tied to esteem needs. This can be an attempt to avoid embarrassment or work due to a student's low expectation of success. The student believes that they lack the skills and/or resources to successfully complete the assignment and therefore misbehave in order to avoid the task.

Table 7.11 Ways Teachers Can Meet Students' Esteem Needs

- Offer praise and acknowledgment for academic and nonacademic achievements ("I heard you did _____ in music/gym/art/computer class today. Nice job." "You did a really nice job on your test yesterday. All that studying really paid off.").
- Provide specific positive and negative feedback ("I like how you did _____, but remember _____."
- Praise persistence ("I know this is hard, and I like that you keep trying." "I noticed you _____, and I like the effort you are putting into this.").
- Foster student ownership in the classroom.
  - Offer students choices and allow them to make minor decisions.
    - "Who wants to _____?"
    - "Would you rather _____ or _____?"
    - "What do you think about _____?"
    - "How should we _____?"
    - "Which would you rather do first, _____ or _____?"
- Establish leadership roles in the classroom, such as line leader and teacher's helper.
- Spotlight students (star of the week, giving students options for displaying their work in the classroom).
- Promote independence (task analysis or checklists of steps to be completed, have students set goals and track their progress toward meeting those goals).

For instance, Michael struggles to read and knows that his reading ability is below that of his peers. When given an assignment that requires reading, Michael has a low expectation of success and will therefore try to avoid the assignment and the potential embarrassment of being a poor reader. Michael does not want to look "dumb" in front of his classmates. If Michael misbehaves (gets sent to the office, thrown out of class, puts his head down and takes a nap), he can avoid having to read and looking "dumb" in front of his classmates. Michael would rather get attention from being "bad" than from being "dumb." Students may choose to engage in inappropriate behaviors that draw attention away from their academic struggles (withdrawal, act out, or not complete a task) in an attempt to maintain their sense of self-worth and avoid the embarrassment. It is the teacher's responsibility to ensure that they establish a physically and emotionally safe classroom, provide students with the needed academic supports, and praise persistence over achievement in order to meet a student's esteem needs and to maintain an effective classroom environment. See Table 7.11 for ways to meet students' esteem needs in the classroom.

Cognitive Needs

Cognitive needs are based on a person's desire to learn, understand, and make sense of the world around them (McLeod, 2016). Schools are critical for fulfilling this need, but all students do not possess an innate motivation to learn academics and do well in school. Students have different interests, ways of learning, and ability levels that influence their motivation to learn in a school environment. If a school's curriculum is not relevant or a teaching method is misaligned to students' interests, expectancy, and needs, then the motivation to address cognitive needs in school may be lacking. Lessons must be engaging and relevant, with the necessary supports to allow all students to succeed. Both engaging lessons and needed supports are equally critical in meeting cognitive needs and keeping students actively engaged in the learning process. When students are actively engaged in the learning process, they are also more likely to behave in an appropriate manner. When students are busy learning, they are less likely to have the time or desire to misbehave.

One method of teaching that incorporates components of both engagement and support is Universal Design for Learning (UDL). UDL works to support and interest students by promoting flexibility within the classroom and allows teaching, learning, and engagement to happen in multiple ways within the same lesson. It is based on the concept that teachers should incorporate a variety of ways to present materials, allow students to demonstrate their knowledge, and keep them engaged in the learning process. For example, Jeremy struggles to read and therefore has difficulty being engaged and successfully completing a history lesson that requires him to read (as well as having a low expectation of success based on expectancy theory). The objective of the lesson is to learn history, and Jeremy's difficulties with reading interfere with his ability to meet this objective. Jeremy's failure to meet the objective is primarily due to his inability to access the information rather than a lack of ability in learning history. He cannot successfully complete the history assignment because he has difficulties reading. If his teacher were to provide options for different ways to access the information covered in the text (audio textbooks, guided notes, and videos), then Jeremy would have options that allow him to access the history material without the interference of his reading difficulty. He could learn history by listening to an audiobook or watch a movie and complete guided notes. His ability to learn history would not be dependent on his ability to read. Jeremy is more likely to be engaged (and better behaved) in a classroom where he has a means to access and learn the material in a manner that supports his skills, needs and interests.

When multiple options are provided for all students, then all students are more likely to be successful in meeting the objective and more engaged in the process. When students are engaged in learning, they tend to be better behaved. This approach benefits not only Jeremy but also all students who may or may not have barriers to learning, need supports, and/or prefer different ways to access material. This flexibility is a key concept found in the three main principles of UDL: Multiple Means of Representation, Multiple Means of Action and Expression, and Multiple Means of Engagement (The IRIS Center, 2009).

Multiple Means of Representation addresses the way a teacher presents information or lessons to the class. Just as in the previous example with Jeremy, these multiple ways to represent and present material allow students to access information in a manner that supports their learning needs and interests. For example, in a math lesson, a teacher may supplement the lesson with a brief video that reiterates and restates the material and use manipulatives and modeling to demonstrate the concept in a more concrete manner. The teacher could also provide guided notes for the lesson, have students highlight the formula or steps for the math problem, use closed-captioning on the video, and clarify any needed vocabulary and academic language. The more supports provided and built into the lesson, the greater accessibility it has for all students. A student who struggles with receptive language, is an English language learner, or just prefers to have concepts reinforced will benefit from hearing the lesson from the teacher and again in the video. Guided notes help students follow along in the lesson and summarize the main points. Highlighting the formula or steps draws all students' attention to what is important or necessary for completing the assignment. Closed-captioning can be used to support students with hearing issues and to support comprehension with all students. Clarifying vocabulary and academic language helps connect the lesson to students' background knowledge and schema while helping facilitate comprehension. UDL promotes multiple ways for information to be presented or represented in order for the information to be accessible to all students (The IRIS Center, 2009).

Multiple Means of Action and Expression allows students to demonstrate their knowledge and abilities in multiple ways. Rather than a pen-and-paper test or assignment, this principle advocates flexibility in means of assessment (The IRIS Center, 2009). For example, James is a student with poor fine motor skills and horrible penmanship. His teacher uses multiple means of action and expression by allowing James to take his spelling tests in two ways. James takes the written test with the rest of the class, and afterward his teacher reassesses him orally on the words he missed on the written portion. This second oral test allows James to demonstrate his knowledge without the barrier of poor penmanship since the objective is to assess spelling rather than penmanship. Chase, like many students with learning needs, has difficulty memorizing information, including basic math facts. His teacher allows him to compensate for the barrier of memorizing by using a multiplication facts chart on long division problems. In order to receive credit for the problems, Chase must document or show each step in problem (rather than just the answer), but uses the multiplication table to support his difficulty with memorizing math facts. Chase's difficulties with memorizing limits his ability to demonstrate what he knows in terms of long division. Allowing him and all students to use supports increases the expectancy of success and helps address cognitive needs. The key is that these supports are available to all students and not just those identified as having specific learning needs. Multiplication (or addition) charts also help students who may have the facts memorized but are slower to recall them or may be used to self-check answers before submitting the assignment. The objective remains that same (learning spelling and long division), but the supports are provided to all students and allows them to demonstrate their knowledge.

The third principle of UDL is Multiple Means of Engagement. This principle incorporates a variety of different components into lessons to enhance the interest and engagement of individual students (CAST, 2011). Some students are engaged by lessons that are relevant to their lives, culture, and/or connect to their background knowledge and prior learning. Other students need to establish goals or are motivated by learning that is tied to their interests, incorporates projects, or uses different resources or manipulatives. Offering a variety and giving students a choice facilitates

Table 7.12 Ways Teachers Can Meet Students' Cognitive Needs

- Foster an inclusive and supportive classroom.
- Implement teaching strategies, such as Universal Design for Learning.
- Use the ongoing cycle of assessment, analysis, decision-making, and instruction to provide students with the appropriate instruction.
- Connect lessons and learning to students' lives and prior knowledge.
- Incorporate student discussions, activities, and lessons.
- Provide the accommodations and resources as needed and as identified on Individualized Education Programs.

greater engagement in the learning process. Flexibility in providing engagement is necessary to address the needs of each individual student. What interests and engages Juan will not necessarily be what interests and engages Juanita. Juan may be motivated to work independently on a science project while Juanita prefers to work in a group. Allowing students choices in how they complete the project helps further the engagement of Juan, Juanita, and the rest of the class. Linking the lesson to the students' lives, culture, future and prior learning, and interests fosters the sense that the teacher cares about them and motivates them to achieve academically rather than to behave inappropriately.

Making sense of the world is the basis of a student's cognitive needs. Math, science, social studies, and language arts are all attempts to help fulfill these needs, but students must have the needed resources and support to do so. Expectancy theory defines why supports, resources, and strategies, such as UDL, are essential to meeting a student's cognitive need. If motivation is partially based on the expected outcome, as suggested by expectancy theory, then students must believe that they have the skills and resources to be successful and make that outcome positive. When a student believes that the expected outcome will be positive and that they have the skills and support to be successful, then they are more likely to be motivated to perform the task. When teachers incorporate engagement and support into learning, then students tend to achieve academically and behave in a more appropriate manner. See Table 7.12 for ways to meet students' cognitive needs in the classroom.

Aesthetic, Self-Actualization, and Transcendence Needs

The final three types of needs identified by Maslow are aesthetic, self-actualization, and transcendence. These needs help a person appreciate the beauty around them, reach their potential, and give back or support others in reaching their potential. These are lifelong processes that develop over time and with experiences rather than an immediate need that can quickly be meet in the classroom. Schools can help support and address these needs in students through academics, upholding high expectations, and fostering a sense of community and support.

Aesthetic is the need to appreciate the beauty in the world through feeling and enjoying something aesthetically pleasing (McLeod, 2016). Teachers can nurture this through lessons that incorporate and teach an appreciation for nature, arts, and beauty. This can be accomplished through field trips, science and art projects, literature, integrating art, drama, and music into lessons, and allowing students to expand their experiences and appreciation of the beauty of the world around them. Teachers have a unique opportunity to share their own aesthetic appreciation with their students, which in turn helps foster students' aesthetic needs.

Fulfillment of needs (having basic needs meet, feeling safe, loved, and worthy, and developing an understanding of the world) allows a person to progress toward becoming self-actualized. A self-actualized person reaches their full potential and is a lifelong learner. Not everyone becomes self-actualized, and how a person becomes self-actualized differs based on individual interests and abilities (McLeod, 2016). A musician's path toward self-actualization may look different from an accountant's, bus driver's or a teacher's path. Self-actualization does not mean a person is perfect or an expert but that they are achieving their potential. Self-actualization is a goal for schools and the educational system, but is not something a student is likely to achieve during one year in a classroom. It is typically a lifelong process, which few people actually ever achieve. Teachers can help students along the path to self-actualization by setting high expectations, offering support and encouragement, and helping to address other needs (basic survival needs, a feeling of safety, love, and worthiness, and an understanding of the world), which supports them on this journey.

Transcendence is the final or highest of Maslow's needs. It is a person's need to give back and to help others on their own path to self-actualization. This stage allows a person to focus on a higher goal outside of one's self and to become altruistic and principled. In this stage, a person begins to focus on the needs of others rather than on the needs of themselves (McLeod, 2016). Teachers can begin providing a basis for this by teaching collaborative skills, empathy, and compassion. Establishing a cohesive and inclusive classroom environment that encourages and enriches all students can help foster an appreciation and a desire in students to support one another. Teachers and schools can use a curriculum that teaches tolerance and social justice and can encourage students to give back to their schools and community.

It is important for teachers to realize that people across cultures and nationalities experiences the human needs identified by Maslow. When a teacher proactively assists in meeting these needs, it increases a student's motivation to achieve academically and behaviorally. When teachers are not proactive in meeting needs, students may behave in a less than an ideal manner in an attempt to fulfill them. A student may yell out in class in an effort to fulfill a need for attention (love and belonging) or be afraid to ask a question or seek help for fear of being teased or made fun of (safety). Another student may become disengaged and lose focus near lunchtime because they are hungry (physiological and biological) or become a class clown in a desire for prestige (esteem). When teachers proactively meet these needs (providing attention for positive things, building authentic relationships, establishing a safe, secure, and inclusive classroom environment, providing snacks, and using specific feedback for students' strengths and areas of need), students are more likely to be academically engaged and to behave in a manner more conducive to learning.

APPLICATION CASE STUDY 7.2: MASLOW'S NEEDS

Charlie is a student in Mr. Basil's math class. In speaking with Charlie's previous teachers before the beginning of the school year, Mr. Basil learned that Charlie barely passed math last year. He had multiple missing assignments as well as low test scores. These teachers reported that Charlie acted out during lessons in an attempt to be the class clown. He was often sent to the office for disrupting class and had multiple detentions for missing assignments. This year, Mr. Basil decided to be proactive in his approach with Charlie and with all his students. His goal was to design and foster a classroom environment and academic lessons that supported his students in meeting their needs.

Beginning on the first day of class, Mr. Basil worked hard to build authentic relationships with all his students. He greeted them at the door and took an interest in their lives outside the classroom. Extra effort was given to form an authentic relationship with Charlie. Mr. Basil knew that developing this relationship will help Charlie feel more comfortable and cared about in the classroom.

The classroom environment was another area on which Mr. Basil focused additional attention. It was his belief that part of Charlie's motivation to misbehave was due to an embarrassment over his poor math skills. Mr. Basil, therefore, placed emphasis on ensuring that students felt safe, which allowed them to put forth effort and take risks without the fear of embarrassment. Students were encouraged to be supportive, and lessons were often collaborative in nature. This type of environment aided all students, including Charlie, and helped them overcome any discomfort they felt academically.

Mr. Basil knew that relationships and environment were not enough to help students succeed and that providing academic support was also essential. Mr. Basil began the year by screening all his students to determine their strengths and areas of need. Based on those results, he developed lessons that were challenging yet achievable and implemented teaching strategies, such as Universal Design for Learning, to allow students to overcome barriers to their learning. He used an ongoing cycle of assessment and analysis to align lessons to his students' specific needs and provided supports to allow his students to be successful. Although the feedback he provided was specific and allowed students to determine their strengths and needs, he also praised their persistence when faced with challenging problems and situations.

While making a conscious effort to meet Charlie's and the rest of the students' needs, Mr. Basil was increasing the likelihood that all would succeed both academically and behaviorally. Although at times Charlie still had behavioral issues, they were far fewer than in previous years, and his academic gains were far greater. Mr. Basil knew that an ounce of prevention is worth a pound of cure when meeting the needs of his students.

Case Study Comprehension Check

1. Identify the needs Mr. Basil addressed in his classroom and how he proactively designed his classroom to meet those needs.

> *Comprehension Check*
> 1. How do Maslow's needs affect motivation in the classroom?
> 2. Why is it important for teachers to have a proactive plan for helping students meet their needs?
> 3. What can teachers do to proactively address students' physiological and biological needs? Safety needs? Love and belonging needs? Esteem needs? Cognitive needs?

Motivation is one of part of a person's decision to behave in a certain way, but it is not the only contributing factor (Maslow, 1943). It is important, however, for teachers to be aware of the effects of motivation and to proactively address them through intrinsic and extrinsic motivators, student expectations, and providing supports.

> **APPLICATION CASE STUDY 7.3**
>
> Ms. Pepper is a teacher who believes in structure in the classroom. She is very firm in her expectations and strives to have a well-managed classroom. At the beginning of the year, she worked with her students to develop the class rules and procedures, which she strictly enforces. She plans her lessons precisely and details specifically what her students will do and how they will do it. Her students are to sit quietly in their seats and to do their work to the best of their ability. The behavioral and academic expectations in the classroom are high. Ms. Pepper is quick to intervene when behavioral expectations are not met and believes that students should be motivated by an innate and internal desire to learn.
>
> Although most of the students in Ms. Pepper's class adhere to her structure, they often complain that she is mean and her classroom is boring. For the most part, the majority of her students do not have behavioral concerns, with the exception of three students in particular, Rachel, Adam, and Cara.
>
> Rachel is a quiet, shy student. She tends to keep to herself and does not interact often with either Ms. Pepper or her peers. She sits quietly, does not disturb the class, and is not considered a behavior problem, but is on the verge of failing. Rachel is missing numerous in-class and homework assignments, but the work she does complete typically receives a passing grade. Ms. Pepper has observed that if Rachel does not appear to believe she can do well, then she does not attempt the assignment or ask for help. In a parent-teacher conference with Rachel's guardians, Ms. Pepper stated that she believed Rachel would do better if she would ask for help when she needed it. Rachel's guardian shared with Ms. Pepper that last year Rachel was often teased by classmates and made fun of for her looks and academic ability.
>
> Adam is a behavior problem in the classroom. He often talks when he is supposed to be quiet or when the teacher is talking. He is often off task, playing with

items in his desk or bothering a classmate when he is supposed to be working quietly. He is friends with everyone and seems to enjoy being with and talking to other students. He usually completes his assignments and is passing, but Ms. Pepper feels he could do much better if he would just focus on his assignments rather than on what everyone else does in the classroom. Ms. Pepper recently moved Adam's seat to the back of the room and away from his peers in hopes of getting him to work quietly, but this seems to have a limited effect on Adam's behavior and he continues to disrupt the class.

Cara is also a behavior problem. She speaks out in class when she is supposed to be quiet and mumbles under her breath when the teacher is talking. She does not appear to have many friends, but interacts with most of her classmates. Cara is a struggling reader and reads several grades below that of her average peer. She hates to read in the classroom, has failed multiple reading assignments, and appears to have low self-esteem. Ms. Pepper has noticed that Cara's behavior concerns are less apparent in math than in her other academic classes. Cara is passing math but is missing multiple assignments in other classes. Ms. Pepper feels that Cara does not even try academically.

Case Study Comprehension Check

Use expectancy theory and Maslow's needs to answer the following questions from the case study.

1. What could Ms. Pepper do to further motivate the students in her class to achieve both academically and behaviorally?
2. Which of Maslow's needs is Rachel struggling to fulfill in school? Provide specific examples to support your answer.
3. How can Adam's behavior problems be tied to the fulfillment of Maslow's needs?
4. How does expectancy theory relate to both Rachel and Cara's failing grades?

APPLICATION ACTIVITIES

1. Have candidates identify strategies to intrinsically motivate students, and then list extrinsic motivators they could use in their classrooms.
2. Have candidates observe a classroom and identify ways that the teacher motivates students. Identify these strategies as intrinsic or extrinsic motivators, expectancy theory, and/or Maslow's needs.
3. Discuss ways to motivate the following students:
   a. In science class, Josie refuses to do any assignment that involves reading. At times she will complete assignments, such as lab reports, but none that require her to read.

b. Emma often tries to get the teacher's attention. She is usually the last student to leave the classroom and regularly hangs out around the teacher's desk. While academically she is passing, she frequently disrupts class with her comments and questions.
c. At around 1:30 most afternoons, Marc seems to lose focus and has difficulty completing assignments. He does not seem to have the same difficulties in the morning or just after lunch.

CHAPTER SUMMARY

Motivation Influences Behavior

- Humans are typically more motivated to perform behaviors that fulfill a need and/or provide the greatest satisfaction or pleasure.
- Motivation influences behavior but does not necessarily determine which behavior is chosen.

Types of Motivation

- Intrinsic motivation means that the inspiration to complete the behavior comes from the task or behavior itself.
- The person completes the task because the task itself fulfills a need or provides satisfaction.
- Students are intrinsically motivated through engaging and interesting lessons.
- If students are engaged in the lesson, then they are less likely to engage in inappropriate behavior.
- Extrinsic motivation is when the task is not inspiring but a means to an end or leads to something that is inspiring.
  - A teacher may use the Premack principle as an extrinsic motivator for a less desirable behavior. If a student does what the teacher wants, then the student can do what they want.
  - Teachers often use positive and negative reinforcers.
  - Extrinsic motivators can be effective but tend not to permanently change behavior.

Theories of Motivation

- Expectancy theory focuses on the outcomes and whether a person views the effort to perform a task is worth the outcome it may bring.
  - The motivation is based on three variables.
    - Expectancy
      - Based on one's belief in their skills or ability as well as the resources and supports available.
      - The key is the student's, not the teacher's, belief in the possibility of success.
      - Students must believe that their efforts will result in some academic or behavioral gain and, if they struggle, that the teacher will provide support.

- Instrumentality
  - Deals with the recognition and whether the effort to complete the task will actually produce the anticipated results.
  - Instrumentality influences motivation by examining the anticipation of an outcome or result.
  - Based on a person's degree of confidence that their performance or behavior will result in the anticipated outcome or lead to the expected consequence.
- Valence
  - The value a person attributes to that outcome.
  - Determines the significance of the anticipated outcome to a person, which helps determine if the task or behavior is worth the effort.
  - Valence can be intrinsic, such as a feeling of satisfaction for a job well done, or it can be extrinsic, such as a positive reward or negative consequence.
- A person decides which behavior to perform based on their belief in their ability to perform the task (expectancy), the predicted recognition or outcome of that task (instrumentality), and the value, either positive or negative, of the anticipated outcome (valence).
- Maslow's hierarchy of needs states that motivation is based on a desire to fulfill certain needs. The needs include the following:
  - Physiological and biological needs are the essential survival needs of the human body.
    - If a student is deficient in any of these needs, then the motivation to fulfill that need may overpower other needs.
    - Some physical needs can and must be fulfilled within the classroom and school.
  - Safety needs
    - Student must feel safe and secure both physically and emotionally at school.
    - Teachers must be the authority figure who ensures students' sense of safety.
  - Love and belonging needs
    - This means that students need an inclusive classroom where all students feel a sense of affiliation, acceptance, and support.
  - Esteem needs
    - Students must feel that they are worthy.
    - Teachers contribute to meeting this need through their interactions and relationships with students and also by acknowledging students' strengths and accomplishments.
    - Esteem needs can also be met by providing specific feedback on students' strengths and needs.
    - Ownership in the classroom can be made by giving students the opportunity to make choices.
  - Cognitive needs
    - These needs are based on a person's desire to learn.

- Teachers must have engaging lessons and provide needed support.
    - Universal Design for Learning is based on flexibility in the classroom that allows teaching, learning, and engagement to happen in multiple ways within the same lesson in order to support and interest students.
    - The three principles in Universal Design for Learning include Multiple Means of Representation, Multiple Means of Action and Expression, and Multiple Means of Engagement.
- Aesthetic, self-actualization, and transcendence needs
    - An appreciation of the beauty in the world.
    - The purpose for fulfilling a person's needs is that it allows them to progress toward becoming self-actualized.
    - Transcendence is a person's need to give back and to help others on their path to self-actualization.

REFERENCES

Cambridge English Dictionary. (2018). *Motivate.* Retrieved from https://dictionary.cambridge.org/us/dictionary/english/motivate

CAST. (2011). *Universal design for learning guidelines version 2.0.* Wakefield, MA: Author.

The IRIS Center. (2009). Universal design for learning: Creating a learning environment that challenges and engages all students. Retrieved from http://iris.peabody.vanderbilt.edu/udl/

Maslow, A. H. (1943). A theory of human motivation. *Psychological Review, 50*(4), 370–396.

Maslow, A. H. (1970a). *Motivation and personality.* New York, NY: Harper & Row.

Maslow, A. H. (1970b). *Religions, values, and peak experiences.* New York, NY: Penguin. (Original work published 1964)

McLeod, S. A. (2016). Maslow's hierarchy of needs. Retrieved from www.simplypsychology.org/maslow.html

Sachau, D. (2016). *Salem press encyclopedia of health.* Database, Research Starters. Hackensack, NJ.

Tay, L., & Diener, E. (2011). Needs and subjective well-being around the world. *Journal of Personality and Social Psychology, 101*(2), 354.

Vroom, V. H. (1964). *Work and motivation.* San Francisco, CA: Jossey-Bass.

Weinstein, C., Tomlinson-Clarke, S., & Curran, M. (2004). Toward a conception of culturally responsive classroom management. *Journal of Teacher Education, 55*(1), 25–38.

8

GROUP STRATEGIES FOR IMPROVING AND MAINTAINING APPROPRIATE BEHAVIOR

Jennifer T. Christman

CHAPTER OBJECTIVES

After reading this chapter, students should be able to:

1. Describe the importance and use of group strategies to improve and maintain positive behavior.
2. Explain common causes of problem behaviors.
3. Name and describe several academic and behavioral interventions to improve behavior.
4. Distinguish between types of group contingency plans and the benefit of each.
5. Discuss social skills that influence school behavior and how to teach these social skills in a group setting.
6. Identify critical questions regarding behavior management to seek answers prior to the first day of school as a new teacher.

As you have learned from previous chapters, the three-tiered model allows for increasing levels of support provided for students to meet different needs. In Chapter 4, you learned about whole-school positive behavior supports. The supports, when effectively implemented in a schoolwide program, provide enough structure to meet the needs of 80% to 85% of the student body. Most students comply with schoolwide rules, understand procedural protocols, demonstrate effective self-control, and are behaviorally successful in the school setting. However, for the remaining 15% to 20% of the student body, more supports are needed, and this additional scaffolding comes from group strategies designed to improve or maintain positive behaviors. Often whole-group or class-wide plans are implemented for all students, but there are modifications made for a smaller set of students who require more specific behavioral supports.

Throughout this chapter, we will examine group strategies for management. These strategies may be implemented in a whole-class setting or among other small subgroups of the student body. These strategies are in addition to the schoolwide supports explained in Chapter 4. Remember, as you increase in intensity in a three-tier system, the supports in each tier supplement the previous supports; they do not replace the supports from previous tiers.

GROUP STRATEGIES TO INCREASE POSITIVE BEHAVIORS

Research has shown that with the effective implementation of Schoolwide Positive Behavior Support (SWPBS), rule infractions, office referrals, and bullying can be reduced (Sugai & Horner, 2006). However, SWPBS strategies do not eliminate all problem behaviors. There remains a need for teachers to implement effective classroom and group strategies in addition to schoolwide strategies. Before addressing the components and strategies for group behavior management, it is necessary to identify *why* there is a need for continued behavioral supports. Chapter 4 introduced functional behavioral assessments, and you will learn about these assessment tools in detail in Chapter 14. However, it is necessary to have a preliminary understanding that functional behavioral assessments provide a framework to identify the purpose (function) behind a behavior that a student repeatedly performs. It is important to understand that any behavior that is occurring repeatedly over time is being reinforced.

CASE STUDY 8.1

Andrew is a sixth-grade student. He consistently does not turn in his homework. When he has not turned in his homework, he is told to stay in from recess to complete his missing work. He satisfactorily completes the work in the amount of time given to him. After several weeks of noticing a pattern of this, Mrs. Watkins talked to Andrew about his repeated missing assignments and, after a lengthy conversation, she discovered that he was being bullied at recess when he was permitted to play. Staying in from recess to complete his missing assignments allowed him to avoid the bullying on the playground.

Sometimes a simple conversation can lead to answers as to why a student is performing a problem behavior repeatedly. At other times, functional behavioral assessment is needed to look for patterns. This process allows the behavior assessor (classroom teacher, school psychologist, special education teacher, administrator) to discover patterns in the behavior to identify the function for an undesirable behavior and then, ideally, to determine a behavior that is more desirable to replace it. Throughout this process, there remains a need to recognize that a statistically significant predictor of school performance is engagement (Appleton, Christenson, & Furlong, 2008). The more students are engaged in learning, classroom activities, and school community, the less frequently behavior problems occur and the greater degree of school achievement and success is attained.

In response to the knowledge that positive engagement decreases the need for behavioral supports, teachers must be sure to implement evidence-based practices in their instruction to reduce the need to provide additional behavioral supports. We will discuss several practices that support academic engagement and then discuss practices for behavioral support within group settings. In conclusion of this chapter, we will discuss how to plan for the start of a new school year as an entry-year teacher.

Comprehension Check
1. When would a teacher use group or class-wide behavior strategies?
2. What is a function of behavior?
3. What trait is a significant predictor of school achievement?

GROUP STRATEGIES TO INCREASE ACADEMIC ENGAGEMENT

Academic engagement reduces the need for behavior supports in the classroom (Appleton et al., 2008). To engage students, content presented must be appropriate to their readiness (based on skill and development) and presented in authentic ways. Many times, students lack engagement in academic content because the material does not seem accessible to them. This may be because the material is too difficult or is presented in a way that does not meet the needs of students or the students do not have background experiences to relate to the new content. It is the teacher's job to connect the subject matter to each student. This is achieved by providing strategies that increase engagement, thus making the new content accessible to all learners and simultaneously reducing behavioral interruptions in the classroom.

Evidence-based practices (EBPs) were created in response to the increased accountability demands on teachers. Teachers must justify what they are teaching (through curriculum) and how they are teaching and intervening (through EBPs). However, EBPs are difficult to define. To date, researchers and professional organizations have been working to clearly define what constitutes an EBP. The community agrees that EBPs are research-validated practices that consistently yield positive results for students (Simenson, Fairbanks, Briesch, Myers, & Sugai, 2008); however, it is debatable as to what constitutes research validated. Horner et al. (2005) determined parameters for single-subject design research to be identified as EBP, yet there are other types of research methods that are not included within these parameters. It would be impossible to provide an exhaustive list of academic supports that increase student engagement in the classroom, but we will identify several commonly used practices. In this next section, we will consider group strategies to increase academic engagement that are evidence-based.

Guided notes are teacher-created notes with blanks throughout the notes and are designed for the students to record an appropriate answer as the teacher is lecturing, reading aloud, or the student is reading independently. This increases the student's attentiveness by requiring engagement in the content presented and highlights the

> Providing a worksheet such as this to students during lectures can help to increase academic engagement and can lead to fewer disruptive behaviors. This is an example based on a junior high or high school chemistry lecture. This can be modified to have more blanks, fewer blanks or a word bank also.
>
> 1. All elements in the periodic table are _____ into groups based on similar _____.
> 2. All elements are listed in order of increasing _____ number.
> 3. The atomic number is the number of _____ in each atom.
> 4. Each element has its own _____ and _____.
> 5. An element is a _____ substance made from a single type of _____.

Figure 8.1 Guided Notes—Chemistry Lesson

main ideas; after the lesson, the student has a complete set of notes. This is similar to the cloze procedure in which a teacher provides a paragraph with key words eliminated. Students are required to complete the paragraph by filling in appropriate words using context clues. (See Figure 8.1 for an example of guided notes.) For teachers who find themselves dealing with repeated problem behaviors during lectures, presentations, independent reading, or whole-class read aloud, guided notes could be helpful in providing students with a requirement for active engagement.

The use of computer and application technology has increased the accessibility of curriculum for many students. Along with increased accessibility, technology also provides teachers with opportunities to increase engagement (Wardlow, 2016). Students are drawn to this type of technology, and as quickly as this field has grown, we know that technology skills have become lifelong skills. Advanced education and many professions require the use of computer and/or application technology, and the prerequisite skills are being taught as early as elementary school. With this in mind, allowing students access to different types of technology for various purposes is beneficial. Many classrooms are equipped with interactive white boards. These displays are touch sensitive, connected to the internet, and allow students to engage in content in new ways. Students can write on worksheets, manipulate objects, solve problems, browse the internet, hear stories read aloud, use their bodies to interact with subject matter, and much more, all on a large projection screen. This style of learning increases engagement because students are using different parts of their brain (along with their bodies) through movement, music, physical interactions, and the like to increase understanding. In addition to interactive white boards, many classrooms also have student computers, and some are one-to-one devices (one piece of technology per student). The accessibility of these devices allows for unlimited access to students. When students are unsure of how to solve a problem, answer a question, or confirm a hypothesis, the technology resources are available to do so, therefore allowing students greater access to and engagement in the content presented.

Peer tutoring is another EBP that has been shown to increase academic engagement (Simenson et al., 2008). When students are struggling with material, often it is the presentation of the material that provides the greatest hindrance to their understanding of the content. When an alternative teacher (a peer tutor) presents the same information but in a different format, comprehension can increase. Although this benefits the learner, it also benefits the peer tutor. Students who understand a concept can help other students, deepening understanding for the tutor because teaching increases the teacher's own understanding and engagement. The tutoring relationship increases engagement because the student who is the tutor feels the need to maximize their understanding of the concept in order to effectively reteach the information. For the recipient, the content is presented again but in a different style that optimizes the opportunities to learn. Coinciding with peer tutoring is the concept of pre-teaching and re-teaching. These two techniques are used to increase engagement because students have greater access to and understanding of the content presented. Pre-teaching is a technique used with students who are at risk of struggling with a concept. The teacher can anticipate this struggle because of pre-test data, previous knowledge of student weaknesses, knowledge of a learning disability or other academically challenging disability, knowledge of challenges because the student is an English language learner, and so on. It occurs prior to the presentation of the content to the whole class, focuses on vocabulary and content development, and prepares students for upcoming lessons, thereby leveling the playing field in advance of the lesson for students who may be at risk of struggling. Once pre-teaching has occurred, engagement increases during whole-class presentation of information because students are able to make connections to what is being taught. Re-teaching is similar in that students who are at risk of academic challenges receive the content again after the lesson. This provides an opportunity to emphasize critical information, expand student understanding to an application level (by posing such questions as "What does this mean to you?" or "Why is this important to know?"), and answer clarification questions.

A common, overarching theme among these group strategies to increase academic engagement is that these strategies are techniques recommended in the Universal Design for Learning philosophy. Universal Design for Learning is an approach to teaching that provides a variety of ways for students to represent, engage, and express content and assessments and allows them to work to their personal strengths in order to optimize learning. It is important to again recognize that such enhanced academic engagement techniques decrease the need for behavioral supports in the classroom.

Comprehension Check
1. Describe one evidence-based practice that can be used to increase academic engagement in the classroom.
2. How is peer tutoring beneficial to both the provider and the recipient?
3. Why is it important to examine the academic engagement of students when assessing behavioral needs?

MOVING BEYOND ACADEMIC SUPPORTS TO BEHAVIORAL SUPPORTS

As the teacher continues to work with academic interventions in the classroom and to use an ongoing assessment cycle, as shown in Figure 8.2, they may recognize that additional supports are needed. Conversely, they may realize that students are successful and, in this case, more intensive supports are not needed. However, if SWPBS strategies are insufficient, behavior management supports and EBPs have been implemented to assure engagement in the content and the behavior problems persist, there are specific behavior change strategies that may now be implemented. These strategies are used to increase positive behaviors and to decrease negative behaviors in the classroom and other school settings. A teacher may choose to implement whole-class strategies for all students but may need to modify the plan to meet the needs of students who require more intensive supports. The following strategies have been used to increase desired behaviors in a group setting.

Reinforcing positive behaviors is an ethically and fundamentally sound strategy to increase desirable behaviors. It is important to identify desirable behaviors, notice when they are occurring, and reinforce them. As discussed in Chapter 4, it is necessary to establish what is reinforcing for students. There may be some students who are reinforced with a sticker and others who do not care about stickers, so using them as reinforcement would not be effective. Likewise, some students seek teacher attention and acknowledging behaviors with praise is effective ("Lucy, great job completing the spelling test with excellent handwriting. I can tell you tried your best!") while others may shy away from adult attention and withhold positive behaviors to avoid the attention given through praise. Knowing what is most effective with individual students is essential to attaining the greatest benefits from reinforcement.

One strategy of group positive behavior supports that uses reinforcement is the Good Behavior Game. Originally researched in 1969, the Good Behavior Game uses a team approach of competing for a reward (Barrish, Saunders, & Wold, 1969). This game is an EBP and claims successes in improved behavior and school readiness skills, along with substance abuse prevention, reduction of criminal activities, and improved academic output (see goodbehaviorgame.org). In the classroom setting, students are divided into two teams, and teams receive points when any one of the team members engages in behaviors that do not follow the predetermined classroom rules. At the end of a designated time, the team with the fewest points is rewarded. If both teams keep

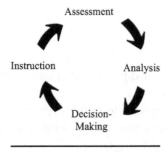

Figure 8.2 Ongoing Cycle of Response to Intervention

their point accumulation below a predetermined standard, both are rewarded. This system teaches "self-regulation, self-control, and self-management in the context of collaborating with others for peace, productivity, health and happiness" (Paxis Institute, 2018). Discussed previously as a key to successful positive behavior supports, the essential elements to the Good Behavior Game are that the students generate the list of rules to be followed and the teacher systematically teaches what is expected of the students through examples and non-examples.

Another group strategy to increase positive behaviors and to decrease negative behaviors in the classroom is the use of a token system. Tokens are used in many classrooms and most often are part of a token economy system. A token economy system is a procedure of earning coins or tokens that are accumulated and redeemed to purchase a reward. This system encourages students to delay gratification because the rewards that are received in exchange for tokens increase in perceived value as the number of earned tokens increases over time. These tokens (coins, poker chips) can be exchanged for tangible items, such as a small trinket or piece of candy, or non-tangible items, such as lunch with the teacher or a positive phone call home. There are digital versions of this system available through internet applications. In such formats, students receive points, and student avatars are projected on a large screen. Students watch as classmates earn points, and parents can check on how many points their child has earned throughout the day from their own digital devices. On a more basic level, a sticker chart for positive behaviors serves a similar purpose for younger students. Students keep sticker charts at their desks or on folders and can earn stickers for positive behaviors. The value of stickers earned transfers to opportunities to "shop" for items. This process can be modified to meet the individual needs of students. See Application Case Study 8.2 for an example of this differentiation. See Figure 8.3 for an example of a token economy plan with differentiation.

Possible ways to earn tokens:
- Completed homework
- Planner signed
- In seat before bell rings
- Quiet work
- Helping a classmate
- Excellent work
- Honorable behavior (stopping bullying, helping someone in need, reporting a serious problem)

Shopping occurs on Fridays and some rewards may include:
- Piece of candy: 10 tokens
- Trinket: 10 tokens
- Homework pass: 15 tokens
- Positive phone call/note home: 20 tokens
- Extra recess with a friend: 30 tokens
- Lunch with a favorite teacher: 30 tokens
- Lead the Pledge of Allegiance on the morning announcements: 30 tokens
- Principal for the Day: 50 Tokens

Figure 8.3 Token Economy Plan for Fifth Grade

> Here are some sensory support ideas that can be implemented in a whole class setting or a smaller group setting:
> - Jumping jacks
> - Push-ups (on the floor or on the wall)
> - Walk in a figure 8 around the classroom
> - Play with playdough, clay or putty
> - Moving heavy objects
> - Passing a weighted ball
> - Resistance bands
> - Going outside for a walk
> - Playground time
> - Calming music
> - Dance music
> - Gum or other chewy candy

Figure 8.4 Group Sensory Break Ideas

Another strategy that can be used to increase engagement and to decrease undesirable classroom behaviors is the use of sensory breaks. These breaks are often called brain breaks and provide students with a respite from the cognitive demands of school and, upon refocusing, an improved the ability to concentrate. The use of sensory breaks has been researched over time, and there are various opinions as to the value in them. However, there is an agreement that there is no harm in them and that they are implemented unintentionally by children and adults alike. Often when adults are in stressful situations, working hard on a project, or attempting to complete a difficult task, they may chew gum, pace the hallway, take a brief walk, or take a few deep breaths. All these strategies help refresh the body and refocus the mind. Similar strategies can be taught to students as a means of self-regulation. Teachers have found that encouraging students to take a break and to regulate their bodies through systematic movements provides them with a greater ability to maintain focus on work. There are class-wide benefits when this type of break is intentionally scheduled into the routine. See Figure 8.4 for a list of possible sensory break activities.

Several of these strategies can be implemented through a group contingency system. With group contingency, all students in a group are presented with an opportunity, and attaining the opportunity is dependent on performance. There are three types of group contingency plans: dependent, independent, and interdependent. In dependent contingency plans, every student must meet a predetermined standard or none of the students receive the opportunity that is being worked toward. An independent contingency plan requires each student to work toward a predetermined standard, and those students who meet the standard receive the opportunity presented. Those students who do not meet the standard do not receive the opportunity. Finally, an interdependent contingency plan outlines individual tasks or standards that must be met, and for anyone to earn the opportunity provided, everyone must meet their standard or complete their task (Litoe & Pumro, 1975).

> *Comprehension Check*
> 1. Why is it important to know what is reinforcing to individual students?
> 2. Explain one group strategy to increase positive behaviors in the classroom.
> 3. Explain the differences among dependent, independent, and interdependent group contingency plans.

SOCIAL SKILLS TRAINING TO INCREASE POSITIVE BEHAVIORS IN A GROUP SETTING

As discussed in previous chapters, direct instruction on skills that enhance positive behaviors becomes necessary. Improved social skills can increase positive behaviors among students, and they may be taught at a schoolwide level (see Chapter 4) as well as at classroom or group levels. Some of the skills that can be addressed through social skills training are empathy, self-regulation, and de-escalation.

Empathy allows a person to understand and share the feelings of another (*Merriam-Webster Dictionary*, 2018). Also referred to as emotional intelligence, empathy is present when someone feels sad when a friend is suffering. This ability is essential in friendships and in inclusive classrooms. When individuals lack empathy, they are often seen as uncaring, insensitive, or thoughtless. Teaching empathy through direct instruction can improve the classroom climate and encourage an acceptance of differences. A few strategies that are helpful in teaching empathy at an elementary level are to label feelings, talk about feelings, encourage problem-solving, model empathetic behaviors, and talk about similarities between students ("Yes, you look different from a classmate, but let's look at how many ways you are similar."). With older students, many of the elementary strategies can be helpful combined with teaching moral development, encouraging internal motivation rather than external motivation, discussing antagonists and protagonists in literature and the traits that categorize them as such, and the messages portrayed through nonverbal communication ("What are you communicating to a teacher when you put your head down during class and play on your phone?" "How would that make you feel if you were having a conversation with someone and that is how they behaved?")

"Self-regulation is the ability to monitor and control our own behavior, emotions, or thoughts, altering them in accordance with the demands of the situation" (Cook & Cook, 2009). This skill is developmentally advanced for many students; however, it is encouraged at a young age because it is the impetus to self-control and self-management. Self-regulation is often taught through simulations and direct instruction. An example of self-regulation is the awareness that when on the basketball court a person makes the winning shot at the final second of the game, because they are thrilled with excitement, it is appropriate to jump up and fist pump the air and scream, "Yes!" However, when the teacher passes back final exams and, after studying for very long hours, a student has earned a fantastic score on the final, it is not appropriate to show excitement in a manner similar to the situation on the basketball court. In this case, a small smile, perhaps a deep breath and sharing this good news with your parents when you arrive home after school, is much more appropriate for the latter situation. The ability to recognize feelings and to adapt personal responses to those feelings in varying social contexts is necessary to be a socially adept member of society. Concurrently, although recognizing feelings and situationally appropriate responses is important, it is also important to analyze personal de-escalation techniques. Personal de-escalation is the prevention technique individuals use to calm themselves down. In avoiding personal escalation, they are encouraging themselves to remain in control of themselves and to be peaceful. Teaching students to walk away from an upsetting situation, take deep breaths, ask for a break to bounce on a sensory ball, request a break to walk to the drinking fountain, or even, if necessary, request a pass to visit the school counselor can all be beneficial. Personal de-escalation techniques are skills and learning strategies that are effective at a young age and that can prove to be helpful throughout life.

It is important to recognize how social skills affect behavior in school. Social behavior is influenced by many factors (culture, teacher behavior, experiences, academic readiness, social aptitude), and some of these dynamics can be enhanced through direct instruction. Social skills instruction is an area of behavior management that can be influenced by a proactive rather than a reactive approach. As social aptitude increases among students, the classroom culture becomes more positive and there is an increase in access to more challenging content because more time and attention is spent on academic learning rather than on behavior management.

The First Week of School

The tone of the school year is set in the first several days. The teacher's role in designing an inclusive classroom and teacher behavior motivates or discourages students. Uniting that knowledge with the previous content about group strategies, begin to formulate a personal classroom. What elements create an inclusive classroom? What strategies are important to implement from day one to ensure that positive behaviors shine in your classroom? What approaches are effective in teaching social skills? As teachers begins to formulate answers to these questions, it is important to recognize that some of the answers will come through trial and error. Some strategies work consistently; some work with some students but not with others; some will work some years of teaching and will not in other years. Students will change, and the work environment will change. However, what does remain constant is that students rely on the teacher for consistency and that consistency begins on day one.

Before the first day of school in a new building, inquire about how SWPBS strategies are implemented. When unfamiliar with the program that is used, spend time researching it, ask to be trained, talk to veteran teachers about how it runs, and educate yourself. Next, seek out suggestions on how classroom and group strategies are run in the building. Do teachers decide what strategies will be used in their classroom, or is there an expectation that a protocol will be followed? How should data be taken when there are concerns about student behavior? Who provides supports in such situations? What behavior problems are typically seen in the school? Are there any children in your classroom who have specific behavior needs or plans that must be addressed? After gathering as much information as possible (without gossiping about students' reputations and the like), design a plan that will fit the needs of the students, that will align with the philosophy of the building and your knowledge and preferences, and that you feel confident implementing. Remember, it can be a work in progress, but having some foundation from day one is important.

> *Comprehension Check*
> 1. Discuss one social skill that can be taught through direct instruction that can yield positive behaviors in the classroom. How would you teach this skill in your classroom?
> 2. How is personal de-escalation used throughout life?
> 3. Why is it important to be proactive in teaching social skills in the classroom?
> 4. What knowledge regarding behavior management should you seek out prior to the first day of school?

> **APPLICATION CASE STUDY 8.2**
>
> Mrs. Laurel has 26 students in her first-grade classroom at West Putnam Elementary. It is an eclectic group of six and seven-year-olds. She has students who are working above grade level, those working at grade level, and those working below grade level as well as five students who receive special education services, two students who are English language learners, and one student who is currently receiving home instruction because of a significant medical issue. West Putnam Elementary School implements a Schoolwide Positive Behavior Support system that uses stickers to reinforce positive behaviors.
>
> In Mrs. Laurel's classroom, all students have opportunities to earn stickers on a sticker chart. Each student tapes their sticker chart on their take-home folder. This serves as a strategy for parent communication as well as for classroom behavior management. Four of Mrs. Laurel's students receive special education services in a resource room for language arts and mathematics. The students take their folders to the resource room and can earn stickers there as well. Of the four students who receive instruction in the resource room, two, Molly and Ben, are on specific behavior plans and receive behavioral support through a behavioral intervention plan. As documented on their plans, Molly and Ben are permitted to shop at the treasure box with their stickers on Mondays, Wednesdays, and Fridays. They must earn 10 stickers per day to be able to shop. The other students are required to have earned 40 stickers throughout the whole week to shop at the treasure box. Mrs. Laurel fills her treasure box with homework and lunch passes and donated restaurant child's meal prizes, trinkets, stickers, and candy.
>
> Mrs. Laurel builds in supports for one student, Fiona, who is struggling to attend during whole-class instruction. Fiona currently receives special education

services for a learning disability but does not receive behavioral support and is fully included in the general education classroom setting. Fiona gets out of her seat often, wanders around the classroom, requests visits to the restroom multiple times during a class, doodles in textbooks, and chats frequently to her neighbors. Mrs. Laurel is frustrated with these behaviors and is not sure how to proceed because she feels that the special education teacher should be removing Fiona from the general education classroom and teaching her in a small-group setting in the resource room.

At 10:00 every day, the students transition from math instruction and independent work to literacy centers. During the transition, Mrs. Laurel plays a song that requires the students to move in certain ways (walk in a circle, crawl like a bear, hop like a frog) and then tip-toe to their assigned literacy centers. During this transition time, the students wiggle, giggle, and relax prior to refocusing when the literacy centers begin. Mrs. Laurel has found that this proactive strategy serves as a positive influence on students and improves concentration during literacy centers. When literacy centers are over, before transitioning to lunch Mrs. Laurel has a group read aloud. Mrs. Laurel emphasizes a certain character trait each month beginning at the start of the school year. (This month the students are working on empathy.) During group read aloud, Mrs. Laurel reads a book about empathy and then has a class meeting to talk about the importance of empathy.

At the end of the day, Mrs. Laurel feels like she has done what she can to teach the necessary academic skills, challenge the students who are achieving above grade level, support those students who are learning below grade level, manage behaviors in the classroom and throughout the school building, and encourage positive character development among her class. She knows that there is always room for improvement and approaches each day as a fresh start.

Case Study Comprehension Check

Apply what you have learned in Chapter 8 to this case study.

1. Is it fair that Ben and Molly get to shop at the class treasure box more often than the other students? Why or why not?
2. Is it fair that Molly and Ben have to earn more tickets, on average, than the other students? Why or why not? Why would a teacher make the number of tickets required for a prize different for some students?
3. Mrs. Laurel feels that Fiona should be pulled out for specialized instruction with the special education teacher. Assume the role of the general education teacher, Mrs. Laurel, or the special education teacher and have a debate with a classmate. Where should Fiona be educated? How is this decision made? Who is "right" in this situation?
4. Provide Mrs. Laurel with a suggestion to improve her classroom.

APPLICATION ACTIVITIES

1. In a field experience, identify group plans for positive behavior support. What strategies do teachers use to increase engagement with students, and what strategies are used to specifically address behavioral concerns? Are proactive group contingency strategies implemented in the classroom?
2. Continue to research evidence-based practices for positive behavior supports in the classroom. What are three new strategies you learned that are not covered in this text? How would you use these new strategies to help learners in your classroom?

CHAPTER SUMMARY

Increase Positive Behaviors

- There is a need for teachers to implement effective classroom and group strategies to increase positive behaviors.
  - Why is there a continued need for behavior supports?
- The functional behavioral assessment provides a framework to identify the purpose behind the behavior the student is exhibiting.
  - Any behavior that occurs repetitively is being reinforced.
  - The functional behavioral assessment is needed to discover challenging behavior patterns and to identify more desirable replacement behaviors.
  - A key predictor of school performance is engagement.

Increase Academic Achievement

- The teacher must make the content accessible to each student.
  - Provide strategies to increase engagement, making all content to be accessible to all learners, which in turn will reduce the negative behavior that may arise in the classroom.
- Teachers must justify their teaching strategies through evidence-based practices.
- Group strategies that increase engagement in the classroom include the following:
  - Guided notes are teacher-created notes with blanks throughout the notes for students to follow along and write in the appropriate answers.
  - In the cloze procedure, the teacher provides a paragraph with key words eliminated for students to fill in the appropriate words using context clues.
  - Application technology has increased the accessibility of curriculum for students.
  - Allowing students access to different types of technology is beneficial to their learning experience and enhances engagement in class content.
  - Peer tutoring is another way to improve student engagement.
  - Comprehension can increase when students hear the same content from a different person in a different format.
  - This provides further opportunities for both the tutor and the learner to engage in the content a second time, in a fresh way that enhances knowledge on the information.

- All these strategies are techniques used in the Universal Design for Learning philosophy.
  - Universal Design for Learning is an approach to teaching that provides a variety of ways to represent, engage, and express content to optimize learning.

Strategies Used to Increase Desired Behaviors in a Group Setting

- Reinforcing positive behaviors is a sound strategy that increases desirable behaviors.
  - Knowing what is most effective for your students is vital.
- The Good Behavior Game is an evidence-based practice.
  - This strategy uses a team-based approach to compete for rewards.
  - It teaches students to work toward valued goals, how to cooperate, and how to self-regulate while learning and having fun.
- A token economy system is a procedure of earning tokens that are accumulated and used to purchase rewards.
  - Digital versions are available through internet applications.
  - A sticker chart can serve a similar purpose for younger students.
- Sensory breaks, also known as brain breaks, are used to provide students with a break from the cognitive demands of school and a chance to refocus after.
- In a group contingency, all students in the group are given an opportunity, and the availability to achieve this opportunity is based on performance.
  - The three types of group contingency plans include dependent, independent, and interdependent.

Social Skills Training

- Empathy
  - Teaching empathy through direct instruction can improve the classroom climate and encourage an acceptance of differences.
  - At an elementary level, strategies that are helpful in teaching empathy are to label feelings, talk about feelings, encourage problem-solving, model empathetic behaviors, and talk about similarities between students.
  - With older students encourage internal motivation, discuss antagonists and protagonists, and review the messages portrayed through nonverbal communication.
- Self-regulation
  - Self-regulation is often taught through simulations and direct instruction.
  - It is the ability to recognize feelings and adapt responses to those feelings in an appropriate manner that is necessary to be socially aware.
- Personal de-escalation techniques
  - These techniques are used to calm down and to remain in control.
  - They are lifelong skills.
  - Learning these strategies at a young age can be helpful when personal escalation arises.

REFERENCES

Appleton, J., Christenson, S., & Furlong, M. (2008). Student engagement with school: Critical conceptual and methodological issues of the construct. *Psychology in the Schools, 45*, 369–386.

Barrish, H. H., Saunders, M., & Wold, M. M. (1969). Good behavior game: Effects of individual contingencies for group consequences on disruptive behavior in a classroom. *Journal of Applied Behavior Analysis, 2*, 119–124.

Cook, J. L., & Cook, G. (2009). *Child development: Principles and perspectives.* Upper Saddle River, NY: Pearson.

Horner, R. H., Carr, E. G., Halle, J., McGee, G., Odom, S., & Wolery, M. (2005). The use of single subject research to identify evidence-based practice in special education. *Exceptional Children, 71*, 165–180.

Litoe, L., & Pumroy, D. K. (1975). Brief technical report: A brief review of classroom group oriented contingencies. *Journal of Applied Behavior Analysis, 2*, 341–347.

Merriam-Webster Dictionary. (2018). *Empathy.* Retrieved from www.merriam-webster.com/dictionary/empathy

Paxis Institute. (2018). *What is it about?* Retrieved from http://goodbehaviorgame.org/about

Simenson, B., Fairbanks, S., Briesch, A., Myers, D., & Sugai, G. (2008). Evidence-based practices in classroom management: Considerations for research to practice. *Education and Treatment of Children, 31*, 351–380.

Sugai, G., & Horner, R. (2006). A promising approach for expanding and sustaining school-wide positive behavior support. *School Psychology Review, 35*, 245–259.

Wardlow, L. (2016). *How technology can boost student engagement.* Retrieved from www.pearsoned.com/education-blog/technology-can-boost-student-engagement/

9

STRATEGIES FOR DECREASING BEHAVIOR CHALLENGES IN THE CLASSROOM

Jennifer T. Christman

CHAPTER OBJECTIVES

After reading this chapter, students should be able to:

1. Discuss several strategies used to decrease the occurrence of behavior challenges in the classroom.
2. Initiate several strategies used to decrease the occurrence of behavior challenges in the classroom.

When you consider classrooms in which you have observed, you will recognize that not all problems are solved through the strategies provided to you in this text thus far. There will be students whose behavioral needs are not yet met with the best practices implemented in the classroom. Challenging behaviors occur in all classrooms. Some classrooms have more challenging behaviors, and some have behaviors that are of greater intensity or severity, but all classrooms have some form of challenging behaviors. The teacher's response, interventions implemented, and the supports executed shape whether these behaviors continue or discontinue. As you have learned in previous chapters and will continue to explore in depth in Chapter 14, every behavior serves a purpose or has a function. When the intervention is linked to the same function that the problem behavior served, the success of the intervention increases (Gable, Park, & Scott, 2014). Knowing this, it is difficult to say, "If this is the problem in your classroom, then fix it by doing this" because the same behavior can serve different functions for different students or even the same student at different times. However, the strategies we will discuss in this chapter are commonly used and can help reduce challenging behaviors.

STRATEGIES FOR ALL LEARNERS

Behavior problems increase when students do not comprehend content or engage in instruction. The use of visuals in the classroom can increase both comprehension and engagement. This is especially important for students who are non-readers, emergent readers, or those students for whom English is not their native language. Items in the classroom can be labeled (see Figure 9.2 for an example), the class schedule can have both words and pictures (see Figure 9.3 for an example), and individual student schedules can have visuals (see Figure 9.4 for an example). Small pictures can be embedded into instructions, simple sign language can be used to communicate silent needs (a student signing "restroom" rather than disrupting class to announce the need to use the restroom), a teacher using a universal sign for "quiet" (one hand in the air and one finger from the other hand over lips rather than "sssssshhhhhhhhh" and adding additional noise to the classroom), or color-coding (green folders go home daily, or all red items belong to Thomas). All these examples are strategies to help increase comprehension and/or engagement in the classroom.

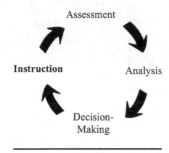

Figure 9.1 Ongoing Cycle of Response to Intervention

Figure 9.2 Labeled Classroom Item

Figure 9.3 Class Schedule With Words and Pictures

The Picture Communication Symbols © 1981–2015 by Mayer-Johnson LLC a Tobii Dynavox company. All Rights Reserved Worldwide. Used with permission. Boardmaker © is a trademark of Mayer Johnson LLC.

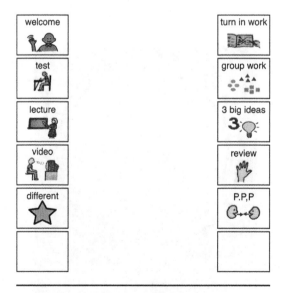

Figure 9.4 Individual Student Schedule

The Picture Communication Symbols © 1981–2015 by Mayer-Johnson LLC a Tobii Dynavox company. All Rights Reserved Worldwide. Used with permission. Boardmaker © is a trademark of Mayer Johnson LLC.

When power struggles are a problem in the classroom (student wants control but teacher needs control), choices are often presented to students. Offering students two or more options and allowing students to make a choice is not relinquishing control to the students, although they may interpret it as so. The teacher must carefully select the options presented to the student and be sure that all possible outcomes still achieve the goal in the situation. For example, "Nick, would you like to complete your worksheet at your desk or on the floor with a clipboard?" or "Rasheed, would you like to do your science experiment first or complete your geography project first?" Another option would be: "Class, we need to do our silent reading, partner math flash cards, and literature circles before lunch. What activity would you like to start with?" In these situations, regardless of which option the student(s) select, the teacher's goal (task completion) is achieved. See Illustrative Case Study 9.1 for an example of how providing choices is beneficial to all.

ILLUSTRATIVE CASE STUDY 9.1: PROVIDING CHOICES

Mr. Jackson is having a difficult time with two students in his eighth-grade civics class. He recognizes that Liz and Hendrix are both resisting seatwork. Mr. Jackson has tried to use schedules, positive reinforcement, time-out procedures, and punishment but with no success. He asks his colleague, Ms. Jacobs, if she has these problems, and she reports that she has seen this behavior but has recently started to provide choices as to how, where, or in what order to complete independent seatwork, and both students are much more receptive to the work demands now. Mr. Jackson decides to try providing choices.

The following Monday, at the start of class, Mr. Jackson reviews the content that was discussed last week and provides an agenda for the day. Liz and Hendrix are engaged during the review (a short video clip and then a group activity writing down key words they remember from last week). Next, Mr. Jackson explains that during class today, the students must complete three tasks: an internet scavenger hunt worksheet, decide which amendment they are going to debate in the upcoming oral assessment and notify Mr. Jackson of their selection, and, finally, practice reciting the Preamble with a partner. Mr. Jackson wrote these three tasks on the board, explained his expectation for academic and behavioral performance during these tasks, and set a timer for 40 minutes (leaving the class with eight minutes to wrap up before the bell rings). He encourages the students to get started with one of the activities and reminds them to pace themselves so that all three tasks are completed when the timer goes off. Mr. Jackson then walked around the classroom, answering questions and monitoring student performance. He noticed that both Liz and Hendrix got right to work and did not complain about the upcoming tasks (complaining and refusal have been their normal response to classroom demands). When the timer went off, Mr. Hendrix collected the internet scavenger hunt worksheets and praised the students for how well they worked during class. As the bell rang, Mr. Jackson was sure to provide Liz and Hendrix with individual praise, acknowledging both their hard work and their positive attitude during class today, and then he immediately emailed Ms. Jacobs, thanking her for sharing her classroom strategy and bragging about the successful day he had with Liz and Hendrix!

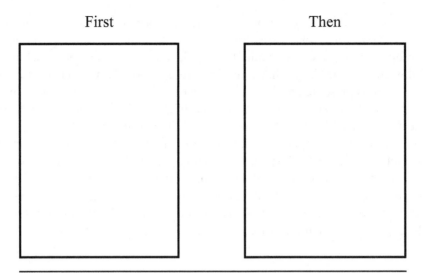

Figure 9.5 First/Then Board

Another strategy that is similar to offering choices is called the Premack principle. The Premack principle is a presentation of two tasks, one desirable and one less desirable. The less desirable task precedes the more desirable task, using the more desirable task as a reinforcement to completing the less desirable task (Premack, 1961). For example, if the student likes to complete work on the computer and does not like to complete paper-and-pencil tasks, then using the Premack principle, the teacher would present the two tasks in the following way: "Annie, you need to complete your worksheet first, and then you may play Math Blaster on the computer." This is helpful for students who desire control and can understand a delay in gratification (if you complete the worksheet, then you get what you want). This "first this, then that" strategy is effective with students of all ages. Visuals can be incorporated if the student needs this to increase comprehension. See Figure 9.5 for an example of a first/then board. With this example, a picture would be attached or words written in each box.

Social Stories, originally documented by Carol Gray, can help with challenging behaviors as well. Social Stories are short, positively written stories to help a student through a difficult social situation (see www.carolgraysocialstories.com). These are commonly used with students with autism but can also be used with students who are neurotypical but are displaying challenging behaviors. These stories are authentically written and frequently read with the student to increase their understanding of how to navigate challenging situations. Read Illustrative Case Study 9.2 and Ryan's Social Story in Figure 9.6 for further understanding of the use of Social Stories.

ILLUSTRATIVE CASE STUDY 9.2: SOCIAL STORIES

Ryan is a seven-year-old student who has a history of behavioral challenges at school, but he is not identified as having a behavior disorder. Daily, Ryan runs through the hallway to his bus when school is dismissed. This is a problem in the school because he frequently bumps into other students and is loud in the hallway. He is now continuing to run once he is outside, running into the parking lot and to his school bus. This is a safety concern, and the staff at his school are addressing how to slow Ryan down. The school counselor, Mrs. Klein, wrote a Social Story because Ryan loves to read and enjoys the attention he receives in one-on-one situations with Mrs. Klein. The plan is that 10 minutes prior to the end of each school day, Mrs. Klein will meet Ryan at his locker. Once he gathers his belongings to go home, she will walk with him to her office. In her office, Ryan and Mrs. Klein will read his Social Story before the bell rings and Ryan proceeds to his bus. Mrs. Klein has printed out the pages and laminated and bound them into a book.

Figure 9.6 Ryan's Social Story

Video modeling has emerged as another evidence-based practice supporting students in a variety of ways (National Professional Development Center on Autism Spectrum Disorders, 2010). One way that video modeling is used is to change behaviors (Bellini & Akullian, 2007). Video modeling is an intervention used to support observational learning. With video modeling, the teacher records a video of a desired behavior. This video can be digitally recorded and viewed on a mobile device that has a camera and a screen. The teacher then shows the video to the child who is struggling with the desired behavior. See Figure 9.7 for step-by-step directions on how to create a video model. Intentionally showing the video of desired behaviors to a struggling student can help to increase the desired behavior for the struggling student. For example, if Lily is struggling to wait to be called on when she is in small-group teacher time, Mrs. Abel, Lily's teacher, can record a classmate of Lily's raising her hand, waiting to be called on, and then contributing to the class discussion. Mrs. Abel can also "catch" Lily raising her hand and record her performing the desired behavior and then show it to Lily in the future when she needs reminders. Once Mrs. Abel has a video of Lily or a classmate raising their hand to indicate a desire to be called on, Mrs. Abel can show the video to Lily before her small-group teacher time to remind Lily of the behavior expectation. Bringing Lily's attention directly to the desired behavior can increase Lily's performance of the desired behavior.

Behavior contracts are helpful in defining the expectation and formalizing the behavior change process. A behavior contract is an authentically written agreement between the student performing the behavior to change and an adult (teacher, principal, school counselor) implementing the intervention. This contract is written, agreed upon, and signed (and sometimes even posted as a visual reminder) to solidify a behavior change agreement. See Figure 9.8 for an example of a behavior contract.

Step 1- Identify a target behavior or skill that the learner needs to be taught.

Step 2- Prepare the video equipment prior to recording.

Step 3- Plan the video recording session by setting up a time and environment without distractions.

Step 4- Collect baseline data.

Step 5- Create the video.

Step 6- Arrange the environment to watch the video.

Step 7- Show the video.

Step 8- Monitor the progress.

Step 9- Troubleshoot if the learner is not making progress.

Step 10- Fade the video and prompting

Note: If using commercially prepared video model, skip steps 3 and 5. These VM steps are consistent with the recommendations from the National Professional Development Center (2010).

Hall, C., Hollingshead, A., & Christman, J. (in press) Implementing video modeling to improve transitions within activities in inclusive classrooms. Intervention in School and Clinic.

Figure 9.7 Steps for Video Model Creation and Implementation

> Today, February 13, 2014, Tracy Edwards and Mrs. McDwyer have come to a formal agreement regarding Tracy's performance and behavior in 5th grade social studies class. Tracy and Mrs. McDwyer have agreed that:
>
> 1. Tracy will complete his homework every night.
> 2. After Tracy completes three consecutive nights of homework, he earns a 15 minute pass to listen to music during class.
> 3. By the end of the quarter, if Tracy has earned his music pass 5 times, he will earn a homework pass.
>
> Signed:
>
> Tracy Edwards   *Mrs. S. McDwyer*

Figure 9.8 Sample Behavior Contract

When a student is performing an acceptable behavior but too frequently (raising a hand to ask or answer a question, sharpening a pencil, getting a tissue, filling up water bottle), a visual representation system is helpful. Provide the student with three (or any appropriate quantity) tokens and require the student to turn in one token every time they perform the behavior (asks a question, sharpens a pencil). When the tokens are gone, there are no more opportunities to perform the behavior. If tokens are not handy, stickers, coins, tickets, or even small trinkets can be used. This visual system helps young children and older students with developmental disabilities to see the use of their opportunities diminish and to increase their ability to delay gratification. This can be a process that is completed for the whole day or for a partial day—for example, three tokens before lunch and three tokens after lunch. This system can be used for older students as well, perhaps using check marks in a plan book for a more appropriate image to the plan.

A check in/check out (CICO) procedure can also be helpful when slowing a student down or when a student requires more adult contact than their peers. Executing a CICO requires the student to stop their work, transition, or proceed at specified intervals and to make contact with an adult. This adult may check work, remind of upcoming situations, discuss behavioral expectations, provide a sensory time, and so on. There is not a defined expectation to occur during that check-in time. At this point, the student may self-monitor behavior, academic performance, and the like. After this check-in time, the student will do something to indicate a "check out." This may be to present a card to the teacher, receive a sticker, get a high five, and so forth. Again, there is no standard as to what occurs during the CICO procedure; rather, it is an opportunity for extra adult contact that helps some students to proceed appropriately.

STRATEGIES SPECIFICALLY FOR THOSE WITH DISABILITIES

The previously mentioned intervention strategies can be used with typical developing students and with students with disabilities. The following interventions are used specifically with students with disabilities.

Sensory diets are provided to a student to help regulate sensory needs. In these prescribed plans, according to Baranek (2002), "systematically applied somatosensory stimulation (i.e. brushing with a surgical brush and join compression) is followed by a prescribed set of activities designed to meet the child's sensory needs that are integrated into a child's daily routine" (p. 407). Contrary to the name, a sensory diet includes activities, exercises, and protocols, not food limitations. Other strategies that are commonly used to support students' sensory needs are playing with a fidget toy, bouncing on an exercise ball, wearing a weighted vest, eating a chewy candy, or pushing a heavy cart. An occupational therapist can help design a plan that best fits the needs of the student. Such a plan is often used with students with autism or other students requiring sensory regulation; however, many other students can benefit from the advantages of sensory supports.

The use of visual timers is an effective means of easing transitions for children with autism (Hume, 2008). A visual timer is a timer that visually represents the passing of time. This visual representation could be with sand through an hourglass, a light getting dimer as time passes, a screen decreasing in size as time passes, or even, on mobile technology, bubbles popping (when the bubbles are gone, the time is up). These strategies visually represent the passage of time, helping a student learn to wait, or speed up, as their time awareness increases. Transitions are often hard for young children, students with autism, attention deficit hyperactivity disorder, or other developmental disabilities because shifting attention from one task to another is a complex undertaking. Using visuals can ease this transition.

One behavioral concern that can lead to significant problems related to students with disabilities is the lack of a functional communication system. Everyone needs some way to communicate, and without that functional system, behavior problems vastly increase. When a student cannot tell an adult that something hurts, or when a student needs to use the restroom, challenging behaviors emerge out of frustration. A functional communication system may be the use of words, pictures, a communication device, or sign language. Often the functional use of these systems requires direct instruction over time, but if a student enters the classroom without a way to communicate, addressing this must be a top priority. It is worth noting that not all forms of communication are functional. If a student uses modified sign language but only the student and the student's father know the meaning behind these signs, then the system is not functional. If the student has vocalizations and only one teacher has learned to interpret these utterances, this system is not functional because it requires one teacher to interpret for meaning. Consult with a speech and language pathologist or the school psychologist to assess the student's abilities and needs regarding functional communication systems.

One strategy that is often used to support students with behavior challenges is assigning a paraprofessional to a student. Giangreco, Broer, and Suter (2011) wrote about the benefits and hindrances that are caused by one-on-one assistance (when one paraprofessional, or assistant, is assigned specifically to a certain student for the school day), and the hindrances were more significant than the benefits. In one-on-one situations, the benefits are that the paraprofessional is available to coach the student through challenging behaviors, remove the student when behaviors cause significant problems, encourage the student to interact in socially appropriate ways, and facilitate positive learning interactions for the student. However, such outcomes as decreased self-esteem, increased self-reliance, and overall negative long-term effects were more detrimental to the student (Giangreco et al., 2011). Paraprofessionals are, often, invaluable resources to a school community and provide vital services to both students and teachers, but assigning one adult to one student for the school day in the hopes of decreasing problem behaviors has not been shown to be an effective intervention (Giangreco et al., 2011).

SELF-MONITORING

Once a behavioral intervention is in place and success is seen through data analysis, it is important to think about a long-term intervention plan. How will this intervention be maintained over time? How will this skill or behavior be generalized to occur in different environments or with different people? How will the student absorb responsibilities and the teacher wean away? One strategy to address these questions is through self-monitoring. Self-monitoring is the ability to observe and evaluate one's own performance. This is a life skill. Adults regularly track and monitor their own behavior. This may occur when someone is trying to lose weight and they track their food intake and monitor their exercise progress. This may also happen when someone is looking to cut personal spending. This person may track how they have spent their money for the last few months and then revise their personal budget to increase their savings. It is important to teach children how to monitor their own behavior as well. This may mean that students reflect on whether they have raised their hands to gain the teacher's attention or have spoken out without raising their hands. Or this may mean that students review their previous test scores and analyze what personal behaviors resulted in a difference in earning satisfactory grades and unsatisfactory grades. It is important that students of all ages learn how to self-monitor, especially when recognizing and remediating problem behaviors. Some students may be successful if they color in a chart representing how many times they have successfully met their goals. A check mark on a ticket indicating a successful week may be appropriate for other students. Be sure that the process to wean away from adult support and toward independence is gradual, planned, and individualized. This will allow for greater success in the process.

Comprehension Check
1. Name three intervention strategies, how each could be implemented in the classroom, and when each would be used in the classroom.
2. Discuss how and when social stories are best used.

APPLICATION CASE STUDY 9.3: LETTER OF STRATEGIES

Mrs. Manfield is a fourth-grade teacher at Laycraft Elementary School. She is known in her building as being a very effective classroom teacher, employing extremely effective behavior management techniques, implementing the curriculum in a highly engaging fashion, and yielding very high test scores from her students. Mr. Bradford, the superintendent of Laycraft City Schools, has asked Mrs. Manfield to write a letter explaining her practices. Mr. Bradford hopes to use this letter to encourage other teachers to employ some of the same techniques, and he is also using this letter in an application to nominate Mrs. Manfield for Iowa Teacher of the Year. The following letter is Mrs. Manfield's response to Mr. Bradford.

Dear Mr. Bradford,

Thank you for asking about my classroom. I am so proud of my students! I really feel that it is an honor to be a Laycraft Lion!

I have a diverse group of learners in my fourth-grade classroom. I use this diversity to teach lessons. I celebrate this diversity on the first day of school when I teach my students that being fair does not mean that every student will receive the same treatment every day. We do an activity in which I hand each student a notecard with an ailment on it (headache, upset stomach, scraped elbow, etc.). The first student reads his card aloud: "blister on my toe." To help with this ailment, I wrap a Band-Aid around his toe. Then the next student reads his card: "earache." In response to this, I wrap a Band-Aid around his toe also. The next student reads her card, and I again wrap a Band-Aid around her toe. This continues, and as each student reads their card, I wrap a Band-Aid around their toe. This activity demonstrates for my fourth graders how, if everyone is treated the same, many students do not receive what they need. I refer to this activity throughout the year as students question why their peers may receive different treatment. I remind them that I am being fair and that fair does not mean everyone receives the same treatment but rather that everyone gets what they need.

In my experience, when I make lessons interesting and exciting, I have far fewer behavior problems to manage in my classroom. This motivates me to be creative in every lesson I teach. However, for a few of my struggling students, I know that their engagement is not dependent solely on my creative approaches but rather also on comprehension. For two of my students who struggle with written words (I have one student who has recently moved to the United States from Saudi Arabia and one student who has an intellectual disability and is included with the general education population for half of the school day), I combine visuals (either images I find on the internet or photos I have personally taken) with written words. I do this on written directions, worksheets, class and individual schedules, and classroom materials. Using visuals to support written words increases their comprehension and engagement.

Beyond making materials more comprehensive to increase engagement, I have also implemented specific strategies that I use throughout my classroom. I start the school year with a routine and, for the most part, stick to it! The students come to know the schedule, and the predictability helps several of my students to feel calmer throughout the day. I use a visual timer during most activities throughout the day. This allows the students to see the passage of time without having to ask me how much longer we are doing an activity. This visual timer also helps my students to pace themselves on independent work.

I have one student in my classroom who receives special education services for a behavior disorder. The special education teacher and I have worked collaboratively to create a plan that works for him and is conducive to the general education setting because his academic needs are best met in my classroom. He has a "break card" that he can present throughout the day when he feels himself getting agitated. After he presents his break card to me, he can select from a menu what he will do for his break. His choices are computer time, sensory room, walk to the office to deliver mail, put his head down and listen to music for 10 minutes, do a crossword puzzle (which he really enjoys doing) while he sits in a beanbag chair, or read a book. After his break (usually about 10 minutes) he returns to his work and completes the task. Currently, he is allowed three breaks a day. When we started this plan last year, he was averaging 12 breaks in his school day. He was missing a lot of instructional time, so we have slowly weaned him away from breaks and he is doing really well.

The final intervention that I have seen provide significant positive changes to my classroom is the use of video modeling. I have been using video modeling in my classroom for three school years, and I have quite a bank of models to use in various situations. Currently, I am using a video model for the transition inside after recess. I have one student who has autism, and this is a challenging time of the day for him. He enjoys recess and struggles to come back inside and to refocus after lunch and recess. After we line up on the playground, I show him a model (on an iPod Touch so it is easy for me to slip into my pocket before I head outside) of a 50-second video of a student performing the transition. In the video, he watches as a classmate calmly leaves the playground, walks appropriately into the school in a line with the class, puts his empty lunchbox into his locker, takes a quick drink of water at the drinking fountain, walks into the classroom, takes a seat at his desk, takes his reading book out of his desk, and begins silent reading. Each day at the end of the silent reading time, the student takes out a small calendar and gives himself either a check mark (indicating that he transitioned like the video showed him) or an X (indicating that he did not transition as the video showed him). At the end of the month, he analyzes his progress. We have noticed strikingly fewer episodes of resistance since this intervention began. I know the special education teacher has collected data on this intervention and has been very pleased with the positive changes she has seen.

Overall, I feel strongly that it is my job to do what is needed for each student in my classroom. Fourth graders like to be entertained, and I try my best to make the curriculum as fun and exciting as I can. I work hard to ensure that my classroom is a safe haven for everyone, regardless of their learning styles, family life, and previous experiences with school. By using evidence-based practices in my teaching and intervening, I have witnessed positive changes in my overall management and student test scores.

Thank you, again, for acknowledging my hard work!

Sincerely,
Jenny Manfield

Case Study Comprehension Check

Apply what you have learned in Chapter 9 to this case study.

1. Identify three strategies that are used in Mrs. Manfield's classroom to decrease behavior problems. Discuss these strategies.
2. What theme do you see present in most of the options that the student with the behavior disorder is presented with on the break menu? Why do you suppose several options have similar characteristics? What do you think led the special education teacher to make a menu that has these similarities?
3. Find an example of data-based decision-making and discuss.
4. Think of other ways you can teach fairness in your classroom. Share your ideas.
5. Discuss connections between Mrs. Mansfield's knowledge of overall development with the strategies she employs in her classroom. What evidence do you find in this application that Mrs. Manfield has a strong understanding of both fourth-grade typical development and the development of some of her individual students?

APPLICATION ACTIVITIES

1. Identify a student with whom you work or have worked with. Think of a strategy explained in this chapter that could assist the student to enhance quality of life. Design the intervention as if you would implement it with the student. What challenges would this intervention help?
2. Visit a school (in person or virtually) and discuss strategies that teachers use in the classroom. Compare strategies used in an elementary school to a high school. What strategies cross over age ranges, and what strategies are specific to certain ages? How could you modify elementary strategies to be appropriate at the high school level, and how could you modify high school strategies to be appropriate at the elementary school level?

CHAPTER SUMMARY

Strategies for All Learners

- The use of visuals can increase comprehension and engagement.
  - Items in the classroom can be labeled with pictures.
  - The class schedule can have words and pictures.
  - Individual student schedules can have visuals.
- Give students the opportunity to make choices or decisions in the classroom.
  - Students are able to make decisions while the teacher's goal is achieved.
- The Premack principle is a presentation of two tasks, one desirable and one less desirable.
  - The less desirable task precedes the more desirable task.
  - The more desirable task is used as a reinforcement to completing the less desirable task.
- Social Stories are short, positively written stories that are used to help a student through a difficult social situation.
  - These are commonly used for students with autism but can also be used with any student who has a challenging behavior.
- Video modeling is an intervention used to support observational learning.
  - The teacher records a video of a desirable behavior for a student struggling with the desired behavior.
  - Focusing the student's attention directly to the desired behavior can increase the student's performance of that behavior.
- Behavior contracts are written, agreed-upon, signed agreements between the student and the teacher.
  - This is a helpful strategy to define the expectation and to solidify a behavior change.
- For students who perform an acceptable behavior too frequently, teachers can develop a visual representation system.
  - An example is providing students with three tokens and requiring the student to turn in one token each time they perform the behavior. When the tokens

are gone, there are no more opportunities for the student to participate in that behavior.
- A check in/check out procedure requires students to stop what they are doing, transition at specified intervals, and contact an adult.

Strategies Specifically for Those With Disabilities

- Sensory diets are provided to students to help regulate sensory needs.
- A visual timer is an effective strategy to ease transitions for students.
  - These visually represent the passing of time, helping a student learn to wait or speed up.
- A functional communication system can be the use of words, pictures, a communication device, or sign language.
- Students may be assigned a paraprofessional.
  - In one-on-one situations, the paraprofessional is available to coach the student through challenging behaviors, remove the student when behaviors cause significant problems, encourage the student to interact in socially appropriate ways, and facilitate positive learning interactions for the student. This one on one support has not been proven in research to be effective in encouraging social independence.

Self-Monitoring

- Self-monitoring is the ability to observe and evaluate your own performance.
- It is important to teach students how to monitor their own behaviors.
  - This can be done using a color chart or a checklist.
- It is vital for teachers to wean away from adult support and toward independence gradually.

REFERENCES

Baranek, G. (2002). Efficacy of sensory and motor interventions for children with autism. *Journal of Autism and Developmental Disorders, 32*, 396–421.

Bellini, S., & Akullian, J. (2007). A meta-analysis of video modeling and video self-modeling interventions for children and adolescents with autism spectrum disorders. *Exceptional Children, 73*, 264–287.

Gable, R. A., Park, K. L., & Scott, T. M. (2014). Functional behavioral assessment and students at risk for or with emotional disabilities: Current issues and considerations. *Education and Treatment of Children, 37*, 111–135.

Giangreco, M., Broer, S., & Suter, J. (2011). Guidelines to selecting alternatives to overreliance on paraprofessionals: Field testing in inclusion oriented schools. *Remedial and Special Education, 32*, 22–38.

Hume, C. (2008). Transition time: Helping individuals on the autism spectrum move successfully from one activity to another. *The Reporter, 13*, 6–10.

National Professional Development Center on ASD. (2010). *Evidence based practice brief: Video modeling.* Retrieved from http://autismpdc.fpg.unc.edu/sites/autismpdc.fpg.unc.edu/files/imce/documents/VideoModeling_Complete.pdf

Premack, D. (1961). Predicting instrumental performance from the independent rate of the contingent response. *Journal of Experimental Psychology, 61*, 163–171.

Part III

Application of Classroom and Behavior Management Strategies: Tier 2

Part III

10

TIER 2

Catherine Lawless Frank

CHAPTER OBJECTIVES

After reading this chapter, students should be able to:

1. Understand the main components of Tier 2.
2. Identify the referral process from Tier 1 to Tier 2.
3. Explain the ongoing cycle of assessment, analysis, decision-making, and instruction used in Tier 2.

The previous six chapters have examined the components necessary for developing general behavior management strategies fundamental to all classrooms. These classroom management components are necessary to provide the structure for effective Tier 1 instruction to occur. Just as effective instruction is fundamental to all classrooms no matter the tier, the behavior management components found in the previous chapters is also fundamental to all classrooms, no matter the tier. All classrooms need routine and structure. All teachers must work to develop authentic relationships. All teachers should be aware of student motivation, develop strategies for improving and maintaining appropriate behavior, and be able to effectively intervene on common behavioral issues. These components are fundamental to all classrooms, but for some students these components may not be enough. Those students may require Tier 2 behavioral supports.

Approximately 20% to 25% of students will need additional support academically and/or behaviorally beyond what is provided in Tier 1. This support is typically provided in Tier 2 and, if additional intensive support is necessary, Tier 3. Tier 2 is designed for students who do not meet the expected levels of proficiency in Tier 1 but who are not currently considered in need of special education services (Shapiro, n.d.). The needs of these students are assessed using the ongoing cycle (assessment, analysis, decision-making, and instruction) to determine the appropriate instruction to meet the student's individual needs. Chapter 10 will begin to examine the components of Tier 2 while Chapters 11 and 12 will provide strategies for addressing both externalizing and internalizing behavior concerns.

OVERVIEW OF TIER 2

Tier 2 typically begins when an individual student is not making adequate progress in Tier 1. In Tier 1, teachers provide effective instruction and an inclusive classroom environment that focuses on the needs of the entire class, but sometimes this whole-classroom approach is not enough to meet the individual needs of specific students. When an individual student struggles, the teacher implements academic and/or behavior interventions to help mitigate a student's area of concern. Teachers may do research, attend professional development, or seek advice from a mentor, other teachers, parents, former professors, and/or other school staff members for strategies and resources to help a struggling student. Although most often this approach is successful, other times teachers need additional assistance in meeting the needs of an individual student. This help is provided in Tier 2.

Tier 2 is designed to meet individual students' needs after the options in Tier 1 have been exhausted and the student continues to struggle. This tier involves a collaborative process that provides additional resources, training, and/or support to the teacher to help meet the distinct academic and/or behavioral needs of the student. The student receives more individualized intervention and support than what is currently provided to the whole class.

For example, Ms. Alexander loves teaching and works hard to establish a classroom community that is structured and supportive in meeting the needs of all her students. She works to ensure that all her students feel supported, included, and valued. She is flexible in her approach to meeting students' needs and has very few significant behavioral problems in her classroom. This year, however, Ms. Alexander is struggling to meet the needs of one of her students named Becca. Ms. Alexander's concerns about Becca have evolved as the year has progressed. Becca is a quiet student who appears withdrawn and anxious. She is quiet to the point of rarely communicating either verbally or nonverbally. Ms. Alexander has seldom seen Becca initiate any form of verbal communication or make eye contact with others. She does not typically engage with her classmates and will often sit and watch them but will rarely participate or join in the activities. Ms. Alexander worked to develop an authentic relationship and tried numerous times to talk to Becca with little success. At most, Becca responds to these attempts with a shoulder shrug and little to no eye contact. Becca also has failed to complete or turn in multiple homework and class assignments. Currently, she is failing because of these missing assignments. Due to Becca's lack of interaction in the classroom and multiple missing assignments, Ms. Alexander is unsure of Becca's academic abilities. She wonders if the work is too difficult and that is causing Becca to be withdrawn or if there is a sensory processing disorder, mental health disorder, and/or a hearing or vision problem. Ms. Alexander researched and consulted with other teachers and staff for ideas and suggestions on how to help Becca (quietly praising even small accomplishments, encouraging one-word or short responses, offering encouragement, one-on-one assistance, and peer tutoring) but those interventions have resulted in limited progress. Becca still appears withdrawn and anxious and rarely completes assignments. After Ms. Alexander tried all the interventions available with limited success, she referred Becca Tier 2.

In this case, Ms. Alexander provided a structured and supportive Tier 1 classroom that met the majority of her students' needs, and she implemented additional supports to meet Becca's individual needs with limited success. At this point, Ms. Alexander realized that she had tried everything that she could and needed additional assistance to support Becca.

Although Tier 3 and special education disabilities have a federal definition that establishes specific criteria to determine eligibility, no such established criteria exist for Tier 2. Tier 2 support is provided when the teacher has implemented interventions in a whole-group setting that have attempted to meet the student's individual needs with limited success. Specific criteria, such as the number and type of interventions or qualifying academic and/or behavioral characteristics, are not defined for a Tier 2 referral and are left to the discretion of the teacher and school. Behavioral referrals are typically initiated on individual teachers' informal assessments and observations. Each classroom, school, district, and state may establish different criteria to determine Tier 2 eligibility. A student who qualifies for Tier 2 services in one school may have different characteristics than a student who qualifies in another school.

Tier 2, in part, constitutes what has previously been referred to as the pre-referral process. It does not constitute a referral into special education but is designed to remediate difficulties by providing additional and more individualized services, supports, and/or interventions before a referral to special education becomes necessary. It is a pre-referral process intended to remediate areas of concern and prevent inappropriate referrals and placement into special education (Richards, Lawless Frank, Sableski, & Arnold, 2016).

A student in Tier 2 typically receives the majority of their instruction through Tier 1 but has additional Tier 2 support to meet specific needs. The resources and supports provided to Becca in Tier 2 from the previous example will be different from those of a student whose primary concern is reading fluency, disrupting the class (speaking out of turn, refusing to follow directions, defiance), or understanding borrowing in two-digit math subtraction.

Due to the nature of Tier 2, it tends to be more collaborative than Tier 1 and typically requires a team approach. This team may consists of special education and general education teachers, parents, administrators, counselors and/or the school psychologist, and possibly the student, a behavioral consultant, or other related service personnel. This team-based pre-referral process has existed prior to the RTI movements and may have a variety of different titles depending on the school or district. This team may be referred to as an intervention assistance team, problem-solving team, teacher assistance team, RTI team, mainstream assistant team, pre-referral intervention team, or child study team. No matter the name, the team collaborates in the assessment, analysis, decision-making, and instruction cycle in order to meet the academic and/or behavioral needs of individual students (Richards et al., 2016; Nellis, 2012).

Although a behavioral referral to Tier 2 tends to be more informal than a referral to Tier 3 or special education, it also uses the same ongoing assessment cycle (assessment, analysis, decision-making) as well as effective data-driven instruction and inclusive classroom environment fundamental to all three tiers.

Tier 2 uses individualized pre-referral assessments and interventions. The assessments are conducted to determine a student's strengths, areas of need, and appropriate interventions. Tier 2 also incorporates fidelity assessments, which are designed to ensure that the agreed-upon Tier 2 interventions are implemented in the designated manner. This is a safeguard method in which a person (administrator, co-teacher, and/or school counselor) familiar with the intervention observes the teacher administering it in order to verify that it is done in the appropriate manner. This may consist of a school counselor observing a teacher conduct a social skills lesson to ensure that the lesson follows the valid and reliable curriculum requirements. Or co-teachers observe each other to verify that they each are implementing a behavior management plan in the agreed-upon manner. It may require a school principal to observe a teacher to make certain that the components of an intervention plan are being properly administered or followed. This fidelity assessment is necessary for the success of Tier 2 by ensuring that the student receives the agreed-upon intervention in the designated manner (NJCLD, 2005).

Academic referrals to Tier 2 tend to be more objective in nature than behavioral referrals. Academic referrals are often based on a student's failure to meet grade-appropriate benchmarks or standards (Shapiro, n.d.). For example, if a student scores on a reading fluency assessment at 48 words per minute (wpm), and the grade-level benchmark or expected level of competency is 65 wpm, then the student may qualify for Tier 2 services in reading. The referral is based on clear, predetermined, and measurable criteria. Any student whose fluency rate is less than 65 wpm may also qualify while those whose reading fluency is at or above 65 wpm would not qualify. These academic criteria and assessments can be predetermined, clear, and specific. Each school or district establishes their own benchmark criteria as well as the interventions provided based on the needs of the students and the resources available.

Although some schools may establish certain criteria or benchmarks for behavioral referrals (number of office referrals or a benchmark in a schoolwide behavioral system), that is generally not the case. Identifying students for Tier 2 behavioral support tends to be more subjective in nature and occurs when the teacher has run out of available options and is in need of additional support. Because students' behaviors and teachers' expectations differ widely, it is difficult to establish a set behavioral referral criteria, and therefore referral points vary depending on teachers, schools, and administration.

Referrals to Tier 2 may concern externalizing (yelling out, disrupting class) or internalizing (withdrawn, anxious) behaviors or deficits in organization or social skills.

These behaviors can be exhibited throughout the school day (any time or during any class) or be limited to a specific period of time or class (after lunch or during math class). They may occur with all faculty, administrators, or staff or with one particular teacher, administrator, or staff member (the math teacher, the school counselor, the principal). The referral can be based on one teacher's experiences and observations or multiple teacher or staff member recommendations. A referral means that a student is struggling and that their teacher needs additional assistance or support in meeting that student's needs. This typically occurs after the teacher has implemented additional interventions beyond what has been implemented for the general classroom populations without adequate success. See Case Study 10.1 for an illustration of this process.

ILLUSTRATIVE CASE STUDY 10.1

Mr. Johnson is struggling to meet the behavioral needs of a student named Tony. Mr. J., as the students often call him, works hard to develop authentic relationships with all his students and plans lessons that keep them actively engaged. Although he is successful most of the time with most of his students, that is not always the case. There is one student in particular, Tony, who Mr. Johnson has had difficulty reaching.

Tony is disruptive. He yells out during lessons, wanders the classroom during independent work time, taps pencils, rocks in his chair, and seems to do whatever is necessary to cause a disruption in the classroom. His behaviors often affect other students in the class. When Tony is disruptive, it causes some of his peers to watch Tony's antics (and sometimes even to join in) rather than complete assignments or focus on Mr. J.'s lesson. When this happens, Tony has a larger audience, which seems to inspire him to continue and at times to escalate his behavior, further disrupting the class. Some days Mr. Johnson feels like he spends more time dealing with Tony's behaviors than he does teaching the rest of the class.

Mr. Johnson has tried multiple strategies in an attempt to refocus and engage Tony. He has conferenced with Tony about his behaviors, changed his seating assignment, spoken with his parents, attempted to redirect his behavior, and incorporated additional strategies to better engage him in lessons. Although some of the approaches seemed to have some short-term positive effect, none has significantly influenced Tony's overall behavior.

Although Mr. Johnson truly cares about Tony and wants him to be successful, he is tired of Tony's disruptions. He is frustrated and knows that his frustration is affecting his level of patience and his relationship with Tony. Mr. Johnson realizes that he has run out of options and ideas and makes a referral to the Tier 2 referral team to receive further assistance in meeting Tony's behavioral needs.

All schools, whether they use a multi-tier system of support such as RTI or not, should have in place a process and procedure that allows all teachers (general education, special education, art, music, physical education) access to a pre-referral team for support in addressing the academic and/or behavioral needs of a student. All teachers need assistance at times, and this school-based team is designed to provide teachers with support and assistance to meet individual students' needs. A referral to Tier 2 does not mean that a student is in need of special education or will eventually be referred to special education. It simply means that a teacher is in need of assistance in meeting a student's needs. Referral to Tier 2 does not negate the possibility of eventual referral to special education but is designed to remediate areas of concern and eliminate inappropriate referrals.

A behavioral referral to Tier 2 should include a description of the area of concern (missing 17 out of 24 assignments, appears withdrawn, speaks out of turn or calls out). This description should be specific and include such information as when (independent math work time, during a history lecture, in the morning before lunch, transition times), where (classroom, hallway, cafeteria), and with whom (math teacher, all teachers and staff, bus driver) the behavior is most likely to occur. If possible, it should also include a hypothesis as to why the behavior may be occurring (get attention, avoid work, avoid embarrassment). The interventions previously attempted (changing student's seat, conference with student, praising or rewarding positive behavior, loss of privileges) by the teacher(s), as well as the degree of success of each intervention (decrease in problem behavior, increase in problem behavior, seemed to have no effect on the behavior), should also be detailed. In a behavioral referral, teachers should identify the goal or what they would like to accomplish as a result of this Tier 2 process (for the teacher to learn strategies to better meet the student's needs, for the student to learn and/or employ different behaviors) as well as any other relevant information the team should be aware of. (See Table 10.1 for an example of a Tier 2 behavioral referral form.) The information provided to the Tier 2 referral team should be as clear, specific, and objective as possible in order to facilitate the team process in understanding and assisting the student and teacher in reaching the desired outcome.

For example, if a referral form simply states that the student of concern is disruptive in class, then the team has limited information to analyze in order to determine the appropriate intervention. If the referral is specific and states that the student disrupts learning by talking out during math class and the hypothesis is because the student struggles in math and is attempting to avoid work, then the team may have sufficient information (an informal evaluation from the teacher as well as academic background information) to begin developing strategies or interventions (use of accommodations, such as addition or multiplication charts, math tutoring). In the first example, the team needed more information in order to begin developing the appropriate interventions. In the second example, although the team may eventually need more information, they had sufficient information to immediately begin developing the necessary supports and interventions. Being clear and specific allows teams to more effectively and efficiently analyze the information and determine an appropriate course of action.

Table 10.1 Example of a Tier 2 Behavioral Referral Form

Tier 2 Behavioral Referral Form

Name(s) of person(s) making the referral:

Student of concern: Grade:

Description of area(s) of concern (be as specific as possible):

    Specific time(s) or subjects when the behavior is most prevalent:

    Specific locations where the behavior is most prevalent:

    Identify with whom the behavior is most likely to occur:

Hypothesis as to why the behavior is occurring (its purpose or cause):

Complete the following chart and identify at least three (3) interventions previously attempted and the degree of success for each one.

Intervention	Degree of Success
1.	
2.	
3.	

Goal for the final resolution for the referral:

Other relevant information:

A behavioral referral to Tier 2 typically occurs based on a teacher's informal observations of a student's behavior in comparison to their peers and the classroom expectations. Depending on the nature of the class and the classroom environment, it may be difficult for teachers to provide the specific information and details necessary to determine the appropriate interventions. In those cases, further assessment, analysis, and decision-making must occur before the proper course of action is determined.

> *Comprehension Check*
> 1. How is Tier 2 like Tier 1? How are they different?
> 2. Why is Tier 2 considered part of the pre-referral process?
> 3. What is the purpose of the pre-referral team?

THE ONGOING CYCLE ON TIER 2

Assessment

A behavioral referral to Tier 2 is often based on informal observations that compare a student's behavior to that of his or her peers and/or the classroom expectations. Although at times the information provided by a teacher for a referral will be sufficient in determining a proper course of action, that is often not the case. Due to the demands of teaching, it is often difficult for a teacher to conduct a specific and objective observation of an individual student while at the same time teaching an entire class. Although more informal than a referral to Tier 3 and special education, a referral to Tier 2 typically requires multiple sources of assessment data to clearly determine a student's needs and the appropriate interventions (see Figure 10.1).

In Tier 2, the assessments focus on the needs of an individual student rather than on those of the entire class. These assessments are used to specifically and objectively determine the student's strengths and baseline data (or current levels) on the frequency, duration, and intensity of the area(s) of need(s). The assessment process should also indicate the environmental components, teacher's behavior, peer involvement, cultural components, and any other factor that may be influencing the student's behavior. A student's strengths are considered in determining the appropriate interventions while the baseline information is necessary to measure growth. The environmental factors, teacher's behavior, peer involvement, cultural components, and other factors are analyzed to help determine the suitable course of action.

For example, a teacher's informal evaluation may conclude that a student is off task and disruptive during class. The teacher may also be able to report what they have done to help the student stay on task and to stop disrupting class (moving the student's desk, redirecting the student, proximity, contacting parents) as well as the degree of success (moving the desk was somewhat successful but redirecting the student has not been). Although helpful, these informal teacher evaluations typically are not specific enough to define the behavior (what off task specifically means in terms of the student's behavior and its frequency and/or duration) and the appropriate intervention to meet the student's specific needs. Other assessments, such as formal observations, behavior rating scales, adaptive behavior scales, hearing and vision screenings, parent interviews or questionnaires, medical background, and school history, may be necessary to develop a clear understanding of the student and his or her specific needs.

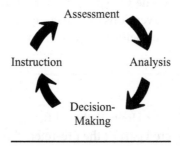

Figure 10.1 Ongoing Cycle of Response to Intervention

The most commonly used form of pre-referral assessment is a formal observation for data collection purposes. Because it is difficult, if not impossible, for a teacher to teach and to formally observe a student for data collection purposes, this is typically done by another member of the team, such as a teacher, administrator, counselor, or other school personnel. The use of an outside observer also helps to minimize any potential bias in specifically identifying the behaviors and its potential cause. An outside observer may offer a different perspective and additional information, such as peer involvement, cultural differences, or environmental factors, that may be contributing to the student's behavior. The observer will use one or more of the four types of data collection methods (anecdotal, event, duration, and latency) discussed in Chapter 3 (see Table 10.2 for a review of the data collection methods) to help clearly and objectively define the behavior.

Table 10.2 Observational Data Collection Methods

Method	Definition	Example
Anecdotal	Objectively journaling the specific actions of an individual student during a given amount of time	A school counselor observes Gerry during math class and specifically journals what he observes. 8:05 Gerry enters the classroom. 8:07 The teacher directs the class to get out their math books. 8:10 Gerry appears to be playing with a pencil—his math book is not out—and the majority of his peers have their books out. 8:13 Gerry still appears to be playing with a pencil, and his math book is not out—all other peers have their math books out and open to the appropriate page. 8:15 The teacher redirects Gerry to get his book out and opened. 8:16 Gerry gets out his math book and opens it to the appropriate page. 8:17 Gerry asks and receives permission to go to the restroom. 8:25 Gerry returns from the restroom. 8:26 Gerry breaks the lead off his pencil and gets up to sharpen his pencil. 8:27 Gerry finishes sharpening his pencil and stops to talk to a peer on his way back to his desk. 8:29 The teacher redirects Gerry to return to his desk.
Event	The number of times a behavior occurs within a given amount of time	A tally of the number of times Gerry interrupts class during a math lesson.
Duration	The amount of time a specific behavior occurs	The amount of time Gerry spends out of his seat during math class (restroom, sharpening pencil, talking to peer).
Latency	The amount of time it takes for a student to follow a specific command	The amount of time it takes for Gerry to follow a teacher's directions. Gerry took 11 minutes (8:07–8:18) to follow the teacher's original direction to get out his math book, with one teacher prompt or redirection. Gerry took three minutes to follow the teacher's redirection (815–8:18).

The observation should be conducted at the time of day and location where the behavior has the greatest frequency or intensity. For example, if a student is more likely to exhibit a behavior in Mrs. Paxson's classroom in the morning than in Mr. Rigouski's classroom in the afternoon, then the student should be observed in Mrs. Paxson's class in the morning. It is often beneficial for multiple observations to be conducted while possibly using different data collection methods to better clarify and define behaviors. The student may be observed using an anecdotal method (objectively journaling the detailed actions of an individual student during a given amount of time) to determine an overall picture of the student's behavior and the classroom environment. Once the assessment data are analyzed and a specific behavior(s) of concern is identified, it may then be beneficial to conduct a second observation using event, duration, and/or latency to determine a baseline for the behavior. Baseline information is necessary to determine student progress.

It may also be beneficial to compare observations of when and where a student is most likely and least likely to exhibit the behavior of concern to help identify possible triggers. It may be beneficial to observe the student in both Mrs. Paxson's and Mr. Rigouski's classroom to determine similarities and differences between the environments that may potentially be affecting the student's behavior.

Although the assessments used are primarily observations, behavior rating scales and/or adaptive behavior scales may also be used. Behavior ratings scales assess how often a student exhibits specific behaviors and to what degree or intensity. Adaptive behavior scales focus on a student's strengths and needs in terms of general (daily living skills, community participation) or specific skills (social skills, pragmatics) that are essential to daily life. Both types of scales are typically completed by the student's teacher(s), and possibly the parents, in order to rank the student's behavior and to more specifically and objectively determine their strengths and needs (Rosenburg, Westling, & McLeskey, 2010). Rating scales may also assist educators in concretely and specifically defining a student's area(s) of concern(s).

Hearing and vision are other factors that should be considered during the Tier 2 assessment process. Not being able to hear the teacher or to see the board clearly can influence a student's academic and behavioral performance in school. Hearing and vision are often routinely screened in schools using a short assessment that is designed to identify any potential problems. If a problem is detected, then the student is referred to a doctor or medical specialist for a more thorough evaluation (Rosenburg et al., 2010).

Other assessment information may include parental input and medical and school history. Parents often have insight into home life, medical history, school experiences, peer relationships, and community factors that may affect their child's behavior in the classroom. Parents should be an essential component in the Tier 2 process. During the assessment phase, parents should be interviewed or provided a questionnaire that helps identify possible factors that may be influencing a student's behavior and their progress in the classroom. This interview should be conducted by the school personnel who has the strongest rapport with the parents and can lead the discussion in an objective and supportive manner (Richards et al., 2016).

The student, their school records, and their prior teachers can also provide insight as to the cause, longevity (new concern or a preexisting one), and any academic issues as well as the degree of success of previous interventions. Interviewing the student and previous teachers as well as examining school records may provide a wealth of information into the behavior itself and help determine the appropriate intervention.

The purpose of this assessment is to determine a clear picture of the student's present levels of the behavior as well as any factors that may influence the behavior. Specific, observable, and measurable assessment data facilitates the ease of the analysis and decision-making process and allows the instruction and intervention to better align with the student's needs. The information gathered should not focus solely on the behavior itself but also on the student's strengths and other factors that may be influencing or contributing to the behavior. The assessment data are used to help the team analyze and hypothesize as to why the behavior is occurring in order to determine the instruction and intervention that is best suited to remediate the behavior. Multiple sources of assessment data are typically necessary for an accurate analysis of the student's strengths and area of need.

APPLICATION CASE STUDY 10.2

In Mr. Johnson's referral of Tony for Tier 2 support, he provides the following information:

Tier 2 Behavioral Referral Form
Name(s) of person(s) making the referral: **Mr. Johnson**
Student of concern: **Tony Aberdeen**

Description of area(s) of concern (be as specific as possible):

Tony yells out during lessons, wanders the classroom during independent work time, taps pencils, rocks in his chair, and seems to do whatever is necessary to cause a disruption in the classroom.

Specific time(s) or subjects when the behavior is most prevalent:

Tony's behavior tends to be worse in the morning, especially during language arts, but is apparent throughout the day.

Specific locations where the behavior is most prevalent:

The behavior is most prevalent in the classroom during instructional time.

Identify with whom the behavior is most likely to occur:

The behavior is most likely to occur with Mr. Johnson but has also been present with Mr. Shoemaker (gym teacher) and Mr. Arnett (school counselor).

Hypothesis as to the cause or purpose of the behavior:

I am not sure. I think he wants attention, but he may just be trying to avoid doing schoolwork.

Complete the following chart and identify at least three (3) interventions previously attempted and the degree of success for each one.

Intervention	Degree of Success
Contacted Tony's grandmother (primary custodian) about his behavior and possible interventions	This seemed to help for a while, but the effects were only short term. Tony reverted back to his previous behaviors.
Changed his seat and moved him closer to my desk and where I teach from	Limited success. He now tries to speak with me throughout class and independent work time, but most of his other behaviors still continue.
Tried to make lessons more engaging and hands-on in hopes of focusing Tony on the lesson	This was somewhat effective but not something I can do for every lesson. He does tend to be more engaged in those lessons but only during those lessons.

Goal for the final resolution for the referral:

I would like to learn strategies to better work with Tony and for Tony to learn ways to behave in class that do not cause a disruption to the rest of the class.

Other relevant information:

Tony is new to our school, so I was unable to speak with his previous teacher.

Case Study Comprehension Check

Use the information in Case Study 10.1 and Case Study 10.2 to answer the following questions.

1. What other information does the team need in order to make an informed decision about the appropriate interventions for Tony and Mr. Johnson?
2. What assessments should be conducted to determine this needed information?

Analysis

In the analysis phase, the team establishes a hypothesis as to the cause of the behavior (why the student is exhibiting the behavior) and to specifically define the behavior in observable and measurable terms. This process is also used to verify the student's strengths and baseline (current levels of the student's performance) in terms of duration, frequency, and/or intensity of the behavior. When the referral is first initiated, the behavior of concern is often generally, rather than specifically, stated (as in the case of Tony in Application Case Study 10.2). It is the role of the assessment and analysis phase to clarify that behavior in observable and measurable terms and to examine any factors that may be contributing to or reinforcing it. This information is then used to determine the necessary interventions and progress monitoring (Richards et al., 2016).

Data from parents may be especially valuable in the analysis process. Parents are often able to offer insights into their child's behavior as well as factors that may be contributing to or influencing it, such as home life, school information as reported by the child (problems with peers, like or dislike of a particular subject or teacher, anxiety), and their academic history beyond assessment results and report cards. It may also be beneficial to include the student in the analysis. Students, at times, can provide insight as to the reason they behave in a certain manner as well as interventions that may be beneficial.

If a referral contains more than one behavior of concern (missing assignments, disruptions in class, tardy, unprepared or without needed materials for class), then the team should identify one specific behavior as the primary behavior of concern. This primary behavior of concern is the behavior initially targeted for intervention. Interventions tend to be more effective and successful if they are focused on one particular behavior rather than on multiple behaviors. Focusing on one behavior allows the team to identify specific interventions, facilitates progress monitoring, and provides the student greater clarity in terms of behavioral expectations. Identifying a primary behavior does not negate the need to address the other secondary area(s) of concern but allows the intervention to be more focused and to increase the chance of success. For example, Charlie's areas of concern include disrupting class, missing assignments, and both arriving late and unprepared to class. It would be difficult for a team to develop interventions for each of these behaviors individually in a manner that facilitates successful implementation and assessment by her teacher. It would also be difficult for Charlie to successfully address all these multiple behaviors at one time. Both the teacher's and Charlie's focus and energy would be divided over multiple behaviors, interventions, and means of progress monitoring, making it cumbersome to implement in an effective manner. It is more effective for a team to evaluate those behaviors of concern and to choose one behavior to initially focus on to ease the implementation process and to increase the chances of success.

Often the problem behaviors are related, and addressing the primary behavior influences and helps rectify secondary behaviors. In Charlie's case, the team may choose missing assignments as the primary behavior of concern. In evaluating the data, it may be determined that the potential cause of Charlie's secondary behaviors (disrupting and being late and unprepared for class) is related to her primary behavior (missing assignments). The hypothesis may be that Charlie's missing assignments are due to academic difficulties, poor study habits, and/or mismatch in teaching and learning styles. Charlie's secondary behaviors may also be rooted in the same cause. Charlie may be disrupting class and arriving late and unprepared in order to avoid the academic challenges of the classroom or to avoid being embarrassed about her academic difficulties. Focusing the intervention on Charlie's primary behavior may also have a secondary positive effect on her other areas of concern. If after remediating the primary behavior other concerns still exist, then the team begins addressing those needs. A second behavior becomes the area of focus, and once it is remediated then a third behavior becomes the area of focus, and so on.

Before establishing the primary behavior, it is beneficial to first determine the cause or why the behavior is occurring. Behaviors serve a purpose and determining that purpose is fundamental to providing the appropriate intervention. The purpose of the behavior is often to avoid something (work, embarrassment) or to get something (attention from peers or teacher). The purpose for Charlie's behavior may be an attempt to avoid embarrassment or work due a deficit in academic skills or a mismatch between her learning style and the teaching style. It may be that Charlie's behaviors were an attempt to get attention from the teacher or other students. Whether it is to avoid something or to get something, it is important to consider why a behavior is occurring in order to adequately define it and to determine the appropriate interventions. An intervention for a student with deficit in an academic skill may be significantly different from that of a student seeking attention even though the behaviors of concern may look similar.

It is also important to examine cultural influences, the classroom environment, and other factors that may be contributing to the behavior. The team should also determine if the student is aware of the behavioral expectations of the classroom and how their behavior deviates from those expectations. The teacher's expectations in the classroom may have been inconsistent or poorly communicated, leading the student to be unsure of the exact expectations. There may be cultural differences that influence a student's behavior. For instance, Charlie's culture may have a different value for time, which affects her behavior in regard to due dates for assignments and arriving to class on time. Charlie and the teacher may both be unaware of this cultural difference, leading them to be frustrated about the other person's behavior. A peer may be teasing or provoking Charlie, or there may be factors in her life outside of school (job, extracurricular activities, family situation) contributing to her behaviors. Without considering the cause or contributing factors to the behavior, it will be difficult for the team to determine an effective intervention.

In this phase, the primary behavioral concern is defined in observable and measurable terms and the baseline is established. These are necessary for determining student growth. When a behavior is not clearly defined, it is difficult to assess, especially objectively. The baseline, before the implementation of the intervention, is necessary to determine the degree of success of the intervention. The baseline may be established based on the frequency, intensity, and/or duration of the behavior as compared to the student's peers or to a certain behavioral criterion or standard. The extent to which a student's behavior deviates from the norm may affect the types of decisions made in regard to the behavioral goal and interventions.

Decision-Making

The purpose of the decision-making phase is to establish a goal and the intervention necessary to reach that goal. Goals may be established for the student, the teacher(s), or both the student and the teacher. The interventions should include the needed instruction and supports for the student and/or teacher to reach the goal.

The purpose of the goal is to clearly and positively state the expected or desired behavior as a result of the intervention. Setting a goal allows the team and the student to be clear on the expectations in terms of what the student (or teacher) will know and be able to do. Goals are essential to measuring and determining the success of an intervention. Writing behavioral goals will be covered in more detail in Chapters 14 and 15 in Individualized Education Programs and behavioral intervention plans, but they are also an important component in Tier 2 to establish the expectations for both the student and the teacher. See Table 10.3 for the main components of a behavioral goal.

It is often necessary for teachers to adjust their own behavior in order to help a student change their behavior, which may make it appropriate to establish goals for both the student and the teacher. For example, if a team believes that a student's

Table 10.3 Components of a Behavior Goal

A **goal** is a clear, positive statement of the expected or desired behavior as a result of the intervention.

Goals should be **SMART**
- **Specific**—clear and specific about what is to be accomplished
- **Measureable**—allows for a clear, predetermined way to measure progress
- **Attainable**—with the necessary support, something that can reasonably be accomplished within the allotted amount of time
- **Realistic**—doable and focused on what the student and teacher are capable of and willing to work toward
- **Time bound**—attainable within a specific time frame

Components of a goal
- **Conditions**—the conditions under which the target behavior will be assessed
- **Target behavior**—the specific, measurable, and observable behavior the student is working toward
- **Criteria**—the manner in which the target behavior will be assessed to determine when the goal has been met

Example

Given a lecture or teacher instructional time, Steve will follow the class procedures for answering a question (raise hand, wait quietly, answer the question if called on, quietly lower hand if not called on) with zero teacher prompts in four out of five consecutive trials within a three-month time frame.

Components
- **Condition**—given a lecture of teacher instructional time
- **Target behavior**—Steve will follow the class procedures for answering a question (raise hand, wait quietly, answer the question if called on, quietly lower hand if not called on)
- **Criteria**—with zero teacher prompts in four out of five consecutive trials

SMART
- **Specific**—clearly states that the student will follow the specific procedure when answering a question during a lecture or teaching time in four out of five consecutive trials
- **Measurable**—progress can be measured using a frequency chart tallying whether Steve followed each step of the procedure
- **Attainable**—the goal is reasonably attainable by students; whether it is truly attainable is dependent on being more familiar with Steve's strengths and areas of need
- **Realistic**—this is typically a realistic goal but is dependent on being more familiar with Steve's strengths and areas of need
- **Time bound**—goal is to be accomplished within a three-month time frame

inappropriate classroom behaviors (arriving late, slow to transition between subjects, off task, missing assignments) are an attempt to avoid class work, then it may be appropriate to establish goals for both the student and the teacher. The student's goal may be based on work completion (given an in-class assignment, the student will be able to complete the assignment in the allotted amount of time with no more than one teacher prompt in four out of five consecutive trials) while the teacher's goal may be to make the assignment expectations clearer and to provide more specific supports (given an in-class assignment, the teacher will state directions orally and in writing, model the correct way to answer the first assigned question, offer guided practice for the second question, and display using a timer the amount of time students are allotted for the assignment in four out of five assignments). Having a goal for the student and teacher holds them both accountable for meeting specific expectations in order to more successfully address the target behavior.

Although the goal states the expected behaviors, the interventions provide the instruction and support necessary to achieve the goal. It is inappropriate to assume that a student (or teacher) can reach a goal without additional support or intervention. These interventions can be designed for the student to learn and implement behaviors that better conform to the expectations of the school and classroom. This may include self-monitoring strategies, task analysis, reinforcements, social skills classes, a behavior contract, anger management classes, or multiple other means to assist a student in meeting the goal. The interventions may also be designed for the teacher to better meet the student's needs, such as providing more academic, learning different ways to react or respond to the student's behavior, making adjustments to the layout and/or culture of the classroom, or learning other behavior management techniques. It may also be necessary for the intervention to address both the student and the teacher. The student may receive intervention on alternative and more positive ways to gain the teacher's attention while the teacher may receive instruction on ways to appropriately respond to a student's inappropriate demands for attention. How Tier 2 is specifically implemented may differ from school to school, but there are two common approaches used in this decision-making process, standard protocol and problem-solving.

Standard Protocol

In standard protocol, the school has predetermined the types of interventions used based on the general needs of students. Students are identified and grouped according to the nature of their Tier 2 area of concern, and predetermined interventions are then implemented for the group of students with similar characteristics (Shapiro, 2009). Although this approach tends to be more common in academics (all students with reading fluency concerns in second grade receive the same reading fluency intervention), it may also be used to address some behavioral concerns, especially in terms of social skills and anger management. All students referred to Tier 2 and determined to have a deficit in social skills would then attend the same social skills classes. All students would receive the same instruction, no matter the individual differences in the specific type of social skills needed.

The advantage of the standard protocol approach is that it requires fewer resources and less time. The interventions in standard protocol are often conducted in small groups rather than individually, requiring fewer faculty to implement. The faculty or staff responsible for conducting fidelity checks must be knowledgeable only about the components of a smaller number of previously agreed-upon interventions. In this approach, because a set procedure for interventions has previously been established, the team spends less time brainstorming and deciding on the course of action. Students may also benefit from this approach in that they may begin receiving the interventions in a timelier manner because the interventions have already been determined (Shapiro, 2009).

The disadvantage of this approach is that it is not designed to meet the specific needs of individual students but rather the general needs of a small group of students (Shapiro, 2009). Although this approach may be effective for some, it may be ineffective for others. If a student's specific needs only generally align with the intervention, then its positive effects may be limited. This approach may cause some students to not receive the individualized interventions necessary to fully address the areas of concern.

Problem-Solving

The second approach used is problem-solving, which identifies interventions based on the specific needs of each individual student (Shapiro, 2009). This is a more collaborative approach that requires the team to brainstorm and devise individualized interventions to best meet individual student's needs.

The advantage of this approach is that interventions are designed to meet the individual needs of the student and ensures that their academic and behavioral needs are specifically addressed (Shapiro, 2009). If a student's problem behavior is turn taking (alternating taking turns in an activity or conversation), then the intervention specifically addresses turn taking rather than all social skills, as would be the case in standard protocol.

The disadvantage of the problem-solving approach is that it requires more resources and is more time consuming. Because each intervention is individualized, more resources are required in implementation. For example, in standard protocol a group of six students with social skills concerns would require one faculty member to teach a general class on social skills. In problem-solving, multiple faculty members would be required to teach each student (rather than the small group) the individualized skills they need. The person responsible for conducting fidelity checks would have to be knowledgeable about many different types of interventions rather than the limited number used in standard protocol. The problem-solving approach is also more time consuming. The team collaborates on each individual student to make informed decisions about the appropriate interventions for the student, teacher, or both.

The advantages of one approach are the disadvantages of the other and vice versa. The standard protocol benefits are in the needed time and resources while the disadvantages are in meeting students' needs in a general way. The advantage of problem-solving is that the individual needs of the student are addressed while the disadvantages are the necessary time and resources to do so. Some schools therefore implement a blended approach where there are options for both standard protocol and problem-solving based on the student's needs. There may be a standard protocol for some behaviors (social skills, anger management) while also having options for problem-solving based on a student's individual needs (following directions, getting attention). Some behaviors are more easily addressed in a small-group setting while other behaviors need a more individualized approach.

No matter the approach used, the purpose of the decision-making phase is to determine the appropriate intervention and instruction for the student, teacher, or both. This decision is based on the needs of the student and the resources available in the school.

Instruction

The final phase of the ongoing cycle is instruction. It is important to remember that all interventions involve instruction. Although addressing a student's individual needs may be referred to as an intervention, the key component to that intervention is instruction. No intervention will be effective in addressing a student's needs without further instruction for either the student, the teacher, or both.

In this phase, the results of the assessment, analysis, and decision-making are implemented through standard protocol, problem-solving, or a combination of both. The instruction in Tier 2 continues to provide the same components as found in Tier 1. The role of the teacher (Chapter 5) in establishing a structured inclusive environment (Chapter 6) that motivates and engages the student (Chapter 7) and implements group management strategies (Chapter 8) continues to be core a component in Tier 2 instruction.

Team members in the instruction phase can assume the role of a collaborator, consultant, or a combination of both. The role of a collaborator is to assist in the implementation of the intervention. For example, a school counselor may serve as a collaborator by providing instruction in social skills classes to the targeted students. A consultant, on the other hand, provides direction or instruction to the teacher primarily responsible for providing the intervention but does not directly provide the intervention itself. For example, a special education teacher could provide instruction on behavior management techniques to a general education teacher. A general education teacher could provide content-specific instruction (math, social studies) and resources to a special education teacher to make a class more engaging to students. A behavioral consultant could provide strategies to teachers that are then implemented in their classroom. At times, a combination of both collaboration and consultation may be used. A special education teacher may consult with a general education teacher about different strategies and also co-teach in order to implement some of those strategies.

The type of instruction provided is a team-based decision that requires ongoing fidelity checks to ensure that it is implemented in the manner in which it is designed. These fidelity checks should be conducted by a faculty or staff member familiar with the processes and procedures of the intervention. This is typically done through an observation where the person conducting the fidelity check observes the person implementing the intervention to ensure that it is completed in the manner in which it is designed. This facilitates accountability and allows the team to clearly determine if the prescribed intervention is working.

The type of instruction provided is based on the needs of the student as well as the resources and procedures of the school. The following chapters will provide specific strategies and interventions designed to meet a diverse range of behavioral needs including both externalizing and internalizing behaviors.

Progress Monitoring and the Ongoing Cycle

It is important to remember that the assessment cycle is ongoing. Once the instruction is provided, the student is reassessed on an ongoing basis to evaluate its effects. A student's progress is typically evaluated on a weekly or biweekly schedule. The initial baseline information, along with the results of the progress monitoring, are graphed in order to visually examine the effect of the intervention. After a set period of time, the team reconvenes to analyze the results of the progress monitoring. If the analysis determines that the intervention is successful and that the student is progressing toward the goal, then the team may decide to continue the intervention using the ongoing cycle until the goal is reached or the team determines the intervention is no longer effective or necessary. If the analysis determines that the intervention is not effective and that the student is not progressing in meeting their goal, then the team must decide the appropriate course of action. The team may decide to continue the intervention and allow it more time to make the necessary effect or change the intervention in some way to better meet the student's needs. Whatever decision is made, the instruction is implemented and continues to be progress monitored. The team continues to analyze the data and to determine the appropriate course of action until the goal is met or until the team decides that a referral to Tier 3 and special education is necessary.

Comprehension Check

1. How does the assessment phase in Tier 2 differ from that in Tier 1? How are they alike?
2. Why should the analysis focus on more than just the frequency, duration, and intensity of the behavior? What other factors should be considered?
3. What are the advantages and disadvantages of standard protocol and problem-solving in regard to the decision-making process?
4. Why is it necessary for Tier 2 to consist of the ongoing assessment cycle?

APPLICATION ACTIVITIES

1. Have candidates develop a step-by-step flowchart on the main components of Tier 2. Make sure the candidates include aspects of each phase of the ongoing cycle.
2. Have candidates assume specific roles (general education teacher, special education teacher, parent, administrator, and student) and role-play a Tier 2 meeting.
3. Have candidates attend a Tier 2 meeting in an area school and reflect on each phase of the process.

CHAPTER SUMMARY

Overview of Tier 2

- Tier 2 typically begins when an individual student is not making progress in Tier 1.
- For assistance, teachers may reach out to others for strategies and resources to help a struggling student.
- Tier 2 is a collaborative process where the student receives individualized intervention.
- There are no criteria established that qualify a student for need of Tier 2 support.
  - Each classroom, school, district, and/or state may have different criteria for Tier 2 eligibility.
- It is known to be a pre-referral process because it is intended to prevent students from inappropriately being referred into special education.
- It requires a team approach, which consists of teachers, parents, administrators, school counselors, and/or school psychologists.
  - This team collaborates using the ongoing cycle of assessment, analysis, decision-making, and instruction.
- Individualized pre-referral assessments and interventions are used.
  - Fidelity assessment consists of an observation of the teacher to ensure the intervention is provided properly.
- Academic referrals are typically more objective compared to behavioral referrals.
  - The criteria for academic referrals are typically established by the school or district.
  - Behavioral referrals typically do not have an established criterion.
- Behavioral referrals should include a description of the area of concern.
  - This description should be specific and include when, where, and with whom the behavior is most likely to occur.
  - The referral should include a hypothesis as to why the behavior may be occurring, previous interventions and their degree of success, and identify a goal to be accomplished as a result of the Tier 2 process.
  - Being clear and specific allows the team to effectively analyze the information and to develop a plan of action.

The Ongoing Cycle on Tier 2

- Assessments are used to specifically and objectively determine the student's strengths and baseline data in terms of frequency, duration, and/or intensity.
  - The assessment process should indicate the environmental components, teacher's behavior, peer involvement, cultural components, and any other factor that may be influencing the student's behavior.
  - Other assessments may need to be used, such as observations, behavioral rating scales, adaptive behavior scales, hearing and vision screenings, parent interviews or questionnaires, medical background, and/or school history.
  - Most common is a formal observation for data collection purposes.
  - Observations should be conducted at the time of day and location where the behavior has the greatest frequency or intensity.

- The purpose of assessment is to determine a clear picture of the student's present levels of the behavior as well as any factors that may influence the behavior.
- The analysis phase consists of the team establishing a hypothesis and defining the behavior in observable and measurable terms.
  - Data from parents may be useful in this process.
  - If the referral contains more than one behavior of concern, then the team should identify a primary behavior on which to focus.
  - Often focusing on one behavior affects and helps resolve secondary behaviors.
  - After the primary behavior is resolved, the second behavior becomes the area of focus.
- The purpose of the decision-making phase is to establish a goal and the intervention necessary to reach that goal.
  - Clearly and positively state the expected or desired behavior as a result of the intervention.
  - Having a goal for the student and teacher holds them both accountable for meeting expectations.
  - Two approaches used in the decision-making process include standard protocol and problem-solving.
  - In standard protocol, the school has a predetermined type of intervention used based on students' needs.
    - The advantages to this approach are that it requires fewer resources and less time.
    - A disadvantage is that it is not designed to meet the specific needs of individual students.
  - Problem-solving identifies interventions based on the specific needs of the individual student.
    - The advantage is that it focuses on the individual student.
    - The disadvantage is that it requires more time and resources.
- Instruction is the key component to the intervention.
  - The results of the assessment, analysis, and decision-making are implemented through the standard protocol, problem-solving, or both.
  - The type of instruction provided is a team-based decision that requires ongoing fidelity checks for accurate implementation.
- The assessment cycle is ongoing.
  - After a set period of time, the team reconfigures to analyze the results of the progress monitoring.

REFERENCES

National Joint Committee on Learning Disabilities (NJCLD). (2005). *Responsiveness to intervention and learning disabilities*. Retrieved from www.ldonline.org/article/11498

Nellis, L. (2012). Maximizing the effectiveness of building teams in response to intervention implementation. *Psychology in the Schools, 49*(3), 245–256. doi:10.1002/pits.2159

Richards, S. B., Lawless Frank, C., Sableski, M. K., & Arnold, J. M. (2016). *Collaboration among professionals, students, families and communities*. New York, NY: Routledge.

Rosenburg, M. S., Westling, D. L., & McLeskey, J. (2010). *Types of tests used in special education*. Retrieved from www.education.com/reference/article/types-tests-used-special-education/

Shapiro, E. S. (n.d.). *Tiered instruction in a response to intervention model*. Retrieved from www.rtinetwork.org/essential/tieredinstruction/tiered-instruction-and-intervention-rti-model?tmpl=component&print=

Shapiro, E. S. (2009). *The two models of RTI: Standard protocol and problem solving*. Retrieved from http://doe.virginia.gov/support/virginia_tiered_system_supports/response_intervention/two_models.pdf

11

STRATEGIES FOR EXTERNALIZING BEHAVIORS

Jennifer T. Christman

CHAPTER OBJECTIVES

After reading this chapter, students should be able to:

1. Describe three externalizing behavior disorders.
2. Plan interventions to address challenging behaviors associated with externalizing behavior disorders.
3. Distinguish between a child with typical challenging behaviors and a child with an externalizing behavior disorder.
4. List classroom implications of students with attention deficit hyperactivity disorder, oppositional defiance disorder, and conduct disorder.

The child who pushes you away the most likely needs you the most. This is said to be true when working with children, and it especially pertains to children with externalizing challenging behaviors. Often when a student is demonstrating behaviors that are difficult to accept, teachers want to look for an easy solution (removal from the classroom), take away privileges ("You are staying in from recess."), and struggle to build a relationship with that student. However, these teacher behaviors are detrimental to the student's overall development and may increase the challenging behaviors rather than decrease them.

Externalizing behaviors are behaviors that are directed toward others, reflect the child negatively, or show aggression toward the environment (Campbell, Shaw, & Gilliom, 2000). These are opposite types of behaviors to internalizing behaviors, those behaviors reflected internally, that you will learn about in Chapter 12. Examine Illustrative Case Study 11.1 for how these behaviors manifest in school and the process toward identification of an externalizing behavior disorder.

222 • Jennifer T. Christman

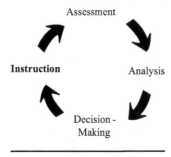

Figure 11.1 Ongoing Cycle of Response to Intervention

ILLUSTRATIVE CASE STUDY 11.1: STACY

Lola is an eighth-grade student. She is new to Mount Middle School and, since her arrival two months ago, has had eight after-school detentions, six office referrals, and an in-school suspension for two days. All her infractions are a result of missing work or disrespect toward an adult. For example, when a teacher requested that she answer a question at the board in math class, she refused to get out of her seat. In gym class, she sits in the corner and states that she "doesn't care about gym," refusing to change into her gym uniform or to participate in the class, other than walking laps for the warm-up (and she puts very little effort in when she does walk). She does not have an Individualized Education Plan, there is not a behavioral intervention plan in place, and her parents and her previous school do not report that behavior has been a problem in the past. She is maintaining passing grades but only by a few points in language arts, geography, and earth science. During her school day, she spends quite a bit of time socializing with peers and communicating on her phone. She makes excuses about adjusting to her new school when homework is not turned in, grades are poor, or behavior is unacceptable.

Lola is referred to as a troublemaker and as defiant. The school staff look at providing her more structure in a Tier 2 framework (allowing Lola to work for time on her phone or to sign a behavior contract with her gym teacher regarding her participation) while collecting data on the success of the interventions in place and analyzing the functions of her problem behaviors (defiance and missing work). As the staff members collect data on setting events and antecedents to her problem behaviors, on the frequency of the problem behaviors prior to the implementation of the interventions, the response to the interventions, and consequences that occur, staff members are also reaching out to Lola's parents to gain insight into any changes at home regarding Lola's behavior, health, and overall conduct. At the conclusion of a six-week Tier 2 trial in which supplementary supports were implemented, evidence-based practices were executed, and data were collected, Lola's behavior has not changed. The school is prepared

> to present this information to Lola's parents, discuss the interventions that have been implemented without success, and suggest a referral for a medical diagnosis because the school has intervened and demonstrated efficacy in their practices and because behavioral problems continue to negatively affect Lola's education (and, at times, the education of her peers).

Sometimes children who have an externalizing behavior disorder that adversely affects their educational performance are identified as having an emotional and behavioral disorder and can receive support services under the Individuals with Disabilities Education Act (IDEA). Other children do not receive federally funded formal services because their disorder may not negatively affect their education; however, these students may struggle with both the manifestation of the disorder and the secondary consequences that also occur. It is important to note that all children display some external behaviors during their childhood, but those who perform these behaviors over time and to a marked degree are said to have a behavior problem.

COMMON EXTERNALIZING DISORDERS

Common disorders that are classified as externalizing behavior disorders are attention deficit hyperactivity disorder (ADHD), oppositional defiance disorder (ODD), and conduct disorder (CD). Be careful to note that the abbreviation of CD as an IDEA disability category means cognitive disability, but when referring to externalizing disorders, CD means conduct disorder. All three of these disorders are currently described in the *Diagnostic and Statistical Manual of Mental Disorders (DSM-5)* (American Psychiatric Association, 2013) and are seen in children and adults. The *DSM-5* is a resource published by the American Psychiatric Association (APA) that compiles all diagnosable mental disorders. This resource is updated regularly, provides symptoms, signs, treatments, and characteristics, and is used throughout the United States and beyond (APA, 2018).

> *Comprehension Check*
> 1. What are the defining characteristics between a child who is typically developing and demonstrating challenging behaviors and a child who has a diagnosis of an externalizing behavior disorder?
> 2. Describe externalizing behaviors.
> 3. What are three common externalizing behavior disorders?
> 4. How are externalizing behavior disorders diagnosed?
> 5. What is the *Diagnostic and Statistical Manual of Mental Disorders*?

ATTENTION DEFICIT HYPERACTIVITY DISORDER

ADHD is very commonly documented in schools. According to Hinshaw (1992), ADHD is defined by "developmentally inappropriate levels of inattention, impulsivity and overactivity" (p. 128). The *DSM-5* reports that 5% of children are diagnosed with ADHD (APA, 2013), although the National Survey of Children's Health reports that almost 9% of children ages 4 to 17 have a current diagnosis of ADHD, and that accounts only for those diagnosed (Children and Adults with Attention-Deficit/Hyperactivity Disorder, 2018). The true prevalence is likely higher because there are children who are not diagnosed for a variety of reasons. The rates of diagnosis vary across cultures, races, and religions. It is suspected that the reason for this is because of the rater influence on the perception of expected behaviors. Notable is that twice as many boys are diagnosed than girls (APA, 2013). According to the diagnostic criteria in the *DSM-5*, "ADHD is a persistent pattern of inattention and/or hyperactivity-impulsivity that interferes with functioning or development" (APA, 2013, p. 59). The diagnosable criteria included in the *DSM-5* also states that "individuals must present symptoms prior to age 12, exhibit the symptoms in more than one setting, have clear evidence that symptoms interfere with social, academic or occupational functioning, and symptoms cannot be explained by another mental disorder" (APA, 2013, p. 60).

ADHD is classified with either predominately inattention or predominately hyperactivity and impulsivity. Attention deficit disorder (ADD) is no longer a diagnosis. Since the *DSM-5* launched in 2013, every new diagnosis is ADHD, with a prominence in inattention or a prominence in hyperactivity/impulsivity. Both an inattention and a hyperactivity/impulsivity diagnosis must show inconsistencies in developmental level and negatively effect social and academic/occupational activities (APA, 2013). ADHD is diagnosed when there is evidence of at least five characteristics over a six-month period. Some of these characteristics include the following (APA, 2013):

- Fails to give close attention to details
- Makes careless mistakes
- Displays difficulty in maintaining attention over time in tasks or play activities
- Appears distracted
- Fails to finish schoolwork
- Displays difficulty organizing tasks or activities
- Avoids tasks perceived as difficult
- Displays difficulty keeping materials or belongings orderly
- Exhibits poor time management
- Loses things easily
- Appears easily distracted
- Forgetful

Individuals diagnosed with ADHD with predominately hyperactivity and impulsivity must exhibit at least six characteristics over a six-month period of time. Some of the characteristics include the following (APA, 2013):

- Fidgets hands or feet
- Squirms in seat

- Leaves seat when staying in seat is expected
- Runs or climbs at inappropriate times
- Plays in noisy fashion when quiet play is appropriate
- Talks excessively
- Blurts out answers
- Struggles to wait turn
- Interrupts
- Takes over activities that others are playing

The cause of ADHD is unknown, but there is an increase in individuals diagnosed who had a very low birth weight, experienced maternal smoking during pregnancy, have a history of child abuse or neglect, have resided in multiple foster placements, and experienced neurotoxin exposure, infections, or alcohol exposure in utero. However, there is not a direct causal link between the aforementioned conditions and ADHD. ADHD is hereditable as evidenced by the elevated link among biological relatives (APA, 2013).

Classroom Implications

In the classroom, ADHD manifests itself in the same way as the characteristics just listed. When students are predominantly affected by inattention, they often have incomplete work, miss details in class work or assignments, lose materials, and do not appear to be engaged in classroom activities. As a teacher, this can be very frustrating, but it is important to remember that the child is not doing this intentionally. Adding to the frustration of the behaviors in the classroom is that, with a diagnosis of ADHD, some students qualify for special education services under IDEA while others do not. When students qualify for special education services, there must be evidence that the student's behaviors adversely effect their educational performance. In such a situation, the student can receive special education services under the qualifying disability category of Other Health Impairment (OHI). However, in some situations, the student's behaviors are controlled by medication, coping strategies, therapy, successful interventions, and so forth and do not negatively influence their school day. In cases in which a student is diagnosed with ADHD but does not qualify for a federally supported Individualized Education Plan through IDEA, a student can receive accommodations with a 504 Plan through Section 504 of the Rehabilitation Act. A 504 Plan is agreed upon by all teachers and recognized as an educational plan for student success. See Illustrative Case Study 11.2 for an example of how ADHD may manifest in the classroom.

ILLUSTRATIVE CASE STUDY 11.2: GERI (ADHD)

Geri is a five-year-old at Central Calhoun Elementary School. Geri is social, seems to enjoy being at school, has a gregarious personality, and makes friends easily but is struggling with school readiness skills. Geri has attended a daycare center since birth, and the center incorporated preschool skills into his day; however, he did not attend a formal preschool setting.

Geri's day starts at the daycare center at 6:00 a.m. He then has a 30-minute bus ride to school in which he often falls asleep because he has been awake since 5:30 a.m. On this particular day of observation, after being woken up upon arriving at school, Geri ran into school with his backpack loosely tossed over his shoulder, at times running into other students and appearing unaware of the large groups of students who were walking into the school building. Once Geri arrived at the classroom, he haphazardly tossed his backpack toward his cubby and slid, one knee tucked under his bottom and one leg straight out front, into his center of choice (he is supposed to remove his Velcroed name card from a board and place it at the center of his choice). He then participated in the center for three minutes (he is supposed to stay at one center for 10 minutes until the teacher begins the next activity) and then proceeded to move on to the next center of his choice without asking permission, moving his name tag, recognizing if the center was available or occupied, or cleaning up the materials he was previously working with. At this point, Ms. Clermint was in the hallway greeting other students, so she was not closely supervising all the students in the classroom. Once the bell rang, Ms. Clermint entered the classroom, turned off the lights to indicate the transition time, and asked the children to quickly and quietly clean up their centers, place their name cards back on the board, and sit at their desks. Geri jumped up and ran to his desk. When at his desk, Geri took out his pencil and began to erase his desk, holding the pencil with a very hard grip and rubbing the eraser until the eraser broke off. Geri then blew the eraser shavings until Ms. Clermint asked him to stop. Ms. Clermint began with a good morning song, and as soon as Ms. Clermint walked away from Geri's desk, he continued to blow the eraser shavings. He clapped along with the good morning song intermittingly, singing a word or two at a very loud volume, and then stood up and took a bow after the song. The students are expected to sing along at the teacher's pace and volume and clap to the beat for the duration of the song, and when the song concludes, place their hands quietly in their laps (as the lyrics of the song suggest). At this point, the principal began the morning announcements. Geri immediately got out of his seat to sharpen his pencil, walked around the classroom, and used his pencil as a drumstick on different objects (and students' heads). He then ran to his backpack, seemingly realizing that he did not hang it up upon arriving to the classroom, and hung it up, then crawled back to his desk and sat in his chair.

Ms. Clermint is feeling frustrated with this pattern of behavior and starting the day with so many redirections for Geri, all prior to the start of the academic day. Geri's day does not improve much, and Ms. Clermint finds herself exhausted by Geri's behaviors. She recognizes that Geri's needs are occupying a disproportional amount of her time, and the other 26 kindergarteners are losing time on instruction and attention because of Geri's actions.

Response to challenging behaviors in the classroom can have a significant effect on the continuation or discontinuation of the behaviors. Medication is the most commonly reported form of intervention for children with ADHD (Purdie, Hattie, & Carroll, 2002). Parents may choose to address the behaviors related to ADHD from a pharmacologic standpoint, medicating the child to decrease the problems associated with the challenging behaviors. Although a teacher may be asked to provide a perspective on the student's behavior from a school standpoint, to medicate or not to medicate is not a decision in which teachers are involved. Another parent-based decision is the use of behavioral therapies. Parents may seek support from outside of school therapy-based programs to decrease the presence of challenging behaviors. In school, teachers implement interventions to decrease the manifestation of the behaviors associated with ADHD, and in turn they hope to increase the student's engagement as well as academic and social success. Common interventions that have proven to be successful are environmental supports (Purdie et al., 2002), class-wide peer tutoring, computer-assisted instruction, and daily behavior report cards (Vannest, Reynolds, & Kamphaus, 2015).

Interventions

Environmental supports that help students with ADHD are preferential seating, frequent breaks (Purdie et al., 2002), and increased opportunities for movement (Loe & Feldman, 2007). Students who struggle with attentiveness, impulse control, and/or hyperactivity may benefit from sitting close to the teacher or to a responsible peer. They may also benefit from sitting away from the doorway in which other students are walking by or away from a window that affords a distracting scene. This preferential seating helps to set the student up for success in the classroom. Frequent breaks may help with the behavioral concerns of students with ADHD. When proactively built into the daily schedule, the use of frequent breaks can provide the student with an opportunity to move about, exert energy, practice mindfulness, and regain focus on a task. Students benefit from knowing that a break is coming and is available to the student regardless of their behavior. When students are provided with a break as a reaction to out-of-seat behavior, carelessness, exhibiting a lack of control, and other behaviors, students may inadvertently associate the performance of such behaviors to earn a break. However, if students recognize that the break is available to them under other circumstances, these behaviors will be better managed.

Class-wide peer tutoring is a strategy used to increase opportunities to respond. Within a diverse classroom setting, some students receive significantly fewer minutes engaged in academics than others. This is caused from individual student needs, work habits, and independence levels. From this concern came the idea of class-wide peer tutoring (Delquadri, Greenwood, Whorton, Carta, & Hall, 1986). In one example, through the implementation of class-wide peer tutoring, students received upward of 10 minutes of engagement, as compared to 2 minutes in the traditional model with 30 students in a classroom (Delquadri et al., 1986). In class-wide peer tutoring, students are paired together: a tutor and a tutee. During the first rotation, the tutor listens while the tutee reads or completes other work. The tutor critiques the tutee, coaches the tutee, and provides feedback on both the learning process and the academic product. After a designated amount of time, the roles are reversed and the tutor becomes the tutee and the tutee becomes the tutor. This increase in engagement and opportunities to respond have been shown to increase reading levels as well (Delquadri et al., 1986). This strategy is helpful in building an inclusive classroom because it enables students to work collaboratively, see individual strengths, and provide support on an individualized level. Students of different ability levels, cultural backgrounds, or genders work together in a productive and supportive way. This inclusivity is best met through student training and social skills awareness.

Computer-assisted instruction is an intervention strategy in which content is presented to the student on a computer and supplements direct instruction from a teacher (Vannest et al., 2015). With computer-assisted instruction, students receive frequent and exciting feedback while being provided with activity and stimulation. This combination has yielded positive results for students with ADHD, but it does require the teacher to obtain computers if they are not provided by the school. The teacher also must learn about programs that are appropriate for the student and the content presented.

Lastly, daily behavior report cards are effective for students with ADHD (Vannest et al., 2015). The use of daily behavior report cards requires the teacher or another adult to identify critical behaviors to be changed, set a goal for the desired outcome, create a rating system ("When you stay seated for 15 minutes during math instruction, you earn 10 minutes on the computer."), directly teach how to perform the intended behavior, monitor and analyze the progress and communicate the outcomes (Vannest et al., 2015). A way to formalize the daily behavior report is through a behavioral contract. See Chapter 9 for details on this intervention.

While working through behavioral intervention changes, it is important to plan for generalization. This is necessary for the comprehensive success of the student. This generalization allows the student to perform the behavioral change in a variety of settings, with a variety of adults, and under a variety of circumstances. This is critical for independence of the behavior change. One strategy to effectively do this is through self-management plans. Self-management plans are strategies implemented to help students learn how to increase independence in tasks by overseeing the monitoring and reinforcing of their own behaviors (University of Kansas, n.d.). This increased independence helps students to generalize the behavior change, which in turn, increases the probability that the behavior change will become permanent and decreases the demand on the teacher. When students take an increased responsibility in the monitoring, evaluation, and reinforcement of their own behaviors, they feel more in control (University of Kansas, n.d.).

Comprehension Check
1. There are two types of ADHD; explain the difference.
2. What are two commonly implemented interventions to help students with ADHD? Describe the implementation of these interventions.
3. Discuss generalization. Why is it important to plan and implement strategies to work toward generalization?

OPPOSITIONAL DEFIANCE DISORDER

ODD is another externalizing behavior disorder. According to the *DSM-5*, this disorder is classified as externalizing because it manifests in behaviors that "violate the rights of others and/or bring the individual into significant conflict with societal norms or authority figures" (APA, 2013, p. 461). A diagnosis of ODD comes after evidence of "a pattern of angry/irritable mood, argumentative/defiant behavior, or vindictiveness lasting at least 6 months as evidenced by at least four symptoms from any of the following categories, and exhibited during interaction with at least one individual who is not a sibling" (APA, 2013, p. 462). The symptoms include the following:

- Often loses temper
- Often touchy or easily annoyed
- Often angry and resentful
- Often argues with authority figures or, for children and adolescents, with adults
- Often actively defies or refuses to comply with requests from authority figures or with rules
- Often deliberately annoys others
- Often blames others for their mistakes or behavior
- Has been spiteful or vindictive at least twice within the past six months

Along with the alarming frequency and persistence of these behaviors, when these behaviors lead to distress in the individual or others around them, or negatively influences the social, educational, occupational, or other important areas of functioning, this is cause for a diagnosis. Also, these behaviors must not occur as a result of another mental health crisis (APA, 2013). Again, it is critical to recognize that these behaviors are seen among most children at some time; however, the increased frequency, persistence, and pervasiveness is what distinguishes a child with a diagnosis of ODD.

A diagnosis of ODD often comes during childhood or adolescence, is one and a half times more prevalent in males than females, is consistent across cultures, and occurs in about 4% of the population. The causes of ODD are not clearly identified, but they have been related to a harsh, inconsistent, or neglectful childhood, poor frustration tolerance, and other neurobiological markers (APA, 2013).

Classroom Implications

A student diagnosed with ODD can qualify for specialized instruction under the emotional disturbance and behavior disorder category of IDEA if the behaviors adversely influence the student's education. If this is the case, the student can receive special education services and will likely need a behavioral intervention plan in place to help with the management of challenging behaviors. In the classroom, a student diagnosed with ODD may exhibit aggression and struggle to follow directions, take commands from an authority figure (teacher, paraprofessional, bus driver), comply with school rules, or accept one's own actions (Frick, 2016). See Illustrative Case Study 11.3 to see how ODD and CD may manifest in the classroom.

ILLUSTRATIVE CASE STUDY 11.3: JAMAR (ODD)

Jamar is a sixth-grade student. He was diagnosed with ODD at the age of seven and, due to his ODD negatively affecting his education on a consistent basis, has qualified for special education services under IDEA. He was later diagnosed with a conduct disorder after repeatedly running away from home, getting into several physical fights, and starting a fire at an abandoned warehouse. He has an Individualized Education Program and a behavioral intervention plan, receives support from a paraprofessional and a special education teacher throughout the day, and is taught in the general education classroom for most of his academic subjects. Jamar had a very difficult start to life, living with abusive relatives in several different homes prior to being removed by the state to live in foster care. Before his diagnosis and the start of his treatment, Jamar lived with four different foster families in a matter of six months; each family would return him to social services when they felt his behavior was more than they could handle. Jamar moved in with his current foster family when he was ten years old; he is now fourteen. This is the longest he has ever lived with one family.

Jamar's foster mom and dad take him to family counseling and individual counseling weekly. These sessions help Jamar to recognize his behaviors, how these behaviors affect him socially and academically, and how his behaviors affect his family and friends. Although he is resistant to go at times (he must miss football practice to go), he knows that this is what he needs.

During the school day, Jamar's teachers provide him with breaks throughout the day, options on how to complete his work, smaller tasks when necessary, and the support of additional adults at times. He demonstrated specifically negative behavior towards one of the paraprofessionals who was previously assigned to him, but he no longer works with that individual because of this pattern of behavior. Jamar's behaviors are inconsistent. He attends different classes for each period, and there are some classes in which he performs as expected and other classrooms in which his behavior is consistently a problem. The special education teacher is working to identify the triggers in the classrooms that are consistently a problem for Jamar and is working with the general education teachers to build rapport with Jamar because that seems to be a significant influencer on his behavior.

Jamar, his foster family, and his teachers hope that he can continue a positive behavioral track. His behaviors are negatively affecting his social life. He rarely asks to hang out with friends on weekends, participate in after-school activities, or attend school functions. He does play on the school football team, but his counselors are not sure this is a good idea for him because of a pattern of more aggression after being at practice or a game. Participating in this activity may not be an option for Jamar after this season. When his teachers try to set up social situations for Jamar, his peers get frustrated after Jamar blames them for his actions, makes fun of them, or even shows aggression toward them. The school counselor wants to start a social skills group for Jamar and a few other students who struggle with friendships, but Jamar's grades are very poor and the counselor feels she cannot justify taking Jamar out of an academic class for this support when his grades are so low.

Interventions

Addressing behaviors related to ODD is challenging. One essential component to this is relationship building. As mentioned previously, students who struggle with ODD often come from unpredictable backgrounds (inconsistent parent responses to behaviors, various foster home placements, neglectful situations) and building a relationship that is consistent and predictable is essential (Minahan & Rappaport, 2012). Strategies to building rapport with students were previously outlined in this text.

Throughout this text, you have learned about the importance of identifying the function of behaviors. This identification allows a replacement behavior to be effectively implemented. This is important when analyzing the challenging behaviors of students with ODD. It is likely that the functions of behaviors associated with ODD are related to obtaining control or attention or escaping a task or demand (Minahan & Rappaport, 2012). Based on this, it is important to provide opportunities throughout the day for the child to feel in control, gain positive attention, and have breaks. These interventions are directly related to serving the functions previously listed. Providing these opportunities, along with positive teacher-to-student rapport and social skills training, all in a structured environment, can provide the greatest opportunities for success for the student with ODD.

Providing a student with opportunities to feel in control is difficult in a classroom. However, everyone desires the feeling of control, especially students with ODD. One strategy to permit students to be in control is to provide choices. Chapter 9 discussed the importance of providing choices to students as a commonly used intervention strategy. These choices can be related to where students complete their work (on the floor with a clipboard, at the teacher's desk, or at the group table in the back of the classroom), in what order students complete their work ("You may complete your independent worksheet first or your spelling assessment, but both need to be completed before eleven o'clock."), how the work is completed (paper-and-pencil task, typed on a computer, or orally presented to the teacher), or, at times, with whom the work is completed (individually, in pairs, or in small groups). The teacher maintains control over all these circumstances by providing acceptable options, but the students feel in control because they can make a choice.

Opportunities to gain positive attention are essential to the well-being of all developing students. Acknowledging a student when they are doing what is asked of them and making it be known to others (if the student likes positive attention), for example, can be very encouraging to the student and can help to build the positive rapport that is essential in behavior management. Behavior-specific praise is a praise statement that draws attention to the behavior the student is performing that is desired by the teacher. Behavior-specific praise is reinforcing when it is delivered immediately after the performance of the desired behavior because the teacher's praise allows the student to hear exactly what the behavior is that is desired (Haydon & Musti-Rao, 2011). Besides providing verbal reinforcement through praise, positive rapport can also be built in other ways. Displaying student work on a classroom or hall bulletin board, providing opportunities to be a leader (line leader, class helper, team captain), or sending positive notes home regarding classroom accomplishments (not always specifically academic or behavior) are authentic strategies to build rapport. These positive affirmations benefit the student's overall well-being and development.

Providing a student with ODD designated breaks in the schedule is beneficial (Minahan & Rappaport, 2012). It is important to provide the breaks proactively by building these into the schedule, not as a response to challenging behavior. When used as a response to challenging behaviors, the student may interpret the break as an escape from the current demand (likely schoolwork), and if escape is the intended function of the challenging behavior, the function has been served and the student has been reinforced. To prevent this from occurring, it is important to schedule breaks for the student. This break should be an opportunity to be relieved from adult demands (Minahan & Rappaport, 2012)—for example, participating in a free-choice activity, engaging in computer time, running a school errand (if it is safe to allow the student in the hallway independently), or completing a classroom chore.

Students with ODD often have warning signs that allow the teacher to know that the student is feeling frustrated. The teacher should recognize the behaviors that lead to an escalation of problems. Many of the strategies previously mentioned can be implemented proactively, but if they have not been and a student is performing warning sign behaviors, the teacher must begin to react appropriately. It is also worth noting that children with ODD struggle with both emotions and behaviors (APA, 2013), so teachers must be attentive to both needs. Emotionally escalating responses may include crying or inappropriate laughing, and behaviorally escalating responses may include voice volume increases, pacing, or laying their head on the desk. As discussed with ADHD, it is essential to plan for generalization and independence with the maintenance of problem behaviors associated with ODD.

Comprehension Check

1. Define ODD and explain how it manifests in the classroom.
2. Explain strategies to provide students with opportunities to feel in control.
3. If a student does not like peer attention, how else can you provide them with praise?
4. Why is it important to build breaks into the schedule for a student with ODD and not solely use them reactively?

CONDUCT DISORDER

According to the *DSM-5*, CD is a repetitive and persistent pattern of behavior in which the basic rights of others or major age-appropriate societal norms or rules are violated, as manifested by the presence of at least three of the following: 15 criteria in the past 12 months from any of the following categories, with at least one criterion present in the past six months (APA, 2013, pp. 469–470):

Aggression to People and Animals

1. Often bullies, threatens, or intimidates others.
2. Often initiates physical fights.

3. Has used a weapon that can cause serious physical harm to others (e.g., bat, brick, broken bottle, knife, gun).
4. Has been physically cruel to people.
5. Has been physically cruel to animals.
6. Has stolen while confronting a victim (mugging, purse snatching, extortion, armed robbery).
7. Has forced someone into sexual activity.

Destruction of Property

8. Has deliberately engaged in fire setting with the intention of causing serious damage.
9. Has deliberately destroyed others' property (other than by fire setting).

Deceitfulness or Theft

10. Has broken into someone else's house, building, or car.
11. Often lies to obtain goods or favors or to avoid obligations (i.e., cons others).
12. Has stolen items of nontrivial value without confronting a victim (shoplifting but without breaking and entering, forgery).

Serious Violations of Rules

13. Often stays out at night despite parental prohibitions, beginning before age 13.
14. Has run away from home overnight at least twice while living in the parental or parental surrogate home or once without returning for a lengthy period.
15. Is often truant from school, beginning before age 13.

The *DSM-5* also states that "the disturbance in behavior causes clinically significant impairment in social, academic, or occupational functioning" (APA, 2013, p. 470). Children with CD often show a lack of frustration tolerance, self-control, remorse, guilt, empathy, and concern for the behaviors they exhibit (APA 2013).

The prevalence of CD behaviors are usually present in more than one setting and observed by various people. CD effects about 4% of the population and, again, is more prevalent among males than females and crosses races and ethnicities equally (APA, 2013). There are several risk factors for CD that include, but are not limited to, lower than average IQ, parental rejection, harsh discipline, physical or sexual abuse, parental criminal activity, a parent with CD, a biological parent with severe alcohol disorder, a biological parent with ADHD, and a slower resting heart rate (APA, 2013).

Classroom Implications

A student diagnosed with CD can qualify for special education services under the emotional disturbance and behavior disorder category of IDEA if the behaviors negatively influence their education. If this is the case, the student will likely need a behavioral intervention plan in place to help with management of challenging behaviors.

In the classroom, a student diagnosed with CD may demonstrate the aforementioned characteristics as well as struggle with social skills, specifically maintaining friendships (APA, 2013; Vannest et al., 2015).

Interventions

Unlike other disorders, CD is difficult to treat, so the emphasis must be on proactive strategies and prevention (Mrazek & Haggerty, 1994). Often there are early-warning signs that, eventually, become comprehensive CD. Addressing these early-warning signs with early intervention is imperative. Most of the successful early-intervention approaches for students with conduct disorders are family- based therapy interventions and not school-based intervention. Family-based therapy programs are aimed at teaching parents appropriate responses to the challenging behavior and building positive relationships within the family (Frick, 2016). Parent training is highly effective (Hawes & Dadds, 2005).

In school, it is important to create positive classroom climates and to build a positive rapport with students with any type of emotional or behavioral disorder. When building rapport, teachers must take a personal interest in students (Brown & Skinner, 2007). Attending a sporting or musical event outside of the school day, asking about a family party or new pair of shoes, or inviting a student to join you for lunch in the classroom are strategies to demonstrate to a student that the teacher is taking a personal interest. Engaging in meaningful communication with students with emotional disturbance and behavior disorder is another effective strategy for building rapport (Brown & Skinner, 2007). Listening to students, being empathetic and supportive, and using nonverbal communication (eye contact, smiles, high fives) are all effective and meaningful communication strategies. Information on building rapport with students was explained in Chapters 5 and 6.

Anger management and social skills training are critical for students with CD (Vannest et al., 2015). Anger management training in school teaches students not to change their emotions but to respond more appropriately to the emotions they are feeling. Anger management training components vary; however, many use journaling, role-playing, and personal reflection to identify triggers and response strategies, illustrations, and maintenance sessions over time (Kellner, Bry, & Colletti, 2002). Social skills training is another advantageous approach to remediating the challenges of CD. Similarly to anger management programs, social skills training approaches vary, but there are consistent elements, including, but not limited to, modeling, problem-solving training, peer training, and self-monitoring (Maag, 2006). Perspective taking is another component to social skills training that aids students in the behavior change process (Frick, 2016). Perspective taking is observing the behaviors of another individual and predicting the individual's response to a situation (LeBlanc et al., 2003).

Students with externalizing behavior disorders struggle with their emotional and behavioral problems in all aspects of their lives. They struggle with social situations (Frick, 2016), academics (Hinshaw, 1992), and family life (Jianghong, 2004) and are often dually diagnosed with other types of mental health impairments, along with externalizing behavior disorders, such as anxiety and depression (Frick, 2016). Longer term research shows that childhood aggression is a robust precursor to adult crime

(Jianghong, 2004). This is important for teachers to recognize because the behavioral problems may be one layer of the challenges in their day-to-day life but may be only the tip of the iceberg when looking at the whole student.

> *Comprehension Check*
> 1. Define and describe a student with CD.
> 2. What are some strategies to help students with CD manage their anger?
> 3. Discuss perspective taking and why it is important in social skills proficiency.

When acknowledging how challenging the lifestyle of an individual with an externalizing behavior disorder may be, it is important to maintain the perspective that the behavioral challenges are not always a choice. The child's behaviors are a means of communication, and teacher behavior can make a significant difference in the overall well-being of every child.

APPLICATION ACTIVITIES

1. In a field experience, discuss with your cooperating teacher the strategies used in the classroom to help students with externalizing behavior disorders. Then talk to a counselor, psychologist, or physician about the challenges these disorders place on children through their development. Combine ideas from the professionals and discuss how can teachers set up a classroom for optimal success for these students.
2. With your college class, examine the case studies in this chapter. In small groups, have each person take on a role—general education teacher, special education teacher, parent, and school counselor—and discuss one of the students described in the case studies (Lola, Geri, or Jamar). Collaborate on a plan to best teach Lola, Geri, or Jamar. What strategies should be in place? Who is responsible for execution and data collection?

CHAPTER SUMMARY

Externalizing Behaviors

- These are behaviors that are negatively executed on the environment, are visually observable, and reflect the child negatively.
- Some students can receive support under the Individuals with Disabilities Education Act (IDEA) while others do not receive federally funded services. Because of this, they may struggle with disorders and secondary consequences.
- All children display some external behaviors during their childhood, but those who perform these behaviors over time and to a certain degree may be identified has having a behavior problem.

Common Externalizing Disorders

- Attention Deficit Hyperactivity Disorder (ADHD)
  - ADHD is a persistent pattern of inattention and/or hyperactivity/impulsivity that interferes with functioning or development.
  - ADHD is classified with either predominately inattention or hyperactivity/impulsivity.
  - Rates of diagnosis vary across cultures, races, and religions.
  - Twice as many boys are diagnosed than girls.
  - Both inattention and hyperactivity/impulsivity diagnosis must be inconsistent with developmental level and negatively influence social and academic or occupational activities.
  - The cause of ADHD is unknown but is hereditable.
  - In the classroom, these students often have incomplete work, miss details in class work or assignments, lose materials, and do not appear to be engaged in classroom activities.
  - In some situations, the student's behaviors are controlled by medication, coping strategies, therapy, or successful interventions and do not negatively affect their school day.
  - Students can receive accommodations with a 504 Plan through Section 504. This plan is not legally binding and holds less weight than an Individualized Education Program.
  - Environmental supports for the student are preferential seating, frequent breaks, increased opportunities for movement, organizational supports, and visual reminders.
  - In class-wide peer tutoring, students are paired together as tutor and tutee. The tutor listens, critiques, and gives feedback.
  - This strategy builds an inclusive classroom and enables students to work together, identifies strengths, and provides individualized support.
  - Computer-assisted instruction is an intervention strategy where students receive frequent and exciting feedback while provided activity and stimulation.
  - A daily behavior report card is a beneficial intervention that requires the teacher to identify a behavior to change, set a goal for the desired outcome, create a rating system, and directly teach how to perform the behavior, then monitor and analyze the progress.
- Oppositional Defiance Disorder (ODD)
  - ODD is an externalizing behavior that violates the rights of others and/or brings the individual into significant conflict with societal norms or authority figures.
  - The diagnosis comes after a pattern of angry/irritable mood, argumentative/defiant behavior, or vindictiveness lasting at least six months.
  - The diagnosis most often comes during childhood or adolescence.
  - Students who are diagnosed can qualify for specialized instruction under the emotional disturbance and behavior disorder category of IDEA.

- In the classroom, a student may struggle to follow directions, take commands from an authority figure, refuse to comply with school rules, or frustrate peers.
- Build a relationship with these students that is consistent and predictable.
- Provide opportunities for students to feel in control by offering choices.
- Provide positive attention through verbal praise.
- Schedule breaks throughout the day.
- Students with ODD often display warning signs prior to problematic behaviors.
- Conduct Disorder (CD)
    - CD is a repetitive and persistent pattern of behavior in which the basic rights of others or major age-appropriate societal norms or rules are violated.
    - Some risk factors for this disorder include lower than average IQ, parental rejection, harsh discipline, physical or sexual abuse, parental criminal activity, a parent with CD, a biological parent with severe alcohol disorder, a biological parent with ADHD, and a slower resting heart rate.
    - In the classroom, students demonstrate the aforementioned characteristics and struggle with social skills, specifically maintaining friendships.
    - CD is difficult to treat, so emphasis is placed on proactive strategies and prevention, which can be done through therapy programs.
    - Building a positive classroom climate and positive rapport with students is important.
    - Anger management and social skills training are critical for these students.
- The emotional and behavioral problems of students with externalizing behavior disorders influence all aspects of their lives.
    - Students are more prone to delinquency, adult crime, substance abuse, and violence.

REFERENCES

American Psychiatric Association. (2013). *Diagnostic and statistical manual of mental disorders* (5th ed.). Arlington, VA: Author.

American Psychiatric Association. (2018). *DSM-5: Frequently asked questions*. Retrieved from www.psychiatry.org/psychiatrists/practice/dsm/feedback-and-questions/frequently-asked-questions

Brown, D., & Skinner, D. (2007). Brown-Skinner model for building trust with at-risk students. *National Forum of Applied Educational Research Journal, 20*, 1–7.

Campbell, S., Shaw, D., & Gilliom, M. (2000). Early externalizing behavior problems: Toddlers and preschoolers at risk for later maladjustment. *Development and Psychopathology, 12*, 467–488.

Children and Adults with Attention-Deficit/Hyperactivity Disorder (CHADD). (2018). *General prevalence*. Retrieved from www.chadd.org/understanding-adhd/about-adhd/data-and-statistics/general-prevalence.aspx

Delquadri, J., Greenwood, C., Whorton, D., Carta, J., & Hall, R. (1986). Classwide peer tutoring. *Exceptional Children, 52*(6), 535–542.

Frick, P. (2016). Current research on conduct disorder in children and adolescents. *South African Journal of Psychology, 46*, 160–174.

Hawes, D., & Dadds, M. (2005). The treatment of conduct problems in children with callous-unemotional traits. *Journal of Consulting and Clinical Psychology, 73*, 737–741.

Haydon, T., & Musti-Rao, S. (2011). Effective use of behavior specific praise: A middle school case study. *Beyond Behavior, 20*, 31–39.

Hinshaw, S. (1992). Externalizing behavior problems and academic underachievement in childhood and adolescence: Causal relationships and underlying mechanisms. *Psychological Bulletin, 111*, 127–155.

Jianghong, L. (2004). Childhood externalizing behavior: Theory and implications. *Journal of Child and Adolescent Psychiatric Nursing, 17*, 93–103.

Kellner, M., Bry, B., & Colletti, L. (2002). Teaching anger management skills to students with severe emotional and behavioral disorders. *Behavioral Disorders, 27*, 400–407.

LeBlanc, L., Coates, A., Daneshvar, S., Charlop-Christy, M., Morris, C., & Lancaster, B. (2003). Using video modeling and reinforcement to teach perspective-taking skills to children with autism. *Journal of Applied Behavior Analysis, 36*, 253–257.

Loe, I., & Feldman, H. (2007). Academic and educational outcomes of children with ADHD. *Journal of Pediatric Psychology, 32*, 643–654.

Maag, J. (2006). Social skills training for students with emotional and behavioral disorders: A review of reviews. *Behavioral Disorders, 32*, 5–17.

Minahan, J., & Rappaport, N. (2012). *The behavior code: A practical guide to understanding and teaching the most challenging students.* Cambridge, MA: Harvard Education Press.

Mrazek, P., & Haggerty, R. (Eds.). (1994). *Reducing risks for mental disorders: Frontiers for preventative intervention research.* Washington, DC: National Academy Press.

Purdic, N., Hattie, J., & Carroll, A. (2002). A review of the research on interventions for attention deficit hyperactivity disorder: What works best? *Review of Educational Research, 72*, 61–99.

University of Kansas. (n.d.). *Teaching self management skills.* Retrieved from www.specialconnections.ku.edu/?q=behavior_plans/positive_behavior_support_interventions/teacher_tools/teaching_self_management_skills

Vannest, K., Reynolds, C., & Kamphaus, R. (2015). *BASC 3: Behavior intervention guide.* Bloomington, MN: Pearson.

12

INTERNALIZING BEHAVIORS

Joni L. Baldwin

CHAPTER OBJECTIVES

After reading this chapter, students should be able to:

1. Define internalizing behaviors.
2. Explain how students with internalizing behaviors may be identified and helped.
3. Discuss intervention and treatment options for internalized behaviors.
4. Identify the members of a school-based team for internalizing behaviors and discuss their roles.

Everyone likes the good kid. You know, the one who sits anywhere in the room, follows directions, seldom asks or answers questions, but that's okay because you can tell by their work that they are paying attention. But what if there is an *internalizing behavior* that really is affecting their work, interactions with others, and general functioning in life? And if we don't know there is a problem, how do we refer the student for help?

Research shows us that if internalizing behaviors (anxiety, depression, eating disorders, post-traumatic stress disorder) are not addressed, they may intensify and start interfering with students' learning (Crundwell & Killu, 2010; Smith, 2014). Kern, Hilt-Panahon, and Mukherjee (2013) report "negative outcomes, including low self-esteem, social withdrawal, sadness, physical health problems, lack of concentration, poor academic performance in school, disrupted day-to-day functioning, and, in severe cases, even suicide" (p. 60).

Internalizing disorders are not noticeable like externalizing disorders. Those with externalizing behaviors make themselves known by being verbal, destroying property, getting in fights, and spending much time in the principal's office. Their education is under scrutiny, and a referral to special education will likely happen if strategies at Tier 1 and Tier 2 are unsuccessful. Students with internalizing disorders prefer not to call attention to themselves. They may actually be overachievers, struggling to take advanced courses, and their grades do not indicate an academic problem. They are seldom referred for special education and may have not been identified as having an academic or behavior problem in Tier 1; thus, they have not been a part of Tier 2 interventions.

The Individuals with Disabilities Education Act (IDEA) defines emotional disturbance as follows:

> A condition exhibiting one or more of the following characteristics over a long period of time and to a marked degree that adversely affects a child's educational performance:
>
> 1. An inability to learn that cannot be explained by intellectual, sensory, or health factors.
> 2. An inability to build or maintain satisfactory interpersonal relationships with peers and teachers.
> 3. Inappropriate types of behavior or feelings under normal circumstances.
> 4. A general pervasive mood of unhappiness or depression.
> 5. A tendency to develop physical symptoms or fears associated with personal or school problems.

As defined by IDEA, emotional disturbance includes schizophrenia but does not apply to children who are socially maladjusted, unless it is determined that they have an emotional disturbance (IDEA, 2004).

But what constitutes a "marked degree," and is every child who does not play with others at recess, always seems to be sad, or frequently complains of stomachaches going to be identified as having an emotional disturbance? Probably not, but as with other concerns, this student should be identified in early screening for Tier 1 and progress monitored to see if the symptoms go away. If Karen's grandpa just died, her best friend moved to another state, or she didn't get to go on vacation as the family had planned, then the symptoms of sadness, wanting to be alone, and feeling sick to her stomach likely will go away in a short time. Or it could take longer and she may need some help. For example, if Karen's mom just deployed to Afghanistan for a year, she could have these symptoms until her mom returns safely. In these first few examples, progress monitoring will help identify if the symptoms are improving, but in the case of a parent going to war, a support group at the Tier 2 level would likely help Karen and other students in that building who have parents deployed. Moving to Tier 3 and/or a referral to special education would occur if sufficient progress was not identified with Tier 2 interventions. Internalizing behaviors can affect academics and social skills and result in medical issues. Think of yourself; have you ever been sick to your stomach because you were so worried about something (like a final exam that you know is going to be hard) or just could not make yourself go to a party because you had a bad week? Or not be able to pay attention in class because a relative was very ill and in the hospital? We all have had experiences like this, but multiply these little episodes into weeks, or months, or even years, and a person's functioning will suffer in several areas of life.

Figure 12.1 Ongoing Cycle of Response to Intervention

Comprehension Check
1. Why can internalizing behaviors go unnoticed in a school setting?
2. What should be done to ensure that those with internalizing behaviors are identified?
3. What criteria in the IDEA definition could be used to identify a student with internalizing behaviors as a student with an emotional disturbance?

In the ongoing cycle of the Response to Intervention process, working with students with internalizing behaviors involves all the components of the cycle. Assessment will be needed to identify the problem, analysis of the data will be necessary, decision-making as to what interventions are needed, and finally instruction in the strategies identified will occur. See Figure 12.1 for a review of the cycle.

WHAT ARE INTERNALIZING BEHAVIORS?

Kern et al. (2013, p. 61) summarized the fourth edition of the *Diagnostic and Statistical Manual of Mental Disorders* (*DSM-IV*) as including the following diagnoses as internalizing disorders:

- Adjustment disorder
- Anorexia nervosa
- Bulimia nervosa
- Dysthymic disorder
- Generalized anxiety disorder
- Major depressive disorder
- Obsessive-compulsive disorder
- Post-traumatic stress disorder
- Reactive attachment disorder of infancy or early childhood
- Selective mutism
- Separation anxiety disorder
- Social anxiety
- Somatization disorder

However, in the fifth edition of the *Diagnostic and Statistical Manual of Mental Disorders* (*DSM-5*), clusters have been developed as the "clustering of disorders according to what has been termed *internalizing* and *externalizing* factors represents an empirically supported framework" (American Psychiatric Association [APA], 2013, p. 13). The *DSM-5* includes in the *internalizing* group, diagnosis of "prominent anxiety, depressive and somatic symptoms" (APA, 2013, p. 13). In the *DSM-5*, the following diagnoses are clustered with the anxiety, depression, or other disorders (see Tables 12.1, 12.2, and 12.3).

Anxiety

According to the National Institute of Mental Health (NIMH), 25.1% of 13- to 18-year-olds have or have had an anxiety disorder. The prevalence rates reported as of September 2017 are included in Table 12.1. Anxiety disorders include separation anxiety disorder, selective mutism, specific phobia, social anxiety disorder (social phobia), panic disorder, agoraphobia, generalized anxiety disorder, substance/medication-induced anxiety disorder, anxiety disorder due to another medical condition, other specified anxiety disorder, and unspecified anxiety disorder (APA, 2013).

Table 12.1 Anxiety Disorders

Separation anxiety disorder	Anxiety related to leaving home or loved ones. Affects the ability to attend school or other activities.
Selective mutism	"Selective Mutism is a complex childhood anxiety disorder characterized by a child's inability to speak and communicate effectively in select social settings, such as school. These children are able to speak and communicate in settings where they are comfortable, secure and relaxed" (Shipon-Blum, 2017).
Specific phobia	Intense fear and anxiety when exposed to a specific situation, place, or object (15.1% prevalence).
Social anxiety disorder (social phobia)	Anxiety related to social situations that require interactions with others, with a fear of being negatively evaluated by others (5.5% prevalence).
Panic disorder	Recurring panic attacks and fear of additional panic attacks that limits functional behavior (2.3% prevalence).
Agoraphobia	An anxiety disorder characterized by illogical fear of certain places or situations (2.4% prevalence).
Generalized anxiety disorder	Excessive anxiety and worry about everyday life events, with no particular reason to worry, always expecting disaster (1.0% prevalence).
Substance/medication-induced anxiety disorder	Anxiety as a side effect to a particular medication or substance, such as illegal drugs or alcohol.
Anxiety disorder due to another medical condition	Some medical disorders, such as thyroid disease or heart issues, can cause anxiety as part of the diagnostic symptoms.
Other specified anxiety disorder	When a person experiences panic attacks but does not have all the symptoms of a panic disorder and the anxiety causes impaired functioning.
Unspecified anxiety disorder	Anxiety without a known cause.

Symptoms of anxiety vary, but the predominant symptoms are irrational fear and worries. Vannest, Reynolds, and Kamphaus (2013) describe anxiety as a "complex set of interactions between experiences and genetics" (p. 143), and Aschenbrand and Kendall (2012) report that anxiety can be learned from parents or other caregivers. Irrational fears and worries can be about leaving family, certain places, schoolwork, peer relationships, health issues, performance anxiety, or natural disasters. Children are unable to concentrate on schoolwork or personal relationships due to the reoccurring thought patterns that fuel their anxiety.

Identification of anxiety disorders can occur through observations, interviews, check sheets, or self-rating scales. Often a medical doctor will be involved in the diagnosis and treatment options for a student with an anxiety disorder and will recommend that the school nurse and/or school counselor be involved with the student at school.

Within the school and classroom, anxiety will affect a variety of skills. Dependent on their fears, students may be wary of the cafeteria or auditorium. Large groups can be daunting, as well as a form of sensory overload, leading to increased anxiety and possibly avoidant behavior (leaving the area, causing an interruption to be removed from the setting). Assignments or activities that draw attention to the student, such as reading aloud, solving a math problem on the board, or small-group work, may trigger an increase in anxiety symptoms. Less structured tasks, such as a writing assignment without specific parameters, can be more anxiety provoking than a math worksheet with a defined set of problems and directions. Organizational skills can be impaired, leading to more anxiety because the student can't find their paper or doesn't know what to do for homework.

Interventions for anxiety include cognitive behavioral therapy, cognitive restructuring, contingency management, exposure-based techniques (phobias and posttraumatic stress disorder), family therapy, modeling, and self-monitoring and/or self-assessment (Vannest et al., 2015).

Comprehension Check

1. What are the primary symptoms of anxiety?
2. What are some triggers in a classroom setting that may increase student anxiety?
3. Do you know others with anxiety? What are their triggers?

Depression

According to the NIMH, 25.1% of 13- to 18-year-olds have or have had a depressive disorder. The prevalence rates as of September 2017 are included in Table 12.2. Depressive disorders include major depressive disorder (depression), persistent depressive disorder (dysthymia), premenstrual dysphoric disorder, substance/medication-induced depressive disorder, depressive disorder due to other medical condition, other specified depressive disorder, and unspecified depressive disorder (APA, 2013).

Table 12.2 Depressive Disorders

Major depressive disorder (depression)	Sad, depressed mood for at least two weeks, feelings of low self-worth, and loss of interest in former pleasurable activities that affect all areas of functioning.
Persistent depressive disorder (dysthymia)	A continuous long-term form of depression (prevalence 11.2%).
Premenstrual dysphoric disorder	Severe form of premenstrual syndrome. Severe irritability, tension, and depression. Is cyclic in pattern but interferes with life functioning while occurring.
Substance/medication-induced depressive disorder	The use of certain medications (abuse) that cause symptoms of depression.
Depressive disorder due to another medical condition	Certain medical diagnoses can result in depressive symptoms as a part of the disorder/disease.
Other specified depressive disorder	Depressive episodes lasting four or more weeks, but the symptoms present do not meet the criteria for major depressive disorder.
Unspecified depressive disorder	Depression that exhibits some or all of the symptoms of other depressive categories but does not meet the full criteria.

Depression results in a student having impaired functioning in all aspects of their life. This can occur after a specific event, or it can have no evident trigger. Genetics have been proven to be a factor in depression, and depression has been shown to cause changes to the brain, either temporary or permanent (APA, 2013). Depression is considered a brain illness, with irrational and distorted thoughts, characterized by dysfunctional thinking, behaviors, and emotions (Vannest et al., 2015). It can also result in self-defeating thoughts and self-doubt (Minahan & Rappaport, 2013).

For example, Sarah is a 13-year-old freshman in high school. She has been refusing to get out of bed to go to school. She reported to her mother that everyone hates her, and she is failing all her classes. Sarah is sobbing uncontrollably as she speaks with her mom. When Sarah's mom (Jan) meets with the school counselor, Jan discovers that Sarah received a C on one of her papers in history class and a B on a math test. The school counselor also tells Jan that Sarah has isolated herself at lunch, refusing to sit with students who considered themselves her friends before this current episode of withdrawn behavior. Because of her depression, Sarah is not reading social cues accurately and has irrationally characterized all her studies as failing. Intervention will be needed to help Sarah alter her thought patterns.

Students with depression may have trouble eating or sleeping, be irritable or moody, and have feeling of worthlessness, suicidal ideation, or extreme fatigue. Somatic complaints (feelings of illness or pain) may be present, including the request not to go school because they have a stomachache or headache. Depression can affect executive functioning skills, including task initiation, working memory, initiative, attention span, and organizational skills. These difficulties affect the ability to learn new material, retrieve learned material, and participate in class or other activities of the school day. The student may not make the effort to do schoolwork or ask for assistance if needed, and grades will deteriorate. The teacher may be the first person to notice differences in the student and may need to refer the student to an early intervention team.

Although depression has generally been classified as an adult disorder, research is occurring focusing on depression in adolescents and children (Allison, Nativio, Mitchell, Ren, & Yuhasz, 2014; Crundwell & Killu, 2010; Smith, 2014). Smith reports that depression in children and adolescents presents differently than in adults, so depression may be hard to recognize to start the referral process. Allison et al. (2014) reported findings by school nurses in sixth and ninth grades through a screening process during mandatory physical screenings, and Crundwell and Killu offered a school team approach to helping adolescents.

Tandon, Cardeli, and Luby (2011) studied preschool-age children and diagnosis of depression and anxiety disorders. Concern for younger children begins with their inability to express their feelings and the lack of language skills to communicate their concerns. Modified interventions are needed for children, such as play therapy with puppets (Tandon et al., 2011). Additionally, sadness, isolation, and loss of interest for a persistent period of time are typical markers for identifying depression, and those feelings must be evident for at least two weeks. However, for some forms of depression, such as social phobia, six months of displayed symptoms are required for diagnosis. Tandon et al. (2011) argue that six months is a very long time in the life of a preschooler and that duration requirement should be adjusted. Identification of depressive disorders includes observation, checklists and self-rating scales, interviews with the student and those around them, and general overall regulatory state (physically and emotionally).

Interventions that have been successful in treating depression include cognitive behavioral therapy, problem-solving skills training, cognitive restructuring, pleasant activity planning, relaxation therapy, self-management training, family involvement, and interpersonal psychotherapy (Vannest et al., 2015).

Comprehension Check
1. How will depression affect a person's functioning in life?
2. List 10 symptoms of depression and categorize them per physical, emotional, and functional.
3. Why do you think depression has expanded to include preschoolers, children, and adolescents?

Other Internalizing Disorders
Eating Disorders

According to the NIMH, 2.7% of 13- to 18-year-olds have or have had an eating disorder. Eating disorders include anorexia nervosa, bulimia nervosa, and binge-eating disorder. Each of these will harm the heart, digestive system, and teeth (Mayo Clinic, 2018). Anorexia refers to excessive weight loss over the fear of being fat, bulimia refers to overeating and purging after eating, and binge-eating is extreme overeating. Those engaged in bulimia and binge-eating report feeling out of control with their ability to monitor their food intake. Eating disorders affect both genders, but girls are two and a half times more likely to be affected (NIMH, 2018). Intervention will include psychotherapy and medical treatments. School faculty and staff are often the first to notice anorexia, based on extreme weight loss and possibly over-requesting to go to the restroom. The school and faculty roles will be determined by the severity of the disorder and the possible need to be hospitalized or to attend therapy programs.

Somatic Symptom Disorder

Catherine is always complaining of a stomach ache and asking to go to the school nurse. The nurse will take her temperature and talk with her to find out where it hurts on a scale of 1 to 10. The nurse has tried having Catherine use the restroom, lay down with a heating pad on her stomach, and giving her some ice to chew. Following three weeks of almost daily documented visits to the nurse, Catherine's parents are called and they follow up with doctor visits and tests. All the tests come back negative. Although Catherine's pain is real, it is related to a mental health condition identified as somatic symptom disorder, not a medical disorder. The pain and subsequent excessive thought patterns interrupt daily functioning, including learning. Psychological services will be necessary, and the school will play a major role in Catherine's interventions.

Obsessive-Compulsive Disorder

Obsessive-compulsive disorder (OCD) can have a debilitating effect on a student's functioning in school and society. Obsessions are repeated thoughts that cause anxiety, and compulsions are repetitive behaviors that are performed based on the obsessive thought. Gina turns off the wall light switch but checks it three more times or else the house will catch on fire and her family will die. This is an irrational thought, and Gina knows it is irrational, but she feels she *must* check that light switch three times before she can leave the room.

A frequent obsession displayed is a fear of germs, resulting in numerous hand-washing episodes to the point of requiring medical help for chapped and bleeding hands. Compulsions, the repetitive behaviors, occur from a few times a day to several times an hour. Having things in order or organized in a particular way, such items on the desk in specific spots, is another common compulsion based on the person's obsession. According to the NIMH (2016), those with OCD often spend more than one hour a day on their compulsions, experience relief from the anxiety caused by the obsession once the compulsion has been performed, and cannot control their thoughts and behaviors, even when they know the thoughts (obsessions) are irrational.

Research has shown that there may be a correlation between brain abnormalities and OCD, but this research is not conclusive yet (NIMH, 2016). Additionally, studies with twins and families reflect a greater risk for OCD if there is a direct family member with the disorder. For example, Wala has an older sister with OCD, so she is at greater risk than her friend Amy who does not have a family history of OCD.

Attending school and being present to learn is affected by OCD. Psychotherapy and medication are generally the interventions used for OCD, and as in other conditions, the school's medical staff and faculty will be a part of the intervention plan.

Post-Traumatic Stress Disorder

Post-traumatic stress disorder (PTSD) is the result of an individual witnessing or being involved in a violent, traumatic event. Symptoms include reliving the event (flashbacks or nightmares), avoiding any activity that reminds the person of the event, having negative beliefs and feelings, and feeling anxious that an event will occur again (US Department of Veterans Affairs, 2017). Children can be identified with PTSD, and it is common for children who live in poverty in urban settings to develop PTSD as a result of the violence witnessed in their daily lives.

Treatment for PTSD also involves psychotherapy and medication, although there are a few different interventions used for PTSD. Trauma-focused psychotherapy returns the student to the traumatic event and helps them process the event. This can be done through cognitive processing therapy, where the student learns to understand how the trauma changed their life, and prolonged exposure therapy, which has the student talk about the event numerous times until it becomes less painful and anxiety producing. Places that remind the student of the trauma, but that are safe, are visited to help the student understand that the event likely won't happen again (US Department of Veterans Affairs, 2017). For younger children, puppet or dramatic play related to the trauma may help the child talk about the event, share feelings, and/or offer details they cannot provide because their language and communication skills are continuing to development (Tandon et al., 2009). As with other internalizing behaviors, the school should be a part of the intervention plan.

Comorbidity

Many internalizing behaviors can be present together (comorbidity), such as OCD with ADHD, conduct disorder, anxiety, or depression (Boylan, Vaillancourt, Boyle, & Szatmari, 2007). Eating disorders are often accompanied with anxiety and/or depressive disorders, and those identified with anxiety or depression may have symptoms of both. Interventions for these comorbid disorders must be individualized to the student, with the family and school staff actively participating in the interventions.

Bullying

Although bullying has not been identified as a mental health disorder, the process of bullying or being a bullied victim has been identified as a cause of depression, anxiety, and other internalizing disorders. Bullying is identified as an imbalance of power where individuals are intentionally intimidated, physically harmed, or socially harassed. A study by Lemstra, Nielsen, Rogers, Thompson, and Moraros (2012) indicated that being bullied led to poor health outcomes, including depression, and that the more frequently a student was bullied, the more their risk of depression increased. Kutcher and MacCarthy (2011) report bullying as a possible indicator of internalizing behaviors. Various other studies have also linked bullying to depression, especially for girls who are victims of cyberbullying.

Table 12.3 Other Internalizing Disorders

Eating disorder: anorexia nervosa	Anorexia is characterized by extreme weight loss based on a fear of being fat, not eating, eating very little, over exercising, and taking laxatives.
Eating disorder: bulimia nervosa and/or binge-eating	Bulimia refers to overeating and then purging after eating (vomiting and/or bowel elimination), and binge-eating is overeating without the purging.
Somatic symptom disorder	This disorder "emphasizes diagnosis made on the basis of positive symptoms and signs (distressing somatic symptoms plus abnormal thoughts, feelings and behaviors in response to these symptoms) rather than the absence of a medical explanation for somatic symptoms" (APA, 2013, p. 309).
Obsessive-compulsive disorder	"OCD is characterized by the presence of obsessions and/or compulsions. Obsessions are recurrent and persistent thoughts, urges, or images that are experienced as intrusive and unwanted, whereas compulsions are repetitive behaviors or mental acts that an individual feels driven to perform in response to an obsession or according to rules that must be applied rigidly" (APA, 2013, p. 235).
Post-traumatic stress disorder	Caused by experiencing or witnessing a traumatic experience, which can result in flashbacks, severe anxiety, nightmares, and uncontrolled thoughts about the event (4% prevalence; US Department of Veterans Affairs, 2017).

> *Comprehension Check*
> 1. What health issues can occur for a person with an eating disorder?
> 2. How are obsessions and compulsions connected in OCD?
> 3. Why are children who live in high-poverty urban settings more likely to develop PTSD?

INTERVENTIONS

Interventions are needed to help individuals manage their internalizing behaviors. Often a behavioral approach is used, but that may not be enough in the beginning to address the issue, and medication may be considered. Teachers are not generally going to be involved in these interventions, but knowing what they are and being able to support the therapy is important for the student to be successful. The following are some of the successful intervention programs for internalizing behavior.

Cognitive Behavioral Therapy

Cognitive behavioral therapy (CBT) is a combination of cognitive and behavioral interventions. The student is taught to self-reflect and to think of how to alter their behavior before a behavioral outburst or withdrawing from a situation. According to Kern et al. (2013), "the goal of cognitive therapy is to confront, challenge and modify maladaptive thought processes" (p. 61); "behavioral interventions . . . are designed to teach skills and provide opportunities to increase positive social experiences and pleasurable activities (i.e. reinforcers)" (p. 62). Minahan and Rappaport (2013) label maladaptive thoughts as thinking traps, such as "They all hate me," "If I don't finish this paper, I'll fail the class," and "If I leave the house, it will burn down and my parents will die." Teaching a student to identify those thoughts, analyze them, and recognize how unrealistic they are, and replace those thoughts with realistic expectations, is the purpose of CBT.

CBT is taught in five to 16 sessions either individually or in small groups. The students are taught cognitive techniques to help them cope with distressing situations, and then they practice those techniques as they are gradually desensitized to the trigger (Vannest et al., 2015). The behavior/problem is identified and operationally defined for the student to understand the behavior, and then a treatment plan is developed. The student practices the replacement behavior and self-monitors their behavior. Relaxation activities are sometimes paired with CBT. CBT is generally developed and monitored by someone trained in the intervention, but school personnel can be taught to provide assistance to the student at school.

Forms of CBT include the following:

Cognitive restructuring. This involves challenging negative irrational thoughts about themselves and their environments to replace them with realistic thoughts. For example, a student thinks he is going to fail all his midterm exams. Various strategies can be used, including thinking the worst and what it could mean (if he did fail all the exams, he would not be failing the class because he has As in all his other assignments), thinking about the accuracy of the thought (Would he really fail the test? He knows some of the information, so he probably won't fail, but he might not get an A.), and positive self-thought ("I know this material, and I won't fail."). Specific training in cognitive restructuring is necessary to work with the student, but the teacher can be informed about the strategies being used so that they can help the student when the negative or irrational thoughts are affecting their functioning.

Problem-solving. The student is instructed to face the problem, determine alternative strategies for handling the problem through research, and then choose a more socially acceptable response to the problem.

Pleasant activity training. The student is taught to create a schedule for pleasant activities to be included in their day. For example, if lunchtime is stressful for the student, resulting in anxiety-related behaviors, immediately after lunch a quiet break in the school courtyard is scheduled.

Contingency management. This is the use of natural consequences and reinforcement to reduce anxiety associated with behaviors or events (Vannest et al., 2015). The purpose of the behavior is identified (escape, attention) and a replacement behavior is identified. Rewards are provided for the replacement behavior (tangible fading to social attention, gradually faded to self-management), and consequences focus on requiring a change in behavior. For example, Dennis is afraid to go into the gym at school, but for safety reasons he cannot remain in the hall while the rest of the class and the teacher are in the gym. This is explained to him, and Dennis agrees to sit inside the door of the gym. He is reinforced with stickers for participating in this replacement behavior, and he gradually begins to move forward into the gym. Within a month, he was participating in activities with his peers. Positive reinforcement continued through all the gradual steps to replace the challenging behavior.

Modeling. Both live or video can be used to show the student that what makes them anxious is in fact not a concern for others. For example, in the previous scenario, while Dennis is being praised for gradually coming into the gym, other students are modeling going into the gym without any harm occurring.

Self-management is critical for CBT to be successful. The student must be able to review their thoughts, actions, and feelings in order for CBT to work. Jarrod is a bright four-year-old with anxiety, and his response to overstimulation is to run the halls of the school. Behavioral intervention strategies have not been successful in addressing his behavior, so a medical consult was requested and Jarrod was placed on medication. Once he had the ability to process the situation and to respond to strategies, he learned to remove himself from overstimulating situations and go to his "quiet chair" in the classroom or to go across the hall to a smaller, quieter classroom. Jarrod learned to monitor himself, to both take himself out of a situation and to know when he was ready to return. This ability to self-assess and self-monitor allows Jarrod to be mostly independent in his intervention.

Anxiety Management/Relaxation Training

Students are first helped to understand the relationship between life stressors and anxiety and/or depression. Although anxiety management/relaxation training is not a traditional depression intervention, there have been studies that prove it is an effective strategy for improving depression (Kern et al., 2013). Students are taught to tense and release progressive muscle groups, including hand/arm, head/face/neck, chest/shoulders/upper back, and leg/calf/foot (Kern, et al.). This is taught in individual or small-group sessions, with the student taught to take control of when they are feeling stressed and to implement some or all of the muscle groups to improve relaxation and to decrease feelings of anxiety and/or depression. This technique has been successful in several clinical trials.

Social Skills Training

Many students with internalizing behaviors have not had the opportunity to learn pro-social behaviors. Their shy, withdrawing behavior has not allowed them to interact with others to learn the necessary developmental skills of interacting, collaborating, sharing, or communicating. This leads to deficits in interpersonal relationships and social acceptance by others (Gresham, Libster, & Menesses, 2013), adding to internalizing self-doubt and negative self-assessment. Educational goals are also affected by deficit social skills because the student is not engaging with others to learn.

Social skills training is a process to teach students how to interact with others. The steps in this process include defining the skill, giving examples of the skill, and helping the student understand the importance of the skill. Modeling exemplars and non-exemplars of the skill, practicing the skill in a safe setting, and setting up a self-monitoring system are next, followed by actual implementation of the skill. Data collection and monitoring are implemented to ensure continued use of the skill (Gresham et al., 2013).

Replacement Behavior Training

Replacement behavior training would be a Tier 3 intervention, as it follows the steps of a functional behavioral analysis (see Chapter 14) and develops a plan to teach a replacement behavior (behavioral intervention plan—see Chapter 15). Please refer to those chapters for greater detail on developing a replacement behavior for a challenging behavior.

Interpersonal Psychotherapy

Interpersonal psychotherapy focuses on working on relationships with other people. This is particularly helpful for depression and has been shown to work well with adolescents (NIMH, 2018). The Interpersonal Psychotherapy Institute (n.d.) reports that this form of therapy is an effective treatment for internalizing disorders from ages 9 to 99+.

Family Therapy

Involving the family in the interventions for the student has been proven to be helpful in most cases. A primary factor for involving the family is to observe the student's interaction with their caregivers and to determine if there are behaviors from the family that are contributing to the internalizing behavior. For example, Farra, a seven-year-old in second grade, is displaying fears of leaving the house. Her dad wants to allow her to stay home and has even talked about homeschooling. Her mom feels that she is being ridiculous and just needs to go to school. Both parents will need to engage in education and training to determine what is best for Farra and how to help her in her therapy.

The first step is to identify the problem behavior, and then to educate the family and child on the disorder. Several therapy sessions might be necessary to teach common causes of the disorder as well as strategies to address the behavior. The parent will become a coach and supportive figure to the child, and as with any coaching training, the parent must be given time to observe the desired strategy (modeling), practice the strategy, and be given support as they implement the strategy to help them maintain fidelity.

For Farra, through conversations with her therapist, it was discovered that Farra began to get worried about her family when her grandfather died suddenly. She feels that if she is home with her family, then nothing will happen to them and they won't die. Interventions to help Farra return to school included having a parent take her to school and walk her to her classroom. At morning recess, Farra is permitted to call a parent, or both parents if needed, to reassure herself that they are alive. In the beginning of the intervention, one of her parents came to school for lunch with Farra and a few of her friends in the classroom, but this was gradually faded out as Farra became less fearful during long separations (a full school day). Farra was also given a phone card that she could use anytime during the day to call home but only once. She also continued to receive psychotherapy outside of school, and Farra gradually was able to reduce the number of contacts she needed with her parents each day.

Pharmacologic Intervention

Medications, particularly psychotropic drugs, are used in conjunction with behavioral or cognitive therapies. Although many medications for anxiety and/or depression (and other internalizing behaviors) were developed for adults, these medications are being prescribed to children and adolescents. De Andres-Trelles (2015) continued to warn of the difficulty of determining how children would function on medication trialed on adults, including the concern that symptoms are different in children than adults for many internalizing behaviors and therefore they may not react to the medication in the same manner as adults. A study of the prescribing of off-label drugs (drugs prescribed for a disorder or age group it was not clinically trialed on for Food and Drug Administration approval) completed in a Danish outpatient clinic for one day revealed off-label prescribing of the majority of medications, with only ADHD medications being prescribed as indicated by the manufacturer (Nielsen et al., 2016). Concerns related to adverse drug reactions were raised, along with questions of appropriate dosages. Suggestions that additional clinical studies of children and medications need to occur were offered.

Despite the concern raised by many studies, medication may be necessary for management of symptoms to then apply cognitive or behavioral interventions. Our four-year-old, Jarrod, could not concentrate until his anxiety was controlled by the use of medication. Once medicated, he was then able to learn techniques to manage his anxiety and need to escape from situations and to use those techniques appropriately.

Medications used for internalizing behaviors include selective serotonin reuptake inhibitors (SSRIs), serotonin-norepinephrine reuptake inhibitors (SNRIs), and monoamine oxidase inhibitors (MAOIs). Each of these works with the biochemical system in the brain that is affected. Teachers must know the side effects of the medications and monitor the student for any possible difficulties.

Comprehension Check

1. What are the key components in all forms of CBT?
2. Why is self-management critical to the majority of interventions for internalizing behaviors?
3. Why is medication prescribed to children and adolescents when the clinical trials were done only with adults?

SCHOOL AND TEACHER ROLES

According to the (NIMH), in 2010, 46.3% of 13- to 18-year-olds had mental health issues during their lifetime. Although this includes externalizing and internalizing disorders, this figure is staggering when it is often the teacher or school nurse who identifies behaviors that might be indicators of a serious disorder. The use of a tiered model of identification for social/emotional skills, in addition to academics, may help with identifying students with mental health issues. This will allow for early diagnosis and interventions to help the student with mental health issues be more success in school and life.

A school with a strong Schoolwide Positive Behavior Support program will be helpful for students with internalizing behaviors. The philosophy of "catching students when they are being good" creates a mindset for teachers, administrators, and staff to be positive role models for the students. Teachers are also more likely to be observant of all students, including the quiet ones. Universal screening of behaviors and emotions should be a part of the schoolwide plan, with those considered at risk placed on progress monitoring of their behavior, just as would be done with academics. Some key behaviors to look for include often being alone (recess, lunch, before or after school), not talking with others, somatic complaints (stomachache, headache), attempting to be with an adult instead of peers, coming in late to school, excessive requests to go to the restroom, and other atypical behaviors that are present on a consistent basis.

A positive classroom climate would provide the student with behavioral and emotional needs with a solid base of support for learning. In earlier chapters, you learned the role of the teacher as the guiding force in the classroom (Chapter 5), how to structure an inclusive classroom (Chapter 6), strategies to motivate and engage students (Chapter 7), and how to implement strategies for improving and maintaining overall classroom behavior (Chapter 8). With all these strategies in place, if the student continues to exhibit difficulties, a referral to Tier 2 would be appropriate. In Chapter 10, the role of the school's pre-referral team was discussed as well as the difference between standard and problem-solving protocols. The school either has a standard procedure for handling specific referral types (small-group instruction for trouble in math, small-group social skills training, check in/check out) or they problem solve each referral to determine what would be best for the student. With either of these methods, the pre-referral team will provide strategies to help the student learn and to engage in more positive behaviors to facilitate learning in the classroom. See Table 12.4 for strategies to help students with internalizing behaviors. Progress monitoring must continue to determine whether the interventions are working. If not, a functional behavioral assessment (see Chapter 14) is needed, with individualized help provided for the targeted behaviors.

The school nurse should be a key member of a team working with mental health issues in the school. The nurse may be one of the first people to determine a concern, either through required health screenings or an increase in somatic complaints (headaches, stomachaches that cannot be medically explained). Allison et al. (2013) completed a research study on school nurses screening for depression and/or anxiety as part of required health screenings of sixth- and ninth-grade students attending an urban school. The students completed the Patient Health Questionnaire-9 (PHQ-9) to determine depressive features and the Screen for Child Anxiety Related Emotional Disorders (SCARED) to detect anxiety disorders. The screening took little time, and 57 of 182 students (31.32%) received a positive rating on one or both of the scales.

Table 12.4 Strategies to Help With Internalizing Behavior Disorders

Classroom Strategies

Provide a structured classroom with a predictable schedule.

Post visual schedules for the classroom.

Create a supportive, nurturing environment, with an area for calming.

Model calming strategies, and include yoga for transitions.

Provide access to sensory fidgets to help calm or alert (calming box).

Use positive cards—"You can do it," "Happy face," "Just breathe."

Student Specific

Create a relationship with the student to help build trust.

Help students label feelings (use of a visual cue, such as an emotional thermometer).

Help students "read" their bodies (clenched fists, shoulders drawn up toward the ears, clenched teeth).

Incorporate structured, scheduled breaks into the day.

Use concise language when a student is in a heightened state of arousal.

Offer the check in/check out procedure for the student each day.

Help with organizational skills.

Be aware of medication side effects and monitor students' behavior.

Use a timer at the student's desk to provide visuals of the length of activities.

Allow choices of assignments to complete.

Group Strategies

Provide opportunities for small-group work, with each student assigned a role.

Pair the student with one other student (recess buddy, study buddy, lunch buddy).

Create small lunch groups in the classroom.

Those students were referred to the school's early referral team, and further diagnostics were completed. Sixteen of the 57 students were diagnosed with mental/behavioral disorders. Interventions to address the disorders included in-school therapy, out-of-school therapy, and monitoring by the school social worker.

The National Association of School Nurses adopted a position paper in June 2017 on *The School Nurse's Role in Behavioral Health of Students*. The conclusion states,

> School nurses recognize that positive behavioral health is essential for academic success. School nurses are critical to the school mental health team in that they can help address and reduce the stigma of a behavioral health diagnosis, decrease fragmentation of care, and remove barriers to behavioral health services. School nurses, because of their regular access to students and their experience with care coordination, are also uniquely equipped to assist school and community-based behavioral health professionals in providing services including prevention, assessment, early identification/intervention, and treatment of mental illness and substance use disorders.
>
> (p. 3)

Students with internalizing behaviors will need support in the school setting. A team should be in place that includes the school nurse, social worker, psychologist, special education teacher, general education teacher, and school administrator for the purpose of monitoring interventions and providing support as needed. Adults working with students with internalizing behavior may need support themselves, as some students can be unpredictable and fragile at the same time, causing the teacher to question strategies in place. See Illustrative Case Study 12.1 for school interventions for a student with internalizing disorders.

ILLUSTRATIVE CASE STUDY 12.1

Carla is a 16-year-old junior who has always been quiet, but her schoolwork is always turned in on time and is accurate. In fact, her teachers have referred to her as being a perfectionist. She is taking several Advanced Placement (AP) honors classes, which she has done in past years, but her teachers are beginning to notice some changes in Carla. She seems to be losing weight, forgets to bring her books to class, and does not turn in her homework. Carla has stopped participating in class discussions, and in small work groups it is evident she is not doing her share of the work.

Carla's teachers meet to discuss their concerns and invite the school nurse to join them. They all agree there is a concern, and the parents are invited to come in for a conference. Mom is concerned and feels there is a problem. She has noticed Carla going to the restroom more often, especially after dinner. She also is not eating the amounts she used to eat, simply stating, "I'm not hungry." Dad doesn't see any difference in his daughter but is willing for Carla to be evaluated by the school nurse and pre-referral team.

The school nurse meets with Carla and checks her temperature, blood pressure, and weight. Per Carla's records, she has lost about 10 pounds and her blood pressure is elevated. Carla insists there is nothing wrong; she just decided to lose a little weight. She admits to weighing herself daily and occasionally taking laxatives to help her use the restroom. With regard to her schoolwork, Carla reports she just doesn't have time to complete the assignments. The nurse returns to the pre-referral team, including the parents, and the team decides there is enough concern to refer her for a psychological and educational evaluation to determine if there are some psychological and/or learning problems. As these evaluations are being completed, it is decided to place Carla into a Tier 2 support group for a group of students with eating disorders and a Tier 2 small group on organizational skills.

Her assessment results reflect that Carla has average intelligence and academic abilities. Because she has chosen to take AP honors classes, she is struggling to meet the higher academic demands of an AP course. Self-reporting rating scales reflect that Carla is anxious about her grades, what other people think about her, her weight, and her relationship with others. Her anxious thought patterns have affected her ability to concentrate, resulting in her academic organizational difficulties.

Although Carla does not qualify for special education services, several services at the Tier 2 level are available for her, including the eating disorders support group and organizational skills group. Additionally, Carla's parents consult their family doctor, and he recommends a more intense eating disorders group at the local hospital. The hospital will work with Carla's parents, as well as Carla, to help them understand eating disorders and to provide strategies they can use to help Carla with her anxieties. The hospital consults with the school as part of Carla's interventions, encourages the eating disorders support group at the school, requests monitoring of Carla's weight by the school nurse, and offers to meet with Carla's teachers to explain eating disorders, the anxiety that is a part of the disorder, and teach them interventions that will help Carla in her schoolwork.

Carla attends the in-patient hospital support group for six weeks, learning about her anxiety and eating difficulties as well as strategies to manage both. The medical team decides that Carla does not need anti-anxiety medications at this time but suggests a daily multivitamin. While in the hospital, Carla continues with her schoolwork and is also taught study skill strategies that can help her with the higher demand of AP courses. When Carla returns to school, she returns to the Tier 2 eating disorders and organization skills groups and is placed on a Tier 3 strategy of meeting individually with the school psychologist, nurse, and special education teacher once a week. This is to monitor and provide support for the anxiety, eating disorder, and possible difficulties with schoolwork. Carla continues to recover, and by the end of the school year she is not meeting individually with the school psychologist and special education teacher, but she does meet once a month with the nurse to be weighed. Her schoolwork has improved as well, and Carla has learned that a B is an acceptable grade for an honors course.

Comprehension Check
1. How will a Schoolwide Positive Behavior Support program help with identifying students with internalizing behaviors?
2. What type of Tier 2 strategies would be appropriate to help students with internalizing behaviors?
3. Why should the school nurse be a part of the intervention team for students with internalizing behaviors?

APPLICATION ACTIVITIES

1. Go to your state's education website and review the referral and evaluation requirements for emotional disorders in your state. Would students with internalizing disorders qualify for special education? Why or why not?

2. In your field placement, ask to speak to the school nurse about her role in identifying and/or providing support for interventions for students with internalizing disorders.
3. Find a journal article about medication and school-age children. Review the article and write a reflection, including the medication, the rationale for using the medication, the side effects if any, and how successful it has been for helping the student be ready to learn in school.

CHAPTER SUMMARY

Introduction

- Internalizing behaviors include anxiety, depression, eating disorders, and post-traumatic stress disorder.
- Internalizing behaviors are not often noticed in school because students do not display learning or behavioral difficulties.
- The Individuals with Disabilities Education Act requires that a disorder adversely affect a child's educational performance before they can be identified as being a student with an emotional disturbance.
- Most students with internalizing behaviors will not qualify for special education.

What Are Internalizing Behaviors?

- The *Diagnostic and Statistical Manual of Mental Disorders* (*DSM-5*) is used to diagnose internalizing disorders.

Anxiety

- Anxiety disorders include separation anxiety disorder, selective mutism, specific phobia, social anxiety disorder (social phobia), panic disorder, agoraphobia, generalized anxiety disorder, substance/medication-induced anxiety disorder, anxiety disorder due to another medical condition, other specified anxiety disorder, and unspecified anxiety disorder (APA, 2013).
- Irrational fears and worries can be about leaving family, certain places, schoolwork, peer relationships, health issues, performance anxiety, or natural disasters.
- Children are unable to concentrate on schoolwork or personal relationships due to the reoccurring thought patterns that fuel their anxiety.
- Interventions for anxiety include cognitive behavioral therapy, cognitive restructuring, contingency management, exposure-based techniques (phobias and post-traumatic stress disorder), family therapy, modeling, and self-monitoring and/or self-assessment (Vannest et al., 2015).

Depression

- Depressive disorders include major depressive disorder (depression), persistent depressive disorder (dysthymia), premenstrual dysphoric disorder, substance/medication-induced depressive disorder, depressive disorder due to other

medical condition, other specified depressive disorder, and unspecified depressive disorder (APA, 2013).
- Depression results in impaired functioning in all areas of life and is considered a brain illness, with irrational and distorted thoughts.
- Depression affects executive functioning skills, including organizational skills, attention, initiation, and learning and retrieval of content information.
- Depression has been considered an adult disorder, but the condition is being discovered in adolescents, children, and preschoolers.
- Interventions that have been successful in treating depression include cognitive behavioral therapy, problem-solving skills training, cognitive restructuring, pleasant activity planning, relaxation therapy, self-management training, family involvement, and interpersonal psychotherapy.

Other Internalizing Disorders

- Other internalizing disorders include eating disorders, somatic symptom disorder, obsessive-compulsive disorder, and post-traumatic stress disorder.
- Eating disorders include anorexia, bulimia, and binge-eating disorders. Anorexia is excessive weight loss due to the fear of being fat, bulimia is overeating and then purging, and binge-eating is overeating without purging.
- Eating disorders can affect a student's health and quality of life.
- Somatic symptom disorder is when a student has somatic complaints (pain) but there are no medical reasons for the pain. The pain is real to the student and is actually a mental disorder.
- Post-traumatic stress disorder is caused by exposure to extreme trauma. Children who are exposed to frequent violence are candidates for this disorder.
- Interventions for other internalizing disorders include psychotherapy and medication.

Interventions

- Cognitive behavioral therapy is a combination of cognitive and behavioral interventions. The student is taught to self-reflect and to think of how to alter their behavior before a behavioral outburst or withdrawing from a situation. Types of cognitive behavioral therapy include the following:
- *Cognitive restructuring.* This involves challenging negative irrational thoughts to replace them with realistic thoughts.
- *Problem-solving.* The student is encouraged to determine a more socially acceptable response to the problem.
- *Pleasant activity training.* Scheduling pleasant moments during the day to reduce stress.
- *Contingency management.* The use of natural consequences and reinforcement to reduce anxiety associated with behaviors or events.
- *Modeling.* Having the student watch others doing the behavior that concerns them with no harm coming to the other party.

- *Self-management.* Teaching the student to self-monitor for signs of distress and implementing a strategy to reduce the distress.
- *Anxiety management/relaxation training.* A technique to teach the student to systematically clench and release muscles to help reduce the stress causing a reaction.
- *Social skills training.* Working with a student or small group of students to teach appropriate behaviors in a social situation.
- *Replacement behavior training.* A Tier 3 intervention with functional behavioral assessment and a behavioral intervention plan (see Chapters 14 and 15).
- *Interpersonal psychotherapy.* Focuses on working on relationships with the student.
- *Family therapy.* This is essential to help support the student by learning about the disorder, training to help the student with irrational thought processes, and being a member of the intervention team.
- *Pharmacologic intervention.* This is often necessary to allow for a reduction of symptoms so that the student can participate in the psychological and/or behavioral approach.
- Many of the medications used with children and adolescents have not been clinically trialed with this population. Research is needed on dosage, side effects, and the matching of symptoms to the right medication.

School and Teacher Roles

- A tiered model of identification for social and emotional skills should be a part of the school culture, just as for academics.
- Tier 1 and Tier 2 can provide assistance, data, and detailed information on interventions used if the student does not make progress and needs to be referred to a physician.
- School nurses are a key component in the intervention for internalizing behaviors to monitor health issues, screen for early intervention for behaviors, and work to remove barriers to obtaining help for the student.
- A team approach is needed in the school to provide support for the student and those working with the student.

REFERENCES

Allison, V. L., Nativio, D. G., Mitchell, A. M., Ren, D., & Yuhasz, J. (2014). Identifying symptoms of depression and anxiety in students in the school setting. *The Journal of School Nursing, 30*(3), 165–172.

American Psychiatric Association. (2013). *Diagnostic and statistical manual of mental disorders* (5th ed.). Washington, DC: Author.

Aschenbrand, S. G., & Kendall, P. C. (2012). The effect of perceived child anxiety status on parental latency to intervene with anxious and nonanxious youth. *Journal of Consulting and Clinical Psychology, 80*(2), 232–238.

Boylan, K., Vaillancourt, T., Boyle, M., & Szatmari, P. (2007). Comorbidity of internalizing disorders in children with oppositional defiant disorder. *European Child & Adolescent Psychiatry, 16*(8), 484–494.

Crundwell, M. A., & Killu, K. (2010). Responding to a student's depression. *Educational Leadership, 68*(2), 46–51.

de Andres-Trelles, F. (2015). Psychiatric disease moving towards adolescents and children: How much room is there for extrapolation? *European Neuropsychopharmacology: The Journal of the European College of Neuropsychopharmacology, 25*(7), 1039–1044. doi:10.1016/j.euroneuro.2014.12.011

Gresham, F. M., Libster, L., & Menesses, K. (2013). Research-based practices for social behavior: Social skills training, replacement behavior training, and positive peer reporting. In K. L. Lane, B. G. Cook, & M. G. Tankersley, *Research-based strategies for improving outcomes in behavior* (pp. 94–103). Boston, MA: Pearson.

Individuals with Disabilities Education Act Regulations. (2004) 34 C.F.R. § 300.307[a][2].

Interpersonal Psychotherapy Institute. (n.d.). *About IPT*. Retrieved from https://iptinstitute.com/about-ipt/

Kern, L., Hilt-Panahon, A., & Mukherjee, A. D. (2013). Strategies to address internalizing behavior problems. In K. L. Lane, B. G. Cook, & M. G. Tankersley, *Research-based strategies for improving outcomes in behavior* (pp. 59–72). Boston, MA: Pearson.

Kutcher, S., & MacCarthy, D. (2011). *Identification, diagnosis, & treatment of childhood anxiety disorders: A package for first contact health providers*. Retrieved from www.teenmentalhealth.org. September 30, 2017.

Lane, K. L., Cook, B. G., & Tankersley, M. G. (2013). *Research-based strategies for improving outcomes in behavior*. Boston, MA: Pearson.

Lemstra, M. E., Nielsen, G., Rogers, M. R., Thompson, A. T., & Moraros, J. S. (2012). Risk indicators and outcomes associated with bullying in youth aged 9–15 years. *Canadian Journal of Public Health, 103*(1), 9–13.

Mayo Clinic. (2018). *Eating disorders: Symptoms and causes*. Retrieved from www.mayoclinic.org/diseases-conditions/eating-disorders/home/ovc-20182765

Minahan, J., & Rappaport, N. (2013). *The behavior code: A practical guide to understanding and teaching the most challenging students*. Cambridge, MA: Harvard Education Press.

National Association of School Nurses. (2017). *The school nurse's role in behavioral health of students (position statement)*. Silver Spring, MD: Author.

National Institute of Mental Health. (2016). *Obsessive-compulsion disorder: Overview*. Retrieved from www.nimh.nih.gov/health/topics/obsessive-compulsive-disorder-ocd/index.shtml

National Institute of Mental Health. (2018). *Teen depression*. Retrieved from www.nimh.nih.gov/health/publications/teen-depression/index.shtml

Nielsen, E. S., Hellfritzsch, M., Sorensen, M. J., Rasmussen, H., Thomsen, P. H., & Laursen, T. (2016). Off-label prescribing of psychotropic drugs in a Danish child and adolescent psychiatric outpatient clinic. *European Child and Adolescent Psychiatry, 25*(1), 25–31. doi:10.1007/s00787-015-0699-z

Shipon-Blum, E. (2017). *Selective mutism: A comprehensive overview*. Retrieved from https://selectivemutismcenter.org/whatisselectivemutism/

Smith, D. D. (2014). *Emotional or behavioral disorders defined*. Retrieved from www.education.com/reference/article/emotional-behavioral-disorders-defined/

Tandon, M., Cardeli, E., & Luby, J. (2011). Internalizing disorders in early childhood: A review of depressive and anxiety disorders. *Child and Adolescent Psychiatric Clinics of North America, 18*(3), 593–610.

US Department of Veterans Affairs. (2017). *What is PTSD?* Retrieved from www.ptsd.va.gov/public/PTSD-overview/basics/what-is-ptsd.asp

Vannest, K. J., Reynolds, C. R., & Kamphaus, R. W. (2015). *BASC3 behavior intervention guide*. Bloomington, MN: Pearson.

Part IV

Application of Classroom and Behavior Management Strategies: Tier 3

Part IV

13

TIER 3 AND SPECIAL EDUCATION

Joni L. Baldwin

CHAPTER OBJECTIVES

After reading this chapter, students should be able to:

1. Understand the connection between Response to Intervention and special education.
2. Know the process for referrals to special education.
3. Understand the criteria for a diagnosis of specific learning disability and emotional and behavioral disorders.
4. Know the components of and be able to write annual goals for academics and behavior.

Students who have not been successful with Tier 1 and Tier 2 interventions for significant learning and academic concerns or challenging behaviors will be referred to Tier 3. Many resources identify Tier 3 as special education, but that is not necessarily true. However, there will likely be a referral made for an evaluation to determine if the student is in need of specialized instruction. The results of this process will determine if the student is eligible for special education. In Chapter 1, you were introduced to the laws protecting individuals with disabilities and briefly walked through the process with Olivia. In this chapter, we will go into more detail to help you understand the process and how it applies to Response to Intervention (RTI).

In the ongoing cycle of the RTI process, the areas of assessment, analysis, and decision-making will all be a part of this Tier 3 process. See Figure 13.1 for a review of this cycle.

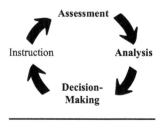

Figure 13.1 Ongoing Cycle of Response to Intervention

IDENTIFICATION OF SPECIFIC LEARNING DISABILITIES

The Education for All Handicapped Children's Act (P.L. 94–142) guaranteed rights to children and families when the child was suspected of having a disability. The 11 categories of disabilities, 13 as of the reauthorizing of P.L. 94–142 and name change to Individuals with Disabilities Education Act (IDEA) in 1990, identified requirements for the diagnosis of a specific disability. In the category of specific learning disabilities (SLDs), a "significant discrepancy" between the students' intellectual and academic ability was required. However, this significant discrepancy was not defined, and it was left up to the states to determine a formula. One state required a two-year gap between academic skills (a fourth-grade student scored at the fourth grade in reading but at only the second grade in math; the student qualified in math). Another state used a 21-point discrepancy between achievement and intellect (an IQ score of 110, required a reading standard score of 89 or below to qualify for special education in reading). The 21-point discrepancy was difficult to reach using just the total score on assessments; thus, evaluators started to compare subtest scores to reach the required 21 points. A third state used a regression analysis, which again left students out who needed help. This resulted in under- and overrepresentation of students who needed special education and required a student to fail before they could receive any help.

In the 2004 reauthorization of IDEA, "states were prohibited from requiring that school districts use a discrepancy formula; instead, states could allow or require that schools use a process that determined whether a student responded to scientific, research-based interventions" (Yell, 2016, p. 70). Per the 2004 IDEA reauthorization, one of the qualifications to be identified as having an SLD is the lack of response to research-based interventions through the RTI process. It must also be determined that the leaning difficulties are not caused by a lack of appropriate teaching in reading or math; a visual, hearing, or motor disability; mental retardation; emotional disturbance; cultural factors; environmental or economic disadvantage; or limited English proficiency (Pierangelo & Giuliani, 2017; Yell, 2016).

IDENTIFICATION OF SEVERE EMOTIONAL DISTURBANCE

IDEA defines emotional disturbance as follows:

> A condition exhibiting one or more of the following characteristics over a long period of time and to a marked degree that adversely affects a child's educational performance:
>
> 1. An inability to learn that cannot be explained by intellectual, sensory, or health factors.

2. An inability to build or maintain satisfactory interpersonal relationships with peers and teachers.
3. Inappropriate types of behavior or feelings under normal circumstances.
4. A general pervasive mood of unhappiness or depression.
5. A tendency to develop physical symptoms or fears associated with personal or school problems.

As defined by IDEA, emotional disturbance includes schizophrenia but does not apply to children who are socially maladjusted, unless it is determined that they have an emotional disturbance (IDEA 2004).

As with SLDs, determining if a student has an emotional disturbance requires ruling out intellectual, sensory, and health factors. Strong documentation from Tiers 1 and 2 will must be reviewed to help develop the assessment plan. Tier 1 data will be from the Schoolwide Positive Behavior Support program and possibly progress monitoring of the student's social/emotional behavior, Tier 2 would have included social group training, possibly a functional behavioral assessment and/or a behavioral intervention plan (see Chapters 14 and 15), check in/check out procedures, or other less intensive interventions than would be offered at Tier 3.

Comprehension Check

1. In 2004, what change was made to the identification process for an SLD?
2. Why would an RTI model in a school system help in the referral of students to special education?
3. Identification of an emotional or behavioral disorder could be said to be subjective. Do you agree or disagree? Explain your answer.

INDIVIDUALS WITH DISABILITIES EDUCATION ACT REQUIREMENTS FOR REFERRALS TO SPECIAL EDUCATION

As part of the referral process for special education, the school system must produce evidence that the student has been educated with "scientific, research-based interventions" (IDEA Regulations, 34 C.F.R. § 300.307[a][2]) during the pre-referral process. A student who has been attending school where the RTI process is in place will have the data through Tier 1 and Tier 2 reflecting that despite quality instruction and additional help at Tier 2, this student has not made the gains necessary to do grade-level work. Progress monitoring, data-based instructional decision-making, and the use of evidence-based practices will have already been documented. It is hoped that the parents have been involved with the school as the student has been engaged in various strategies at Tiers 1 and 2, but to make the referral for a special education evaluation, the parents must give permission.

A multidisciplinary team (MDT) is convened, including the parents, a general education teacher, an administrator, a special education teacher, and usually a school psychologist. An assessment plan is developed based on the needs of the student, and the parents give written permission for the evaluation. This evaluation should include parent and teacher interviews, consultation with anyone else who has worked with the student, formal and informal assessments, and observations of the student in their natural settings by someone other than their teacher. See Illustrative Case Study 13.1 for an assessment plan developed by the MDT for Logan, a third-grade student with problems in integrative reading, writing, and math.

ILLUSTRATIVE CASE STUDY 13.1: INDIVIDUAL ASSESSMENT PLAN

Name: Logan T.   School: St. Henry Elementary
Date of birth: 5/11/2009   Grade: 3.4
Chronological age: 8+6   Classroom teacher: Mrs. Jack
Date of IAP: 11/17/17   Participants:

  1. Mr. and Mrs. T., parents
  2. Ms. Adams, principal
  3. Ms. Giller, school psychologist
  4. Mrs. Jack, classroom teacher
  5. Mrs. Mound, special education teacher

Reason for referral: Logan is having difficulties in integrative tasks, including written language, reading comprehension, and math application problems. It is reported that he works hard, his processing appears proficient, and he enjoys science and hands-on learning. He was targeted for progress monitoring at the beginning of third grade, and his teachers in first and second grade reported no difficulties. Progress monitoring data reflected that Logan was not making progress at the expected rate, so he was referred to Tier 2 and has had small-group instruction for the past two months, again without noticeable gains in his skills. To assess his current levels of performance, the team developed the following individual assessment plan.

Question or Concern	Assessment Procedures	Responsible Person	Timeline	Initial When Complete
Appears to have average sight word identification, but reading comprehension is low for his age.	Woodcock Reading Mastery Test III	Mrs. Mound	Within two weeks	
Integrated writing is difficult for Logan. Obtains 100% on weekly spelling tests, but his spelling in context is poor.	Test of Written Language (4th Edition)	Mrs. Mound	Within two weeks	

Question or Concern	Assessment Procedures	Responsible Person	Timeline	Initial When Complete
Has difficulty with math application problems during seatwork.	Key Math 3	Mrs. Mound	Within two weeks	
Review of vision, hearing, and health	Records review	Mrs. Rea, school nurse	Within three days, before other testing begins	
Intelligence testing for comparison purposes	WISC-V (Wechsler Intelligence Scale for Children, Fifth Edition)	Ms. Giller	Within two weeks	
Parent interviews		Ms. Giller	Within two weeks	
Teacher interview		Ms. Giller	Within two weeks	
Collection of RTI data		Ms. Giller	Within two weeks	
Observation in the classroom		Ms. Giller and Mrs. Mound	Within one week	

> *Comprehension Check*
> 1. Why would an RTI model in a school system help in the referral of students to special education?
> 2. Why develop an assessment plan? Explain your answer.

EVALUATION FOR IDENTIFYING THE NEED FOR SPECIAL EDUCATION

Federal law requires the provision of a nondiscriminatory evaluation for each student referred for special education. This includes the evaluation being completed by an MDT, across multiple settings, and with multiple assessments. The assessments must be (1) free from bias, including bias as a result of a disability; (2) administered by trained staff following the procedures outlined in the assessment; (3) validated for the purpose for which they are being used; (4) all areas of the suspected disability must be assessed; (5) tests are to be given and reports written in the native language of the student; and (6) no one instrument can be used as the sole criterion for determination of the student's educational needs (Pierangelo & Giuliani, 2017). See Table 13.1 for examples of each component of nondiscriminatory evaluations.

Table 13.1 Nondiscriminatory Evaluation Examples

Nondiscriminatory Component	Examples
Free from bias, including disability.	• Give a visually impaired student a written math assessment unless it has been enlarged or modified to meet their needs. • An assessment that requires two-handed bilateral hand use to a student with limited use of one hand or arm is biased. • Watch for cultural considerations and where the assessment was normed—it must match your population.
Administered by trained staff, following procedures outlined in the manual.	• Standardized assessments should be given by individuals who have had a college course or extensive professional development on assessment. • The directions in the manual must be followed or the results will be invalid.
Assessments must be validated for the purpose for which they are being used.	• The PPVT4 is an assessment of receptive language. The student looks at four pictures on a page and points to the one requested by the examiner. Although receptive language is an indicator of intelligence, this test cannot be used as a measure of intelligence.
All areas of suspected disability must be assessed.	• Logan is having difficulty with reading comprehension. Just assessing reading comprehension will not give a clear score of *why* he is having trouble. Fluency, vocabulary knowledge, sight word awareness, and phonemic awareness should all be assessed.
Tests are to be given and reports written in the native language of the child and family.	• This is difficult to do because most assessments are only in English. Some have been translated to Spanish, but most are only published in English. • The assessment can be given to determine a baseline representation of the student's skills, but the scores cannot be reported because it was not in the child's native language, and the norming of the assessment did not include the assessment given in other languages.
Decisions cannot be determined based on the results on one instrument.	• A full evaluation with multiple measures, multiple settings, and multiple people is required for placement decisions.

> *Comprehension Check*
> 1. What is a nondiscriminatory evaluation? And what are the components of a nondiscriminatory evaluation?
> 2. Why do we want to evaluate the whole child, including vision, hearing, communication, and so on, if we are looking at problems in reading? Explain your answer.

TYPES OF ASSESSMENTS

To complete the evaluation for special education services, multiple evaluators, multiple measures, and multiple settings are required. Formal (standardized) and informal (interviews, checklists, criterion-referenced tests, curriculum-based assessments) evaluations should be used, with the results considered by the team to develop a picture of the whole student, not just looking at the apparent disability.

Standardized Assessments

Standardized assessments (sometimes called normative assessments) are normed instruments that allow a student to be compared to other students of their age or grade. The instruments have been validated (assesses what it says it assesses) and proven to be reliable (gives consistent scores). To norm the assessment (develop the scores), the test developers give the assessment to a stratified sample (variety of different people) of the ages covered in the assessment. For the best results, the test developers try to match the US Census information to develop the stratified sample to make their assessment as broadly usable as possible. For example, the test developers look at gender, socioeconomic status, age, race, location (urban, suburban, rural), education level of the parents of the children in the sample, culture and geographic location, and any other possible demographics.

Why is this stratified sample information important? Imagine that you live in rural Montana and you need to find an assessment that will help you determine one of your student's writing abilities. You find an assessment that covers the areas you want to assess: grammar, punctuation, and sentence and paragraph structure. The reliability and validity are good, so you check the normative sample. Gender and age are similar, but you notice that only female students from a private school in New York were in the normative sample. That is not a stratified sample that includes the demographics of your student (male, northwest, public school, rural), and that assessment is likely not going to result in valid results for your student in a Montana public school.

Standardized assessments provide normative data, including standard scores, scaled scores, Z scores, and T scores. All these scores provide a mean and standard deviations that can be used to determine how far a student's scores are from the mean, which is a part of the data used to determine if a student has a disability in any of the defined categories. Stanines and percentile ranks are also scores that can be obtained for the standardized assessment. The scores can be plotted on a bell curve to show relationships between the assessments or subtests of the assessments, and they are used to facilitate documentation of a disability. This visual can also be used to help parents understand the different scores and how they relate to one another. See Figure 13.2 to review the normal curve for assessment scores.

> *Comprehension Check*
> 1. How could you explain to parents their child's strengths and weaknesses if you have a variety of scores from a variety of assessments (standard scores, scaled scores, and Z-scores, for example)?
> 2. Why use standardized assessments as part of a referral to special education?

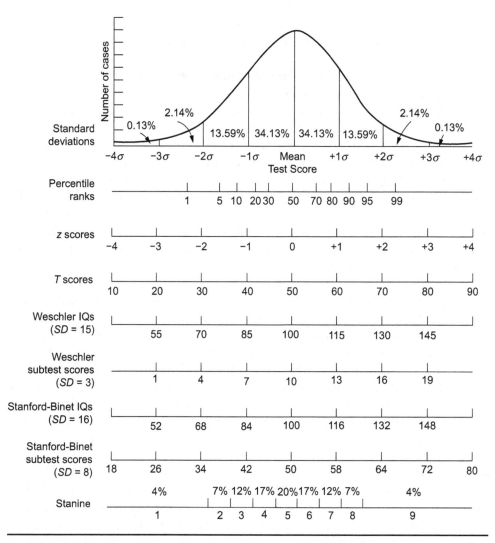

Figure 13.2 Normal Curve

Source: http://www.assessmentpsychology.com/bellcurve.htm

Criterion-Referenced Tests

Criterion-referenced tests (CRTs) measure an individual's performance on a fixed set of criteria. Advanced Placement exams, ACTs and SATs, are CRTs. You make the cutoff score or not, which makes some of these assessments very high stakes. Think of high school students needing to pass the state graduation examination in math and reading to graduate.

On a smaller scale, CRTs look at specific skills a student should have learned, based on the curriculum and standards that have informed the instruction in the classroom. The purpose of the CRT is to determine the student's mastery of content (Taylor, Smiley, & Richards, 2009). Think back to the Tier 1 level in RTI; if at the screening a student did not achieve the expected number of items correct or was in the lower percentages of the class ranks, progress monitoring occurred and if the student did not make progress, they were referred to Tier 2. The assessments used for the progress monitoring were CRTs.

There are also commercial products to assess a student's skills on a particular set of competencies, which can lead to goal setting and instruction. One of the most widely used is the Brigance Development Inventories, available to assess children age two to adult. Many of the Brigance series of assessments have recently been standardized to assist with identification of specific needs and services.

Curriculum-Based Assessments

Curriculum-based assessments (CBAs) measure a student on what they have learned using the current curriculum in the classroom. It is usually a direct assessment of academic skills used to determine the next unit to be taught or the need to go back and reteach some skills. For those students who might need a little more assistance on a particular topic, using a Tier 2 strategy of small-group instruction might provide them with the extra assistance they need to go on with the class. Think about weekly spelling tests or a chapter test in a history class; those are both CBAs.

According to Pierangelo and Giuliani (2017, p. 24), CBA is useful because it

- Can monitor the child's progress frequently
- Can be closely aligned to performance standards
- Can be sensitive to cultural and linguistic diversity
- Links curriculum and instruction
- Helps the teacher determine what to teach
- Can be administered frequently
- Is sensitive to short-term academic gains
- Assists in the evaluation of student progress and program evaluation

CBAs are used in the progress monitoring of a student's learning at all tiers of the RTI process. While assessing curriculum, CBAs can also be used to assess components of learning, such as fluency and processing speed. Deficits in processing skills are a component in the identification of an SLD. For example, the fourth-grade class takes a math fluency test every Monday to help determine if they are learning their multiplication facts. The number of problems the students answered correctly is plotted, and the lower percentages of students who are not making progress are monitored. If the expected improvement is not evident, the students will be moved to Tier 2, and these data will be available as part of the SLD evaluation if the students continue to not make progress.

There are also CBAs that have been written to go along with a specific curriculum. For example, at the early childhood level, there is the Assessment, Evaluation, and Programing System for Infants and Children, Hawaii Early Learning Program, and Carolina Curriculum that provide check sheets for assessing children's strengths and needs, and then the curriculum provides activities for parents or teachers to use to improve the student's skills. The Brigance Transitions Skills Activities is an example of a CBA curriculum that can be used to facilitate the transition of a student from school to the workforce and independent living, planning objectives, and learning tasks following the administration of the Brigance Transition Skills Inventory.

> *Comprehension Check*
> 1. How would you use CRT and CBA in a referral for special education?

DATA ANALYSIS AND INTERPRETING EVALUATION RESULTS

After the assessments are given and scored, the MDT meets to discuss the results. Observations of Logan in his natural environments, and while being assessed, are reviewed and discussed. For example, the school psychologist may have observed Logan in the classroom in the morning and the occupational therapist in the afternoon, and they report completely different behaviors. This discrepancy must be resolved, and if it is not a simple answer (Logan's attention deficit hyperactivity disorder [ADHD] medication had left his system in the afternoon), then perhaps a functional behavioral analysis (see Chapter 14) is needed.

There might also be some questions unresolved, and there may be a need for further evaluations. For example, the school psychologist has completed the intellectual evaluation, the special education teacher has evaluated academics, and the occupational therapist has assessed handwriting and visual processing skills. All three of these professionals feel that there might be a concern with processing language; thus, with parent permission the speech/language pathologist might perform some assessments as well.

Data obtained during the testing then must be reviewed, with discrepancies discussed as well, if there are any. Each team member will have a brief report to share and contribute to the team report. See Illustrative Case Study 13.2 for a brief report from a developmental specialist on Landon, a five-year-old with attention, language, and pre-academic skill concerns. This will be combined with content from the school psychologist, speech/language pathologist, and general education teacher to determine if Landon has a need for special education.

ILLUSTRATIVE CASE STUDY 13.2

Landon
BD: 12/28/08
CA: 4+8

Assessment Summary

Landon participated in assessments from October through December 2013. He was given the Battelle Developmental Inventory (2nd Edition), the Bracken Basic Concept Scale: Receptive (3rd Edition), the Brigance Kindergarten screen, and the Brigance Preschool Screen II—4-year-old.

Results of Landon's Evaluation Are Scattered

Language

Landon's strongest developmental skill is in the area of language. On the Battelle Developmental Inventory, he scored a 12 (10 being average) on receptive communication and a 13 on expressive communication. His composite language score was a 110 (mean 100). Teachers report that Landon can carry on a conversation with turn taking, participate in joint engagement, and has a strong vocabulary. To confirm this strength, Landon was then given the Bracken Basic Concept Scale where there was some variability in his scores but only one area above the mean (10); Landon received an 11 on texture/material. This score is possible because the content requested is concrete and he likely heard words often at the his daycare center (glass, wood, flat, smooth, metal) as they participate in investigations. The lower scores were related to pre-academics (school readiness composite, direction/position, quantity), with each having a scaled score of 7 (mean 10).

Cognition

Cognitive processes of attention and memory, reasoning and academic skills, and perception and concepts again varied. Although Landon has the ability to sort by attribute, recognize differences in printed shapes, letters, and numbers, knows his colors, and has strong picture identification/vocabulary skills, his awareness of letter and number names and concepts is very low. The cognitive skills Landon is strongest in are concrete or rote concepts with greater difficulty related to more abstract concepts, such as giving a certain number of blocks or recalling information from a story. This also could be related to Landon's difficulties with attention. It was reported that his attention span for group activities is five minutes or less and that he is easily distracted by those around him. When playing, Landon moves from activity to activity, although he can stay with a group of children if they initiate the play.

Motor

One of Landon's weakest areas is in motor skills. He is limited in his ability to jump, hop, or balance on one foot and has minimal ball-playing skills (throwing/catching), although he can kick a ball without falling. Fine motor skills are also delayed. Although he can copy simple shapes (circle, cross), he is unable to copy letters or more advanced shapes (triangle, X).

Adaptive

Adaptive skills include self-care (toileting, eating, dressing) and personal responsibility. Landon is strong in his self-care skills, although he does not dress/undress himself. Concerns are related to personal responsibility because he does not show awareness of safety concerns and is limited in his ability to choose and continue an activity independently. Landon is more likely to wander or to dump and fill buckets of toys.

Recommendations
1. Occupational therapy evaluation for motor skills.
2. Focus on pre-academic skills related to letters, numbers, and attention to task.
3. Use picture cues and possibly a timer to help Landon focus on chosen activities.

A written comprehensive assessment report is required at the end of the evaluation, written in parent-friendly language, discussing the assessment findings of each of the professionals in relationship to the student's strengths and needs. Reports should include the reason for referral; background information, including previous interventions (Tier 1 and Tier 2); student observations; test scores; interpretation of the assessments; a summary statement; and recommendations.

The written report for a student suspected of having an SLD, *must, by law*, include the following: whether the student has an SLD; what the decision of SLD is based on; what information was obtained during the observations; whether any medical findings were relevant to the educational findings; whether there was a severe discrepancy between intellect and achievement; whether cultural, environmental, or economic disadvantages were the reason for the student's delay; and whether the student needs special education to learn (Yell, 2016). Team members must sign that they are in agreement with the findings; if not, they must provide a written statement as to why they disagree with the team decision. See Illustrative Case Study 13.3 for a brief SLD report for Logan.

ILLUSTRATIVE CASE STUDY 13.3: SPECIFIC LEARNING DISABILITY EVALUATION

Name: Logan T.
Date of birth: 5/11/2009
Chronological age: 8+6

School: St. Henry Elementary
Grade: 3.4
Classroom teacher: Mrs. Jack
Participants:
Mr. and Mrs. T., parents
Logan T., student
Ms. Adams, principal
Ms. Giller, school psychologist
Mrs. Jack, classroom teacher
Mrs. Mound, special education teacher

Does the student have an SLD: Yes
What information helps determine the presence of an SLD:
Ms. Giller completed interviews with Mr. and Mrs. T. and Mrs. Jack. She also gathered RTI data collected on Logan and provided an analysis of the data. Ms. Giller also completed the WISC-V with Logan to have an intellectual score for comparison purposes with academic findings. Mrs. Mound completed three standardized tests with Logan, the Woodcock Reading Mastery Test III, the Test of Written Language (4th Edition), and the Key Math 3. Results will be discussed next. Ms. Giller and Mrs. Mound also observed Logan in his general education classroom.

Observational information:
Ms. Giller and Mrs. Mound both agreed that Logan is on task in the classroom and actively participates in discussions and group work. He is well organized, has his materials readily available, and follows directions given to the class or individually. There appears to be no behavioral or organizational issues that would affect his learning.

Any medical findings that would affect the diagnosis of SLD: _____ Yes __X__ No
Mrs. Rae, the school nurse, reviewed Logan's records with regard to vision, hearing, and health. He has passed all the vision and hearing screenings, and there is nothing in his record that would indicate a problem with learning.

Was there a severe discrepancy between intellect and achievement:
Logan's scores on the WISC-5 were solidly within the above-average range. There was limited range in his scores on the five full-scale subtests. Standard (composite) and scaled scores ranged from 115 to 121 (standard/composite) and 9 to 13 (scaled scores). Minimal discrepancy in scores was noted.

Academic/achievement testing did show discrepancies between isolated and integrative subtests.

Subtests that measure isolated skills, spelling (SS 115), letter/word identification (SS 118), word attack (SS 121), and math calculations (SS 122) were solidly above average compared to same-age peers. More integrative tasks that required Logan to take information and do something with it to reply scores were much lower than those on the isolated assessments. Passage comprehension (SS 78), writing samples (SS 75), and math application (SS 82) reflected difficulties with integrating content. Based on his lack of progress in Tier 2 intervention, these results indicate that Logan has an SLD.

Were cultural, environmental, or economic disadvantages the reason for the discrepancy:
Ms. Giller conducted interviews with both parents and Logan's teacher. There was no indication of any cultural, environmental, or economic disadvantages that would affect Logan's learning.

Does the student need special education to learn:
Yes, Logan requires special education services to learn to integrate information to improve reading comprehension, written language, and mathematics application.

INDIVIDUALIZED EDUCATION PROGRAM

Since the passage of P.L. 94–142 and the regulations that were published in 1977, every student identified as having a disability has an Individualized Education Program (IEP). This is to be developed by the MDT after the determination of qualification for special education and is to address the learning and behavioral needs of the student. This is a legal contract of the services the student will receive, including what services, how often, the duration of the services, and how the student's progress will be monitored.

Members of the MDT that will develop the IEP must include the parents or guardian, special education teacher, general education teacher, and administrator knowledgeable about services available in the district. The student should be involved unless there is a reason the student could not contribute to the meeting. Others who can be involved include related service personnel, school psychologist or counselor, or others appropriate to add information to the team writing of the IEP. Parents are there to provide expertise about their child and to provide permission for special education services and the least restrictive environment educational placement (Yell, 2016).

Required components of the IEP include (Yell, 2016):

- Individual's present level of performance on academic achievement and functional skills
- Measureable annual goals to address areas of need
- How the student's progress on the goals will be measured and how that progress will be reported to the parents at specific intervals (usually when progress reports are sent home for students in general education)
- What services will be provided: special education, related services, supplemental aids and services, accommodations and modifications
- When and why the student will not be educated in the general education classroom if the student will leave their general education classroom for services
- Accommodations necessary for participation on state- or district-wide assessments or if the student will take alternative assessments
- Projected date for the beginning of service, where services will be provided, and the expected duration of services
- For those students 16 and older, transition services needed to reach college or career-ready success before leaving high schools

---

Comprehension Check

1. Who are the required members of an IEP MDT?
2. What are the required components of the IEP?

WRITING ANNUAL GOALS

IDEA requires annual goals in the IEP to address all areas of need. The US Department of Education (2000) states,

A child's IEP must include measurable annual goals that relate to meeting the child's needs that result from the child's disability to enable the child to be involved in and progress in the general curriculum, and to meeting each of the child's other educational needs that result from the child's disability [34 CFR §300.347(a)(2)]. This may, depending on the child's needs, include annual goals that relate to the child's needs in such areas as behavioral skills, communication, self-determination skills, job-related skills, independent living skills, or social skills.

(p. 31)

The annual goals must have a direct relationship to the Present Level of Performance (PLOP). Each concern expressed in the PLOP must be addressed with an annual goal. The purposes of the goals are to provide the student with the skills needed to participate in the general education curriculum. Each goal must be observable and measureable to be able to collect data and to make informed decisions from that data. Goals are required to identify the target behavior, conditions (or givens, what materials or environments), and criteria for acceptable performance.

For example, Wendy is in the third grade and is functioning at a first-grade reading level. Her sight word identification is strong, but comprehension is significantly below grade level. She has not made adequate progress at Tier 1 or Tier 2; thus, she is moved to Tier 3 and is receiving individualized help as she is evaluated for a learning disability. Results of the evaluations indicate that Wendy's vocabulary awareness, speed of processing written material, short-term memory, and attention to detail, in addition to her reading comprehension, are below expectations for her age compared to her peers on standardized assessments. She is determined to have a learning disability in reading, but the other concerns must be addressed as well in her IEP. Wendy needs annual goals to increase her reading comprehension skills, expand her vocabulary, and improve her short-term memory, speed of processing, and attention to detail. See Figure 13.3 for Wendy's goals.

Concerns identified during the evaluation and documented on the IEP PLOP: reading comprehensive, vocabulary awareness, speed of processing written materials, remaining in her seat for academic work, and following a sequence of tasks.

Given a reading passage at her current level, Wendy will be able to identify the main idea and three supporting details with 75% accuracy in four consecutive trials.

Given five new words a week, Wendy will locate the word definition in a dictionary and will write five sentences (5-7 words each), using the word with 80% accuracy.

Wendy will increase her speed of processing from 40% to 80% accuracy, given monthly reading fluency quizzes, by the end of the school year.

Given one 6 minute break, to be taken during the academic block, Wendy will remain seated for the remainder of a 20 minute academic block, for 4/5 days per week for 4 consecutive weeks.

Given a visual cue card of the steps for arriving to school, Wendy will follow a four step sequence, with 1 or 0 teacher prompts (referring Wendy to her visual cue card), 80% of the time by the end of the grading period.

Figure 13.3 Wendy's Annual Goals

> *Comprehension Check*
> 1. What are the required components of an annual goal?
> 2. Identify the following components of an annual goal as a condition, behavior, or criteria:
>   a. _____ when riding the school bus
>   b. _____ 80% accuracy over three consecutive days
>   c. _____ using a map of the United States
>   d. _____ raise their hand
>   e. _____ complete 15 math problems
>   f. _____ four out of five trials

LEAST RESTRICTIVE ENVIRONMENT

If a student is identified as needing special education, the least restrictive environment (LRE) for the student must also be identified once the IEP has been written. Where is the LRE for Wendy to meet her annual goals? Federal law requires a continuum of services to address the needs of all students. This means that there must be multiple placement options for individuals with special needs to obtain the help they need to learn. Briefly, the continuum includes the general education classroom, general education classroom with supports, resource room, self-contained classroom, special education school or program, and homebound, hospitalized, or residential placement. Each level on the continuum removes the student a little more from their peers and instruction in the general education classroom. Per law, the student must be in the general education classroom to the maximum extent possible (Yell, 2016).

However, it must be remembered that the LRE for any student is the place where they can learn best. Students can be placed within a variety of environments during the day. Harold may be in the general education classroom for the majority of the day, receiving supports from a reading specialist during reading, but may leave to go to the resource room for math because he is several grade levels below his peers. Or there may be a student who has sustained a traumatic brain injury, and to come back to school, he needs a self-contained classroom. But as he continues to recover, he may move to the resource room model, and possibly back to the general education classroom with supports for his learning and behavior.

> ### CASE STUDY 13.4: CONTINUUM OF SERVICES
> Pedro was involved in a skiing accident in January of seventh grade, sustaining multiple fractures and a closed head injury. Two weeks following the accident, he was admitted to a children's hospital rehabilitative program where he remained for three months before returning to school. His continuum of educational services included the following:
>
> Inpatient: Tutoring services through the hospital school once he reached the level of recovery to allow him to participate in academics.

Return to school for the remainder of seventh grade: Self-contained classroom for math, language arts, and study and organizational skills for half the day, with the other half in general education classroom science and social studies. Supports offered in the general education classroom included having a scribe, use of a calendar planner, and reduced assignments.

Summer following seventh grade: Tutoring in math five days a week for eight weeks.

Eighth grade: Attempted all general education classes but was unable to complete the assignments without assistance. Schedule revised to two periods a day in the learning disabilities resource room for assistance, one period remained stable, and one rotated from his other classes (math in the general education classroom four times a week and once in the resource room for extra assistance). Use of a calendar planner continued throughout the year.

Ninth grade: Remained at the middle school instead of transitioning to the high school (optional) and continued with one period a day of assistance from the resource room. Support was offered in the general education classroom if needed, but Pedro was able to remain in the classroom with only the resource room assistance.

The determination of the LRE for each student must be based on the student's needs, not the availability of programming in the school. For example, Harold can stay in his general education classroom for reading, but he needs some support. It is determined that based on the case load of the reading teacher, he cannot take on another student, so the team decides to pull Harold for reading, as well as for math, to the resource room. This is a violation of Harold's right to a free appropriate public education. In reality, the school must find another reading specialist to work in the classroom with Harold.

Comprehension Check
1. What is the LRE for students with learning or behavioral needs?
2. Why is it important to have options for placement for services? Explain your answer.

WHAT IF THE STUDENT DOESN'T QUALIFY FOR SPECIAL EDUCATION?

It is possible that a student will be referred, evaluated, and not be identified as in need of special education or specialized instruction. There could be a variety of reasons, including medical issues, lack of competent instruction in earlier grades, native language concerns, or inconclusive results from the evaluations. Case Study 13.5 and Case Study 13.6 provide examples of some students who did not qualify for special education.

CASE STUDY 13.5: SHANE (ADHD)

Medical Issues

Shane is a 16-year-old student with strong academic abilities, but he cannot get his work done in class and reports that homework takes him three to four hours a night and the work is still not done. He reports having trouble passing the ACT examination because he does not complete enough items in the provided time frame. Shane also shares that he has trouble concentrating in class and often has thoughts triggered by a component of the instruction. For example, the teacher is talking about boats and distance traveled in math class, and his mind drifts to jumping off the boat and swimming in the clear water.

Shane is evaluated and his academic scores are average or above for his age range, but his processing speed is seriously below what is expected for his age. Based on the conversation the examiner had with Shane, as well as observations during the evaluation, it is suggested that Shane see his medical doctor with regard to the possibility of having ADHD. Shane and his parents agree that this is a good idea, they make an appointment, and the doctor provides a trial of stimulant medication to see if this helps Shane to concentrate and work faster. She agrees to write a prescription if the trial works for Shane.

Shane returned to the consultant's office to determine if the medication he was taking was helping him pay attention to details. He felt he was more in control of himself and did not have any side effects from the medication. Shane had been taking the medication for seven days at the time of this reevaluation.

Woodcock-Johnson IV Tests of Cognitive Ability	11/30/16	12/14/16
Cluster: Cognitive Processing Speed Standard Score	62	110
Subtests Standard Scores:		
Letter-pattern matching	67	105
Story recall	95	96
Pair cancelation	73	113

Shane's cognitive processing speed improved greatly from the last evaluation (+ 48). His speed of responding was significantly improved for visual tasks. On the pair cancelation subtest, Shane doubled the amount of items completed accurately, from a raw score of 57 to 107 (SS 73 to 113, +40). Improvement was also noted for letter-pattern matching (SS 67 to 105, +38). Story recall remained consistent between the two evaluations.

Shane does not qualify for special education, but his teachers will be monitoring his behavior in class, as well as the quality of his homework, and will bring Shane back to the RTI team if he begins having difficulty again.

CASE STUDY 13.6: SAMANTHA (POOR TEACHING)

Samantha—Lack of Instruction

Samantha is a third-grade student who has moved from a small rural town to a larger suburban area. Her previous school had a 95% rate of free and reduced lunch. There was an average of 25 students in each classroom, and assistance to the teacher was not available. The majority of the students, including Samantha, did not attend preschool and came to kindergarten with limited pre-academic skills. The kindergarten teacher (Mrs. Evans) worked hard to provide engaging activities for the students but was unable to do individual progress monitoring without help in the classroom. Mrs. Evans discovered in early October that she was pregnant but thought she could make it through the school year. Unfortunately, it was determined it was a high-risk pregnancy, and she was advised to leave school in early January. The kindergarten classroom had three different long-term substitute teachers for the rest of the year, all very kind and loving individuals but not strong in planning lessons and working with young children.

Samantha's first-grade teacher was ready to retire. Mrs. Kelly had been teaching for 38 years, and she had been using the same materials for a long time. Lecture and worksheets were how Mrs. Kelly taught, and when she was working with reading groups, the class was not allowed to ask questions about the worksheets. In the second grade, Samantha was again in a class of 25 students, and Ms. Hamilton was a beginning teacher in her first full-time classroom. She was strong in behavior management and allowed project-based learning but did not understand progress monitoring and based grades on written tests. Samantha had all As on her report card.

When Samantha started third grade at a new school, the teacher immediately noticed she was not able to do the work of her other students. The initial RTI screening placed Samantha at the bottom of the class in all areas assessed. Ms. George added Samantha to her progress monitoring group, and at the end of six weeks, Samantha was moved to Tier 2 for reading and math. She worked with a small group of students with a licensed teacher providing the reading instruction, had a check in/check out contract with her teacher every morning, and was placed in the lowest level math class with 10 other students, a teacher, and two assistants. Despite the help at Tier 2, Samantha was still not doing grade-level work, although she was making steady progress in learning content.

Samantha was referred to Tier 3 instruction for individual reading assistance from the reading specialist and to participate in testing to determine if she required special education/specialized instruction to learn. The results indicated that Samantha was in the average range of intelligence, but 1 to 1.5 standard deviations below the mean in all her academic subjects. Her processing skills were average, and there were no vision, hearing, or health concerns.

> The MDT determined that Samantha had been making progress with Tier 2 support, but she was not on grade level with her peers. However, because she did not have good instruction in her first few years of school and did not have preschool experience before kindergarten, the team decided she did not qualify for special education services, but she would stay at Tier 3 to attempt to continue remediating her deficits to reach grade-level standards.

If the student does not qualify for special education services, there are still a few options to obtain the services the student needs to succeed. A 504 Plan can be developed that specifies additional assistance for the student, or the student can stay on Tier 3 with strategies provided as needed. Generally, a student is on different tiers for different subjects, so additional support may be needed only in a specific area of instruction.

APPLICATION ACTIVITIES

1. Go to your state's education website and find the information on referral, evaluation, and determination of a disability. What is your role as the classroom teacher?
2. In your field placement, ask your cooperating teacher about referral strategies to Tier 3 and special education in your building or district. Bring the information back to class and compare with others in different buildings or districts.
3. Plot Logan's standard scores on assessments on the bell curve and review the strengths and weaknesses of his performance.
4. Review Logan's (Illustrative Case Study 13.3) assessment results and determine if an IEP should be written for special education services. If so, what should his annual goals address?

CHAPTER SUMMARY

Identification of Specific Learning Disabilities and Severe Emotional Disturbance

- A significant discrepancy between the students' intellectual and academic ability was required.
- States were prohibited from requiring that school districts use a discrepancy formula; instead, states could allow or require that schools use a process that determined whether a student responded to scientific, research-based interventions.
- Severe emotional disturbance is identified as a condition exhibiting one of the five characteristics mentioned in this section of the chapter over a long period of time.

Individuals with Disability Education Act (IDEA) Requirements for Referrals to Special Education

- The school must provide evidence that the student has been educated with "scientific, research-based interventions" during the pre-referral process.

- To make a referral for a special education evaluation, the parents must give permission.
- A multidisciplinary team (MDT) is organized and an assessment plan is developed based on the student's needs.
- Evaluations should include parent and teacher interviews, consultation with anyone else who has worked with the student, formal and informal assessments, and observations of the student in their natural setting.

Types of Assessments

- Standardized assessments (normative assessments) are normed instruments that allow a student to be compared to other students of the same age or grade.
  - Test developers give the assessment to a variety of different people.
  - These assessments provide normative data—standard scores, scaled scores, Z scores, and T scores.
  - All these scores provide a mean and standard deviation that can be used to determine how far a students' scores are from the mean.
- Criterion-referenced tests measure an individual's performance on a fixed set of criteria.
  - These tests look at specific skills a student should have learned based on curriculum and academic standards.
  - The purpose of these tests is to determine the student's mastery of content.
  - Examples include Advanced Placement tests, such as the ACT or SAT.
- Curriculum-based assessment is a direct assessment of academic skills used to determine the next unit to be taught or the need to go back and reteach some skills.
  - Used in the progress monitoring of a student's learning at all tiers of the Response to Intervention process.
  - Examples include a spelling test or chapter test.

Data Analysis and Interpreting Evaluation Results

- Once the assessments are given and scored, the MDT meets to discuss the results.
- There could be some unresolved questions and need for further evaluations.
- Scores during the testing must be reviewed, and each team member will have a brief report to include with the team report.
- At the end of the evaluation, a written comprehensive assessment report is required.

Individualized Education Program

- Every student identified as having a disability has an Individualized Education Program (IEP).
- The IEP addresses the learning and behavioral needs of the student.
- Members of the MDT will develop the IEP: parents, special education teacher, general education teacher, and administrator.

IDEA Requires Annual Goals in the IEP to Address All Areas of Need

- The annual goals must have a direct relationship to the Present Level of Performance.
- The purpose of the goals are to provide the student with the skills needed to participate in the education curriculum.
- Must be observable and measurable as well as identify the target behavior, conditions, and criteria for acceptable performance.

Least Restrictive Environment

- This is the place where the student can learn the best.
- Students can be placed in a variety of environments throughout the school day.
- The determination of the least restrictive environment must be based on the student's needs.

What If the Student Does Not Qualify for Special Education?

- A student might not qualify for a variety of reasons—medical, cultural factors, lack of quality instruction in earlier grades.
- If a student does not qualify but needs assistance, a 504 Plan could be developed, or the child could receive help in the area needed in Tier 3, without being identified.

REFERENCES

Individuals with Disabilities Education Act Regulations, 34 C.F.R. § 300.307[a][2].

Pierangelo, R., & Giuliani, G. A. (2017). *Assessment in special education: A practical approach* (5th ed.). Boston, MA: Pearson.

Taylor, R. L., Smiley, L. R., & Richards, S. B. (2009). *Exceptional students: Preparing teachers for the 21st century*. Boston, MA: McGraw-Hill.

US Department of Education. (n.d.). *Building the legacy: IDEA 2004*. Retrieved from http://idea.ed.gov/explore/view/p/,root,regs,300,A,300.8,c,4,i,.html

US Department of Education. (2000). *A guide to the individualized education program*. Retrieved from www2.ed.gov/parents/needs/speced/iepguide/iepguide.pdf

Yell, M. L. (2016). *The law and special education* (4th ed.). Boston, MA: Pearson.

14

FUNCTIONAL BEHAVIORAL ASSESSMENT

Joni L. Baldwin

CHAPTER OBJECTIVES

After reading this chapter, students should be able to:

1. Identify a functional behavioral assessment.
2. Describe when a functional behavioral assessment is useful and when it is required.
3. Identify the purposes of a functional behavioral assessment.
4. Describe how a functional behavioral assessment is used in the context of the Response to Intervention process.

WHAT IS A FUNCTIONAL BEHAVIORAL ASSESSMENT?

Teachers and caregivers have been completing functional behavioral assessments (FBAs) for years, without the title, every time they look at a child and say, "Why is she doing that?" Whether it's mild (tapping her pencil on the desk or lagging behind at a grocery store) or intense (laying on the floor screaming in the classroom or the grocery store), the question is why. Determining the answer, especially to the more challenging behaviors, through an FBA will help ascertain the intervention needed.

FBA is a structured process used to determine the function of a challenging behavior. It is based on the belief that the results (consequences) of the behavior serve as reinforcement to the student; thus, the behavior will be maintained or strengthened. FBAs consist of various methods used to identify environmental variables that cause and maintain challenging behaviors. Early researchers looked at behavior analysis theories to understand the function of antecedents and consequences related to challenging behaviors of persons with severe developmental disabilities (self-injurious behaviors, destruction of property). The use of FBAs has expanded to include individuals with autism, attention deficit hyperactivity disorder (ADHD), and specific learning disabilities, among other disability categories. FBAs have also been helpful in determining the function of behaviors that impede learning for at-risk and typical students (Gable, Park, & Scott, 2014), often in the Tier 2 intervention process. The purpose of the FBA is to accurately identify the function of the behavior in order to provide guidance in determining a behavioral intervention plan (BIP; see Chapter 15) that will reduce challenging behaviors.

LEGAL ASPECTS OF FUNCTIONAL BEHAVIORAL ASSESSMENTS

Prior to 1997, the discipline of students with disabilities was not addressed by federal regulations. However, with the reauthorization of the Individuals with Disabilities Education Act (IDEA) in 1997, discipline for students with disabilities became a very specific part of the law. Before the law changed, students with challenging behaviors were on the same discipline plan as the other students in the building and were thus suspended or expelled for challenging behaviors. Because not being in school resulted in no opportunity for learning, the concept of free appropriate public education was being violated.

The 1997 reauthorization of IDEA specifically stated that students identified with disabilities must have an FBA conducted to determine a BIP to address challenging behaviors, if the behavior resulted in a change of placement (suspension or expulsion) for more than 10 days. Additionally, a manifestation determination was required to identify whether the behavior was the result of the student's disability. Manifestation determination is to be completed by the Individualized Education Program (IEP) team, and "A behavior could be determined to be a manifestation of a student's disability only if the conduct in question is 'caused by' or has a 'direct and substantial relationship' to the student's disability" (Yell, 2016, p. 69). Bringing drugs or weapons to school, or causing bodily damage to another person, does allow for an alternative placement for up to 45 days, but the educational component of the IEP must continue as a manifestation determination is being conducted.

To put this into practice, let's look at Brian, age four, who has been diagnosed with ADHD and exhibits poor impulse control. He does not appear to stop and think before acting on his impulses. He is being evaluated for medication but is not on medication at this time. One day, Brian runs out of the preschool classroom and immediately pulls the fire alarm. He doesn't stop before pulling it, it happens on the go, and he is then off to something else. Pulling the fire alarm is an immediate suspension offense, but Brian has already been suspended a few times during the school year and this would be his tenth day out of school. Thus, a manifestation determination is required. The immediate decision is that Brian does not need to be removed from his current placement while the manifestation decision is being completed, as he did not bring drugs or weapons to school or cause bodily damage to another person. What do you think will be the result of the manifestation determination? The team determines that the incident with the fire alarm was a manifestation of his disability because he has the diagnosis of ADHD, has a history of impulsive actions, and is being evaluated for medication to help him focus and decrease his impulsivity.

> *Comprehension Check*
> 1. What year did the federal government require FBAs for students with disabilities who were demonstrating challenging behaviors?
> 2. What is a manifestation determination, and when must it be done?

FUNCTIONAL BEHAVIORAL ASSESSMENT IN THE RESPONSE TO INTERVENTION PROCESS

In the ongoing Response to Intervention (RTI) cycle, FBAs fall in the assessment phase (see Figure 14.1).

Figure 14.1 Ongoing Cycle of Response to Intervention

FBAs are generally used in the Tier 2 and Tier 3 processes. At Tier 2, the behaviors being assessed may be less intense than those assessed at Tier 3. For example, a 10th-grade student is not turning in his homework every day. During the FBA student interview (see Figure 14.2), Kevin tells the team that his father is now unemployed, and to help with the family budget, Kevin has been working four nights a week and both weekend days at his movie concession job. The team helps Kevin and his teachers prioritize his homework for the times when it may not be busy in the theater and Kevin might have a few minutes to work (with the theater manager's permission). The plan also allows Kevin to give verbal instead of written reports for such tasks as a chapter summary and to complete half of the required assignment for some subjects (such as a math worksheet).

At the Tier 3 level, the behaviors are more challenging, such as fighting or damaging property, and there is likely data already collected at the Tier 1 and 2 levels. Brooke, age 10, identified with an emotional and behavioral disorder, has frequently been sent to the office for disruptive behavior (loud talking and laughing, refusing to work, pushing through other students to get to her cubby) during the school year, and various FBAs and BIPs completed in Tier 2 have not been successful with changing her behavior. This time, Brooke has punched another student and then left the room crying. As Brooke has caused bodily damage to another student, she is removed to an alternative placement while the manifestation determination is being completed, including an FBA. Brooke, her parents, teachers, and school administrators participate in the FBA. It is revealed that the disruptive behavior occurs most frequently in the

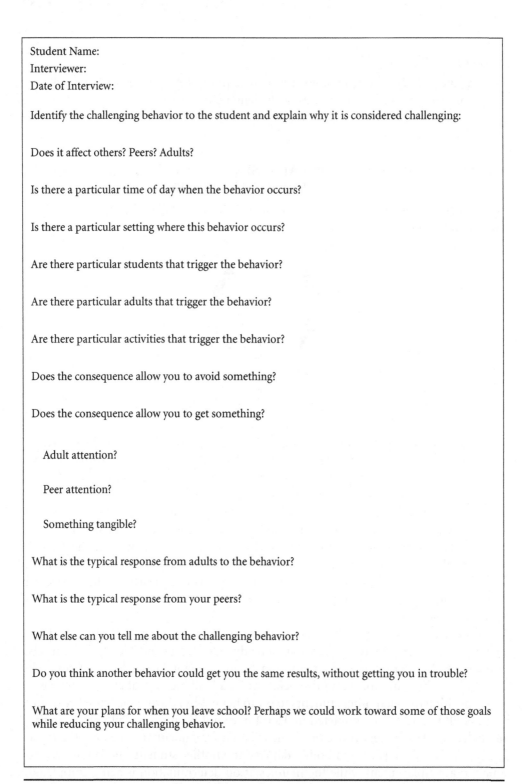

Figure 14.2 Functional Behavioral Assessment Student Interview Form

mornings on days when she has spent the night at her dad's house. Brooke reported going to bed later when she stays with him, comes to school earlier because he goes to work earlier than her mom does, and is in the school's early-morning care with her friend Liz. Their favorite activity is to run around the gym chasing each other. Thus, Brooke is already agitated when she gets to class and does not seem to be able to settle and not be disruptive. The team uses this information to adjust Brooke's schedule and environment by suggesting an earlier bedtime at her dad's house, going to the library instead of the gym for early care, and playing a board game with Liz when they are together. She is also placed on a self-monitoring contract to allow Brooke to keep track of her behavior. Brooke is permitted to return to her classroom once the manifestation determination is complete and it is decided that her behavior was not a result of the identified disability.

> *Comprehension Check*
> 1. How can an FBA be useful in the RTI process?
> 2. FBAs will likely be used at what tier of the RTI process? Defend your answer.

COMPONENTS OF A FUNCTIONAL BEHAVIORAL ASSESSMENT

A simplistic view of conducting an FBA uses an ABC chart. *A* is for antecedent, *B* is for behavior, and *C* is the consequence of the behavior. For example, in an inclusive preschool classroom, the teacher says, "It's time for lunch." A student then falls to the floor screaming and kicking, gets taken to the time-out booth, and when he calms, he eats lunch that is brought to the room by an aide. This happens every day, so let's look at the antecedent (the teacher says, "It's time for lunch."), and the behavior (falling to the floor screaming and kicking), and the consequence (he gets placed in the time-out room instead of going to the cafeteria). A secondary consequence is that when he stops screaming and kicking, the student gets to eat lunch in the room where it is quieter than in the cafeteria (see Figure 14.3) It is generally not this easy, but this format provides a clear picture of the function of a behavior.

Antecedent	Behavior	Consequence
The teacher says "it's time for lunch".	Falls to the floor kicking and screaming	Taken to the time-out room. Someone gets his lunch and brings it to the room. He eats lunch in the room.

Figure 14.3 ABC Chart

In the 1997 reauthorization of IDEA, the federal government mandated the use of FBA and manifestation determination but did not provide specifics as to how this was to be done. States were required to develop a system for conducting FBAs that would be useful for educators. Zirkel (2011) reported that "only 31 of the 50 states have statutory or regulatory provisions for FBAs and/or BIPs that exceed the requirements of the IDEA" (p. 267), leaving 19 states without FBA guidelines. Of the 31 states, Zirkel reported 12 as being "negligible" (p. 267) with regard to providing strong guidelines for school systems. The state of Connecticut (2018) conducted a review of several FBA processes and identified the following 10 common items generally included in an FBA process: (1) the student's identifying information, (2) target behavior, (3) antecedents, (4) concurrent events, (5) consequences, (6) observations, (7) interviews, (8) student records, (9) influencing factors, and (10) hypothesis/function of behavior. To complete an effective FBA, information must be collected from a variety of sources, including school records, interviews with teachers and caregivers, and direct observation. (See Figure 14.4 and Figure 14.5).

Name:	Grade:
DOB:	Preparer:
CA:	Date:

Target Behavior (Measurable & Observable):

Observations and Sources: *What did the ABC observations tell us about the student. Were they different for different sources...attach FBA-ABC Charts completed*

Interviews:
   Teacher:
   Parent:
   Student:
   Others:

Student Records: *Any information gained from the student records that can help with the behavior issues...*

Influencing Factors:
   Medical:
   Family:
   Developmental:
   Other:

Hypothesis/Function of behavior:

Figure 14.4 Functional Behavior Analysis Data Collection Form

| Student: _____ | Time of observation: _____ |
| Teacher: _____ | Place: _____ |

# of students / # of adults: _____ / _____

General climate: Calm < --> Chaotic

Academic Content: _____

A Antecedent	B Behavior	C Consequence	Additional Notes/Concurrent Activities

Observer: _____

Figure 14.5 ABC-Functional Behavioral Analysis Chart

Comprehension Check
1. What did the federal government provide to help states in developing FBAs to use with students who were demonstrating challenging behaviors?
2. What is an ABC analysis? Why is it used?

GATHERING INFORMATION FOR THE FUNCTIONAL BEHAVIORAL ANALYSIS

Methods to obtain this information include indirect (informant) procedures (interviews, checklists, questionnaires, rating scales) and direct (direct observation, descriptive functional assessment—ABC method and functional analysis—manipulating some variables to determine the effect on the behavior) procedures. See Chapter 3 for data collection methods to use as you are collecting data during direct observations.

Indirect Assessments

Indirect (informant) assessments, including interviews or rating scales, rely on the memory and opinions of those who have witnessed the behavior. Using an FBA interview form can help structure the process (see Figure 14.6 and refer back to Figure 14.2) and allows the interviewer the opportunity to see patterns from different informers.

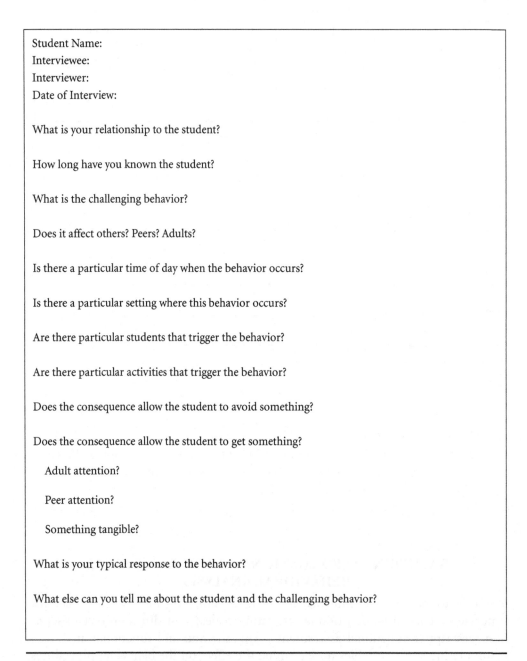

Student Name:
Interviewee:
Interviewer:
Date of Interview:

What is your relationship to the student?

How long have you known the student?

What is the challenging behavior?

Does it affect others? Peers? Adults?

Is there a particular time of day when the behavior occurs?

Is there a particular setting where this behavior occurs?

Are there particular students that trigger the behavior?

Are there particular activities that trigger the behavior?

Does the consequence allow the student to avoid something?

Does the consequence allow the student to get something?

    Adult attention?

    Peer attention?

    Something tangible?

What is your typical response to the behavior?

What else can you tell me about the student and the challenging behavior?

Figure 14.6 Functional Behavioral Analysis Interview Form: Teacher/Caregiver Version

This process can help parents and teachers focus their thoughts about the behavior and facilitate buy-in from the adults who spend the most time with the student. By actively participating in the FBA, greater willingness to implement the BIP is noted. This can also help point out the more difficult times of the day when a direct observation would be the most helpful to the team.

Direct Assessments

Descriptive functional assessment, using the ABC format, is frequently employed to evaluate challenging behaviors in schools. Teachers are often asked to complete this component of an FBA, as they are already observing the student in their classrooms and may be familiar with some of the antecedents that result in challenging behaviors. Mrs. Jones has referred Justin to the school Tier 2 pre-referral team. She reports that Justin is not sitting at his desk during independent work time, is not getting his work done, and is distracting the other students in her classroom. The team asked for specifics of the behavior and gave Mrs. Jones an ABC form (Figure 14.5) to help structure her observations and lead to greater clarity about the behavior. What Mrs. Jones had reported as random behavior was clarified when using the ABC chart. It was determined that the antecedent was returning to his seat after centers or his reading group, with the expectation that Justin would sit at his desk. Consequences for Justin include peer and teacher attention, in addition to escape from his too-small desk. See Illustrative Case Study 14.1 for more details on Justin.

ILLUSTRATIVE CASE STUDY 14.1

Justin is a second-grade student who does not stay in his seat during work time. He is tall for his age, and when he is seated at his desk, his legs always seem to be in the aisle, causing other students to trip. The school counselor came in to observe Justin three times and completed interval time sample recordings. To further help determine why Justin would not stay in his seat, an ABC analysis was completed. See Figure 14.7 for the results of his ABC analysis.

Antecedent	Behavior	Consequence
Justin is called to the reading table by the teacher	Sits at the table with legs under the table	Positive attention by the teacher: work is completed
Justin is sent back to his seat	Does not go to his seat, wanders the room	Work is not completed by Justin and three other students provide peer attention
Class is called to the carpet area to sit on the floor	Justin sits on the edge of the group with his legs out in front of him	Participates in the group activity.
Class is sent back to their seats	Justin sits in his desk, with legs stretched out to the side	Escapes uncomfortable small desk.

Figure 14.7 ABC Illustrative Case Study 14.1 Chart

> An analysis of the data indicate that Justin participates in class if the group is sitting at the front of the room on the carpet, although he always sits on the edge of the circle with his legs straight out in front of him. Justin also participates at the reading table that is set higher than the desks, generally with his legs straight out from the chair, with the heels of his shoes on the floor. When it was seatwork time, quick interval analyses indicated that Justin was out of his seat 79%, 82%, and 92% of the time when he was being observed.
>
> The teacher met with Justin, his mother, and the school counselor who had completed the interval observations. Justin reported that he was not comfortable in his desk, and his mother confirmed that Justin states that his desk is too small. When the teacher had Justin demonstrate by sitting at the desk, it was evident that his knees hit the underside of the desk. The school counselor suggested a different seat for Justin. Justin was provided with an adult-size small round table, with an appropriate-size chair, and was instructed that he could sit or stand, but he had to stay on his "island" in the classroom. When a follow-up meeting was held in three weeks, the teacher reported that Justin is in his seat or at his table 95% of the time dedicated to working independently.

Functional analysis of behavior occurs when one or more environmental variables are manipulated to determine the result of the target behavior. For example, Esther's teacher reported that Esther never completed her math assignment in class because she was always talking with her friends. It was determined that Esther's motivating consequence was peer attention, so that was taken away by sending Esther to the library to do her math assignment. She completed her assignment that day, thus proving the hypothesis was correct.

> *Comprehension Check*
> 1. What is the difference between indirect and direct assessment procedures during an FBA?
> 2. What is a strong reason to use indirect assessment?

WHO CAN COMPLETE A FUNCTIONAL BEHAVIORAL ASSESSMENT?

Remember, FBAs started in clinical settings with students having a developmental disability or autism spectrum disorder diagnosis who were engaging in self-injurious or injurious behaviors. Psychologists, behavior specialists, and special education teachers trained in behavioral principles were generally the ones completing the FBA. However, as the federal law changed (IDEA 1997), FBAs became more common in typical education settings because they were required for some students (those who had been suspended or expelled for more than 10 days), and the number of FBAs needed became overwhelming for those directly trained in the applied behavioral analysis process. Loman and Horner (2014) conducted a small study on training "typical staff with flexible roles in schools" to complete FBAs "when the presenting behavior of the student was not complex" (p. 19). Seven of the 12 participants were counselors, two principals, two learning specialists, and one vice principal/teacher. They participated in four one-hour training events and then conducted an FBA with a student in their school. The procedures included staff interviews and direct observations of the student, ending with a "final summary statement defining the student's behavior, antecedent events triggering the behavior, and hypothesized function of the student's problem behavior" (p. 21). The completed FBA was sent to the researchers who then came to the school to complete a functional assessment. The conditions used that had been identified as antecedents and consequences of the behavior were staged by the researcher to determine the validity of the FBA summary statement. The results of all 10 FBAs that had been completed by school staff were verified to be accurate, thus documenting that other school personnel could learn to conduct FBAs on less complex cases.

In 2015, O'Neill, Bundock, Kladis, and Hawken conducted a survey of special educators and school psychologists on their willingness to participate in FBAs, perceptions of the usefulness of FBAs, appropriateness and feasibility of FBAs, and the desire to use FBAs with students with milder or more severe disabilities:

> Special educators were significantly more likely to endorse the use of systematic direct observation and functional analysis manipulation strategies than school psychologists, although no differences were found regarding the social desirability of FBA procedures for individuals exhibiting mild or severe problem behaviors. The school psychologists were also more worried about the time required to complete the FBA than the special education teachers. Implications of this study imply that pre-service and in-service training in FBAs is important for special education teachers.
>
> (p. 51)

Comprehension Check

1. Who should be involved in conducting FBAs in the school systems? Defend your answer.

STEPS OF A FUNCTIONAL BEHAVIORAL ASSESSMENT

Although various formats for completing an FBA are available, we recommend a practical approach with teachers and caregivers participating in the FBA, along with the students themselves. Usually, a general education teacher or parent will bring a behavior to the attention of a special education teacher or school administrator. This may be broad, such as a student not turning in assignments or talking out loud in class, or it could be more specific, such as a student trying to leave the room during independent math work time. Identifying the behavior might seem like an easy task, but often there is the need to sift through a variety of behaviors in order to identify the main one in measurable and observable terminology (operationalizing a behavior). "Bothering others" is not a measureable statement. How is the student bothering others? Does the student poke others with their pencil? Or make loud, distracting noises? But what is a distracting noise? Can you operationalize "distracting noise?" You must be able to define the behavior you want to change in a way that is not vague or ambiguous and it must be measurable and observable to be able to develop a successful BIP.

After identifying and operationalizing the target behavior, the next step is to collect information from those who know the student well (informants) or have a working relationship with the student (Figure 14.6). Interviewing both the teacher and the caregivers will give insight into the antecedents and consequences that occur as part of the behavior cycle. Interviewing the student is considered appropriate as well, with the purpose to hear from the student (Figure 14.2) what about the behavior is reinforcing and perhaps explore other reinforcements that can be used to reduce the challenging behavior. It is also helpful to ask students about their goals in order to provide some meaning as to why the behavior should be changed. However, it is not unusual for a student not to know what is reinforcing and/or motivating about their behavior.

Direct observation of the student and the behavior is next. An ABC format is suggested, with the observer documenting what is happening before the behavior starts (antecedent) and what happens after the behavior occurs (consequence). Additionally, documenting general classroom climate, concurrent activities, time of day, academic content involved, number of students and adults in the room, or any other distinctive features that could be used to help determine the function of the behavior would be useful (Figure 14.5).

The next step is to analyze the collected data and to form a hypothesis about the function of the behavior. Functions of behaviors generally fall under getting something, such as attention from adults, attention from peers, self-stimulation, or obtaining a tangible object, or avoiding something, such as escape from the cafeteria, math class, or an awkward social situation. Selecting a replacement behavior is next, one that will provide the desired reinforcement (outcome) as the function of the targeted behavior but in a more socially appropriate manner (see Chapter 15 for more information about BIPs). Tom frequently disrupts the class by talking. This gets him the teacher's attention, which is discovered through the ABC process to be what Tom wants, attention from an adult. The intervention plan that is developed recommends that after Tom completes his work quietly for one hour, he may spend 15 minutes with the principal or other office staff. Self-monitoring of his behavior is used to include Tom in developing behavior regulation and increasing replacement behaviors.

Making all teachers, caregivers, and the student aware of the plan is the first step in implementation of the BIP. For some students, this may be the end of the FBA (such as Kevin, earlier in the chapter). But for others (such as Brooke) whose behavior function may be more difficult to pinpoint through hypothesis testing, this cycle may need to be repeated if the BIP does not prove to help reduce the challenging behavior.

> *Comprehension Check*
> 1. What are the steps to conducting an FBA?
> 2. What does it mean to operationalize a behavior?
> 3. What are some typical functions of behavior?

FUNCTIONAL BEHAVIORAL ASSESSMENTS WITH SPECIFIC POPULATIONS

Cultural Considerations

As our culture and schools become more diverse, teachers are employing FBAs to distinguish between challenging (disruptive) behaviors and behaviors influenced or induced by language concerns, lack of content knowledge, or a misunderstanding of cultural norms stemming from family organization, generational status, or social values. Moreno, Wong-Lo, and Bullock (2014) recommend the use of FBAs in the pre-referral process when students are identified as having challenging behaviors. The process is the same for conducting the FBA: indirect assessments that include interviews and rating scales, direct observations using the ABC format, and discussion of the hypothesis as to the function of the behavior. The added component is the need to understand how the student's cultural heritage may influence the behavior. This is done through respectful interviews with family members. By developing an awareness of the family's cultural heritage and demonstrating respect toward that culture while asking questions, a better partnership between family and school can be developed to help address the challenging behaviors of the student. Moreno, Wong-Lo, Short, and Bullock (2014) also caution against "overgeneralization of cultural stereotypes" (p. 351). It is important to remember that the "challenging" behavior might be perceived differently if the behavior is caused by a lack of understanding of the language or not being on the academic level expected in the classroom. See Chapter 6 for additional information on cultural differences.

Early Childhood

At the state and national levels, greater emphasis has been focused on young children with challenging behaviors as the expulsion and suspension rate for preschoolers has climbed. The Division for Early Childhood of the Council for Exceptional Children issued a position paper in 2017 on addressing challenging behaviors of young children. The process for young children follows that of older students, with a three-tier approach involving families, early educators, and behavior specialists. At Tier 3, a functional assessment is recommended to identify the triggers, consequences, and functions of the behavior. Once that has occurred, a behavior plan is developed to be implemented in all the child's environments (home, day care, etc.) by all adults responsible for the child. If the child has an identified disability, the law remains the same for suspension, expulsion, or a change in placement (the goals of the IEP or Individual Family Service Plan must continue to be addressed with related services continuing). During the 45-day change of placement, an FBA is required if the behavior is determined to be a result of the child's disability during the manifest determination meeting. A plan must be put in place to allow the child to be successful when they return to their prior setting (BIP).

Unfortunately, in two recent reviews of the literature (Wood, Drogan, & Janney, 2014; Wood, Oakes, Fettig, & Lane, 2015), it was discovered that early childcare personnel are not usually a part of the FBA/BIP process for young children. Additionally, training and ongoing support to address challenging behaviors is also lacking, making the implementation of behavior intervention strategies problematic. Both studies recommend further research and support related to young children and who is involved in FBAs, development of the BIP, and implementation of the plan.

Work Settings

Kittelman, Bromley, and Mazzotti (2016) proposed that the FBA process be widened to include a work setting, when appropriate, to address challenging behaviors within a work-based learning experience for adolescents and young adults with disabilities. The process remained the same, with indirect data gathering (rating scales, interviews) and direct methods (observation, ABC charting), leading to an analysis of the data and hypothesis formation. The primary difference was the inclusion of the employer as part of the team, with the student also actively participating in the FBA. Once the hypothesis is developed, all team members share responsibility for the implementation of the behavior plan.

Comprehension Check

1. What are the differences when conducting an FBA with individuals from different cultures?
2. Do you think an FBA would be a useful tool to use in early childhood (birth to kindergarten)? Defend your answer.
3. When is an FBA recommended for a workplace setting?

APPLICATION ACTIVITIES

1. In your field placement, be prepared with an ABC form to collect data on a student who has shown challenging behaviors in the past. Collect data on five episodes, then analyze your data to determine a hypothesis of the function of the behavior, and develop an outline of how you would structure an FBA to obtain more information about this challenging behavior.
2. While in one of your college classes, choose a behavior that consistently occurs from either the instructor or one of your classmates. Collect data over five class sessions using the ABC form and then analyze your information to try to determine a hypothesis for the behavior.

Application Case Study

Return to Chapter 7 and read Case Study 7.1. Using Sophie and the information given, develop an FBA for Sophie to determine why she is off task, does not complete assignments, and refuses to work. Complete the ABC form for each of the three challenging behaviors, interview the teacher and Sophie, and identify the function of the behavior. (You will need to be creative, but there is a lot of information presented that you can use.) Then fill out the FBA data collection form (Figure 14.4) for Sophie.

CHAPTER SUMMARY

Functional Behavioral Assessment (FBA) is a process used to determine the function of a challenging behavior.

- One example of a challenging behavior may be when a student is disrupting a class by kicking and screaming on the floor.
- A challenging behavior could also be related to significant difficulties with academics.
- The FBA process is based on the belief that the results (consequences) of a behavior serve as reinforcement to the student and therefore the behavior is likely to happen again.

FBAs are useful and often required for some students.

- FBAs can be useful for students with a variety of needs, including students with severe developmental disabilities, autism, attention deficit hyperactivity disorder, learning disabilities, or at-risk students.
- FBAs are required for students identified with exceptionalities who have been suspended or expelled for more than 10 days.

FBAs serve many purposes that are meant to benefit both students and school faculty alike.

- The main purpose of an FBA is to identify and understand the function of antecedents and consequences related to challenging behaviors.
- FBAs also provide guidance in determining a behavioral intervention plan (BIP).
- The intended outcome of FBAs is to reduce challenging behaviors in students.

The ABC model is a simplified view of conducting an FBA and identifying the function of a behavior.

Antecedent	Behavior	Consequence
The teacher says "it's time for lunch".	Falls to the floor kicking and screaming	Taken to the time-out room. Someone gets his lunch and brings it to the room. He eats lunch in the room.

Figure 14.3 ABC Chart

It is important to know who is able to conduct an FBA as well as the training necessary in order to provide accurate information.

- In the past, functional behavioral assessments were typically completed by psychologists, behavioral specialists, and special education teachers who were trained in behavioral principles.
- As FBAs became more commonly used in schools, the number of FBAs became overwhelming for those few individuals trained in the applied behavioral analysis process.
- Loman and Horner (2014) found that other school personnel, such as counselors, principals, learning specialists, and teachers, are able to learn and conduct FBAs effectively in less complex cases in as little as four one-hour training sessions.

The steps of an FBA are necessary to determine the function of the behavior.

- Using an ABC model of observation allows the team to see what is causing the behavior (antecedent), the behavior itself, and what the behavior provides for the student (consequence).
- Identify the behavior in observable and measurable terminology.
- Conduct interviews with adults, peers, and the student to obtain information about the function of the behavior.
- Analyze the information to develop a hypothesis for the function of the behavior.

There are some adaptations in the FBA process needed for cultural considerations, early childhood, and work settings.

- Cultural values and beliefs must be researched before conducting an FBA interview with members of different cultures to ensure respectful communication.
- Although significant attention has been focused on expulsions and suspensions for early childhood, a review of the literature reports early childhood caregivers are seldom part of the FBA or BIP process.
- The Division for Early Childhood has a "Position Statement on Challenging Behavior and Young Children," discussing the need for collaboration and the use of a tier model for intervention, available at www.dec-sped.org/position-statements.

REFERENCES

Division for Early Childhood. (2017). *Position statement on challenging behavior and young children*. Retrieved from www.dec-sped.org/position-statements

Gable, R. A., Park, K. L., & Scott, T. M. (2014). Functional behavioral assessment and students at risk for or with emotional disabilities: Current issues and considerations. *Education and Treatment of Children, 37*(1), 111–135.

Kittelman, A., Bromley, K., & Mazzotti, V. L. (2016). Functional behavioral assessments and behavior support plans for work-based learning. *Career Development and Transition for Exceptional Individuals, 39*(2), 121–127. doi:10.1177/2165143416633682

Loman, S. L., & Horner, R. H. (2014). Examining the efficacy of a basic functional behavioral assessment training package for school personnel. *Journal of Positive Behavior Interventions, 16*(1), 18–30. doi:10.1177/1098300712470724

Moreno, G., Wong-Lo, M., & Bullock, L. M. (2014). Assisting students from diverse backgrounds with challenging behaviors: Incorporating a culturally attuned functional behavioral assessment in prereferral services. *Preventing School Failure, 58*(1), 58–68.

Moreno, G., Wong-Lo, M., Short, M., & Bullock, L. M. (2014). Implementing a culturally attuned functional behavioural assessment to understand and address challenging behaviours demonstrated by students from diverse backgrounds. *Emotional and Behavioural Difficulties, 19*(4), 343–355.

O'Neill, R. E., Bundock, K., Kladis, K., & Hawken, L. S. (2015). Acceptability of functional behavioral assessment procedures to special educators and school psychologists. *Behavioral Disorders, 41*(1), 51–66.

State of Connecticut. (2018). *Functional behavioral assessment and model form*. Retrieved from http://portal.ct.gov/-/media/SDE/Publications/edguide/FunctionalBehavioralAssessmentandModelForm.pdf

Wood, B. K., Drogan, R., & Janney, D. M. (2014). Early childhood practitioner involvement in functional behavioral assessment and function-based interventions: A literature review. *Topics in Early Childhood Special Education, 34*(1), 16–26. doi:0.1177/0271121413489736

Wood, B. K., Oakes, W. P., Fettig, A., & Lane, K. L. (2015). A review of the evidence base of functional assessment-based interventions for young student using one systematic approach. *Behavioral Disorders, 40*(4), 230–250.

Yell, M. L. (2016). *The law and special education* (4th ed.). Boston, MA: Pearson.

Zirkel, P. A. (2011). State special education laws for functional behavioral assessments and behavior intervention plans. *Behavioral Disorders, 36*(4), 262–278.

15

BEHAVIORAL INTERVENTION PLANS

Joni L. Baldwin

CHAPTER OBJECTIVES

After reading this chapter, students should be able to:

1. Identify a behavioral intervention plan.
2. Describe when a behavioral intervention plan is useful and when it is required.
3. Identify the connection between a functional behavioral assessment and a behavioral intervention plan.
4. Describe how the behavioral intervention plan is used in the Response to Intervention process.

WHAT IS A BEHAVIORAL INTERVENTION PLAN?

A behavioral intervention plan (BIP) is designed to reduce a challenging behavior and to substitute a replacement behavior that is less intrusive to learning for the student and others. If you remember Kevin from the previous chapter on functional behavioral assessments (FBAs), his challenging behavior was failing to turn in homework. The FBA determined that it was because he was working to help support his family, and the BIP was to reduce the size of some of his assignments, allow some homework to be done when he wasn't busy at work, and allow oral reports to the teachers instead of written for assignments like chapter summaries. Some would say that this really isn't a BIP because it wasn't a "challenging" behavior, but it was a problem and it needed to be resolved. Through the FBA with a BIP process, Kevin was able to get back on track with his homework. Granted, when the Individuals with Disabilities Education Act (IDEA) of 1997 required FBA with a BIP for students with exceptionalities, it was focused on behavior, but the use of BIPs has expanded to include academics and is also used with typical students.

The purpose of the BIP is to be proactive, not reactive, to the behavior. The BIP is developed from the information obtained during the FBA. It is based on the hypothesis of the function of the behavior, which leads to teaching a replacement behavior that serves the same function as the problem behavior. The student's preferences are considered, and the plan is to be included as part of the student's daily routine. Parts of a BIP include the following components: the target behavior; the replacement behavior; strategies to teach the replacement behavior; positive and negative consequences; staff training; monitoring of the plan through data collection, maintenance, and generalization (if needed); and crisis intervention.

Legal Aspects of Behavioral Intervention Plans

The reauthorization of IDEA in 1997 required an FBA with a BIP for any student with a disability if the student's challenging behavior resulted in a change of placement for 10 or more days (suspension or expulsion). Specifics as to what was to be included in the BIP were not defined in the law, except that the BIP must be individualized for the student and the settings where the behavior occurs (Yell, 2016). It required that the BIP become a part of the Individualized Education Program (IEP), including the behavioral analysis in the Present Level of Performance, behavioral goals (observable and measureable), and the BIP must include how and when progress reports on the behavioral goals were to be provided to the legal guardians.

This lack of specificity often prevents a student from obtaining a BIP that will truly meet their needs. For several years, Zirkel has published on the varying state requirements, or lack thereof, and subsequent concerns for students in the development and implementation of BIPs. A recent article by Zirkel (2017) summarized that the 2004 IDEA reauthorization relaxed the laws, requiring the IEP team to *consider* using an FBA and a BIP for behaviors that impede the learning of the child or others. It is still required for individuals with disabilities who have been suspended or expelled for 10 or more days. As a result, law cases have been resolved in favor of the school systems. Because the law has minimal requirements, schools can say they are providing services to the level required by law. Unfortunately, the services may not be enough to allow the child to be successful in reducing the challenging behavior.

> *Comprehension Check*
> 1. What is the purpose of a BIP?
> 2. When is an FBA with a BIP required by law?

BEHAVIORAL INTERVENTION PLANS IN THE RESPONSE TO INTERVENTION PROCESS

In the Response to Intervention (RTI) cycle, BIPs are a part of the assessment, analysis, decision-making, and instruction phases (see Figure 15.1).

Just as with FBAs, BIPs can be used in Tier 2 and Tier 3 of the RTI cycle. It is not limited to students with disabilities but can be used with any student exhibiting challenging behavior. It is important to remember that if a BIP is developed for a student

Figure 15.1 Ongoing Cycle of Response to Intervention

identified with a disability and the student has an IEP, then the BIP must become part of the IEP as well as a stand-alone document.

A Tier 2 example might be that of a group of five fourth-grade students who every morning run from their bus to their classroom, drop coats and book bags on the floor, and race to the makerspace area where they work with circuits and Legos to build a working truck. Despite the teacher's continued instructions to walk, hang up their coats, and so on, the girls continue to ignore his instructions. Mr. Caudill discusses the group of girls at his next RTI meeting with his team, and it is decided that a formal FBA is not needed because the function is obvious: quickly getting to play with the circuits. Mr. Caudill reported that the consequence of not being allowed to play with the circuits one day did not stop the behavior on subsequent days. He also acknowledged that he has not been consistent with implementing this strategy because he does not want to take away this creative learning time for the girls. The team decides to implement a Tier 2 strategy of a group meeting with the students when they arrive at school as a check in/check out procedure. As they come indoors from the bus each day, they will go to the conference room next to the entrance and meet with the school counselor for an average of five minutes. They will remove their coats, put away their hats and gloves, pull out the folder that is to be turned in daily, and then be accompanied to their room by the school counselor. When they enter quietly, put their coats and backpacks away, and turn in their folders, they may work with the circuits. Self-monitoring is added for the girls. It consists of ticking off (on laminated check sheets at their cubbies) the completed steps as a reminder of the conditions for working with the circuits. If they miss a step, they must go back and finish that item, losing time from the circuits. Mr. Caudill monitors the check sheets, and if more than two steps are missing, the girl(s) does not get time at the circuit center. Within a few weeks, the replacement behaviors are being displayed daily and parts of the intervention plan can be eliminated (having the school counselor accompany them down the hall), but the self-monitoring check sheets remain as a reminder for the students.

As with Tier 3 intervention discussed in Chapter 14, Brooke's challenging behavior in the classroom also occurred in the mornings. Her schedule, environment, and tasks were revised (these were determined to be antecedents), leading to improved behavior as she entered the classroom each morning. Reinforcing for her was continued time with her friend Liz, and a positive consequence was that when Brooke entered the classroom, she was ready to work and ready to focus on her learning.

WHY USE A FUNCTIONAL BEHAVIORAL ANALYSIS TO DEVELOP A BEHAVIORAL INTERVENTION PLAN?

Many times behavior plans are developed based on the consequences already in place in the school, such as being sent to the principal's office, a phone call home, detention, or other similar punitive consequences. But to the student, these punitive consequences continue to be reinforcement; they have managed to avoid whatever circumstance was the trigger for the inappropriate behavior. This means that the challenging behavior will continue to occur. In Chapter 14, we learned that challenging behavior is often the result of wanting to escape (not going to the lunchroom, avoiding completing a math assignment), obtaining attention from peers or adults, a method of self-stimulation (wanting sensory input), or obtaining a tangible reward. The traditional schoolwide consequences do not address the *function* of the behavior but do serve as reinforcers to the student as they obtain the attention of adults and/or peers or escape from what they didn't want to do, thus the behavior continues.

Gable, Park, and Scott (2014) reviewed several research studies completed from 1997 to 2008 that documented improved behavioral challenges when the student's BIP was completed using the function of the behavior, documenting improved challenging behaviors for typically and atypically developing students. This research has continued over the years, with Trussel, Lewis, and Raynor (2016) again proving that function-based interventions were more successful than non-function-based ones, even when the non-function-based interventions were "universal teacher practices" (p. 262) that have been proven to be evidence-based practices and improve classroom behavior. Trussell et al. defined universal teacher practices as instructional talk, wait time, prompt, and the ratio of positive to negative feedback (p. 266), again based on previous research conducted by several researchers or teams of researchers. With all this documentation, the use of the FBA to develop the BIP has been proven to be critical. The *function* of the behavior is why the behavior is occurring, and finding an acceptable replacement behavior cannot occur if the function is ignored. See Illustrative Case Study 15.1 for an example.

ILLUSTRATIVE CASE STUDY 15.1

Kyra frequently has outbursts (loud talking stating her refusal to complete individual assignments). Ms. Garcia, her second-grade teacher, knows that she is using research-based practices as she engages the students in instructional talk and explanations, uses wait time to allow a student to process a question or answer, is strong in scaffolding through the use of individual prompts, and monitors herself to give positive praise significantly more than negative comments. But none of these strategies seem to have helped Kyra, except for individual attention to provide prompts when she is able to work with Kyra one-on-one. However, with 25 other students in the classroom, this individual time is limited. As Kyra escalates in her verbal refusals, Ms. Garcia finds herself sending Kyra to the office or to the time-out chair in the back of the room. When Kyra calms down and stops making verbal outbursts, she can come back to her desk or return to the classroom. Math period is usually over when she returns to her seat. Kyra's paper goes into her home folder, but it is seldom returned completed the next day. Ms. Garcia believes that escape is the function of her behavior, but she takes Kyra's case to her school RTI team.

Despite the hypothesis of escape being the function of the behavior, the team decides an FBA is needed to determine the function of Kyra's behavior. Using direct and indirect assessments (observation of Kyra in the classroom during math and at other times of the day and interviews with the teacher and Kyra), it is determined that the behavior only happens during math instruction, and then only when it is time to do the independent work for the day. When Kyra works with others in math stations, she participates with the group and does not engage in verbal outburst or refusals to work. Kyra reports that she gets confused when working alone and Ms. Garcia cannot work with her as much as Kyra would like, so she gets angry and starts yelling and refuses to work.

The team decides to move Kyra to a Tier 2 in mathematics, allowing her more time with the teacher and with instruction. She will join this Tier 2 group of four other students three days a week for 45 minutes to work on her math assignments. An adult will be with the group and will be available to provide assistance as needed on the assignments. Her ability to stay on task and completion of math assignments improve, as does a decrease in her verbal outbursts of refusing to work. Kyra was unable to be successful with interventions that did not address her needs, even the strong classroom interventions identified as universal teacher practices. The function of her behavior was escape because she was unsuccessful in working alone in math, so she was provided additional assistance to complete math, a strategy directly based on the function of her challenging behavior. Her outbursts in class were reduced, and her participation in math increased.

Kyra was moved to a maintenance phase where she remained in the small group but had only intermittent help from the teacher. This resulted in a small increase in her behaviors but settled again when she seemed to know help was there, if not directly sitting with her. See Figure 15.2 for her graphed data.

Comprehension Check
1. BIPs are used at what tier(s) of the RTI process?
2. Do you think the FBA should be used in the development of the BIP? Explain the benefits of using FBA with BIP.
3. Why do you think the FBA is ignored in the development of the BIP for some students?

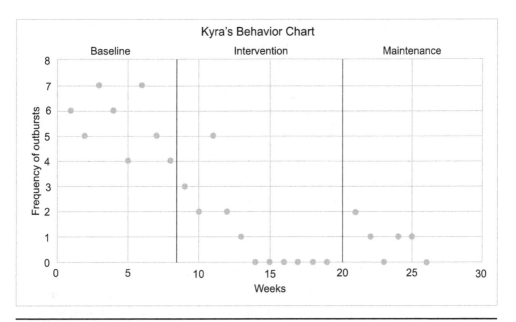

Figure 15.2 Kyra's Behavior Chart

TRAINING STAFF TO IMPLEMENT BEHAVIORAL INTERVENTION PLANS

The classroom teacher is generally the person implementing the BIP, whether a general education teacher, such as Ms. Garcia or Mr. Caudill, or the special education teacher for a more challenging student, such as a student with autism who is engaging in self-injurious behavior. As such, it is essential for the classroom teacher to be a part of the FBA with a BIP process. The teacher has the most information about the student as the FBA is conducted, and we know that the FBA is a critical part of developing the BIP if the interventions are going to change the challenging behavior.

The Office of Special Education Programs (2015) produced a document of classroom behavior support practices that have been empirically proven to improve student behavior in the classroom. This document includes foundational skills of settings, routines, and expectations; practices, including prevention and response; and data systems to document strategies and behavior. However, Myers, Sugai, Simonsen, and Freeman (2017) proposed that preservice and in-service teachers have not been trained on these practices, so their ability to use these practices as part of a BIP or classroom Positive Behavioral Interventions and Supports is limited.

Therefore, the first step is to train teachers in the classroom behavior support practices to improve general classroom behaviors. Refer to Chapters 5, 6, and 8 to learn what the teacher should already have in place for positive classroom strategies. The next step is to then focus on the student with the challenging behavior and the teacher's role in reducing this behavior.

When the FBA and BIP team meets to discuss a challenging student, Trussel et al. (2016) suggest that the team simply ask the teacher if the suggested BIP is doable in the classroom, and if they are comfortable in implementing the suggested strategies. In many cases, a teacher is going to require training to learn how to teach the replacement behavior without responding to the challenging behavior. Mouzakitis, Codding, and Tryon (2015) discuss treatment integrity, the correct implementation of the BIP, including the collection of data to determine if the strategies to increase the replacement behavior are working and that the challenging behavior is decreasing. Many researchers discuss the need for teacher training through sharing and discussing the plan; modeling the plan in as realistic a setting as possible; and providing performance feedback, initially on a daily basis. Teacher self-monitoring is also critical to review the day's events and their own behavior with regard to treatment integrity (Hogan, Knez, &, Kahng, 2015; Mouzakitis et al., 2015; Myers et al., 2017; Trussel et al., 2016).

ILLUSTRATIVE CASE STUDY 15.2

Casey, a seven-year-old boy with severe autism and developmental impairment, is injuring himself by biting on his fingertips during the school day. He frequently makes them bleed and will chew off any bandages that are placed on his hands. He is in a self-contained classroom with a teacher and two paraprofessionals, but there are 11 other students in the class, all with significant exceptionalities. The teacher, Ms. Scheid, requests assistance from the RTI team and an FBA is conducted through direct observations and interviews with the teachers, paraprofessionals, and Casey's family. In addition for this student, the teacher and school psychologist conduct a reinforcement survey to determine what Casey prefers when he is chewing. Through observation of the presenting of items and Casey's responses, it is noted that he is reinforced by soft music (fingers out of his mouth with slight rocking as he is listening), chewy toys instead of hard (a piece of soft rubber tubing instead of a hard plastic ring), warm items instead of cold (chewed longer on a warm washcloth than on the cold one presented), and soft touch (gentle rubbing of his back). From this survey, a reinforcement menu is developed for Casey.

The function of the behavior is sensory input, and it is determined that the chewing occurs when Casey is not in a one-to-one work situation with an adult, usually because the adult is facilitating Casey's use of his hands to complete a task—thus, he cannot put his fingers in his mouth. The team wants to put into place the strategy that Casey has an adult with him at all times so that he is not likely to put his hands in his mouth, and they will provide a soft chewy for Casey to chew on as he works. The teacher says that this is not doable because she has 11 other students who also need instructional time and if one of the adults is always with Casey, then that leaves two for the other 11 students. Ms. Scheid suggests that the school psychologist and assistant principal spend a morning in her classroom so that they can better understand the needs of the students and then offer suggestions. This occurs within the next week, and the team comes back together.

Ms. Scheid was complimented on her use of evidence-based practices, including a structured environment, predictable routines, and modeled expectations. She has a strong data collection system in place, with daily data on behaviors, IEP goals, and learning targets. The three adults are engaged with the students the entire morning, with one large meeting of the whole group, and then small-group and individual work. The student grouping was flexible, dependent on the activity, and some students worked independently for short periods of time, with one of the adults monitoring their work. A plan was developed that Casey would have an adult behind him for the meeting time, with the adult gently rubbing his back and giving him a soft chewy to have during the meeting time. Casey would also not be given independent work time but would always be with a small group with an adult. In this setting, Casey would again be given a soft chewy, encouraged to participate in the activity, and if needed to be left without a close-by adult, would be given the soft chewy and music would be played beside him. Ms. Scheid thought that this plan was doable as it was developed. The school psychologist offered to come into the room to model the strategies and to help Ms. Scheid and the paraprofessionals implement them in the beginning.

Comprehension Check
1. What is the concern regarding teachers implementing strategies defined in a BIP?
2. Why should the teacher be included in the development of the BIP?

DEVELOPING A BEHAVIORAL INTERVENTION PLAN

The first step in developing a BIP is to complete an accurate FBA. Through the FBA process, a hypothesis for the behavior emerges (or perhaps more than one) that has been operationally defined (observable and measureable) and agreed to by all to be the function of the behavior. Umbreit and Ferro (2015) remind us a challenging behavior can be both positively and negatively reinforced at the same time. Remember that Kyra was able to escape math (negative reinforcement) and the teacher's attention served to negatively reinforce it. Everyone involved in the FBA should be a member of the BIP development team. Depending on the function of the behavior, such as escape, attention, sensory input, or tangible reward, the replacement behavior that also serves that function will need to be developed. The BIP should include a summary of the FBA, including sources of information and a list of the student's strengths and personal goals (obtained through the interview during the FBA). Additionally, if the student has an IEP, the laws regarding due process must be considered. The plan should be reviewed by the IEP team, and the BIP becomes a part of the IEP documents.

Part of the BIP process is to look at the environment and to determine if manipulating the antecedents can allow the student to be more successful. Is there a way to change the concurrent activities that are happening when the challenging behavior is displayed? If Johnny always begins to scream and hit himself when four other students return from time in the general classroom, then that concurrent event must be reviewed to determine whether the antecedent is imbedded in that routine. That event (students coming into the room) generally causes the noise level to rise in the room, and Johnny does not like loud noises. Options could be to have Johnny wear noise-reducing headphones or to train the students to enter the room quietly. Transitions are often triggers for challenging behaviors to emerge. Having a smooth transition process in the classroom, perhaps with pictures for younger children or students with disabilities, taught to the entire class, will reduce challenging behaviors (see Figure 15.3).

Clarification of expectations and routines, as discussed in Chapter 6, has been proven to be a proactive strategy to help with whole-classroom behavior support and to reduce the need for individual plans. Examples might include writing the schedule for the day or class on the board, or reminding students daily of the expectations

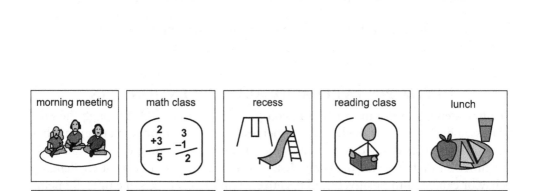

Figure 15.3 Picture Schedules: Preschool and Primary Schedules

The Picture Communication Symbols ©1981–2015 by Mayer-Johnson LLC a Tobii Dynavox company. All Rights Reserved Worldwide. Used with permission.

Boardmaker® is a trademark of Mayer-Johnson LLC.

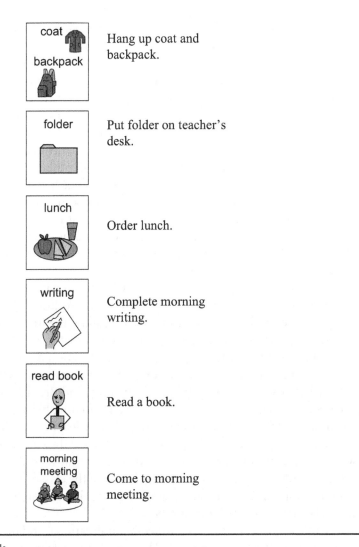

Figure 15.4 Written Schedule

The Picture Communication Symbols ©1981–2015 by Mayer-Johnson LLC a Tobii Dynavox company. All Rights Reserved Worldwide. Used with permission.

Boardmaker® is a trademark of Mayer-Johnson LLC.

of the classroom (raising hands to talk, turning in homework to the basket on the teacher's desk, keeping hands and feet to themselves; see Figure 15.4). Although these might seem like commonsense expectations, some students need support to learn and to continue doing these daily tasks and behaviors. Each teacher must teach the classroom rules at the beginning of the year and review them frequently to maintain a positive classroom environment.

The next step in the BIP is to determine the replacement behavior(s), making sure the behavior is observable and measureable. The behavior must be acceptable to all the individuals in the plan, the teacher and student in particular, with ancillary staff also included in the approval of the plan. To have a successful intervention, the strategies must be functional in the environment where the intervention will occur. The team begins by discussing options for the replacement behavior. The student is to be included in this process when developmentally appropriate for their age and abilities. The student with autism, highlighted earlier, will likely not be a part of the team, but the students in the other examples could be included. These ideas should be reviewed with regard to the ease of implementing the strategies in the natural environment and to determine if the strategies would support the hypothesis of the behavior.

Questions to ask as the replacement behavior is being determined include the following: Will it be functional in the classroom and other daily routines? Is it a skill the student may already have but has not been using? If a student already knows the behavior (raising their hand), is it more likely to occur early in the training process and so does not need to be taught? Does the student need additional instructions in the developmental skills (academic, social, communication) that may be helpful in replacing the challenging behavior? Are there medical issues that should be considered before the behavior can be addressed?

Let's go back to Brian, the student from Chapter 14 with attention deficit hyperactivity disorder (ADHD) who pulled the fire alarm. Although his ADHD and impulsivity were determined to be the cause of his pulling the fire alarm, once he is placed on medication, he must be helped to understand that it is not appropriate to pull a fire alarm unless there is a fire. He also needs instruction on how to safely walk down the hall with his class or when he is alone. The classroom rule is that the children fold their arms across their chests while in the hallway, and Brian needs to learn to do this as well. Strategies include having Brian practice folding his arms, watching the other students as they fold their arms (modeling) before leaving the classroom, or having a peer buddy who can remind Brian what to do when they are in the hall. Brian could also have a picture of himself with folded arms that he holds in his hand to help remind him what to do, and when he gets back to the classroom, Brian will fill out his self-monitoring checklist. Brian's teacher will provide verbal praise several times during the class trip in the hallway and back.

Once the behavior has been identified in observational and measurable terms, ways to teach the behavior are explored. Then the team determines the person who will teach Brian to learn to fold his arms, cue him to watch the other students, remind him to take his picture before leaving the room, and prompt him to use the self-monitoring checklist. In Brian's case, the classroom teacher is the probable choice to help him learn the replacement behavior for not touching things in the hallway. But for Casey, the student with autism, the school psychologist offered to train the teacher and assistants who work with him to learn the methods to reduce the challenging behavior and to increase the replacement behavior. Teacher and staff training is essential to maintain treatment integrity. Without treatment integrity, the BIP will not work and the replacement behavior will not be reinforced, leaving the challenging behavior the student's choice. As Gable et al. (2014) assert, "Training should be case-based, hands-on, and interactive, and embedded and sustained across time as part of a quality program of professional development" (p. 121).

Positive and negative consequences must be clearly defined in observable and measureable terms. What does the student get (positive consequence) or not get (negative consequence) for demonstrating the replacement behavior? While Kyra is completing her math assignments, she is getting positive attention from the adult as the adult provides her with the support to complete the math, but if Kyra refuses to work in that setting, the adult attention will be withheld (planned ignoring). Planned ignoring is often used in BIPs, especially if the reinforcing consequence is adult attention. The attention is given for the replacement behavior but not for the challenging behavior (unless the behavior is dangerous to the student or others). Natural consequences of getting or not getting help support the use of the replacement behavior for the student. But go back to the importance of training: If Kyra gets attention from the teacher for not doing her work, such as more than one reminder to work, then Kyra is getting both positive (gets attention) and negative (gets out of doing math) reinforcement, which means the challenging behavior will continue.

It is important to have data from the FBA to serve as the baseline data of the BIP. Collecting data while engaging in the BIP process is critical to ensure that it is being implemented accurately to reduce the challenging behavior and to increase the replacement behavior. Who is going to collect the data, monitor the data, and address needed changes, if any? What is the review schedule? All of these should be included in the BIP. Reviewing data collections methods in Chapter 3 will be helpful in choosing the type of data to document the reduction and increase in the student's behavior. Self-monitoring of the replacement behavior by both the student and the teacher will help increase the occurrence of the replacement behavior. The teacher will work with the student to facilitate the student continuing the self-monitoring, and there should be someone supporting the teacher in reviewing the self-monitoring check sheets and helping the teacher maintain treatment integrity.

Once the challenging behavior has been decreased and is maintained at the decreased level for a specific length of time, maintenance and generalization occurs. This means that the replacement behavior continues to be reinforced but at a lower frequency than during the full implementation of the BIP. Intermittent acknowledgment of the replacement behavior will be enough to encourage the student to continue to use the replacement behavior. Generalization includes helping the student apply the replacement behavior in a variety of settings with a variety of people. If an eighth-grade student is learning to raise their hand in math class instead of yelling out the answers, this new behavior can be generalized to the student's other classes as well, provided the positive consequences continue.

Crisis intervention is the last item included in a BIP. If the student has the ability (or inclination) to hurt themselves or others, a plan must be developed that ensures everyone is safe. This will likely mean reinforcing the challenging behavior, but safety is the primary consideration, and once the crisis is over, the BIP can be reviewed as to its effectiveness to determine if changes should be made. Michael, a four-year-old who is deaf and blind, bangs his head on the floor for sensory stimulation. A BIP is developed that allows Michael to receive stimulation through other activities, such as playing in water, bouncing on the trampoline, and physical touch/massage from adults. While he is reinforced during the replacement behaviors, if Michael begins banging his head on the floor, that behavior cannot be ignored. If this continues to occur, the BIP should be reviewed as well as the function of the behavior (return to the FBA).

> **Comprehension Check**
> 1. Why is the environment a critical component of the BIP?
> 2. What are the steps to developing a BIP?

WHAT IF THE BEHAVIORAL INTERVENTION PLAN ISN'T WORKING?

Despite knowing the function of the behavior and implementing a written BIP, sometimes the challenging behavior does not change. There are several reasons why this can occur, the first being that the BIP was not developed using the FBA, as discussed earlier in the chapter. Various research studies have proven that the BIP will have greater success when FBA findings are used in the BIP to decrease the challenging behavior and to increase the replacement behavior. However, the FBA findings must be accurate in order to determine the replacement behavior for the challenging behavior. With some of the more severely developmentally delayed students, hypothesizing the function of the challenging behavior may be determined through trial and error. If the student can (and will) participate in the FBA, there is a greater chance of determining the true cause of the behavior.

Another reason the plan is not succeeding may be that the teacher is not implementing the BIP as designed. This lack of treatment integrity will guarantee that the BIP will not work. This may be due to the teacher not understanding the purpose of the BIP, not believing in the BIP plan based on their own teaching style and philosophy (an example might be the use of punishment rather than positive behavior strategies), their relationship with or bias toward the student ("I can't teach if that child is in my room."), or limited positive behavior management training. If a change is requested in how the teacher teaches or manages the classroom, then they may not be willing to work with the BIP team. When teachers are hesitant to change the way they teach or provide information (lecturing), are reluctant to modify an assignment based on their beliefs ("It's not fair."), or prefer that the student leave their classroom, the student has managed to escape what they did not want to do, and the teacher is able to remain in their comfort zone. Learning is interrupted for all students as time is required to address the challenging behavior.

Umbreit and Ferro (2015) and Liaupsin (2015) have begun to look at using the FBA process to determine the reason(s) the teacher is not implementing the BIP with fidelity. This could raise some eyebrows in schools and districts because, as the authors have stated, "Viewing teacher implementation of a BIP from a functional perspective is largely uncharted territory" (p. 92). Just as with students, there is a function to the teacher's behavior as well, and once that function is determined, perhaps the issues with implementing the strategies in the BIP can be addressed. A teacher's behavior could also be categorized as obtaining positive reinforcement (peer, consultant, or administrator attention) or negative reinforcement (escape from the student's behavior). Knowing the function (attention or escape) of the behavior (not implementing the strategies in the BIP) can lead to developing replacement behaviors that will work for the student and the teacher. For example, if the teacher likes positive reinforcement (attention), a check in/check out procedure might be used with the teacher meeting with a coach at the beginning and end of each day to discuss the success of the strategies implemented that day and to plan for the next day. This attention can be decreased as the teacher becomes stronger in implementing the strategies but not taken away entirely to ensure maintenance of the teacher's behavior. It also must be remembered that FBAs and BIPs are more likely to be successful from the start if the classroom teacher is an integral part of the entire process and can provide feedback with regard to the "doability" of the strategies suggested.

Another reason the BIP may not work is that it is too complex, with too many components that make it difficult to monitor and measure. If too many strategies are being used at the same time and the behavior is not decreasing in frequency, it is then difficult to be able to determine which strategy should be adjusted. Simple is best, easy to observe and record, with the teacher and student engaged in self-monitoring behaviors.

Comprehension Check

1. What are three reasons a BIP may not be working?
2. How is a reluctant teacher supported to improve the chances for a successful BIP?

SELF-DETERMINATION, MANAGEMENT, REGULATION, AND ADVOCACY

Self-determination is the individual's ability to make autonomous decisions that lead to a healthy lifestyle and improved quality of life. Decisions are made with regard to employment, education, and social interactions and are motivated by intrinsic rewards, feelings of well-being, pride in your work, or having good health. Self-determination allows individuals to do what is best for themselves without the need for extrinsic rewards. There are usually extrinsic rewards to many decisions we make in life, such as a paycheck for the decisions we made about employment and education or companionship and conversation from social interactions. But the decisions were made by the individuals themselves, hence *self-determination*.

Components of self-determination include self-advocacy, self-management, and self-regulation. For individuals, self-advocacy is the ability to speak up for themselves, self-management means they can control their behavior, and self-regulation is the ability to control their emotions and needs. Students who are able to self-manage and self-regulate their behavior will be more successful in school and later in life.

Many students with challenging behaviors may not understand the effect the behavior has on themselves or others. Including the student in the FBA through interviews allows the student to discuss the behavior in question and to provide some information as to interests and goals. This level of involvement helps the student begin to understand how their behavior is affecting their learning. Involving students helps them to begin to learn self-advocacy skills and also may provide some information as to a successful replacement behavior.

Self-monitoring of one's own behaviors is a source of developing self-management and regulation. By monitoring one's own behavior, the individual manages what they do at a given time and learns to regulate how they react to certain situations. (Remember Brian's monitoring of his behavior in the hallway.) Steps to self-monitoring begin with some of the same steps as developing the BIP. The first is to identify the behavior in observable and measureable terms and to target a replacement behavior. A data collection strategy is next, and then Vanderbilt (2005) suggests a conference with the student.

During the conference, the teacher defines the challenging behavior in terms of how it is affecting the other students and the learning time and provides examples of when the behavior has occurred. The team then discusses the replacement behavior in measurable and observable terms. Once they both agree on the behavior to replace and the one to replace it with, a data table can be provided for the student to monitor use of the replacement behavior. For example, Marie is in the sixth grade and has been on Tier 2 interventions many times in the last two years due to her disruptive behavior in class (talking out, making inappropriate comments). With support, she has been able to improve her behavior, but the behavior always recurs. The RTI team decides to add self-monitoring to Marie's BIP and agrees that she can track her own behavior with support from her teacher. Because the function of Marie's behavior is to gain adult attention, working together should add additional incentive for Marie to improve her skills. Marie and her teacher, Mrs. Davidson, meet together in the classroom while eating lunch to develop the plan.

The behavior is defined as talking when Marie has not been called on, either when raising her hand, when Mrs. Davidson calls her name, or when Mrs. Davidson is teaching the class. The replacement behavior is raising her hand. They will chart Marie's behaviors in five-minute intervals, with Marie marking on her chart when she has honored the plan (not talking out unless called on). Mrs. Davidson will cue Marie by providing her with a chart and a stopwatch before each large-group lesson. The use of the stopwatch is to not disturb the other students, although this may take away from Marie's learning in the beginning of the BIP. At the end of each five-minute interval, Marie will record if she did not call out without a cue from the teacher. When the lesson is over, Marie will tally her score and take the chart to her teacher (providing her with adult attention). If it is at 80% or better, the chart will go in the thumbs-up box. When she has earned a determined number of thumbs-up, she can choose a reward from her reinforcement menu (see Chapter 5).

> *Comprehension Check*
> 1. Why is it important for both the student and the teacher to monitor their behaviors? Provide three reasons.
> 2. How do you teach a student to self-monitor?

BEHAVIORAL INTERVENTION PLANS WITH SPECIFIC POPULATIONS

Cultural Considerations

As with developing and conducting the FBA, working with parents is critical to writing a functional and accurate BIP. For students with a different cultural background, working with the caregivers (parents and other adults) of the student is critical in order to determine how cultural influences affect the student's challenging behavior. Cultural differences in raising the child, expectations for behavior, and beliefs about cooperation and competition and individualism will need to be considered when defining the replacement behavior. (See Chapter 6 for information on working with families from different cultures.)

Work Settings

As with the FBA, the BIP is a useful tool as students transition to the workforce. Employers who hire individuals with disabilities expect the employee to do the work they were hired to do, but sometimes additional assistance is needed with regard to that person doing the job. Frequent difficulties cited include social behaviors of professionalism, social responsibility, collaboration, and communication skills (Casner-Lotto & Barrington, 2006). Despite being trained to do the job, difficulties with the social behaviors may interfere with the job being completed.

To help determine a successful replacement behavior, O'Neill, Albin, Storey, Horner, and Sprague (2014) emphasize that developing a BIP with the student's interests, personality traits, and future plans will be more successful in replacing the challenging behavior. Ecological assessments can be used to develop a better understanding of the student's strengths and needs in addition to determining skills needed in the workforce. Observing the work environment can provide educators with the requirements of the job and the expectations of the supervisor working with the transition student. Additionally, interviewing the student about their interests and goals will lead to a more successful BIP. Although this sounds like an FBA, which it is, by including the development of skills needed to be successful in the workplace, it adds another piece to the data collection process for older students reaching the stage of entering the workforce. See case study 15.3 for an example of a FBA/BIP utilized in the work force.

ILLUSTRATIVE CASE STUDY 15.3

Hank, a young man with Down syndrome, learned to bag groceries in his work experience classroom at the high school. He learned to double bag heavy cans and to bag the eggs separately to keep them from breaking during the trip home from the store. He was quick enough to be considered competent to do the job, and he expressed that he liked bagging groceries and that he was good at it. However, when Hank transitioned into a local retail grocery store, his line was always the slowest and the cashiers and customers were impatient and irritated by his delay. His job coach was called in to complete an FBA to help determine a BIP that would decrease the undesirable behavior (slow bagging) and increase the desirable behavior (faster bagging of groceries).

The job coach used indirect assessments, including informant interviews (cashiers, front manager of the store, other baggers), and direct assessments of observation, including descriptive functional assessment (ABC method) and an interview with Hank. Everyone agreed that Hank knows how to do the job. There have been no complaints about how he bags the food; it is that he is not fast enough to keep up with the pace of the groceries coming down the conveyer belt. It was also noted that Hank was a very social young man; he liked talking with the cashiers, other baggers, and customers.

The job coach observed Hank at his job and agreed with the others that he was significantly slower than the other baggers. But he also noticed that when there were fewer groceries, Hank was less likely to have the customer and cashier waiting on him to bag the groceries so that they could leave or move on to the next customer.

Two hypotheses were developed:

1. Hank was not fast enough to get the groceries bagged at the speed of the conveyor filled with a grocery cart of food.
2. Hank's social skills of talking with the cashier, customer, and other baggers were slowing down his speed.

To help determine which of the hypotheses was accurate, a functional analysis of manipulating a variable to determine the effect of the behavior was attempted. Hank was moved to the 15-item or less line to see if having fewer groceries allowed him to bag items at a pace that was acceptable to the cashier, customer, and store manager. Hank was successful at the limited item lane, despite his continuing to talk with others. Thus, a change to his environment solved the problem and a BIP was not needed. Hank was assigned to the 15-item or less line when he was working.

For the purpose of this case study, let's work with the other hypothesis. Even on the limited item lane, Hank was not successful in keeping up with the groceries on the conveyer belt, but the job coach noted that when Hank was talking, his hands were still. He might be holding a grocery item, but he was not putting it in a bag, or he had the bag in his hand, but he was not putting it in the cart. It was obvious that Hank's talking was slowing down his speed of bagging groceries. A BIP was needed to allow Hank to learn the more desirable behavior of speedy bagging or he would be let go from his job.

Because the function of the behavior was social interaction, restricting Hank from talking could lead to other behaviors that would involve social interaction, perhaps in a negative way (dropping groceries on the floor to allow for interaction through apologizing), so a less restrictive approach was needed. Following a study by Hansen, Wills, Kamps, and Greenwood (2014), it was decided to use self-monitoring (Hank monitors his own behavior with a check sheet) and function-based consequences (attention from others).

To teach Hank the skills he needed to display, his job coach worked with him for two hours each day, and the rest of Hank's shift was completed in the 15-item or less lane to allow him to practice the skills with fewer items on the conveyor belt. The steps in Hank's BIP included the following:

1. Hank was encouraged to be friendly to the customer by looking up and saying hi or good morning but then to look at the conveyor belt as he filled one bag of groceries.
2. Using a variable-interval model, the cashier would provide positive verbal reinforcement with short comments of how fast Hank was working (average of every three bags filled).
3. As the customer was finished, Hank was again encouraged to be courteous and say goodbye or wish them a good day, frequently directing attention back to him by the customer acknowledging his comment.
4. The cashier and the two baggers on each side of Hank would provide high fives and verbal praise for working quickly.
5. Hank gave himself a tally mark on a small white board sitting beside the bags for each successful customer completed.
6. For every 10 tally marks, Hank was rewarded with a snack item of his choice for his break.

To teach these behaviors, Hank's job coach worked with the cashiers, explaining the need for the variable praise. The cashiers felt it was doable to keep an eye on Hank as they were scanning the groceries, offer praise for attention to filling the bags, and offer a high five after each customer where Hank was successful in filling the grocery bags quickly. The other baggers were also requested to offer high fives when they saw the cashier who was working with Hank offer one.

The job coach then worked beside Hank during the training time, modeling the appropriate greetings and farewells and devoting attention to filling the bags. Hank was given positive verbal reinforcement from the coach as well as the cashier, in addition to reminders that Hank became off task by talking with others. The consequence of the need for reminders was not getting a tally mark as that customer was completed or high fives from his coworkers.

To continue to practice the reinforcement behaviors, Hank worked at the 15-item or less line for the rest of his shift, increasing his probability of earning attention and tally marks. After approximately two weeks, the store manager informed the job coach that Hank had improved in his speed of bagging. The variable-interval praise was decreased to approximately every five bags filled, and tally marks on the 15-item or less lane were increased to 15 to earn a reward. Hank continued to improve, with a gradual increase in the number of bags filled for reinforcement from the cashier, but the high fives and tally marks continued as Hank maintained attention to filling bags in a speedy manner.

> *Comprehension Check*
> 1. Why is it important to honor cultural differences when developing a BIP?
> 2. What is different about developing a BIP for a student transitioning to the workforce?

APPLICATION ACTIVITIES

1. Go back to the data you collected on a classmate or instructor from the Chapter 14 FBA application activity. Use the data to determine a BIP for that person. Use the BIP form provided in this book (see Figure 15.5).

Name:	Grade:
DOB:	Preparer:
CA:	Date of Implementation:

Target Behavior (Measurable and Observable):

Functions of Behavior:
    Antecedents:
        Concurrent Activity:
        Environment Concerns:
    Consequences:

Strengths and Goals of the Student:
    Sources:

Replacement Behavior(s):

Environment Adjustment(s):

Antecedent Adjustment(s):

Strategies to teach the replacement behavior(s):
    Who is responsible:

Figure 15.5 Behavior Intervention Plan

```
Self-Monitoring Plan(s):
   Student:

   Teacher:

   Other(s):
---
Reinforcement for Replacement Behavior(s):



Data Collection Strategies and Monitoring Plan:



Review Date:




BIP Development Team:
Name: _____ Position: _____
Name: _____ Position: _____
Name: _____ Position: _____
```

Figure 15.5 (Continued)

2. Develop a self-monitoring checklist addressing a behavior that you would like to increase (exercising, eating more fruit, hanging up your clothes). Monitor your performance for five weeks and determine if monitoring yourself helped you to increase your positive behaviors.

Application Case Study

Return to Chapter 7 and read Case Study 7.1. Using Sophie and the information given, in addition to the FBA you developed in Chapter 14, develop a BIP for Sophie to decrease her off-task behavior, failure to complete assignments, and refusal to work.

CHAPTER SUMMARY

A behavioral intervention plan (BIP) is designed to reduce the challenging behavior and to increase a replacement behavior.

- A BIP is less intrusive to learning for the student and others.
- The purpose of a BIP is to be proactive to the behavior.
  - The BIP is developed from the information obtained during the functional behavioral assessment (FBA).
- Components include the target behavior; the replacement behavior; strategies to teach the replacement behavior; positive and negative consequences; staff training; monitoring of the plan through data collection, maintenance, and generalization; and crisis intervention.
- The 2004 Individuals with Disabilities Education Act reauthorization relaxed the laws of BIPs, requiring the Individualized Education Program (IEP) team to consider using an FBA and a BIP for behaviors that impede the learning of the child or others.
  - The lack of specificity has resulted in many law cases favoring the school systems.

BIPS can be used in Tier 2 and Tier 3 of the Response to Intervention process.

- These can be used with any student with a challenging behavior.
  - If a BIP is developed for a student with a disability and that student has an IEP, then the BIP must become part of the IEP as well as a stand-alone document.
- At a Tier 2 level, the strategy of a group meeting can be implemented with the use of a self-monitoring item.
  - Within a certain amount of time, the replacement behaviors may become more automatic and parts of the intervention plan can be eliminated. The self-monitoring item will remain as a reminder for the student(s).
- At a Tier 3 level, the challenging behavior might be addressed with a change of the student(s) schedule and/or environment, leading to improved behavior. During this level, continuous reinforcers and positive consequences are used to enhance behavior.

Training Staff to Implement Behavioral Intervention Plans

- The classroom teacher is generally the one who implements the BIP.
- Train teachers in behavior support practices to improve general classroom behaviors.
- Focus on the student with the challenging behavior and the teacher's role in reducing the behavior.
  - Treatment integrity includes the correct implementation of the BIP as well as collecting data to determine if the strategies are working.
  - Train teachers and staff through sharing and discussing the plan, modeling the plan, and providing performance feedback.

- Teacher self-monitoring is critical for the teacher to review the day's events and the behavior regarding treatment integrity.

Developing a Behavioral Intervention Plan

- The first step is to complete an accurate FBA.
  - The BIP should include a summary of the FBA, the sources of information, and a list of the student's strengths and personal goals.
  - If the student has an IEP, the laws regarding due process must be taken into consideration.
- Look at the environment to determine if manipulating the antecedents can allow the student to be more successful.
  - It is important to have a smooth transition process to reduce challenging behaviors.
  - Clarifying expectations and routines with students and reviewing them frequently throughout the year helps to maintain a positive classroom environment.
- Next, determine the replacement behavior(s).
  - The behavior should be observable and measurable.
  - The behavior should also be acceptable to all individuals involved with the plan.
  - Questions to ask:
  - Will it be functional in the classroom and daily routines?
  - Is it a skill the student already has but isn't using?
  - Does the student need to be taught developmental skills?
  - Have medical issues been considered before the behavior is addressed?
- Positive and negative consequences must be clearly defined.
  - Attention is given for the replacement behavior but not for the challenging behavior.
- Data from the FBA should be used for the baseline data of the BIP.
  - Collecting data while engaging in the BIP process is important to ensure that it is accurately implemented.
- Once the challenging behavior is decreased and maintained at a decreased level, maintenance and generalization must occur.
  - The replacement behavior continues to be reinforced but with decreased frequency.
- Crisis intervention is the last item to include on a BIP.

What If the Behavioral Intervention Plan Isn't Working?

- The BIP has greater success if the FBA findings are used in the BIP.
  - There is a greater chance of determining the cause of the behavior if the student participates in the FBA.
- The teacher may not be implementing the BIP as designed.
- There could be too many components to the plan, causing it to be hard to monitor and measure.

Self-Determination

- Self-determination is the ability to make autonomous decisions that lead to a healthy lifestyle and improved quality of life.
- Components of self-determination include the following:
  - Self-advocacy is the ability to speak up for oneself.
  - Self-management means that the individual can control their behavior.
  - Self-regulation is the ability to control one's emotions and needs.
- Self-monitoring is a source of developing self-management and regulation.
  - Steps to this include some of the same steps as developing the BIP.

REFERENCES

Casner-Lotto, J., & Barrington, L. (2006). *Are they really ready to work? Employers' perspectives on the basic knowledge and applied skills of new entrants to the 21st century U.S. work force.* Retrieved from www.p21.org/storage/documents/FINAL_REPORT_PDF09-29-06.pdf

Gable, R. A., Park, K. L., & Scott, T. M. (2014). Functional behavioral assessment and students at risk for or with emotional disabilities: Current issues and considerations. *Education and Treatment of Children, 37*(1), 111–135.

Hansen, B. D., Wills, H. P., Kamps, D. M., & Greenwood, C. R. (2014). The effects of function-based self-management interventions on student behavior. *Journal of Emotional and Behavioral Disorders, 22*(3), 149–159. doi:10.1177/1063426613476345

Hogan, A., Knez, N., & Kahng, S. (2015). Evaluating the use of behavioral skills training to improve school staffs' implementation of behavior intervention plans. *Journal of Behavioral Interventions, 24*, 242–254.

Liaupsin, C. J. (2015). Improving treatment integrity through a functional approach to intervention support. *Behavior Disorders, 41*(1), 67–76.

Mouzakitis, A., Codding, R. S., & Tryon, G. (2015). The effects of self-monitoring and performance feedback on the treatment integrity of behavior intervention plan implementation and generalization. *Journal of Positive Interventions, 17*(4), 223–234.

Myers, D., Sugai, G., Simonsen, B., & Freeman, J. (2017). Assessing teachers' behavior support skills. *Teacher Education and Special Education, 40*(2), 128–139.

Office of Special Education Programs. (2015). *Supporting and responding to behavior: Evidence-based classroom strategies for teachers.* Retrieved from www.osepideasthatwork.org/evidencebasedclassroomstrategies

O'Neill, R. E., Albin, R. W., Storey, K., Horner, R. H., & Sprague, J. R. (2014). *Functional assessment and program development for problem behavior: A practical handbook* (3rd ed.). Belmont, CA: Wadsworth.

Trussel, R. P., Lewis, T. J., & Raynor, C. (2016). The impact of universal teacher practices and function-based behavior interventions on the rates of problem behaviors among at-risk students. *Education and Treatment of Children, 39*(3), 261–282.

Umbreit, J., & Ferro, J. B. (2015). Function-based intervention: Accomplishments and future directions. *Remedial and Special Education, 36*(2), 89–93.

Vanderbilt, A. A. (2005). Designed for teachers: How to implement self-monitoring in the classroom. *Beyond Behavior, 15*(1), 21–24.

Yell, M. L. (2016). *The law and special education* (4th ed.). Boston, MA: Pearson.

Zirkel, P. A. (2017). An update of judicial rulings specific to FBAs or BIPs under the IDEA and corollary state laws. *Journal of Special Education, 51*(1), 50–56.

INDEX

Note: Page numbers in italic indicate a figure, and page numbers in bold indicate a table on the corresponding page.

504 Plan 4–5, **5**, 21, 225, 236, 282, 284

ABC model 299–300, *293*, *299*
academic data 53–54, 6
academic engagement 50, 169–171, *170*
accessibility 3, 158, 170, 179
administrators 253, 287; culturally inclusive classroom and 120, 124; RTI and 4; Schoolwide Positive Behavior Support and 67, 70, 76, 82–83; Tier 2 and 201, 203, 218
Americans with Disabilities Act (ADA) 3–5, 7, 24
analysis: culturally inclusive classroom and 128–129, 131–135, *132*, 138–139; motivation and 159, 161; RTI and 8, **9**, 18–19, 21–22, 24; and the teacher's role 87, **88**; Tier 2 and 199, 202, 205, 209–212, 216–219; Tier 3 and 263; *see also* data analysis; functional behavioral analysis
anecdotal records 55–57, *56*, 63
anger management 19, *74*, 214, 216, 234, 237
anxiety 241–243, **242**, 245–250, **248**, 252–253, 256–259
anxiety management 250, 259
application technology 170, 179
assessment: of classroom management plan 128–131, *128*, *131*; criterion-referenced tests (CRTs) 270–271; curriculum-based assessments 271–272; standardized 269, *270*; Tier 2 and 206–210, **207**; *see also* cycle of assessment; progress monitoring; universal screening
attendance and tardy data 52–53, 62
attention deficit hyperactivity disorder (ADHD) 223–228, 232–233, 236–237, 247, 252; and behavioral intervention plans 312; and functional behavioral assessment 285–286; RTI and 4–6; Tier 3 and 272, 280
audiobook 145, **146**, 157
autism: and behavioral intervention plans 307–308, 312; and decreasing behavior challenges 186, 190, 193, 195; functional behavioral assessment and 285, 294, 299; RTI and **6**

behavior *see* behavior management; individual behavioral data
behavioral contracts 26, 32–33, 38, 47–48
behavioral intervention plans (BIP) 302–303, 320–324, *320–321*; developing 309–314, *310*, *311*; and functional behavioral analysis 305–306; legal aspects of 303; plans that aren't working 314–315; in the RTI 303–304; self-monitoring and 315–316; with specific populations 317–320; training staff to implement 307–309, *307*
behavioral rating scales 18, 218
behavioral referrals *see* office and behavioral referrals
behavior management 47–48, 167–168, 177–180, 192–196; behavioral supports 172–175, *173*, *174*; classroom strategies for 182–189, *183–189*; group strategies for 168–169; methods for decreasing behavior 42–47; methods for increasing behavior 26–33, *27*, *28*; strategies for those with disabilities 189–191; *see also* externalizing behaviors; internalizing behaviors; reinforcement; Schoolwide Positive Behavior Support; social skills; three-tiered support model
behavior scales data 54
brain breaks *see* sensory breaks

325

bullying 34, 98, 247; group strategies and 168, *173*; and motivation 142, 152, **153**; prevention of 73, 81, 86

check in/check out (CICO): behavioral intervention plans and 304, 315; and decreasing behavior challenges 189, 196; and internalizing behaviors 253, **254**; Tier 3 and 265, 281
checklists 18, **156**, 196, 245, 268, 291; behavioral intervention plans and 312, 321
check sheets **23**, 243, 271, 304, 313, 319
classroom 136–139; culturally responsive 113–117, **117**, 126; implementation of 126–136; and inclusion 111–117; *see also* classroom design; classroom management plan
classroom design 111, 118, **119**, 138
classroom management plan 111, 117–126, **119–124**, 128, 134, 136–137
class work 132, 214, 225, 236
closed-captioning 157–158
cloze procedure 170, 179
cognitive behavioral therapy (CBT) 243, 245, 248–250, 257–258
color chart 196
color-coding 183
communication: behavioral intervention plans and 312, 317; culturally inclusive classroom and 112–114, **114**, **117**, 137; decreasing behavior challenges and 190, 196; externalizing behaviors and 234–235; functional behavior assessment and 300; group strategies and 175, 177, 180; internalizing behaviors and 247; motivation and 155; RTI and **6**, **21**; Schoolwide Positive Behavior Support and 84; the teacher's role and 87, 95, **98**, **100–101**, 101–102, 104, 108–109; Tier 2 and 200; Tier 3 and 273, 277
comorbidity 247
comprehension: decreasing behavior challenges and 183, 186, 193, 195; group strategies and 171, 179; motivation and 158; RTI and **6**, 10, 16, **21**; SPBS and 72; Tier 3 and 266, **268**, 275, 277
computer-assisted instruction 227–228, 236
conduct disorder (CD) 221, 223, 229–230, 232–235, 237, 247
co-teachers 56, 89, **119**, 202
counselors *see* school counselors
cultural context 54–55, 63
cultural differences: behavioral intervention plans and 317; and a culturally inclusive classroom 112–115, **114**, **117**, 137; functional behavioral assessment and 297; motivation and 151; and the teacher's role 87, 93, **95**, **97**, 99–102, 108; Tier 2 and 207, 212
cycle of assessment: culturally inclusive classroom and 111, 128, 134–136, 138; motivation and **159**, 161; RTI and 10, 15–16, 18–19, 22, 24; SPBS and 69; the teacher's role and 87; Tier 2 and 199, 218

data analysis 69, 78–79, 191, 272–275, 283
data collection 50–52, 62–63; methods 55–62, *56*, *58*, *60*, *61*; Schoolwide Positive Behavior Support and 78–79; *see also* academic data; data analysis; individual behavioral data
daydream 140
decision-making 12–13, *12*; and classroom management plan 133–134, *133*; Tier 2 and 212–214, **213**
depression 239–240, 242–245, **244**, 247, 250–251, 257–258
Diagnostic and Statistical Manual of Mental Disorders (DSM-5) 223–224, 229, 232–233, 242, 257
difference *see* cultural differences
differential reinforcement 26, 42–44, 48
Division for Early Childhood 297, 300
downtime 124, **152**
duration recording 57, 59–61, *61*, *62*, 63

eating disorders 245–247, 255–258
Education for All Handicapped Children Act 5, 8
emotional and behavioral disorders (EBD) 223, 234, 237, 287
empathy 42, 133, 160, 175, 178, 180, 233
engagement: data collection and 50; decreasing behavior challenges and 183, 192–193, 195; externalizing behaviors and 227; group strategies and 168–172, *170*, 174, 179; motivation and **146**, 157–159, 166; SPBS and 69; Tier 3 and 273; *see also* academic engagement
English language learners 71, 89, 127, 177
evidence-based practices 169, 179, 194, 222, 265, 305, 309
expectancy 140, 144–150, **144**, **146–148**, 155–159, 163–165
expectations: and behavioral intervention plans 307, 309–311, 317, 323; culturally inclusive classroom and 113–121, **117**, 124, 126–130, 132, 137; and data collection 50–55, 62; and decreasing behavior challenges 189; and internalizing behaviors 249; and managing behaviors 27, 29, 31–36, *37–38*, 45–48; and motivation 145, 150, **153**, 155, 160, 162; RTI and 12–13, 16; SPBS and 69–73, 75–68, 80–85; and the teacher's role 95, **98**, 99, 103–107, 109; Tier 2 and 206, 211–214, 219; Tier 3 and 277
expulsions 286, 297, 300, 303
externalizing behaviors 221–223, 235–237; attention deficit hyperactivity disorder 224–228; conduct disorder 232–235; oppositional defiance disorder 229–232

fairness 103, 105–107, 109, 194
family therapy 243, 251–252, 257, 259
fidelity assessment **9**, **88**, 202, 218
flash cards 185
flexibility 103, 105–106, 136, 138, 157–159, 166
flowchart 217
frequency recording 57–60, *58*, 63
functional behavioral assessment (FBA) 285–286, 298–300; components of 289–291, *289*, *290*, *291*; gathering information for 291–294, *292*, *293*; legal aspects of 286–287; professionals completing a

294–295; in the RTI process 287–289, *288*; with specific populations 297–298; steps of 295–297
functional communication system 190, 196

generalization 51; behavioral intervention plans and 313, 323; culturally inclusive classroom and 112, 115; externalizing behaviors and 228, 232; and managing behaviors 26, 33, 41–42, 48
Good Behavior Game 172–173, 180
grandma's rule *see* Premack principle
group contingency plans 167, 174, 180
group strategies 168–171, *170*, 176, 179, **254**
guided notes 150, 157–158, 169–170, *170*, 179
guiding principles 118–121, **120**, 124–128, 137–138

handwriting 272
hearing data *see* vision and hearing data
hearing screenings 52, 62, 218, 275
homeschooling 251

individual behavioral data 50, 52–55, 62
Individualized Education Program (IEP): behavioral intervention plans and 303–304, 309, 322–323; functional behavioral assessment and 286, 297; RTI and 4, 7, 20–22; Tier 3 and 276–279, 282–284
Individuals with Disabilities Education Act (IDEA) 3–8, **6, 7**; and behavioral intervention plans 302–303; and externalizing behaviors 223, 225, 229–230, 233, 235–236; and functional behavioral assessment 286, 290, 294; and internalizing behaviors 240; and referrals to special education 264–267; and RTI 20–22; and SPBS 69, 76; and Tier 3 276, 282–284
instruction 13–14, *14*, 134, *134*, 216–217
instrumentality 144, 146–149, **147**, 165
internalizing behaviors 239–242, **248**, 256–259; anxiety 242, **242**; bullying 247; comorbidity 247; depression 243–245, **244**; eating disorders 245–246; interventions for 248–252; obsessive-compulsive disorder 246–247; post-traumatic stress disorder 247; and school and teacher roles 252–256, **254**; somatic symptom disorder 246
internet 137, 170, 173, 180, 185, 193
interpersonal psychotherapy 245, 251, 258–259
interviews 18; behavioral intervention plans and 306, 308, 318; functional behavior assessment and 290–292, 295, 297–298, 300; internalizing behaviors and 243, 245; Tier 2 and 206, 218; Tier 3 and 266–268, 275, 283

Key Math 267, 275

latency recording 60–61, *61*, *62*, 63
law: behavioral intervention plans and 303, 322; functional behavioral assessment 286, 294, 297; and special education 3–8, **5, 6, 7**, 24; Tier 3 and 267, 274, 278
leadership 87, 102–105, 109, **156**

least restrictive environment 6, **7**, 22, 23, 276, 278–279, 284
lesson plans 70, 73, *74*
lunchtime 160, 249

Maslow's hierarchy of needs 150–151, **151**, 161–162; aesthetic, self-actualization, and transcendence needs 159–160; cognitive needs 156–159, **159**; esteem needs 154–156, **156**; love and belonging needs 153, **153**; physiological and biological needs 151–152, **152**; safety needs 152–153, **153**
medical background 206, 218
motivation 140–141, 162–166; and expectancy theory 144–150, **144, 146, 147, 148**; extrinsic 142–144, **143**; intrinsic 141–142, **142**; *see also* Maslow's hierarchy of needs
multidisciplinary evaluation 51, 61–63, **88**
multidisciplinary team (MDT) 265–267, 272, 276, 282–283
Multiple Means of Engagement **146**, 157–158, 166

negative reinforcement *see* reinforcement
nonverbal communication 87, 101–102, 104, 108–109, 175, 180, 234
nurses *see* school nurses

observational learning 188, 195
observations: behavioral intervention plans and 308; culturally inclusive classroom and 130–131, 134, 139; data collection and 54, 59; functional behavior assessment and 290–291, 293–295, 297; internalizing behaviors and 243; managing behaviors and 37; RTI and 12–13, 15, 18–19, 21; SPBS and 79–80; Tier 2 and 201, 203, 206, 208, 218; Tier 3 and 266, 272, 274, 280, 283
obsessive-compulsive disorder 241, 246–247, **248**, 258
office and behavioral referrals 53
oppositional defiance disorder (ODD) 221, 223, 229–232, 236–237

paraprofessional 82, 89, **119**, 190–191, 196, 229–230, 308–309
parents: behavioral intervention plans and 317; and a culturally inclusive classroom 115, 120, **121**, 127–128; data collection and 52, 54, 63; and externalizing behaviors 222–223, 227, 234; functional behavioral assessment and 287, 293; and group strategies 173, 176; and internalizing behaviors 240, 243, 246, 249, 251–252, 255–256; and managing behaviors 35, *37–38*, 41, 43–44, 46; RTI and 4, **5, 7, 7**, 18, 20–22; SPBS and 70, 75–76, 79, 81; and the teacher's role 89, **95, 96, 98**, 98–100, 107–108; Tier 2 and 200–201, 203, 206, 208, 211, 218–219; Tier 3 and 265–266, 269, 271, 274–276, 280, 283
peer tutoring 171, 179, 201, 227, 236
persistence: externalizing behaviors and 229; motivation and **147**, 154, 156, **156**, 161; the teacher's role and 103, 107, 109

personal de-escalation techniques 176, 180
pharmacologic intervention 252, 259
Positive Behavioral Interventions and Supports (PBIS): data collection and 50–51, 57, 62; managing behaviors and 26, 32–34, 36, 41, 47
positive behavior support *see* Schoolwide Positive Behavior Support
positive reinforcement *see* reinforcement
post-traumatic stress disorder (PTSD) 247
praise: behavioral intervention plans and 305, 312, 319; culturally inclusive classroom and 127, 133, 135; and decreasing behavior challenges 185; externalizing behaviors and 231, 237; group strategies and 172; internalizing behaviors and 250; and managing behaviors 28–36, 40–42, 44, 46, 48; motivation and 141, **143**, **147**, 154–156, **156**, 161; SPBS and 73, 75, 77–78, 82; the teacher's role and **96**, **97–98**, 106
Premack principle 133, 142–143, 164, 186, 195; and RTI 26, 30, 32, 47
Present Level of Performance 276–277, 284, 303
problem-solving: externalizing behaviors and 234; group strategies and 175, 180; internalizing behaviors and 245, 249, 253, 258; RTI and **6**, 8; the teacher's role and **97**; Tier 2 and 201, 215–216, 219
procedures 123–124, **123**, **124**; *see also* shaping procedures
progress monitoring 13–18, *15*; data collection and 55, 57–59; externalizing behaviors and 219; internalizing behaviors and 240, 253; managing behaviors and 28–31, 33, 36, *38*, 40, 47–48; RTI and 8, **9**, 11, 22, 24; Schoolwide Positive Behavior Support and 78–79; the teacher's role and **88**; Tier 2 and 211, 217; Tier 3 and 265–266, 271, 281, 283
psychologists *see* school psychologists
punishment: behavioral intervention plans and 314; culturally inclusive classroom and 118, 128; decreasing behavior challenges and 185; managing behaviors and 26, 31, 45–48; motivation and 143, 147; SPBS and 67

questionnaires *37–38*, 206, 208, 218, 253, 291

recognition: managing behaviors and 32, 34, 41; motivation and 148, 165; PBIS and 51; SPBS and 70–71, 76–82, *78*
referral: data collection and 51, 53, 61–62; externalizing behaviors and 222–223; functional behavior assessment and 293, 297; group strategies and 168; internalizing behaviors and 239–240, 245, 253–256; RTI and 4, 8–12, **9**, 17–20, 22, 24; SPBS and 67, 69, 75–76, 79, 81, 84–85; and the teacher's role **88**; Tier 2 and 199, 201–207, **205**, 209–211, 217–219; Tier 3 and 263, 265–266, 264, 282–283
Rehabilitation Act 3–5, **5**, 21, 24, 225; *see also* 504 Plan

reinforcement 133, 172, 296; behavioral intervention plans and 308, 314, 319; differential reinforcement 42–44; extinction 45; positive and negative 27–30, *28*; Premack principle 30; Schoolwide Positive Behavior Support and 76–80, *78*, 81–85; shaping procedures 30–31; token economies 31–33; *see also* reinforcers
reinforcers 32, 44, 46, 48, 77–78; reinforcer menus 37–39, *37–38*; types of 33–36; reinforcement schedules 39–42
relaxation training 250, 259
replacement behavior training 251, 259
Response to Intervention (RTI) 8–10, *9*, **9**, 24, *88*, **88**; *see also* analysis; assessment; decision-making; instruction; Tier 1; Tier 2; Tier 3
rewards 76–80, *78*; behavioral intervention plans and 315–316; group strategies and 172–173, 180; managing behaviors and 30–32, *38*, 39–40, 47; 51, 82; motivation and 141, 143–144, 146–148
role-plays 127, 217
routines 70–72, 77, 84; and behavioral intervention plans 310, 323; and consequences 73–76; and a culturally inclusive classroom 123–124
rules 70–72; behavioral intervention plans and 311–312; classroom rules 120–122, **121**, **122**; and consequences 73–76; and a culturally inclusive classroom 118, 124–130, 132–133, 136–138; externalizing behaviors and 232–233; and managing behaviors 28, 30–31; motivation and 147; SPBS and 67–68, 77, 80–84; the teacher's role and 99, 103–106

school counselors 71, 82–83, 202–203, 218, 243–244, 293–294, 304
school history 208, 218
school nurses 245–246, 252–257, 259
school psychologists 56, 218, 256, 272, 295, 308–309
Schoolwide Positive Behavior Support (SWPBS) 67–69, 81–85, 168; bullying prevention within 81; components of 69–76, *70*, *74*; hurdles to 80
schoolwork 30, 243–244, 255–257; *see also* class work
seatwork 75, 185, 267, 294
self-determination 107, 277, 279, 289, 315–316, 324
self-monitoring 191, 312–313, 315–316, 321–324
self-regulation 133, 173–175, 180, 315, 324
sensory breaks 174, *174*, 180
sensory diets 190, 196
shaping procedures 26, 30–31, 33, 47
skill set 73
social skills 19, 167; behavior management and 175–177; motivation and 153–154; the teacher's role and 90, 92–94, **98**; Tier 2 and 202, 214–216; *see also* social skills training
social skills training 250–251; externalizing behaviors and 231, 234, 237; group strategies and 175–177, 180; internalizing behaviors and 253, 259; SPBS and 73, *74*
Social Stories 186, 195

somatic symptom disorder 246, **248**, 258
special education 264–265, 282–284, 294–295; assessments for 268–275; decreasing behavior challenges and 193–194; evaluation for 267–268, **268**; externalizing behaviors and 225, 229–230; group strategies and 177–178; internalizing behaviors and 239–240, 255–257; referrals to 265–267; RTI and 3–10, **9**, 18–22, **22**; SPBS and 71; students who don't qualify for 279–282; Tier 2 and 201–202, 204, 216–217
standard protocol 214–216, 219
suspensions 83, 222, 286, 297, 300, 303

tardy data *see* attendance and tardy data
teachers 87–89, 107–109; and classroom management plan 126–128; culturally responsive 113–117, **117**; and nonverbal communication 101–102; and relationships among students 97–98, **97–98**; teacher dispositions 102–107; teacher-guardian relationships 98– **100–101**; teacher-student relationship 89–97, **95**, **96**
technology 4, 170, 179, 190; *see also* application technology; computer-assisted instruction; internet
three-tiered support model 67–69, *68*; *see also* Tier 1; Tier 2; Tier 3
Tier 1 9, **9**, 15–18, 199–201; internalizing behaviors and 239–240; and managing behaviors 28–32; SPBS and 68–69, 84
Tier 2 17–20, 24, 217–219, 287; analysis 210–212; assessment 206–210, **207**; behavioral intervention plans and 303, 306; and data collection 52–53; decision-making 212–214, **213**; instruction 216–217; internalizing behaviors and 239–240, 255–256; and managing behaviors 29–30; overview of 199–205, **205**; problem-solving 215–216; progress monitoring 217; and SPBS 68, 84; 222; and special education 265–266, 271, 281–282; standard protocol 214–215
Tier 3 19–23, **21–23**, 68, 287, 322; *see also* special education
time-out 73, 185, 289, *289*, *299*, 305
token economies 26, 31–33, 36–37, 39, 47–48
transitions 77, 178, **254**, 271–272, 310; culturally inclusive classroom and **123**, 124; decreasing behavior challenges and 190, 193–194, 196

United States 3–4, 112–113
Universal Design for Learning (UDL): group strategies and 171, 180; motivation and **142**, **146**, 157–159, **159**, 161, 166
universal screening 10–11, 13, 15, 53–54

valence 144, **144**, 147–149, **148**, 165
video modeling 188, 193, 195
vision and hearing data 52
vision screenings **21**, 52, 62, 206, 218, 275
visuals 183, 186, 190, 192–193, **254**; visual representation system 189, 195; visual timer 190, 193, 196

well-being 41, 91, 231, 235, 315
WISC-V 267, 275

zero-tolerance 67, **98**, 153